CliffsTestPrep®

DAT

CliffsTestPrep®

DAT

An American BookWorks Corporation Project

Contributing Authors/Consultants

Tracy Halward, PhD

Sasheena A. Kurfman

Dai Chinh Phan, DDS, MS, BSAE

Walter Voland, PhD

Mark Weinfeld, MA

Wiley Publishing, Inc.

About the Author

Since 1976, American BookWorks Corporation has been producing and publishing a wide variety of educational books for many of the major publishing houses. The company specializes in test preparation books, as well as K–12 review books and study guides. In its role as a book producer, it functions as a "co-publisher," providing publishers with strong editorial, marketing, and technological expertise, based on more than 30 years of experience.

Publisher's Acknowledgments

Editorial

Project Editor: Donna Wright

Acquisitions Editor: Greg Tubach

Production

Proofreader: Arielle Mennelle

Wiley Publishing, Inc. Composition Services

CliffsTestPrep® DAT

Published by:
Wiley Publishing, Inc.
111 River Street
Hoboken, NJ 07030-5774
www.wiley.com

Copyright © 2007 Wiley, Hoboken, NJ

Published by Wiley, Hoboken, NJ
Published simultaneously in Canada

Library of Congress Cataloging-in-Publication Data

CliffsTestPrep dental admission test (DAT) / an American BookWorks Corporation project ; contributing authors Tracy Halward ... [et al.].

    p. ; cm. — (CliffsTestPrep)

  ISBN-13: 978-0-471-78593-4 (pbk.)

  ISBN-10: 0-471-78593-8

  1. Dental Admission Test. 2. Dental schools—Examinations—Study guides. I. Halward, Tracy. II. American BookWorks Corporation. III. Title: Dental Admission Test. IV. Series.

  [DNLM: 1. Dentistry—Examination Questions. 2. Aptitude Tests—Examination Questions. 3. Educational Measurement—Examination Questions. WU 18.2 C638 2007]

  RK57.C45 2007

  617.60076—dc22

Printed in the United States of America

10 9 8 7 6 5 4 3 2 1

WILEY

Table of Contents

PART III: DAT PRACTICE TESTS

PART I

INTRODUCTION

Introduction

With the purchase of this book you've committed yourself to studying for the Dental Admission Test (DAT). The results of this test will be part of the admission process you will undergo when applying to Dental schools. Obviously, the better you do on this exam, the greater your chances will be to be accepted by the schools of your choice.

In order to apply to take this test, you must contact the American Dental Association (ADA) to request an application. You may either submit your application online, or request a paper application and booklet. You can contact the ADA at www.ada.org.

The DAT battery of tests is computerized, and you can take the test at specified testing centers almost any day of the year. This book will give you the opportunity to study both with the book and on the enclosed CD, to give you a feel for answering questions on the computer.

About This Book

It is also no secret that whenever you take a standardized test such as this one, the more you have prepared for it, the better you will probably do on the test. This book provides you with an enormous amount of preparatory material in all areas of the test. The first part of this book is a series of "review questions and answers." What this means is that as you go through each question presented in these chapters, we give you the answer immediately following each question. In this way you can test your knowledge and receive immediate feedback. The questions are the same type of questions that will appear on the exam, so that you begin your reviewing immediately, while familiarizing yourself with the question-types.

Since you have undoubtedly taken myriad science and mathematics courses throughout your college career, you should be up-to-date on the material that will be covered on this exam. You will already have acquired the appropriate textbooks and review books for the subjects that will be covered on this test, which is why we do not give you hundreds of pages of review material. Instead, we go directly to the heart of the tests—hundreds of questions and answers so that you can find out what you know and what needs additional work. In the Reading Comprehension section we've used shorter paragraphs in order to enable you to get faster feedback from your work, although on the exam there will probably be only three long paragraphs.

The only exception to this is the Perceptual Ability Test (PAT). This portion of the exam is likely to be new material for you. Unless you've taken specialized mathematics courses or engineering courses, most of this material will be new to you. There are six sections to this exam, and they require visual and mental dexterity. The test measures your ability to work with two- and three-dimensional objects, and be able to manipulate them visually and analyze them in different formats. The six sections are aperture passing, orthographic projection, angle discrimination, paper folding, cubes, and form development. We'll discuss more about this later in this section.

Once you've gone through these various practice sections, it's time to turn to the actual tests. We have created three full-length replica exams covering the same type of material and question-types that you will encounter on the actual DAT. It is worth making the effort to take the time to practice on these tests. The tests are timed, and laid out in the same form that the actual exam will be. Find a quiet room in which to work, get a stop watch, and take the tests over a period of a few weeks, if you have the time. When you've completed the tests, check your answers. Remember that all of the questions are fully explained and analyzed for you. If you still don't understand something, do some research in one of your textbooks or online. The more you practice, the better you will do on the test.

About the Test

The Dental Admission Test is actually a set of four tests:

- Survey of Natural Sciences (SNS)
- Perceptual Ability Test (PAT)
- Reading Comprehension Test (RCT)
- Quantitative Reasoning Test (QRT)

The Survey of Natural Sciences test includes biology, general chemistry, and organic chemistry. As we said earlier, the Perceptual Ability Test includes aperture passing, orthographic projection, angle discrimination, paper folding, cubes, and form development. Reading Comprehension Test is just that—reading comprehension. The Quantitative Reasoning Test is a test of mathematics.

These are the four sections that are timed tests. However, you will actually receive eight scores, which include the tests above, but broken down into the various subjects.

1. Biology
2. General Chemistry
3. Organic Chemistry
4. Quantitative Reasoning
5. Reading Comprehension
6. Total Science, which is a combination of the three science subjects
7. Academic Average, which is an average of all of the subject areas except for the PAT section.
8. Perceptual Ability is a separate score

You will have 4 hours and 15 minutes to complete the entire test, which includes a 15 minute break. The test is broken out as follows.

Survey of Natural Sciences	100 questions	90 Minutes
Perceptual Ability Test	90 questions	60 Minutes
Reading Comprehension Test	50 questions	60 Minutes
Quantitative Reasoning Test	40 questions	45 Minutes

A more complete breakdown of all of the subjects that will be covered on the test accompanies each review chapter.

Taking the Test

You can easily see from the above table that you will have to work quickly. In the Natural Science section, you will have less than 1 minute to answer each question, and slightly more than a minute for the other sections. That's why you need to use this book to review the material and question-types. And one of the most important tools in taking a timed test is understanding and memorizing the directions *before* you take the exam. This will save you a considerable amout of time—especially in the PAT section. As you go through this book and take the tests, make sure you read the directions carefully. While it is basically a test that says read the question or paragraph and select the correct answer, you should be fully aware of these directions.

How to Answer Multiple-Choice Questions

In many cases, it's a decided advantage to take a test like this with multiple-choice questions, and the better your skill at answering them, the better your chances are at doing well. Of course, besides the skill, you must also have a basic knowledge of the material.

There are three basic steps to follow.

1. The first approach is to read the question. If you read the question and immediately know the answer, look at the choices given, select the correct one and mark it on your answer page. This is the easiest way to answer the question—you know the answer.

2. The second method is to read the question and if the answer doesn't immediately come to mind, read the answer choices. If you know the material fairly well, the correct answer will be clear to you at once. Or if it is not immediately clear, a little thought will root out the right answer.

3. The third step is to use the process of elimination. Very simply, it involves eliminating the wrong answer choices so that you're left with the correct one, or at least you've narrowed down the choices. When test-developers create questions for multiple-choice tests, there's a process that is often followed. In questions with five choices like those you'll find in the exams in this book, there is always one answer choice that will be undeniably correct. The other choices are called "distracters." There is usually one choice that is completely incorrect and can be quickly eliminated. The other two choices may be similar to the correct answer, but there may be clues in the answers that make them incorrect. The question set up may be something like this:

---

1. Question

   A. Totally Incorrect Choice
   B. Totally Incorrect Choice
   C. Correct Choice
   D. Almost Correct, but not quite correct.
   E. Almost Correct, but not quite correct.

In mathematics, there may be things like decimals in different places in the answer choices. For instance, there's a big difference between .106, 1.06, 10.6, and 106. Keep these things in mind as you solve math problems. They should also all be labeled correctly and consistently.

Look for "give-away words" like *always*, *never*, or *not*. Most things in the world are not *always* or *never*, and you should be careful if a question asks, "Which of the following is NOT . . .!

By using the process of elimination you increase your chances of getting the right answer. Remember that you are not penalized for incorrect answers on the exam, so it's worth taking a chance. What this means is that if you just guess, you have a one in five chance to guess correctly—20%.

But what if you are able to eliminate two of the choices because they just seem wrong to you? You now have a one in three chance of selecting the correct answer. That's 33%, which is surely better than 20%.

If you're able to narrow it down to only two choices, you will then improve to one out of two, or 50%. You just want to improve your odds of increasing your score, and you can see that it doesn't take much.

Scoring

There are two scores that you will receive. One is the raw score, which is the total number of correct answers. The second is the standard score, which is derived by a complex mathematical formula, but suffice to say, that you should be focused on getting the most answers correct as you can. Since you are <u>NOT</u> penalized for incorrect answers, it is definitely to your advantage. The more correct answers you receive, the better your score will be. If you don't know the answers to a question, no matter what you do, just guess at it.

These standard scores range from 1 to 30 and are used to compare your results to those of the performance of the other candidates who took the exam. A standard score of 17 is considered an average score on a national basis.

Because you will be taking the test on the computer, you will immediately receive a test score report and explanation when you have completed the entire battery of tests. These are for your use only, but they will be sent to dental schools within 3 weeks of completing the exam. If you are not happy with your scores, you can take the exam again, but the results of the four most recent sets of scores will be on your official transcript.

There are no secrets to successful test-taking. Try to pace yourself as you go through the book. Review the material, answer all of the questions we've provided, and go back and review again anything you didn't understand the first time around.

PART II

SUBJECT REVIEWS

Survey of the Natural Sciences

Biology

- **Cell and Molecular Biology**—origin of life, cell metabolism (including photosynthesis) and enzymology, cellular processes, thermodynamics, organelle structure and function, mitosis/meiosis, cell structure, and experimental cell biology.

- **Diversity of Life: Biological Organization and Relationship of Major Taxa** (monera, plantae, animalia, protista, fungi, etc.)—using the five-kingdom system

- **Vertebrate Anatomy and Physiology: Structure and Function of Systems**—integumentary, skeletal, muscular, circulatory, immunological, digestive, respiratory, urinary, nervous/senses, endocrine, and reproductive

- **Developmental Biology**—fertilization, descriptive embryology, developmental mechanisms, and experimental embryology

- **Genetics**—molecular genetics, human genetics, classical genetics, chromosomal genetics, and genetic technology

- **Evolution, Ecology, and Behavior**—natural selection, population, genetics/speciation, cladistics, population and community ecology, ecosystems, and animal behavior (including social behavior)

General Chemistry

- **Stoichiometry and General Concepts**—percent composition, empirical formulae, balancing equations, moles and molecular formulas, molar mass, density, and calculations from balanced equations

- **Gases**—kinetic molecular theory of gases, Dalton's, Boyle's, Charles', and ideal gas laws

- **Liquids and Solids**—intermolecular forces, phase changes, vapor pressure, structures, polarity, and properties

- **Solutions**—polarity, properties (colligative, noncolligative), forces, and concentration calculations

- **Acids and Bases**—pH, strength, Brønsted-Lowry reactions, and calculations

- **Chemical Equilibria**—molecular, acid/base, precipitation, calculations, and Le Chatelier's principle

- **Thermodynamics and Thermochemistry**—laws of thermodynamics, Hess' law, spontaneity, enthalpies and entropies, and heat transfer

- **Chemical Kinetics**—rate laws, activation energy, and half life

- **Oxidation-Reduction Reactions**—balancing equations, determination of oxidation numbers, electrochemical calculations, and electrochemical concepts and terminology

- **Atomic and Molecular Structure**—electron configuration, orbital types, Lewis-Dot diagrams, atomic theory, quantum theory, molecular geometry, bond types, and sub-atomic particles
- **Periodic Properties**—representative elements, transition elements, periodic trends, and descriptive chemistry
- **Nuclear Reactions**—balancing equations, binding energy, decay processes, particles, and terminology
- **Laboratory**—basic techniques, equipment, error analysis, safety, and data analysis

Organic Chemistry

- **Mechanisms (Energetics, Structure, and Stability of Intermediates)**—S_N1, S_N2, elimination; addition, free radical, and substitution mechanisms
- **Chemical and Physical Properties of Molecules and Organic Analysis**—inter- and intra-molecular forces, separation, introductory infrared spectroscopy, ^1HNMR spectroscopy, $^{13}CNMR$, chemical identification, stability, solubility, and polarity
- **Stereochemistry**—conformational analysis, geometric isomers, stereoisomers (enantiomers, diastereomers, meso compounds), and optical activity (planes of symmery)
- **Nomenclature**—IUPAC rules and functional groups in molecules
- **Individual Reactions of the Major Functional Groups and Combinations of Reactions to Synthesize Compounds**—carbon-to-carbon bond formation, functional groups conversions, multi-step synthesis, redox reactions, name reactions, grignard, witting, deiels-adlet, aldol reaction
- **Acid-Base Chemistry**—resonance effects, inductive effects, and prediction of products and equilibria
- **Aromatics Arid Bonding**—concept of aromaticity, resonance, atomic/molecular orbitals, hybridization, and bond angles/lengths

Survey of Quantitative Reasoning

- **Mathematical Problems: Algebra**—equations and expressions, inequalities, exponential notation, absolute value, ratios and proportions, and graphical analysis
- **Numerical calculations**—fractions and decimals, percentages, approximations, and scientific notation
- **Conversions**—temperature, time, weight, and distance
- **Probability and Statistics, Geometry, Trigonometry, and Applied Mathematics (Word) Problems**

Biology

Cell and Molecular Biology

---

1. Life on Earth originated

    A. 4.5 billion years ago.

    B. between 3.5 and 4.0 billion years ago.

    C. 2.5 billion years ago.

    D. between 1.7 and 1.9 billion years ago.

    E. between 3.0 and 4.0 million years ago.

(B) The Earth formed approximately 4.5 billion years ago (A), with life originating between 3.5 and 4.0 billion years ago (B). The production of oxygen by early photosynthetic prokaryotes created an aerobic atmosphere approximately 2.5 billion years ago (C). The first eukaryotic organisms originated between 1.7 and 1.9 billion years ago (D), while the first hominids (ancestors of modern-day humans) are thought to have originated between 3.0 and 4.0 million years ago (E).

---

2. The earliest forms of life on Earth are thought to be primitive forms of

    A. paramecia.

    B. amoeba.

    C. bacteria.

    D. fungi.

    E. worms.

(C) Fossil and biochemical evidence suggest that the earliest forms of life were prokaryotic in nature, having a simple cellular structure without a defined nucleus or other organelles. Prokaryotes are represented by various genera of bacteria (C). All other organisms are classified as eukaryotes, having their DNA confined to an organized nucleus and containing various other membrane-bound organelles.

---

3. The cells of eukaryotic organisms contain a variety of organelles that allow for the compartmentalization of specific functions within the cell. The membranes surrounding the various organelles are composed of

    A. a double layer of proteins, within which lipids are embedded.

    B. a double layer of lipids, within which proteins are embedded.

    C. a single layer of proteins, within which lipids are embedded.

    D. a single layer of lipids, within which proteins are embedded.

    E. a triple layer of lipids, within which proteins are embedded.

(B) The cellular membranes of eukaryotic organisms are composed of a double layer of lipids (specifically, phospholipids) with a diverse array of proteins embedded within the bi-layer or attached to the surface. The membranes of different organelles differ in their composition of lipids and proteins, consisting of those most suited to the specific function(s) of the organelle. The lipid bi-layer structure, with embedded and attached proteins, functions to control the movement of substances into and out of the various organelles within the cell, as well as into and out of the cell as a whole.

4. In eukaryotic cells, protein synthesis takes place at the

    A. nucleus.
    B. mitochondria.
    C. chloroplasts.
    D. ribosomes.
    E. lysosomes.

(D) Protein synthesis takes place at the ribosomes of eukaryotic cells. The nucleus of eukaryotic cells (A) contains DNA, packaged into distinct chromosomes, which governs the physical and biochemical properties of the cell. Cellular respiration takes place in the mitochondria of eukaryotic cells (B), while photosynthesis takes place in the chloroplasts of plant cells and some bacterial cells (C). Lysosomes (E) use hydrolytic enzymes to breakdown macromolecules in the cells of some eukaryotic organisms.

5. Plant cells typically contain a large central vacuole. Which of the following is NOT a function of the central vacuole in plant cells?

    A. storage of organic compounds
    B. storage of inorganic ions, such as potassium and chloride
    C. disposal of metabolic by-products
    D. maintenance of water balance within the cell
    E. production of ATP

(E) The central vacuole found in most plant cells has a wide range of functions including the storage of both organic and inorganic compounds, the disposal of metabolic by-products (wastes), the maintenance of water balance and turgor pressure within the cell, and sometimes the storage of pigments, which give color to the cell (for example, the red and blue pigments found in the petals of flowers and the roots of beets). The production of ATP occurs through the process of cellular respiration, which takes place in the mitochondria of plant and animal cells.

6. The chemical interactions among molecules within the cell occur in an orderly array of intricately branched metabolic pathways, which manage the materials and energy resources within the cell. The transformation of energy from one form to another—for example, the conversion of potential energy to kinetic energy—is governed by the laws of thermodynamics. Which of the following is NOT consistent with the laws of thermodynamics governing energy transfer within a cell?

    A. Energy can neither be created nor destroyed within the cell.
    B. Energy transformations increase the degree of entropy within the cell.
    C. Organisms are considered "closed systems" and, therefore, cannot transfer energy between themselves and their environment.
    D. Chemical energy stored in cells is a form of potential energy.
    E. Heat is considered the lowest grade of energy within the cell.

(C) Organisms are considered "open systems" in which energy can be transferred between the individual and its surroundings. For example, plants can take in light energy and convert it into chemical energy in the form of glucose through the process of photosynthesis.

7. Which of the following best describes the process of photosynthesis, which occurs in the chloroplasts of plant cells?

    A. Glucose is broken down to produce oxygen and water.
    B. Glucose is broken down to produce carbon dioxide and water.
    C. Glucose is synthesized from oxygen and water.
    D. Glucose is synthesized from carbon dioxide and water.
    E. Glucose is synthesized from oxygen and carbon dioxide.

(D) In the process of photosynthesis, light energy is used to convert carbon dioxide from the atmosphere, and water is taken up by the plant from the soil to produce glucose, releasing oxygen to the atmosphere as a by-product, as shown in the equation below:

$$6CO_2 + 12H_2O \xrightarrow{\text{light energy}} C_6H_{12}O_6 + 6O_2 + 6H_2O$$

---

8. The most efficient wavelength(s) of light for photosynthesis is/are

   A. green.
   B. green and red.
   C. green and blue.
   D. red and blue.
   E. red and ultraviolet.

(D) Chlorophyll, the pigment involved in the process of photosynthesis and located in the chloroplasts of certain cells found in plants, algae, and some bacteria, absorbs light most efficiently in the red and blue wavelengths. Green wavelengths of light are reflected by chlorophyll, giving the pigment (and most plant leaves) a characteristic green color.

---

9. The breakdown of glucose in the presence of oxygen results in the production of carbon dioxide, water, and energy in the form of ATP. This process, which takes place in the mitochondria of both plant and animal cells, is referred to as

   A. cellular respiration.
   B. alcoholic fermentation.
   C. lactic acid fermentation.
   D. anaerobic respiration.
   E. photosynthesis.

(A) Organisms obtain energy (in the form of ATP) from the breakdown of organic molecules (primarily glucose), in the presence of oxygen, in the mitochondria of their cells through a process known as cellular respiration. (See the equation below). Fermentation involves the breakdown of glucose in the absence of oxygen (anaerobically). In some organisms, such as yeast, the breakdown product is ethanol, through a process known as alcoholic fermentation (B), while in other organisms, such as the muscle cells of humans, the breakdown product is lactic acid, through a process known as lactic acid fermentation (C). (Refer to equations below.) Both types of fermentation, which take place in the absence of oxygen, are often referred to as anaerobic respiration (D). Photosynthesis (E) involves the synthesis of glucose from carbon dioxide and water in the chloroplasts of certain cells found in plants, algae, and some bacteria.

Cellular Respiration (Aerobic Respiration):

$$C_6H_{12}O_6 + 6O_2 \longrightarrow 6CO_2 + 6H_2O + ATP + heat$$

Alcoholic Fermentation (Anaerobic Respiration):

$$C_6H_{12}O_6 + 6O_2 \longrightarrow 6CO_2 + 6H_2O + ATP + heat$$

Lactic acid Fermentation (Anaerobic Respiration):

$$C_6H_{12}O_6 \longrightarrow 2C_3H_6O_3 + ATP$$

10. Which of the following statements regarding enzymes is INCORRECT?

A. Enzymes are a type of protein.

B. Enzymes are substrate-specific, meaning that a given enzyme will only act on a specific substrate and will not catalyze reactions involving similar substrates.

C. Enzymes act as catalysts to speed up chemical reactions by increasing the amount of activation energy required to break the chemical bonds in the reactant molecules.

D. Enzymes act as catalysts by changing the rate of chemical reactions without themselves being changed or consumed by the reaction.

E. Enzyme activity can be affected (increased or decreased) by the physical and chemical environment of the cell in which it is found, with a given enzyme having an optimal temperature and pH range within which it is most efficient at catalyzing reactions.

(C) Enzymes act to *lower* the activation energy required for a chemical reaction to proceed, thereby speeding up the rate of the reaction.

11. Diffusion of molecules across a semi-permeable membrane, such as would occur if a salt water solution was separated from a distilled water solution by an artificial membrane, would ultimately result in which of the following?

A. a dynamic equilibrium in which both solutions would have approximately equal concentrations of salt molecules

B. all of the salt molecules moving to the distilled water solution

C. all of the salt molecules remaining in the salt water

D. all of the distilled water moving into the salt water container

E. all of the salt water moving into the distilled water container

(A) Diffusion involves the movement of molecules from a region of higher concentration to a region of lower concentration, along what is known as a concentration gradient. After the concentration of molecules is similar on each side of the membrane, diffusion would occur at approximately equal rates in both directions across the membrane, resulting in a dynamic equilibrium between the two solutions, with no net movement of molecules in either direction.

12. What would most likely happen to a human red blood cell that was removed from the body and placed in a jar containing distilled water?

A. The red blood cell would take up water and shrivel up.

B. The red blood cell would take up water until it reached a point in which the cell wall would exert turgor pressure against the uptake of water, forcing excess water back out of the cell.

C. The red blood cell would take up water until it swelled and burst.

D. The red blood cell would lose water and shrivel up.

E. The red blood cell would lose water and burst.

(C) A human red blood cell would have a higher concentration of solutes and, therefore, a lower concentration of water than the distilled water into which it was placed. As a result, the cell would take up water by osmosis (the movement of water across a semi-permeable membrane from a region of higher concentration to a region of lower concentration). Because animal cells do not have cell walls, the blood cell would continue to take up water and swell until it bursts (lyses). Plant cells, on the other hand, do have cell walls that exert an opposite pressure against the uptake of water (turgor pressure) forcing any excess water out of the cell and preventing the cell from *lysing*.

13. Metabolic pathways in which complex molecules are broken down into simpler compounds are referred to as

    A.   energetic pathways.
    B.   kinetic pathways.
    C.   anabolic pathways
    D.   catabolic pathways.
    E.   catalytic pathways.

(D) Catabolic pathways involve the release of energy through the breakdown of complex molecules into simpler compounds, such as occurs during cellular respiration when glucose is broken down into carbon dioxide and water. Anabolic pathways (C) involve the consumption of energy as complex molecules are formed from simpler components, such as occurs during the formation of proteins from amino acids.

14. A molecule that binds to an enzyme somewhere other than its active site and results in an inhibition of enzyme activity is referred to as a

    A.   competitive inhibitor.
    B.   noncompetitive inhibitor.
    C.   feedback inhibitor.
    D.   coenzyme.
    E.   cofactor.

(B) A noncompetitive inhibitor reduces enzyme activity by binding to the enzyme at a location other than the active site of the enzyme resulting in a change in the conformation of the enzyme so that the active site is no longer fully functional. A competitive inhibitor (A) reduces enzyme activity by binding to the active site of the enzyme and, thus, competing with the substrate for the binding site on the enzyme. Feedback inhibition (C) occurs when a metabolic pathway is switched off by the presence of its end product, which acts as an inhibitor of the enzyme catalyzing the reaction. A cofactor (E) is an inorganic compound that assists an enzyme with its catalytic activity. A coenzyme (D) is an organic compound that assists an enzyme with its catalytic activity.

15. Prior to cell division, cells go through a phase of the cell cycle known as DNA synthesis, which results in

    A.   a doubling of the number of chromosomes within the cell.
    B.   a doubling of the DNA content within each chromosome of the cell.
    C.   a halving of the number of chromosomes within the cell.
    D.   a halving of the amount of DNA within each chromosome of the cell.
    E.   no change in the amount of DNA within the cell.

(B) During the synthesis phase of the cell cycle, in preparation for cell division, the DNA content of each chromosome doubles, such that each chromosome is represented by two sister chromatids; however, the number of chromosomes in the cell does not change.

16. During the process of meiosis, a single cell gives rise to

    A.   two genetically identical daughter cells.
    B.   two genetically unique daughter cells.
    C.   four genetically identical daughter cells.
    D.   four genetically unique daughter cells.
    E.   four daughter cells, two of which are identical to the parent cell and two of which are genetically unique.

(D) Meiosis is the process of cell division that occurs in the germ cells and gives rise to gametes (for example, eggs and sperm in humans). Each cell that undergoes meiosis produces four genetically unique daughter cells. In contrast, somatic cells undergo a type of cell division referred to as mitosis, which produces two daughter cells that are identical to each other, as well as to the parent cell undergoing division. Mitosis allows for growth and repair of tissues.

Diversity of Life

---

17. Which of the following represents the mode of reproduction that occurs in bacteria?

    A. transformation
    B. conjugation
    C. transduction
    D. binary fission
    E. budding

(D) Bacteria reproduce asexually only through a type of cell division known as binary fission, in which the single chromosome of the parent cell is duplicated, the cell grows in length to separate the two chromosomes, and the plasma membrane grows inward pinching the cell into two equal halves, each with a single copy of the chromosome. Although bacteria reproduce asexually only, genetic variation occurs through the exchange of genetic information by transformation (A), in which genes are taken up by the cell from the surrounding environment; conjugation (B), in which genes are transferred directly from one bacterial cell to another through the formation of a temporary conjugation tube connecting the two cells; and transduction (C), in which genes are transferred between cells by viruses. Budding (E) is a type of asexual reproduction in which outgrowths of the parent cell are pinched off to live independently (as in yeast and hydra) or remain attached to the parent organism to form an extensive colony (as in corals).

---

18. The Gram stain technique is used to determine the cell wall structure of various groups of bacteria. Not only is the Gram stain a useful taxonomic tool, but it is medically important because

    A. Gram-positive bacteria are typically more dangerous pathogens due to the toxins produced in their cell walls.
    B. Gram-negative bacteria tend to be more resistant to antibiotics than gram-positive bacteria.
    C. Gram-positive bacteria have more complex cell walls than gram-negative bacteria and, thus, are more difficult to treat.
    D. Gram-negative bacteria have much peptidoglycan in their cell walls, making them more toxic than Gram-positive bacteria.
    E. Gram-positive bacteria are not pathogenic.

(B) The Gram stain identifies bacterial groups based on differential staining of their cell walls. Gram-positive bacteria have relatively simple cell walls containing much peptidoglycan, while Gram-negative bacteria have more complex cell walls containing less peptidoglycan and much lipopolysaccharide. Although pathogenic bacteria can be found among both Gram-positive and Gram-negative groups, Gram-negative bacteria tend to be more resistant to antibiotics due to the complex structure of their cell walls. Also, Gram-negative bacteria tend to be more dangerous due to the production of toxins from the lipopolysaccharide layer.

---

19. The first photosynthetic organisms that used water and carbon dioxide to make organic compounds, producing oxygen as a by-product and allowing for the eventual development of aerobic cellular respiration among the Earth's organisms, are classified as

    A. plants.
    B. algae.
    C. bacteria.
    D. mosses.
    E. lichens.

(C) Between 2.5 and 3.5 billion years ago, strains of photosynthetic bacteria (cyanobacteria) evolved that were able to utilize water (instead of hydrogen sulfide) and carbon dioxide to make organic compounds, such as glucose. Oxygen was released as a by-product of the reactions.

20. Which of the following organisms is NOT classified as a protist?

    A.   chlamydia
    B.   amoeba
    C.   paramecium
    D.   green alga
    E.   slime mold

(A) Chlamydia are bacteria and, thus, are prokaryotic organisms classified as Monera in the five-kingdom system of classification. Amoebas (B) and paramecia (C) are animal-like protists, green algae (D) are plant-like protists, and slime molds (E) are fungal-like protists.

21. Which of the following statements regarding protists is correct?

    A.   All protists are single-celled.
    B.   All protists are phostosynthetic.
    C.   All protists have cillia.
    D.   All protists are eukaryotic.
    E.   All protists move by pseudopodia.

(D) Kingdom Protista includes a diverse array of organisms that do not fit into any of the other kingdoms of the Five-Kingdom system of classification of organisms. The one characteristic shared by all protists is that they are eukaryotic organisms. Prokaryotic organisms (bacteria) are classified as Monera in the Five-Kingdom system.

22. Which of the following phenomena is explained by the endosymbiont theory?

    A.   The presence of a nucleus in eukaryotic cells.
    B.   The presence of chloroplasts and mitochondria is eukaryotic cells.
    C.   The presence of cell walls in plant cells.
    D.   The presence of a plasma membrane surrounding eukaryotic cells.
    E.   The presence of a large central vacuole in plant cells.

(B) According to the endosymbiont theory, mitochondria and chloroplasts originated as small prokaryotes living as endosymbionts within larger cells. The proposed ancestors of mitochondria are aerobic, heterotrophic prokaryotes, while the proposed ancestors of chloroplasts are photosynthetic prokaryotes.

23. Fungi acquire nutrients by

    A.   photosynthesis.
    B.   chemitrophism.
    C.   ingestion.
    D.   diffusion.
    E.   absorption.

(E) Fungi are heterotrophic organisms that acquire nutrients by absorption. Fungi secrete enzymes that breakdown complex organic molecules into smaller compounds that can be absorbed and used by the organism.

24. There are numerous examples of both helpful and harmful species of fungi. Which of the following organisms is NOT considered a beneficial member of the Kingdom Fungi?

    A.   Rhizobium sp.

    B.   Penicillium roquefortii

    C.   morel

    D.   Saccharomyces cerevisiae (bread / beer yeast)

    E.   puffball

(A) *Rhizobium* species are bacteria that form symbiotic relationships with the roots of plants in the legume family. Through a process known as nitrogen fixation, *Rhizobium* take nitrogen from the atmosphere and convert it into a form usable by the plant, enhancing the uptake of usable forms of nitrogen. *Penicillium roquefortii* (B) is a fungus that provides the color and flavor of roquefort cheese (a type of blue cheese). Morels (C) are a type of fungus that is edible and considered a delicacy by many people. *Saccharomyces cerevisiae* (D) is a yeast (single-celled fungal organism) used in the brewing and baking industries. Puffballs (E) are edible fungi.

25. What part of the fungal life cycle is represented by the common mushrooms we purchase at the grocery?

    A.   asexual reproductive structures

    B.   sexual reproductive structures

    C.   the main vegetative (non-reproductive) part of the body

    D.   the absorptive structures through which the organisms take up nutrients

    E.   the photosynthetic portion of the body

(B) The mushroom portion of a fungus represents the "fruiting body" or sexual reproductive structure of certain groups of fungi (Ascomycota and Basidiomycota). The asexual reproductive structures (A) of most fungi are small and borne on the vegetative part of the body (C), which consists of long, filamentous thread-like structures referred to as mycellia. There are no photosynthetic parts to the fungal body (E).

26. Which of the following statements best describes the movement of water and dissolved sugars in plants?

    A.   Water moves downward through the plant in phloem tissue, while dissolved sugars move upward through the plant in xylem tissues.

    B.   Water moves upward through the plant in the xylem tissue, while dissolved sugars move downward through the plant in the phloem.

    C.   Water moves downward through the plant in the xylem, while dissolved sugars move upward in the plant through the phloem.

    D.   Water moves upward through the plant in the phloem, while dissolved sugars move downward through the plant in the xylem.

    E.   Water moves upward through the plant in the xylem, while dissolved sugars move both upward and downward through the plant in the phloem.

(E) Water is taken up by the roots and transported upward through the plant in the xylem in response to tension created by evapotranspiration of water from the leaves of the plant. Dissolved sugars, made in the photosynthetic tissues of the plant (primarily the leaves), move throughout the plant in the phloem. The direction of movement is from a "source" (where the sugars are made or stored) to a "sink" (areas that need sugars for growth or metabolism). Thus, dissolved sugars may move downward through the plant (for example, from the leaves where it is being made to the roots for root growth or for storage) or upward through the plant (for example, from where it is stored in the roots to new growth occurring at the tips of young branches).

27. The vascular, nonseed-bearing (spore-producing) plants include

    A. pines and firs.
    B. mosses and liverworts.
    C. ferns and horsetails.
    D. mosses and ferns.
    E. ferns and pines.

(C) Ferns and horsetails, along with lycophytes, have vascular tissue (xylem and phloem) and sexually reproduce through spores (as opposed to seeds). Mosses and liverworts are non-vascular, meaning they do not contain xylem or phloem tissue (although some have primitive water-conducting cells) and reproduce sexually via spores. Pines and firs have well-developed vascular tissue and reproduce sexually by seed.

28. Flowering plants undergo a special type of fertilization referred to as double fertilization, which is considered a significant evolutionary advantage over nonflowering plants. In double fertilization,

    A. two sperm cells unite with the egg to produce a more robust triploid zygote.
    B. one sperm cell unites with the egg to form a zygote and one sperm cell unites with the endosperm (nutritive issue) to form the fruit.
    C. two sperm cells unite with the egg cell to form a fruit.
    D. one sperm cell unites with the egg to form a zygote and one sperm cell unites with two polar nuclei to form the endosperm (nutritive tissue).
    E. two sperm cells and two egg cells all fuse to form a more robust tetraploid zygote.

(D) In double fertilization, which occurs in flowering plants, one sperm cell unites with an egg cell to form a diploid zygote, while a second sperm cell unites with two polar nuclei in the embryo sac (female gametophyte) to form triploid endosperm tissue. Triploid endosperm tissue is more robust and has a higher nutritive value than the haploid endosperm tissue of maternal origin found in nonflowering seed plants (gymnosperms).

29. A fruit is most commonly

    A. a mature embryo sac.
    B. a mature ovary.
    C. a fertilized ovule.
    D. a mature female gametophyte.
    E. endosperm tissue.

(B) In flowering plants, after fertilization, the ovule becomes the seed, and mature ovary tissue develops into the fruit, surrounding and protecting the seed. In some fruits, such as apples and strawberries, additional tissue (hypanthium or receptacle tissue) may also become part of the mature fruit.

30. Which of the following animal phyla is mismatched with its description and examples?

    A. Platyhelminthes   no body cavity; flatworms
    B. Porifera   lacking true tissues; sponges
    C. Cnidaria   bilateral symmetry; hydra
    D. Mollusca   determinate cleavage; clams
    E. Chordata   indeterminate cleavage; humans

(C) Members of phylum Cnidaria have a body plan with radial symmetry.

---

31. Which animal phylum is mismatched with its primary characteristics of classification?

A.	Platyhelminthes	dorsoventrally-flattened; acoelomates
B.	Nematoda	segmented; cylindrical
C.	Mollusca	major body parts include a muscular foot, visceral mass, and a mantle
D.	Arthropoda	regional segmentation; jointed appendages; exoskeleton
E.	Chordata	notochord; dorsal hollow nerve cord

(B) Members of phylum Nematoda are unsegmented, cylindrical roundworms.

---

32. The class of chordates whose members are endothermic and nourish their young from mammary glands is the

    A. Amphibia.
    B. Osteichthyes.
    C. Aves.
    D. Reptilia.
    E. Mammalia.

(E) Mammals are endothermic animals that nourish their young from the mammary glands of the female.

---

33. Which of the following organisms is NOT considered a member of the class Reptilia?

    A. toad
    B. snake
    C. lizard
    D. turtle
    E. crocodile

(A) Toads are members of the class Amphibia.

Vertebrate Anatomy and Physiology

---

34. Which of the following is NOT part of the excretory system in vertebrates?

    A. ureters
    B. urethra
    C. kidneys
    D. small intestine
    E. bladder

(D) The small intestine is part of the vertebrate digestive system, which functions in the ingestion, digestion, absorption, and elimination of food. The function of the vertebrate excretory system, which includes the ureters (A), urethra (B), kidneys (C), and bladder (E), is to rid the body of metabolic waste products and regulate the osmotic balance of the blood.

35. Which of the following statements regarding thermoregulation in vertebrates is true?

    A. Reptiles and amphibians are considered ectotherms because they derive body heat primarily from their surroundings and must rely on behavioral adaptations to regulate their body heat, while birds and mammals can regulate their body heat through internal metabolic changes and, thus, are considered endotherms.

    B. All vertebrates are ectotherms, having the ability to regulate their body heat through internal metabolic changes, while invertebrates are endotherms and must rely on adaptations to their surroundings to regulate body temperature.

    C. Birds and mammals have the ability to regulate their body heat through metabolism and are, thus considered ectotherms, while amphibians and reptiles must adapt to their surrounding by behavioral changes to adjust their body temperature and, thus are considered endotherms.

    D. The internal body temperature of an endothermic organism fluctuates according to the temperature of the individual's surroundings, while the internal body temperature of an ectothermic organism remains relatively constant regardless of the temperature of the individual's surroundings.

    E. All vertebrates are endotherms, having the ability to regulate their body heat through internal metabolic changes, while invertebrates are ectotherms and must rely on adaptations to their surroundings to regulate body temperature.

(A) Ectothermic organisms, which include amphibians, reptiles, and fish, must derive body heat from their surroundings and, therefore, must rely on behavioral adaptations to regulate body heat (for example, moving to a sunny spot from a shady spot to increase body temperature). As such, the internal body temperature of an ectothermic organism fluctuates according to the surrounding temperature. Endothermic organisms, which include birds and mammals, control their body heat by internal metabolic changes; therefore, their internal body temperature remains relatively constant regardless of the temperature of their surroundings.

36. Groups of cells with a common structure and function are referred to as

    A. organelles.
    B. organs.
    C. tissues.
    D. systems.
    E. fibers.

(C) There is a hierarchical level of structure in living organisms. The lowest level of organization that can exist independently is the cell. Within the cells of eukaryotic organisms are specialized, membrane-bound structures, called organelles (A), that carry out specific functions. Groups of cells that share a common structure and function are organized into tissues (C). Various tissues are organized into specialized centers of function called organs (B), and groups of organs work together in an organized manner to form organ systems (D). For example, the human digestive system is composed of several organs, including the stomach, small intestine, large intestine, and gall bladder, among others, with each organ composed of different tissue types. Fibers (E) are specialized structures found in many different tissue types of living organisms.

37. In the human digestive system, the primary site of digestion and absorption is the

    A. stomach.
    B. liver.
    C. gall bladder.
    D. small intestine.
    E. large intestine.

(D) When food is ingested and begins to make its way down the human digestive system, it is first processed into small pieces in the mouth and the limited digestion of carbohydrates begins through the action of salivary amylase produced in saliva. With the aid of the tongue, the food is shaped into a ball, called a bolus, and pushed into the pharynx, which leads to both the esophagus and the trachea (windpipe). The act of swallowing pushes the trachea upward so that its opening, the glottis, is blocked by a cartilaginous flap called the epiglottis, thus ensuring that the bolus moves down into the esophagus instead of the windpipe. Muscular contractions, referred to as peristalsis, moves the bolus down the esophagus and into the stomach (A), where food is stored and preliminary digestion begins. As the bolus is mixed and processed by enzymes and acids produced in the stomach, it turns into a broth-like substance called chyme, which moves through the pyloric sphincter connecting the stomach to the small intestine (D). The small intestine is the site at which most digestion occurs and most nutrients are absorbed into the body. The pancreas, liver (B), and gall bladder (C) participate in digestion by producing enzymes that are secreted into the top portion of the small intestine (the duodenum) that help break down the chyme. When digestion is complete, unabsorbed fluids and waste products pass into the large intestine (E) and are eliminated as feces. See diagram below.

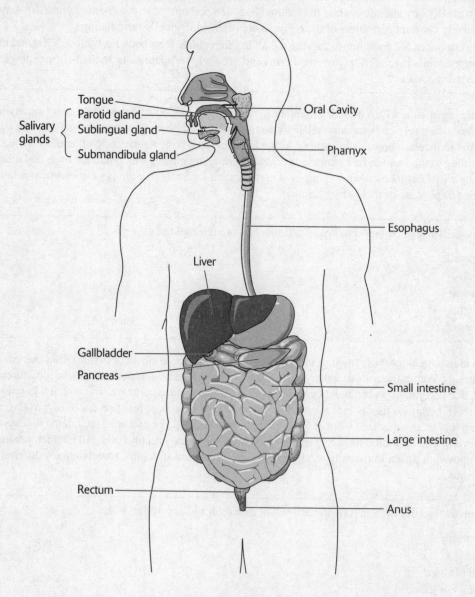

38. An individual whose diet is missing one or more essential nutrients is said to be

    A. undernourished.
    B. malnourished.
    C. anemic.
    D. heterotrophic.
    E. homeostatic.

(B) A malnourished individual is one whose diet is lacking one or more essential nutrients. An individual who is undernourished (A) has a diet that is deficient in caloric intake. An individual who is anemic (C) has insufficient hemoglobin or red blood cells. A heterotrophic individual (D) is one that obtains organic food molecules by consuming other organisms. An individual whose body is in a steady-state physiological condition is said to be in a homeostatic state (E).

39. When taking your pulse, you are actually measuring your

    A. diastolic blood pressure.
    B. systolic blood pressure.
    C. heart rate.
    D. basal metabolic rate.
    E. standard metabolic rate.

(C) By taking your pulse, you can measure your heart rate, or the number of times your heart beats per minute. The diastole (A), the relaxation phase of the cardiac cycle, and systole (B), the contraction phase of the cardiac cycle, must be measured with a sphygmomanometer and a stethoscope. Basal metabolic rate (D), the minimal number of calories an endothermic individual needs when at rest, is determined by the individual's weight and relative level of fitness. Standard metabolic rate (E), the minimal number of calories an ectothermic individual needs when at rest, depends on environmental conditions, such as temperature and relative humidity, as well as the weight of the individual.

40. Which of the following statements regarding blood flow through the human heart is INCORRECT?

    A. Blood that is relatively low in oxygen enters the right atrium of the heart through the vena cava.
    B. The right ventricle of the heart forces oxygen-poor blood to the lungs.
    C. The left ventricle of the heart forces oxygen-rich blood throughout the body.
    D. Blood is supplied to the tissues of the heart by the pulmonary artery.
    E. Oxygen-poor blood from the head, neck, and limbs is emptied into the vena cava.

(D) Blood is supplied to the tissues of the heart by the first two branches of the aorta, referred to as the right and left coronary arteries. The pulmonary artery carries oxygen-poor blood from the heart to the lungs, while the pulmonary veins return oxygen-rich blood from the lungs to the heart. See diagram on the following page.

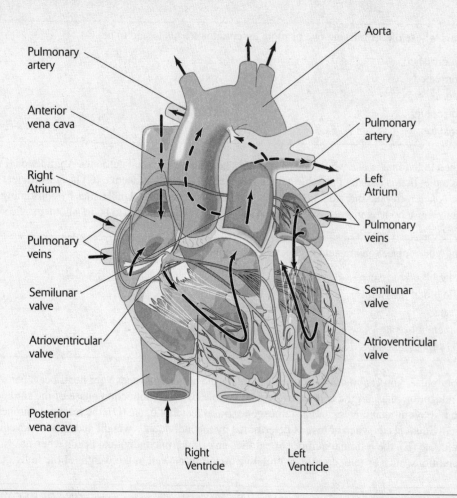

Aorta

Pulmonary artery

Anterior vena cava

Right Atrium

Pulmonary veins

Semilunar valve

Atrioventricular valve

Posterior vena cava

Right Ventricle

Left Ventricle

Pulmonary artery

Left Atrium

Pulmonary veins

Semilunar valve

Atrioventricular valve

41. In humans, the exchange of gases (oxygen and carbon dioxide) occurs primarily across the epithelium of the

    A. alveoli.

    B. bronchioles.

    C. bronchi.

    D. trachea.

    E. windpipe.

(A) When air is inhaled into the human respiratory system, it passes from the nasal cavity into the larynx. From the larynx, air moves into the trachea (D), also called the windpipe (E). The trachea branches into two bronchi (C), one leading to each lung. Within the lung, the bronchi branch into finer and finer tubes called bronchioles (B). The smallest bronchioles terminate into air sacs referred to as alveoli (A), the surface of which serves as the primary site for gas exchange in the human respiratory system. Oxygen in the air inhaled diffuses across the epithelial surfaces of the alveoli into surrounding capillaries. Carbon dioxide diffuses from the capillaries, across the epithelial surfaces of the alveoli and into the air space. See diagram on the following page.

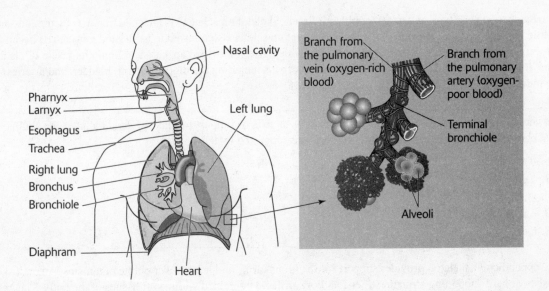

Nasal cavity

Pharnyx
Larnyx
Esophagus
Trachea
Right lung
Bronchus
Bronchiole

Diaphram

Heart

Left lung

Branch from the pulmonary vein (oxygen-rich blood)

Branch from the pulmonary artery (oxygen-poor blood)

Terminal bronchiole

Alveoli

---

42. In vertebrate organisms, oxygen and carbon dioxide are transported throughout the body by binding to

    A.   water molecules in the blood.
    B.   hemoglobin in white blood cells.
    C.   hemoglobin in red blood cells.
    D.   lymph in white blood cells.
    E.   lymph in red blood cells.

(C) Hemoglobin is a blood pigment that gives red blood cells their characteristic color. Hemoglobin consists of four sub-units, each of which contains an iron molecule that can bind to oxygen for transport throughout the body. Hemoglobin also binds and transports carbon dioxide and serves to buffer the blood, preventing harmful fluctuations in blood pH.

---

43. The human tissue system that functions to produce an outer covering for the body, serves as a sense organ and serves as a barrier against pathogens is the

    A.   connective tissue system.
    B.   adipose tissue system.
    C.   muscle tissue system.
    D.   dermal tissue system.
    E.   fibrous tissue system.

(D) The dermal tissue system, the "skin," serves as an outer covering for the body, as well as a barrier to entry for pathogens. It is also an important sensory organ. Connective tissue (A) functions to bind and support other tissues. Adipose tissue (B) is a specialized type of connective tissue that stores fat. Muscle tissue (C) is composed of long cells (fibers) that contract and relax, allowing for movement of various body parts. Fibrous tissue (E) is a dense connective tissue found in tendons and ligaments.

---

44. Which of the following does NOT represent a type of muscle tissue found in vertebrates?

    A.   skeletal
    B.   striated
    C.   smooth
    D.   cardiac
    E.   squamous

(E) Squamous tissue is a type of dermal (epithelial) tissue. Skeletal muscle (A) is attached to bones by tendons and is responsible for voluntary movements of the body. Skeletal muscle is also referred to as striated muscle (B) because of the arrangement of overlapping filaments in the tissue, which give it a striped appearance. Smooth muscle (C) lacks striations; it is found in the walls of most of the internal organs including the digestive tract, bladder, and arteries. Cardiac muscle (D) forms the contractile wall of the heart.

45. In vertebrate organisms, the axial skeleton provides an axis of support for the body and includes the skull, backbone, and rib cage, while the arms and legs are supported by the

  A. appendicular skeleton.
  B. endoskeleton.
  C. joints.
  D. skeletal muscles.
  E. exoskeleton.

(A) The appendicular skeleton provides support for the limbs (arms and legs) of vertebrate organisms. An endoskeleton (B) consists of hard supporting structures (bone and/or cartilage) contained within soft tissues of the body. The appendicular skeleton and the axial skeleton (which provides support for the trunk of the body—the head, backbone, and rib cage) together make up the endoskeleton of vertebrate organisms. Joints (C) allow for flexibility in body movement. Skeletal muscles (D) are attached to the bones and allow them to move through contraction and relaxation of the muscle tissues. An exoskeleton (E) is a hard structure deposited on the surface of an organism, such as is found in mollusks and arthropods.

46. In the vertebrate immune system, all of the following are examples of nonspecific defense mechanisms EXCEPT

  A. secretions of the skin and mucous membranes.
  B. phagocytic white blood cells.
  C. antibodies.
  D. antimicrobial proteins.
  E. inflammatory response.

(C) Antibodies are produced in response to a specific foreign invader (antigen). Each antibody produced by the body works only against a specific antigen. Therefore, the production of antibodies is considered a "specific defense mechanism" or a "specific immune response". Lymphocytes also respond to some specific foreign invaders and, therefore, are also considered a specific defense mechanism. Non-specific defense mechanisms (non-specific immune responses) operate against any foreign invader. Non-specific defense mechanisms include the skin (barrier), mucous membranes, and secretions of the skin (B), phagocytic while blood cells (C), antimicrobial proteins (D), and the inflammatory response (E).

47. Which of the following statements regarding vaccines is INCORRECT?

  A. Vaccines made from killed microorganisms may cause the disease they are designed to prevent.
  B. Vaccines act like antigens to stimulate an immune response.
  C. Vaccines stimulate immunological memory.
  D. Vaccines are considered an active form of immunity.
  E. Vaccines are considered an artificial form of immunity.

(A) Vaccines, whether made from bacterial toxins, parts of microorganisms, viable but weakened microorganisms, or killed microorganisms, are not capable of causing disease; however, they are capable of acting as antigens stimulating both a direct immune response (B) and immunological memory (C). Vaccines are considered an active form of immunity (D) because the immunity depends on a response from the vaccinated ("infected") person's immune system. Vaccines are considered an artificial form of immunity (E) because the immune response is not stimulated directly by the infectious agent.

48. Which of the following glands and hormones produced by the gland is MISmatched?

    A.   pituitary gland   growth hormone

    B.   adrenal glands   oxytocin

    C.   thyroid gland   thyroxine

    D.   ovaries   progesterone

    E.   pineal gland   melatonin

(B) Oxytocin, which stimulates uterine contractions, is produced by the pituitary gland. Other hormones produced by the pituitary gland include growth hormone (A), which stimulates growth; prolactin, which stimulates milk production and secretion; antidiuretic hormone, which promotes water retention by the kidneys; follicle-stimulating hormone, which stimulates production of eggs in females; luteinizing hormone, which stimulates ovaries and testes; thyroid-stimulating hormone, which stimulates the thyroid gland; and the adrenocorticotropic hormone, which stimulates the adrenal cortex to secrete glucocorticoids. The thyroid gland produces thyroxine (C), which stimulates and maintains metabolism; and calcitonin, which lowers blood calcium levels. The parathyroid glands produce parathyroid hormone, which raises blood calcium levels. The pancreas produces insulin, which lowers blood glucose levels; and glucagon, which raises blood glucose levels. The adrenal glands (B) produce epinephrine and norepinephrine, which raise blood glucose levels, increase metabolism, and constrict certain blood vessels; glucocorticoids, which raise blood glucose levels; and mineralocorticoids, which promote reabsorption of sodium and elimination of potassium in the kidneys. The testes produce androgens, which support sperm formation and promote the development of male secondary sex characteristics. The ovaries produce estrogens, which stimulate growth of the uterine lining and promote the development of female secondary sex characteristics; and progesterone (D), which promotes growth of the uterine lining. The pineal gland produces melatonin (E), which assists with the maintenance of biological rhythms. The thymus produces thymosin, which stimulates T-lymphocytes.

49. The junction where one neuron communicates with another neuron within a neural pathway in the human nervous system is referred to as a(n)

    A.   neurotransmitter.

    B.   membrane potential.

    C.   synapse.

    D.   axon.

    E.   dendrite.

(C) A synapse is the junction where one neuron communicates with another neuron within a neural pathway. It is represented by a narrow gap between a synaptic terminal of an axon and a signal-receiving portion (dendrite) of another neuron or effector cell. A neurotransmitter (A) is an intercellular chemical messenger released at a synapse. The membrane potential (B) is a measure of the voltage across the plasma membrane, which is the result of differences in electrical charges on each side of the membrane (the cytoplasm and the extracellular fluid). An axon (D) is a long extension from a neuron that carries nerve impulses away from the cell body toward target cells. A dendrite (E) is a short highly branched extension of a neuron that carries nerve impulses toward the cell body.

50. In vertebrate organisms, the brain and spinal cord make up the

    A.   parasympathetic nervous system.

    B.   somatic nervous system.

    C.   autonomic nervous system.

    D.   peripheral nervous system.

    E.   central nervous system.

(E) The brain and spinal cord make up the central nervous system of vertebrate organisms. The peripheral nervous system (D) is composed of the nerves and ganglia leading from the central nervous system to the rest of the body. The somatic nervous system (B) carries signals to skeletal muscles, usually in response to an external stimulus. The autonomic nervous system (C) conveys signals that regulate involuntary control of the cardiac muscles and the smooth muscles of the digestive, cardiovascular, excretory, and endocrine systems. The autonomic nervous system is divided into two divisions: the parasympathetic division controls activities that conserve energy, such as digestion and a slowing of the heart rate; the sympathetic division controls activities that consume energy, such as increasing heart rate or metabolic function, preparing the body for action.

---

51. Which of the following organs in human males is shared by both the reproductive system and the excretory system?

    A. prostate

    B. testes

    C. urethra

    D. ureter

    E. seminal vesicles

(C) The urethra serves as a conduit for the release of semen from the reproductive system and the release of urine from the excretory system. The prostate (A) is the largest of the glands that secretes semen, secreting it directly into the urethra. The testes (B) are the male gonads (male sex organs, where sperm are produced). The ureter (D) is a duct leading from the kidney to the bladder. The seminal vesicles (E) are a pair of glands that secrete about 60% of the semen produced.

Developmental Biology

---

52. During development of the human fetus, most organ development occurs

    A. during the last trimester.

    B. during the last month of development.

    C. during the first month of development.

    D. during the first trimester.

    E. during the last two weeks of development.

(D) The majority of organ development (organogenesis) occurs during the first trimester of pregnancy in humans. Because of the rapid rate of organ development during this period, the fetus is especially vulnerable to radiation, chemicals, and drugs than can cause birth defects.

---

53. Following fertilization (uniting of an egg and sperm), a special type of cell division referred to as cleavage takes place. Cleavage results in

    A. a three-layered embryo.

    B. the development of rudimentary organs.

    C. an eight-fold enlargement of the zygote.

    D. a partitioning of the zygote from one large cell into several smaller cells.

    E. the development of polarity in the zygote.

(D) After fertilization, a special form of cell division referred to as cleavage occurs. Cleavage involves a rapid succession of cell divisions in which the cells undergo DNA synthesis and mitosis, but not the two growth stages of the cell cycle. The result is a partitioning of the zygote (a single large cell) into several smaller cells, called blastomeres, without an overall increase in the size of the developing embryo. This multi-cellular embryo is called a blastula. Different parts of the cytoplasm are partitioned into different blastomeres during cleavage, setting up the cells for future developmental events. Following cleavage, gastrulation occurs, resulting in the formation of a three-layered embryo called a gastrula (A). The next stage of development, organogenesis, results in the production of rudimentary organs in the embryo (B).

54. Gastrulation results in a rearrangement of the cells in the blastula to form an embryo composed of three layers of tissue referred to as germ layers. The three germ layers produced in gastrulation are the

    A. gastrula, animal pole, and vegetal pole.
    B. ectoderm, endoderm, and mesoderm.
    C. blastula, gastrula, and morula.
    D. protoderm, procambium, and ground meristem.
    E. blastocoel, blastopore, and archenteron.

(B) The three germ layers in vertebrate embryos are the ectoderm (which gives rise to the epidermis of the skin, the lining of the mouth and rectum, the cornea and lens of the eye, the nervous system, tooth enamel, and the epithelium of the pineal and pituitary glands); the endoderm (which gives rise to the lining of the digestive tract, reproductive system, respiratory system, bladder, and urethra, as well as giving rise to the liver, pancreas, thyroid, pararthyroid glands, and thymus); and the mesoderm (which gives rise to the notochord, the skeletal system, the muscular system, the circulatory system, the lymphatic system, the excretory system, the reproductive system, the dermis of the skin, the lining of the body cavity, and the adrenal cortex). The protoderm, procambium, and ground meristem (D) are the primary meristems that give rise to the tissue systems of plants. Other than mammals, most animals have a polarity to their eggs, the animal and vegetal poles (A), which are defined by the distribution of substances within the egg. The blastula, gastrula, and morula (C) represent stages of embryo development in animals: the blastula refers to the multicellular embryo resulting from cleavage of the zygote; the gastrula refers to the three-layered embryo produced by gastrulation of the blastula; the morula refers to the solid ball of cells that results from a series of cleavages of the zygote in some animal embryos, such as frogs and sea urchins. The blastocoel (E) is a fluid-filled cavity that forms in the morula creating a hollow ball stage of development; the blastopore (E) is the open end of the archenteron (E), which is the primitive gut of developing frog and sea urchin embryos.

55. Which of the following statements regarding embryo development in mammals is INCORRECT?

    A. Mammalian eggs have considerable yolk content, which serves as a food reserve.
    B. Mammal eggs do not have cytoplasmic determinants that establish polarity in the egg.
    C. The process of gastrulation in mammal eggs is similar to that found in birds and reptiles.
    D. Organogenesis follows a similar pattern in bird, reptile, and mammal eggs.
    E. Cleavage of mammal eggs occurs at a relatively slow rate, and the cleavage planes are random.

(A) Unlike the eggs of birds and reptiles, which are large and contain a large amount of yolk, mammal eggs are relatively small and contain very little stored food.

56. During the early development of vertebrate embryos, cells with different developmental potential can influence the development of neighboring groups of cells through a process known as

    A. polarity.
    B. organization.
    C. induction.
    D. potency.
    E. determination.

(C) As vertebrate embryos develop, cell division creates groups of cells in different regions. The cells in one region can influence the development of groups of cells in nearby regions through responses to inductive signals (induction). Induction usually involves the switching on of a specific set of genes that causes the cells receiving the inductive signal to differentiate into a specific tissue type. Inductive signals play an important role in the arrangement of organs and tissues (pattern formation) in the developing embryo.

57. Using modern technology, many genetic and congenital disorders can be detected in a developing human fetus while it is in the uterus. Which of the following procedures is NOT used to test the fetus while in the uterus?

    A. amniocentesis
    B. chorionic villus sampling
    C. ultrasound imaging
    D. testing of a blood sample from the mother
    E. in vitro fertilization

(E) In vitro fertilization refers to the uniting of an egg and a sperm outside the mother's body. Typically, an egg is surgically removed from the mother or a donor and fertilized with a sperm sample in a culture dish in the laboratory. When the embryo has reached the eight-celled stage, it is placed in the uterus and allowed to implant in the uterine lining. Technologies that can be used to test for genetic diseases and congenital disorders include amniocentesis (A), an invasive procedure that collects a sample of amniotic fluid for analysis; chorionic villus sampling (B), an invasive procedure that collects a sample of fetal tissue for testing; ultrasound imaging (C), a noninvasive procedure that uses high frequency sound waves to produce an image of the fetus on a computer screen; and testing a sample of the mother's blood (D). The mother's blood contains sufficient fetal cells for testing. The fetal cells, which can be identified using specific antibodies, are separated from the maternal cells and tested for genetic disorders.

58. The ability of embryonic cells to retain the potential to develop into any part of the organism is referred to as

    A. cell fate.
    B. pattern formation.
    C. polarity.
    D. totipotency.
    E. determination.

(D) Totipotency refers to the ability of some embryonic cells to develop into any part of the organism. In some organisms, only the zygote is totipotent. In mammals, the embryonic cells (blastomeres) remain totipotent through the eight-celled stage.

59. Factors that may result in congenital deformities by affecting the embryo during growth and development are referred to as

    A. disrupters.
    B. teratogens.
    C. carcinogens.
    D. deformers.
    E. morphogens.

(B) Many substances (drugs, chemicals, and alcohol) ingested by the mother can pass through the placental membrane into the blood supply of the fetus affecting organ formation, growth patterns, and brain development. Such substances, which affect growth and development of the embryo or fetus, are referred to as teratogens.

Genetics

---

60. The expression of genetic traits in an individual (that is, the physical appearance of the individual) is referred to as the individual's

    A.   genome.
    B.   genotype.
    C.   phenotype.
    D.   genetic make-up.
    E.   allelic make-up.

(C) The physical appearance of an individual, which is an expression of their genetic make-up, is referred to as their phenotype, while the actual genetic make-up of the organism (D) is referred to as their genotype (B). The genome (A) refers to the entire genetic complement of an organism. The allelic make-up (E) of an individual is part of their genetic make-up. For example, if the "P" allele codes for pink flower color and is dominant to the "p" allele, which codes for white flower color, then an individual with a "pink" phenotype could have one of two genotypes: PP (homozygous dominant for pink flower color) or Pp (heterozygous for pink flower color). Homozygous recessive individuals (pp) would have white flowers.

---

61. An individual that is heterozygous for a given trait will

    A.   produce gametes containing one of two different types of alleles for that trait.
    B.   produce gametes containing one of three different types of alleles for that trait.
    C.   only give rise to offspring that have the same genotype as itself when crossed with a homozygous recessive individual.
    D.   only give rise to offspring that have the same phenotype as itself when crossed with a homozygous recessive individual.
    E.   only give rise to offspring that have the same phenotype as itself when crossed with another heterozygous individual.

(A) An individual that is heterozygous for a trait (for example, Aa) will produce gametes that carry either the "A" allele or the "a" allele. When a heterozygous individual (Aa) is crossed with a homozygous recessive individual (aa), half of the offspring will be heterozygous (Aa) and half will be homozygous recessive (aa); thus, some of the offspring will have a different genotype and a different phenotype from the heterozygous parent. If two heterozygous individuals are crossed (Aa × Aa), one quarter of the offspring will be homozygous dominant (AA); one half of the offspring will be heterozygous, like the parents (Aa); and one quarter of the offspring will be homozygous recessive (aa).

---

62. If curly tails are dominant to straight tails in pigs, which of the following represents the correct phenotypic ratio of offspring that would be produced from a monohybrid cross between two pigs that were both heterozygous for curly tails?

    A.   all offspring would have curly tails
    B.   all offspring would have straight tails
    C.   3:1 with 3 curly-tailed : 1 straight-tailed
    D.   3:1 with 3 straight-tailed : 1 curly-tailed
    E.   1:1 with 1 curly-tailed : 1 straight-tailed

(C) A monohybrid cross is one in which the inheritance of a single gene (trait) is followed. If we assign "T" to represent tail shape in pigs, with "T" representing the dominant condition of curly tails and "t" representing the recessive condition of straight tails, then a cross between two pigs, both heterozygous for tail shape (Tt × Tt) would produce ¼ homozygous dominant (TT), ½ heterozygous (Tt), and ¼ homozygous recessive (tt) individuals. If curly tails (T) is dominant to straight tails (t), then both the homozygous dominant offspring and the heterozygous offspring will have curly tails; thus, ¾ of the offspring will have curly tails and ¼ will have straight tails, for a 3 curly-tailed : 1 straight-tailed ratio among the offspring, as illustrated by the Punnett square below.

The heterozygous parents would each produce two types of gametes, in roughly equal proportions: ½ T and ½ t

	½ T	½ t
½ T	¼ TT	¼ Tt
½ T	¼ Tt	¼ tt

Thus, the genotypic ratio among the offspring is 1:2:1 (1 TT : 2Tt : 1 tt), and the phenotypic ratio among the offspring is 3:1 (3 curly-tailed : 1 straight-tailed).

---

63. Which of the following represents the correct ratio of offspring that would be produced from a dihybrid cross between a brown, long-tailed mouse that is heterozygous for both body color and tail length and a white, short-tailed mouse that is homozygous recessive for both traits?

- **A.** 9:3:3:1 with 9 brown, long-tailed : 3 brown, short-tailed : 3 white, long-tailed : 1 white, short-tailed
- **B.** 9:3:3:1 with 9 brown, long-tailed : 3 white, short-tailed : 3 brown, short-tailed : 1 white, long-tailed
- **C.** 9:3:3:1 with 9 brown, short-tailed : 3 brown, long tailed : 3 white, short-tailed : 1 white, long-tailed
- **D.** 1:1:1:1 with 1 brown, long-tailed : 1 brown, short-tailed : 1 white, long-tailed : 1 white, short-tailed
- **E.** All offspring would be brown with long tails.

(D) A dihybrid cross is one in which the inheritance of two genes (traits) is followed simultaneously. If we assign "B" to represent body color, with "B" representing the dominant allele for brown and "b" representing the recessive allele for white, and we assign "T" to represent tail length, with "T" representing the dominant allele for long tails and "t" representing the recessive allele for short tails, then a cross between a mouse that is heterozygous for both traits (BbTt) and a mouse that is homozygous recessive for both traits (bbtt) would result in a 1:1:1:1 ratio of brown, long-tailed : brown, short-tailed : white long-tailed : white, short tailed, as illustrated by the Punnett square below.

The heterozygous individual would produce four types of gametes, with approximately equal frequency (¼ BT, ¼ Bt, ¼ bT, ¼ bt), and the homozygous recessive individual would produce only one type of gamete (bt), resulting in a 4 × 1 Punnett square:

	¼ BT	¼ Bt	¼ bT	¼ bt
bt	¼ BbTt	¼ Bbtt	¼ bbTt	¼ bbtt

The genotypic ratio among the offspring is 1:1:1:1 (1 BbTt : 1 Bbtt : 1 bbTt : 1 bbtt), and the phenotypic ratio among the offspring would be 1:1:1:1 (1 brown, long-tailed : 1 brown, short-tailed : 1 white, long-tailed : 1 white, short-tailed).

---

64. If the offspring from a cross between a red-flowered snapdragon and a white-flowered snapdragon are all pink, the most likely explanation is that

- **A.** the allele for red flower color is completely dominant to the allele for white flower color.
- **B.** the allele for white flower color is completely dominant to the allele for red flower color.
- **C.** there are epistatic interactions occurring between the alleles for red and white flower color.
- **D.** there are pleiotropic interactions between the alleles for red and white flower color.
- **E.** the allele for red flower color shows incomplete dominance over the allele for white flower color.

(E) When the phenotypes of the offspring are intermediate between the phenotypes of the two parents, the most likely cause is that the dominant allele does not completely mask the recessive allele. In the case of the snapdragons in this example, if the dominant allele (for example, "R") produces red pigment, and the recessive allele (for example, "r") produces no pigment, the heterozygous offspring (Rr) may produce less pigment than the red parents (RR), because they have only one copy of the dominant allele that produces the pigment and, therefore, appear pink.

---

65. A trait that is controlled by two or more genes, such as yield in agricultural crops and height in humans, resulting in a continuous array of phenotypes, is referred to as a(n)

    A. epistatic trait.

    B. pleiotropic trait.

    C. polygenic trait.

    D. multi-allelic trait.

    E. discrete trait.

(C) A polygenic trait is one whose inheritance is governed by two or more genes. These quantitative traits, which typically show a continuous array of phenotypes, are usually also highly influenced by environmental factors. Discrete traits (E) are those that are controlled by a single gene, with or without environmental influence, and show a limited number of specific phenotypes. A multi-allelic trait (D) is a type of discrete trait that has more than two possible alleles (for example, the A, B, O blood groups in humans). Epistasis (A) occurs when a gene at one locus alters the phenotypic expression of a gene at another locus (for example the inheritance of coat color in horses). Pleiotropy (B) refers to the condition in which one gene controls the expression of more than one trait (for example, the gene responsible for sickle cell anemia in humans results in the expression of numerous physical symptoms).

---

66. A family tree that shows the genetic make-up of individuals in an extended (human) family, and the relationships among those individuals, is referred to as a

    A. flow chart.

    B. pedigree.

    C. Punnett square.

    D. template.

    E. fingerprint.

(B) The genetic basis of human traits is relatively difficult to study (as compared to fruit flies, plants, mice, and so on) because humans have a relatively long life cycle, typically have relatively small numbers of offspring, and "controlled matings" for which genetic studies cannot be conducted. As a result, geneticists rely on several techniques to study human genes, including the use of pedigree analysis. A pedigree is a family tree that shows the genetic make-up of individuals in an extended family and the relationships among those individuals. Geneticists can use the information contained in a pedigree to determine the mode of inheritance of various traits, determine the genotype of individuals whose genotype (that is , homozygous dominant or heterozygous) is unknown, and predict the probabilities of genotypes and phenotypes of future offspring.

---

67. Sex-linked traits are those traits that are carried on the sex chromosomes. In humans, most sex-linked traits are carried on the X chromosome; very few traits are carried on the Y chromosome. Which of the following statements regarding X-linked traits in humans is INCORRECT?

    A. Females cannot show sex-linked recessive traits.

    B. All daughters born to a father with a sex-linked dominant disorder will show the disorder.

    C. Sons cannot inherit a sex-linked trait from their father.

    D. Males cannot be heterozygous for sex-linked traits.

    E. All sons born to a mother who is homozygous dominant for a sex-linked dominant trait will show the disorder.

(A) The sex chromosome complement of human females is XX, and the sex chromosome complement of human males is XY. Daughters receive one X chromosome from their mother and one X chromosome from their father. With two X chromosomes, sex-linked recessive disorders are less common among females than males, as there is a chance that a female will carry at least one unaffected X chromosome (with the dominant allele), masking the presence of the recessive allele. However, it is possible for a daughter to inherit the recessive allele from both parents and show the homozygous recessive trait. Sons inherit their X chromosome from their mother and their Y chromosome from their father. Thus, even an unaffected, heterozygous mother has a 50-50 chance of producing an affected son.

---

68. Aneuploidy (the condition of having extra copies or missing copies of individual chromosomes) results from errors that take place during meiosis. This type of error is referred to as a

- **A.** linkage.
- **B.** translocation.
- **C.** crossover.
- **D.** non-disjunction.
- **E.** transition.

(D) Mistakes that occur during meiosis often result in non-disjunction, in which the members of a pair of homologous chromosomes fail to separate in meiosis I and move to the same pole of the cell, or sister chromatids fail to separate in meiosis II and move to the same pole of the cell. The result in either case is one or more gametes with an incorrect complement of chromosomes, containing either too much genetic information (having two copies of the same chromosome) or missing genetic information (missing a chromosome).

---

69. Some human genetic disorders are due to chromosomal aberrations resulting from the breakage of chromosomes leading to changes in the normal structure of the chromosome. Which of the following is NOT the result of chromosome breakage and altered chromosome structure?

- **A.** deletion.
- **B.** duplication.
- **C.** inversion.
- **D.** translocation.
- **E.** polyploidy.

(E) Polyploidy results from mistakes that take place during meiosis that result in non-disjunction of entire sets of chromosomes, such that the resulting gamete (egg or sperm) is diploid instead of haploid. A deletion (A) occurs when a piece of a chromosome that does not include the centromere is broken off and lost during cell division. A duplication (B) occurs when a piece that was broken off of one chromosome attaches to the homologous chromosome, resulting in a duplication of the information contained on the chromosome fragment. An inversion occurs when a fragment broken off of a chromosome reattaches to the same chromosome, but in the opposite orientation, which results in the inability for the genes to be read properly during transcription and protein synthesis. A translocation (D) occurs when the fragment from a broken chromosome attaches to a non-homologous chromosome.

70. Genes present in the mitochondria of both plants and animals, and in the chloroplasts of plants, are inherited independently of the nuclear genes and are inherited in a non-Mendelian manner. Inheritance of traits carried on genes present in the mitochondria or chloroplasts is referred to as

    A. embryonic inheritance
    B. paternal inheritance
    C. maternal inheritance
    D. zygotic inheritance
    E. genomic inheritance

(C) The genes present in the mitochondria and chloroplasts are inherited through the cytoplasm during cell division. Because the egg cells of both plants and animals have a considerable amount of cytoplasm, and the male gametes (pollen or sperm) have a negligible amount of cytoplasm, most of the genes in the mitochondria and chloroplasts are inherited through the maternal parent and, therefore, the inheritance of mitochondrial and chloroplast genes is referred to as maternal inheritance.

71. DNA is composed of chains of nucleotides. Each nucleotide consists of

    A. a ribose sugar, a nitrogenous base, and a phosphate group.
    B. a deoxyribose sugar, a nitrogenous base, and a phosphate group.
    C. a ribose sugar, a nitrogenous base, and a sulfur group.
    D. a deoxyribose sugar, a nitrogenous base, and a sulfur group.
    E. a ribose sugar, a phosphorus base, and a mitogenous group.

(B) DNA (deoxyribonucleic acid) is a polynucleotide composed of a chain of nucleotide units. Each nucleotide unit consists of the sugar deoxyribose, a phosphate group, and one of four nitrogenous bases (adenine, thymine, cytosine, guanine). The phosphate group of one nucleotide is attached to the sugar of the next nucleotide, forming a backbone of alternating sugar and phosphate molecules with the nitrogenous bases projecting inward and held together by hydrogen bonds, as depicted in the diagram on the following page.

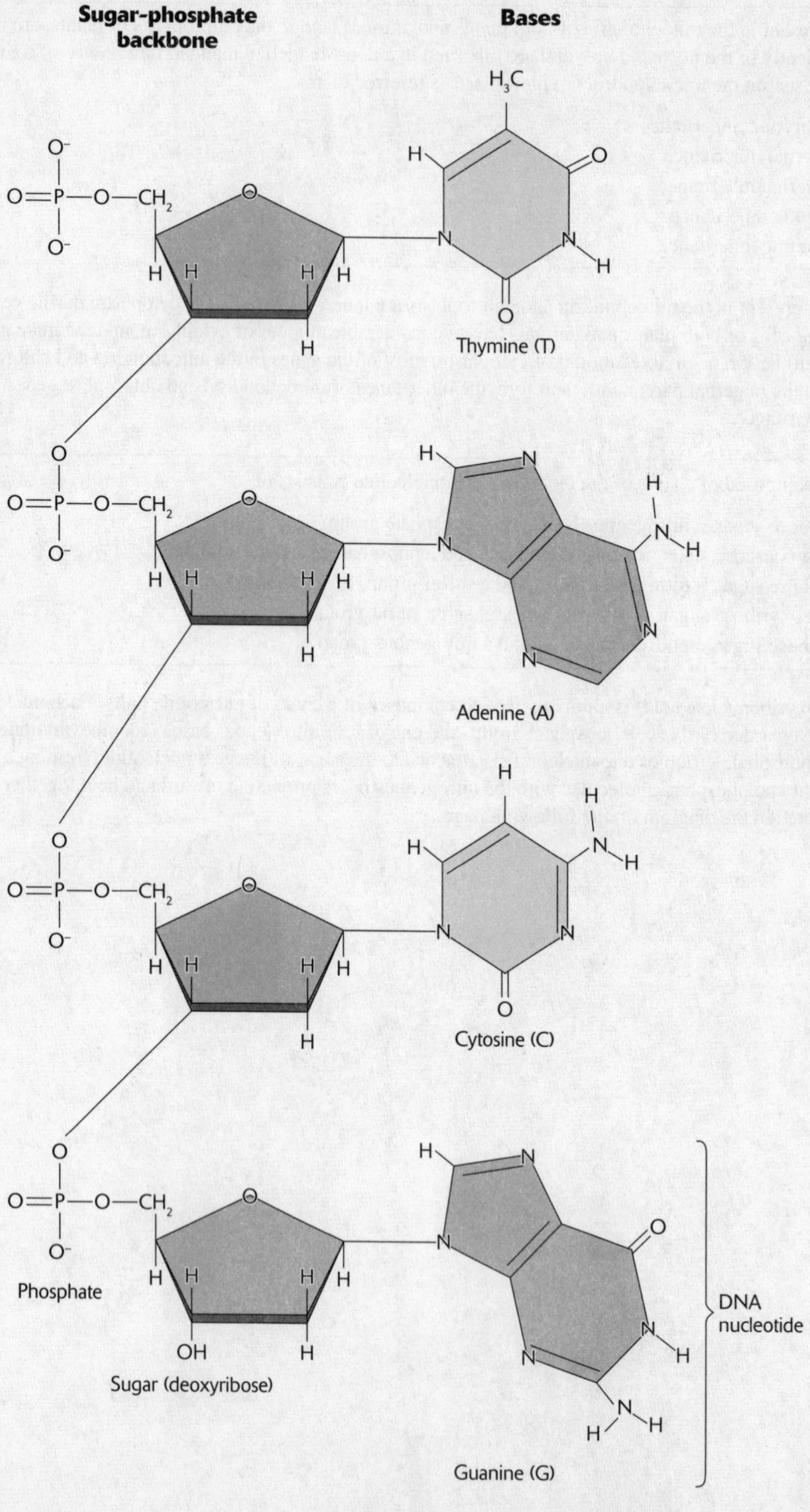

Sugar-phosphate backbone

Bases

Thymine (T)

Adenine (A)

Cytosine (C)

Phosphate

OH

Sugar (deoxyribose)

Guanine (G)

DNA nucleotide

72. Adenine makes up approximately 30% of the nitrogenous bases found in human DNA. Thus, the percentages of the other bases in human DNA are

    A. 20% guanine, 30% thymine, and 20% cytosine
    B. 30% guanine, 20% thymine, and 20% cytosine
    C. 20% guanine, 20% thymine, and 30% cytosine
    D. 15% guanine, 30% thymine, and 25% cytosine
    E. The percentages of the other bases cannot be determined from the information given.

(A) In DNA, the sugar—phosphate backbone is held together by paired nitrogenous bases that project inward from the backbone. The bases are held together by hydrogen bonds, and the molecular structure of the bases is such that adenine only pairs with thymine and guanine only pairs with cytosine. Thus, the percentages of adenine and thymine in a DNA molecule will be equal, as will the percentages of guanine and cytosine. **Note:** There is no thymine in RNA; adenine pairs with uracil in RNA molecules. The pairing rules (Chargaff's rules) ensure that DNA is replicated properly prior to cell division, and that DNA is transcribed properly onto mRNA prior to protein synthesis.

73. The synthesis of a polypeptide is accomplished through the process of

    A. DNA replication.
    B. RNA processing.
    C. transcription.
    D. splicing.
    E. translation.

(E) Each gene on a molecule of DNA codes for one polypeptide, a component of proteins. DNA in the nucleus is read and copied onto a complementary mRNA (messenger RNA) molecule through the process of transcription (C). Following transcription, the non-coding regions of the mRNA molecule (introns), which lie between the coding regions (exons), are excised and the exons are spliced together through RNA processing (B). The processed mRNA molecule moves out of the nucleus into the cytoplasm and attaches to a ribosome, where the synthesis of polypeptides takes place through the process of translation (E). DNA replication (A) is the process by which DNA molecules are duplicated prior to cell division. Refer to the diagram below.

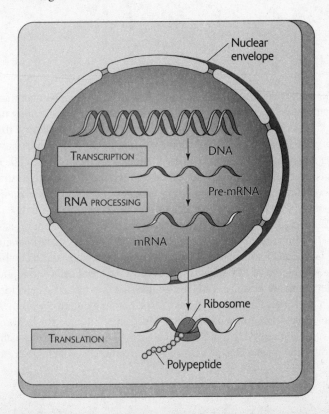

74. The genetic code refers to

    A. the genetic make-up of an organism.
    B. the genetic make-up of a population.
    C. nucleotide triplets that code for amino acids.
    D. the specificity of base pairing that holds the DNA molecule together.
    E. the DNA template strand.

(C) Series of three nucleotides (triplets) on the DNA molecule are transcribed onto a mRNA molecule, where they are read by a transfer RNA (tRNA) molecule during translation. Each triplet of bases on the DNA molecule codes for a specific amino acid. When these triplets are transcribed onto a mRNA molecule, specific tRNA molecules, carrying amino acids, read the triplet code on the mRNA molecule and insert the appropriate amino acid into the growing polypeptide chain.

75. Most cells in the human body contain proto-oncogenes that can be stimulated to become cancerous (oncogenes) through mutations. The normal function of proto-oncogenes in human cells is to

    A. stimulate protein synthesis.
    B. repair damaged regions of DNA.
    C. produce antibodies against invading pathogens.
    D. control normal cell growth and division.
    E. splice introns from mRNA during RNA processing.

(D) Proto-oncogenes are normal genes present in the human genome that code for proteins that regulate cell growth and cell division. Mutations (either spontaneous mutations, or those caused by exposure to radiation, cancer-causing chemicals, and certain viruses) occurring in the proto-oncogenes may cause them to no longer regulate normal cell growth and division. Uncontrolled cell growth and division may lead to cancer.

76. DNA molecules, made in vitro in the laboratory, that contain DNA from two or more organisms are referred to as

    A. DNA clones.
    B. recombinant DNA.
    C. plasmids.
    D. vectors.
    E. phages.

(B) DNA molecules that contain segments from different sources / organisms can be manufactured in vitro in the laboratory. This is usually done by cutting two sources of DNA with restriction enzymes and putting them together in solution. Restriction enzymes are isolated from various bacterial strains where they function to destroy foreign DNA or bacterial viruses (bacteriophages) entering the bacterial cell. Restriction enzymes cut DNA molecules at specific locations, with each restriction enzyme recognizing a unique base sequence where it cuts the DNA molecule. The restricted DNA molecules are double-stranded with at least one single-stranded end, called a *sticky end*. These single-stranded ends will form hydrogen bonds with strands containing complementary sticky ends, even if the complementary strand is from a DNA molecule from a different organism. The fused DNA molecules are sealed together with the enzyme DNA ligase, creating a recombinant DNA molecule that has been spliced together from DNA of different organisms. (Refer to the diagram on the following page.) DNA from one organism, for example a human DNA segment containing the gene coding for human growth hormone, may be spliced into a plasmid using restriction enzymes and recombinant DNA technology. (**Note:** Plasmids are small, circular pieces of DNA that reside in most bacterial cells and replicate themselves independently of the bacterial cell.) Recombinant plasmids can then be inserted into bacterial cells through transformation, the uptake of DNA (in this case, in the form of a plasmid) from the surrounding culture medium. As the bacterial cells reproduce, the recombinant plasmids, containing the gene for the production of human growth hormone, are replicated along with the bacterial cells. After sufficient reproduction, the human growth hormone proteins can be isolated from the cell colony. (See diagram on the following page.) This procedure is one method by which DNA can be cloned.

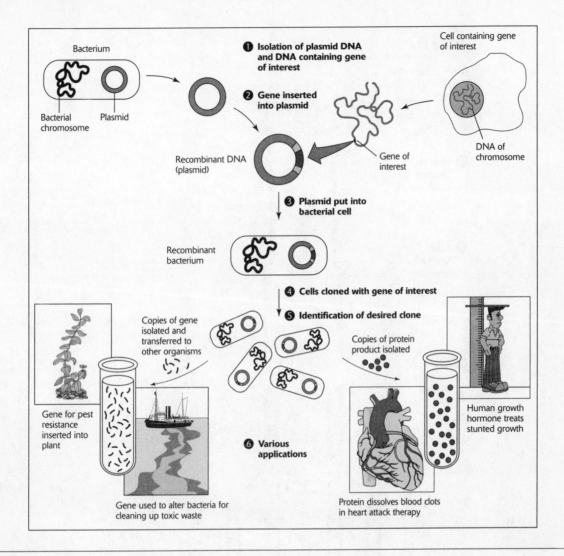

Bacterium

Bacterial chromosome

Plasmid

❶ Isolation of plasmid DNA and DNA containing gene of interest

❷ Gene inserted into plasmid

Recombinant DNA (plasmid)

Gene of interest

Cell containing gene of interest

DNA of chromosome

❸ Plasmid put into bacterial cell

Recombinant bacterium

❹ Cells cloned with gene of interest

❺ Identification of desired clone

Copies of gene isolated and transferred to other organisms

Copies of protein product isolated

Gene for pest resistance inserted into plant

Human growth hormone treats stunted growth

❻ Various applications

Gene used to alter bacteria for cleaning up toxic waste

Protein dissolves blood clots in heart attack therapy

77. A method for cloning DNA segments without using recombinant plasmids and bacterial colonies is referred to as

    A. transformation.

    B. transduction.

    C. conjugation.

    D. genetic engineering.

    E. polymerase chain reaction.

(E) The polymerase chain reaction (PCR) allows for the amplification (making of hundreds or thousands of copies) of a DNA segment without using plasmids and bacterial cells. This technique is especially useful when small quantities of DNA are available to work with, such as the case with evidence (for example, blood or semen) found at a crime scene. The amplification of the DNA allows for the production of a large quantity of DNA from a small sample relatively quickly. The PCR procedure is outlined in the diagram on the following page. Transformation (A) refers to the uptake of DNA from the surrounding environment. Transduction (B) refers to the uptake of DNA by bacterial cells through infection of the cells with a bacteriophage (bacterial virus). Conjugation (C) refers to the transfer of DNA between two bacterial cells through the formation of a temporary connection (conjugation tube) between the cells. Genetic engineering (D) refers to any direct manipulation of genes for research or practical purposes.

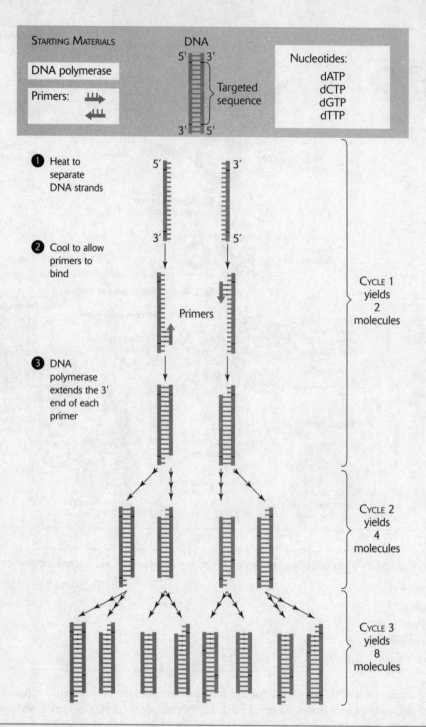

78. Genetic engineering and DNA technology have already been used for many practical applications. Which of the following applications is NOT currently being used?

    A. insertion of genetically engineered genes into human gametes (eggs and sperm)

    B. insertion of genetically engineered genes for disease resistance into agriculturally important crop species

    C. production of large quantities of human growth hormone and insulin

    D. prenatal detection of genetic disorders

    E. the production of DNA fingerprints for use in criminal cases

(A) To date, genetic engineering and gene technology have not been used to insert genetically engineered genes into human eggs and sperm. Such a use of the available DNA technology is still highly controversial.

Evolution, Ecology, and Behavior

79. Which of the following is NOT one of the principle observations used by Charles Darwin in the development of the theory of evolution by natural selection?

- **A.** Most species have such a great potential for reproduction that population sizes would increase exponentially if all individuals that were born successfully reproduced.
- **B.** Environmental resources are limited.
- **C.** Populations sizes naturally tend to fluctuate significantly from year to year.
- **D.** Individuals within a population show a high level of variability for physical characteristics.
- **E.** Much of the variation seen among individuals in a population is heritable (can be passed on to their offspring).

(C) Despite the great reproductive potential of most species (A), their population sizes do NOT fluctuate significantly from year to year. These observations, combined with the observation that environmental resources are limited (B), led Darwin to infer that the production of more individuals than the environment can support, led to a struggle for survival among the individuals of a population such that only a small percentage survive and reproduce. From the observation that there is quite a bit of variability among individuals in a population for most characteristics (D) and the observation that much of the variability was heritable (passed on from parent to offspring) (E), Darwin inferred that the struggle for survival was not random, but rather due at least in part to inherited characteristics—those individuals who inherited characteristics that made them best adapted to their environment were the most likely to survive and produce offspring. Darwin also inferred that the ability of the best-adapted individuals to survive and reproduce would lead to a gradual change in the genetic make-up of the population, with favorable traits increasing in frequency in the population over time. These inferences led Darwin to the development of the Theory of Evolution by Means of Natural Selection.

80. Natural selection can best be defined as

- **A.** an interaction between the environment and the genetic make-up of an individual.
- **B.** the adaptation of organisms to their environment.
- **C.** descent with modification.
- **D.** differential success in reproduction (different abilities of individuals to survive and reproduce).
- **E.** heritable variation.

(D) The differential success in reproduction among individuals in a population, in which the "most fit" or "best adapted" individuals are most likely to survive and reproduce is, by definition, the process of natural selection. The process of natural selection is *influenced* by an interaction between the genetic make-up of an individual and environmental conditions (A) and is based in part on the presence of heritable variation (E). Natural selection allows for the adaptation of populations of organisms to their environment (B). The process of evolution is often defined as "descent with modification" (C).

81. Which of the following fields of evidence in support of evolution is MISmatched with its description?

- **A.** Fossil Record—the study of the succession of fossil forms discovered around the globe.
- **B.** Biogeography—the study of the geographical distribution of species.
- **C.** Comparative Anatomy—the study of anatomical similarities among species grouped together in the same taxonomic category.
- **D.** Comparative Embryology—the study of the process by which human embryos go through a fish stage, an amphibian stage, and a reptile stage before reaching a mammalian stage during development.
- **E.** Molecular Biology—the study of DNA and proteins to determine relationships among species.

(D) The field of Comparative Embryology studies the similarities and differences in embryo development among different species. The research in this field shows that closely related organisms go through similar stages of embryonic development. For example, embryos of all vertebrates go through a stage in which they have gill pouches. As development continues, these structures diverge greatly in the different taxonomic groups. For example, in fish the gill pouches develop into gills, while in humans, the gill pouches develop into the Eustachian tubes that connect the middle ear with the throat. Although humans and fish both go through a stage during embryo development in which gill pouches are present, humans do NOT go through a fish stage during embryo development. Humans also do not go through an amphibian stage or a reptile stage during embryo development.

---

82. A group of individuals of the same species that live within the same geographic area is referred to as a(n)

   A. population.
   B. community.
   C. gene pool.
   D. evolutionary unit.
   E. geographic unit.

(A) A population refers to a group of individuals of the same species that share a common geographic area. A community (B) refers to all of the populations of different species that share a common geographic area and have the potential to interact with each other. A gene pool (C) refers to the total complement of genes in a population at any given time.

---

83. Which of the following is NOT one of the conditions required for a population to maintain Hardy-Weinberg equilibrium?

   A. large population size
   B. no gene flow into or out of the population from other populations (for example, by migration into or out of the population)
   C. no net mutations
   D. no natural selection
   E. no random mating

(E) For Hardy-Weinberg equilibrium to be maintained, mating must occur randomly. If individuals seek mates with certain characteristics, then the random mixing of gametes (necessary to maintain Hardy-Weinberg equilibrium) will not take place. A population in Hardy-Weinberg equilibrium will not undergo evolution. Although most populations fail to meet one or more of the conditions required to maintain Hardy-Weinberg equilibrium, the principles underlying Hardy-Weinberg equilibrium provide a basis for understanding the processes controlling microevolution. For each of the five conditions required for maintaining Hardy-Weinberg equilibrium, there is a corresponding force allowing for microevolution to occur:

(1) **Large population size:** If a population is very small, its gene pool might not reflect the gene pool represented in the entire species. In addition, the existing gene pool of a small population may not be accurately represented in the next generation, due to random chance or sampling error, if all of the alleles are not passed on. This force of microevolution is referred to as genetic drift—changes to the gene pool of a small population due to random chance.

(2) **No gene flow into or out of the population:** Certain alleles may be lost from a population, or their frequencies may be changed, if a high proportion of individuals with those alleles migrate out of the population. On the other hand, the frequency of certain alleles may be increased, or new alleles may be introduced into the gene pool, if individuals from another population (with different allelic and genotypic frequencies in the gene pool) migrate into the population.

(3) **No net mutations:** Random mutations that are transmitted in gametes will alter the allelic composition of the gene pool. If there are more mutations in one direction (for example A → a) than the reverse direction (a → A), then the allelic frequency of the gene pool may be altered.

(4) **No natural selection:** Natural selection for or against specific alleles will alter their frequency in the gene pool. Mutations combined with natural selection for or against the mutations provides the strongest driving force for evolution. Natural selection results in alleles being passed on to the next generation disproportionately to their frequency in the current gene pool, and it is the only evolutionary force that allows a population to become more adapted to its environment.

(5) **Random mating:** Most organisms select mates based on certain phenotypic characteristics. In addition, individuals often mate with other individuals that are physically close by. These types of non-random mating patterns often favor specific alleles over others, leading to changes in the allelic frequencies in a population over time.

---

84. In a population that is in Hardy-Weinberg equilibrium, if 9% of the individuals show the recessive trait and there are only two possible alleles for the trait, what is the frequency of the dominant allele in the population?

    A. .09
    B. 0.3
    C. 0.7
    D. 0.49
    E. 0.42

(C) According to the Hardy-Weinberg theorem, the allelic and genotypic frequencies of a population in Hardy-Weinberg equilibrium will remain constant from generation to generation (that is, the population will not evolve). Population geneticists have developed an equation to determine the allelic and genotypic frequencies in a population, and have defined p to represent the frequency of the dominant allele and q to represent the frequency of the recessive allele. If there are only two allelic possibilities for the trait, then the frequencies of the dominant and recessive alleles must equal 100%. Thus, $p + q = 1$. A homozygous dominant individual would inherit a dominant allele from each parent; the odds of two dominant alleles being present in an individual would be $p \times p = p^2$. Thus, the frequency of the homozygous dominant genotype would be p^2. Similarly, the frequency of the homozygous recessive genotype would be q^2. The frequency of heterozygotes would be $p \times q$; however, since there are two ways a heterozygote can occur (inheriting the dominant allele from the mother and the recessive allele from the father or inheriting the dominant allele from the father and the recessive allele from the mother), the overall frequency of heterozygotes would be $2pq$. Because the genotypic frequencies must equal 100%, the equation representing genotypic frequencies can be written as $p^2 + 2pq + q^2 = 1$. From these Hardy-Weinberg equations, we can determine the allelic and genotypic frequencies present in a population by observing phenotypic frequencies. We typically use the recessive phenotype, because we know that the individual must be homozygous recessive for the trait, so we can easily determine the frequency of the recessive allele from the frequency of the recessive phenotype. Conversely, with complete dominance, the homozygous dominant and heterozygous individuals will have the same phenotype, so their genotype cannot be determined by observing their phenotype.

In our example, we observed that 9% of the population shows the recessive phenotype. Thus, the frequency of the homozygous recessive individuals (q^2) would be **.09**, and the frequency of the recessive allele would be $q = \sqrt{.09}\ a = 0.3$. Because $p + q = 1$, then $1 - q = p$. In our example, $p = 1 - 0.3 = 0.7$. From these allelic frequencies, we can determine the frequencies of the genotypes in the population. We already know the frequency of the homozygous recessive genotype is $q^2 = .09$. The frequency of the homozygous dominant genotype is $p^2 = 0.7^2 = .49$, and the frequency of the heterozygous genotype is $2pq = 2(0.7)(0.3) = .42$.

---

85. There are several different acceptable scientific definitions of what constitutes a species. Which of the following species concepts is MISmatched with its description?

    A. Biological species concept–emphasizes reproductive isolation between species.
    B. Morphological species concept—emphasizes anatomical differences between species.
    C. Recognition species concept—emphasizes recognition of potential mates within a species.
    D. Evolutionary species concept—emphasizes evolutionary lineages and relationships between species.
    E. Ecological species concept—emphasizes the genetic mechanisms that maintain a species as a distinct phenotype.

(E) The ecological species concept emphasizes a species niche or role within the ecosystem.

86. The evolutionary history of a species, or groups of related species, is referred to as

    A. phylogeny.
    B. speciation.
    C. the fossil record.
    D. paleontology.
    E. pedigree analysis.

(A) Phylogeny traces the evolutionary history of species or related groups of species. Reconstructive phylogeny is part of the discipline of systematics, the study of biological diversity on a global evolutionary scale.

87. If two organisms belong to the same class, they must also belong to the same

    A. family.
    B. phylum.
    C. order.
    D. genus.
    E. species.

(B) Classification of organisms follows a hierarchical approach, with the highest level being the domain and the lowest level being the species. The hierarchical classification proceeds as follows: domain, kingdom, phylum (or division, for plants), subphylum, class, order, family, genus, species.

88. All of the organisms existing in a particular location, along with all of the abiotic factors with which they interact is referred to as a(n)

    A. ecological niche.
    B. population.
    C. ecosystem.
    D. biome.
    E. community.

(C) An ecosystem includes a local community and the physical surroundings (abiotic factors) with which the organisms interact. A community (E) includes all the organisms living in a given area, which have the potential to interact with each other. A population (B) refers to a group of individuals of the same species living in a defined geographic location. A biome (D) refers to one of the major global ecosystems, which are typically defined by the predominant vegetation found in the region. An ecological niche (A) can be defined as the biotic and abiotic resources used by an organism in a given environment, or the functional role of an organism in its environment.

89. Interactions between species occur on several levels. One type of interspecific interaction, in which one species benefits from the relationship while the other species is neither hurt nor harmed by the relationship, is referred to as

    A. competition.
    B. predation.
    C. mutualism.
    D. parasitism.
    E. commensalism.

(E) An example of commensalism would be the presence of an epiphytic orchid living on a tree. This relationship benefits the orchid because the tree branches provide a place for the orchid to rest while absorbing water and nutrients from the atmosphere, whereas, the tree is neither helped nor harmed by the orchid. Competition (A) involves two (or more) species competing for limited resources (food, water, shelter, and space) and usually results in detrimental effects to the populations of both species. Predation (B) involves one organism (the predator, such as a mountain lion) benefiting by capturing and eating another organism (prey, such as a deer). Parasitism (D) involves one organism (the parasite) living on or in another organism (the host). Although the parasite usually doesn't kill its host outright, it usually weakens it, leading to a reduction in fitness and reproductive potential of the host. An example would be mistletoe living on a host tree. Unlike epiphytic plants (such as the orchid in the example on the previous page), mistletoe puts down root-like projections into the living tissue of its host tree, absorbing water and nutrients at the expense of the host. Mutualism (C) describes an interspecific interaction in which both species benefit from the relationship. An example of mutualism can be found in lichens, which are composed of a fungal organism and a green alga or cyanobacteria living symbiotically, in which the green alga or cyanobacteria provides energy (carbohydrates) to both organisms through photosynthesis, while the fungus provides the alga or cyanobacteria with shelter from the elements, as well as a source of water and dissolved nutrients through absorption of broken down organic matter from the soil.

---

90. The base (first trophic level) of most food chains is occupied by

    A. grasses.
    B. algae.
    C. primary consumers.
    D. producers.
    E. herbivores.

(D) Producers are organisms that are capable of manufacturing their own food, usually through the process of photosynthesis. Producers in terrestrial ecosystems include any plant that is consumed by another organism. Producers in aquatic ecosystems are usually small, often single-celled forms, of algae and photosynthetic bacteria (phytoplankton). Organisms that feed on the producers are referred to as primary consumers. Because they eat plant material, the primary consumers are often referred to as herbivores. Organisms that feed upon the primary consumers are referred to as secondary consumers. The secondary consumers, which feed on other animals, are also referred to as carnivores. There may be several trophic levels of consumers present in a given food chain. Many organisms feed at several layers of the food chain—for example, a hawk might consume a mouse, or it might consume a snake that has consumed a mouse. Organisms that feed on both producers and consumers are referred to as omnivores. Decomposers, which include fungi, bacteria, and slime molds, break down dead and decaying material and recycle the nutrients back into the ecosystem. The decomposers are often depicted as being at the end of a food chain; however, they actually operate at all levels of the food chain, breaking down waste.

---

91. Water, nutrients, and carbon are cycled through an ecosystem, moving from non-living (abiotic) components to living (biotic) components, and back to non-living components. One of these biogeochemical cycles is the carbon cycle. Which of the following statements regarding the carbon cycle is INCORRECT?

    A. The processes of photosynthesis and cellular respiration account for the majority of transformations and movement of carbon through an ecosystem.
    B. Theoretically, on a global scale, the return of carbon dioxide to the atmosphere through cellular respiration should be approximately balanced by the removal of carbon dioxide from the atmosphere through photosynthesis.
    C. Globally, the amount of atmospheric carbon dioxide is steadily increasing due to the burning of wood and fossil fuels, which adds more carbon dioxide to the atmosphere than can be taken back out of the atmosphere through photosynthesis, disrupting the balance of the carbon cycle.
    D. During the winter months, there may be a seasonal spike of carbon dioxide in the atmosphere due to a lower rate of photosynthesis, especially among deciduous plants.
    E. Aquatic ecosystems do not include a carbon cycle among the biogeochemical cycles present.

(E) The carbon cycle present in aquatic ecosystems is similar to the terrestrial system, except that it is more complicated due to the interaction of carbon dioxide with water and limestone, resulting in a series of intermediates including carbonic acid, bicarbonate, and carbonate. Terrestrial and aquatic carbon cycles are illustrated on the following page.

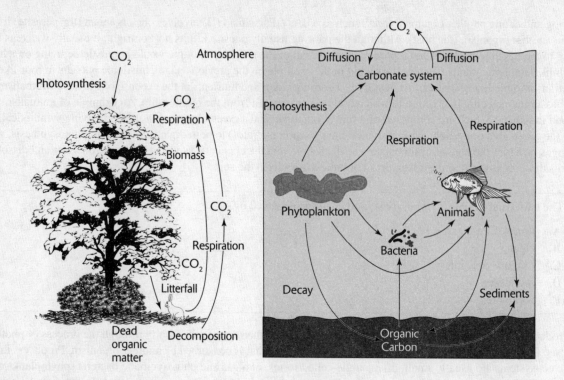

---

92. Movement of energy through an ecosystem occurs,

    A. in a cyclical fashion, similar to the water, carbon, and nutrient cycles.
    B. in one direction, with a gain of energy at each trophic level.
    C. in one direction, with a loss of energy at each trophic level.
    D. bidirectionally, with a gain of energy at each trophic level.
    E. bidirectionally, with a loss of energy at each trophic level.

(C) Unlike water, carbon, and nutrients (nitrogen, phosphorus, and so on), energy moves in one direction through an ecosystem, with a loss of energy at each trophic level. The producers usually constitute the largest biomass at a trophic level in a terrestrial food chain (see diagram on the following page). When consumers feed on the producers, not all of the energy contained in the producers' biomass is available as usable energy to the consumers. Some of the energy contained within the producers is used up by the producers themselves for metabolic activity, while additional energy is lost as heat. This loss of energy continues at each successive level of the food chain, with approximately 10% of the available energy converted to new biomass at each successive trophic level. The inefficiency of energy transfer through a food chain limits most terrestrial food chains to about four trophic levels. In some aquatic ecosystems, which have a large turnover of microscopic producers, the producers may not have the greatest biomass in the food chain; the herbivorous zooplankton typically have greater overall biomass than the phytoplankton (producers).

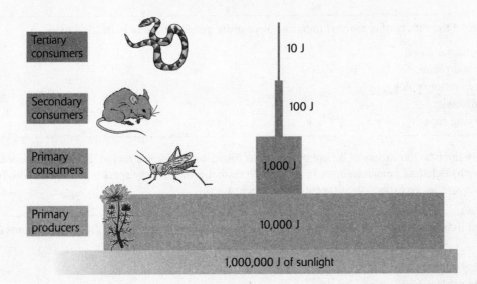

93. Many chemicals, such as DDT, become more and more concentrated at each successive trophic level of a food chain. This phenomenon is known as

   A. biological control.
   B. biological magnification.
   C. eutrophication.
   D. toxin accumulation.
   E. biological synthesis.

(B) Biological magnification refers to the phenomenon in which many chemicals become more and more concentrated at each successive level of a food chain. The magnification occurs because the biomass at any given trophic level is produced from a much larger biomass at the trophic level below it. The top carnivores in a food chain are the most likely to show detrimental effects from the biological magnification of toxic substances. Such was the case with DDT, a chemical that accumulates in fatty tissues, which was in such high concentrations in raptors (often at or near the top of a food chain) that it interfered with calcium deposition in the birds' egg shells. As a result, the eggs' shells were weak, and the eggs often broke when the birds tried to incubate them in the nest.

94. Runoff of animal waste from feedlots and stockyards, as well as runoff of excess fertilizer from agricultural and urban areas, has resulted in an excessive quantity of inorganic nutrients (especially nitrogen and phosphorus) entering many streams, rivers, and lakes. The excess nutrients disrupt the normal nutrient cycles and lead to excessive growth of photosynthetic organisms. The excessive nutrient enrichment of bodies of water is referred to as

   A. eutrophication.
   B. biological magnification.
   C. fertilization.
   D. nutrient runoff.
   E. biological runoff.

(A) Eutrophication, the accumulation of excessive quantities of nutrients in lakes, streams, and rivers, usually results in the excessive growth of photosynthetic organisms, especially algae and cyanobacteria. These *algal blooms* produce considerable oxygen during the day (as a byproduct of photosynthesis); however, at night, cellular respiration by these same organisms cause a significant reduction in oxygen content. In addition, as the photosynthetic organisms die, the organic material accumulates at the bottom of the water body. As decomposers breakdown the organic matter, they use up most of the available oxygen, potentially leading to the death of fish and other organisms.

95. A measure of the variety of organisms found within a given geographic area is referred to as

    A. genetic variation.
    B. polymorphism.
    C. conservation biology.
    D. biodiversity.
    E. carrying capacity.

(D) Biodiversity refers to the variety of different organisms found within a given region. Biodiversity is vital to the health of the Earth, including human welfare. In addition to aesthetic value, many species provide us with food, fiber, and medicine. As species go extinct, their potential value is lost.

96. The use of living organisms, particularly bacteria, fungi, and plants, to detoxify polluted ecosystems is referred to as

    A. biological restoration.
    B. sustainable detoxification.
    C. bioremediation.
    D. bioassimilation.
    E. habitat restoration.

(C) Bioremediation uses living organisms to detoxify polluted ecosystems. Certain bacterial and fungal species have the ability to break down toxic substances into inert, nontoxic substances. In addition, certain fungi, lichens, and plant species take up toxic chemicals and concentrate them in their tissues. The organisms can then be harvested, removing the toxic substances from the area as the organisms are removed. In some instances, the accumulated toxins (for example, accumulated heavy metals) can be extracted from the organisms and used commercially, preventing them from needing to be discarded as hazardous waste.

97. Behavior is controlled by

    A. the genetic make-up of the individual only.
    B. nature.
    C. both the genetic make-up of the individual and environmental influences.
    D. environmental influences only.
    E. nurture.

(C) There are still common myths being perpetuated in society that behavior is controlled either by the genetic make-up of the individual (nature) or environmental influences (nurture). Most scientists today agree that behavior is controlled by both the genetic make-up of an individual and by environmental influences. The degree of genetic versus environmental influence varies among individuals for different behaviors.

98. A method of learning that is limited to a certain period in an animal's life, and is generally irreversible, is referred to as

    A. imitation.
    B. habituation.
    C. maturation.
    D. conditioning.
    E. imprinting.

(E) Imprinting is a form of learning that is connected to innate behavior. Imprinting occurs at a specific stage in an organism's life and is usually irreversible. A well-known example is the imprinting of baby ducks and geese on their mother, or a substitute mother figure. In nature, baby ducks and geese imprint on their mother and follow her around until they are mature. They grow up to interact with others of the same species. The results of several experiments in which goose eggs were artificially incubated and hatched, and the baby geese spent their first few critical hours with the researchers, showed that these geese did not recognize other members of their species. Instead, they imprinted on the researchers, following them around, as other baby geese follow the mother goose. Even as adults, the experimental geese preferred to spend time with the researchers than with other geese.

99. Animals often learn by association, such as learning to associate one stimulus with another. Learning by trial-and-error, in which an animal learns to associate one of its behaviors with either a reward or a punishment, is referred to as

   A. operant conditioning.
   B. experimental conditioning.
   C. experiential conditioning.
   D. learned conditioning.
   E. classical conditioning.

(A) Operant conditioning is a type of associative learning that involves trial and error. An animal learns to associate a particular behavior with either a reward or punishment and then tends to either repeat the behavior or avoid the behavior accordingly. Another form of associative learning involves the association of an arbitrary stimulus with a reward or punishment. This type of learning is referred to as classical conditioning.

100. The discipline of sociobiology is primarily concerned with the study of

   A. competitive behaviors.
   B. mating behaviors.
   C. modes of communication among individuals within a species.
   D. modes of communication among individuals of different species.
   E. the evolution of social behavior.

(E) Sociobiology examines the evolution of social behavior, which includes competitive behaviors, mating behaviors, diverse modes of communication and social interactions within and between species.

PERIODIC TABLE OF THE ELEMENTS

1	2	3	4	5	6	7	8	9	10	11	12	13	14	15	16	17	18
1 **H** 1.0079																	2 **He** 4.0026
3 **Li** 6.941	4 **Be** 9.012											5 **B** 10.811	6 **C** 12.011	7 **N** 14.007	8 **O** 16.00	9 **F** 19.00	10 **Ne** 20.179
11 **Na** 22.99	12 **Mg** 24.30											13 **Al** 26.98	14 **Si** 28.09	15 **P** 30.974	16 **S** 32.06	17 **Cl** 35.453	18 **Ar** 39.948
19 **K** 39.10	20 **Ca** 40.08	21 **Sc** 44.96	22 **Ti** 47.90	23 **V** 50.94	24 **Cr** 51.00	25 **Mn** 54.93	26 **Fe** 55.85	27 **Co** 58.93	28 **Ni** 58.69	29 **Cu** 63.55	30 **Zn** 65.39	31 **Ga** 69.72	32 **Ge** 72.59	33 **As** 74.92	34 **Se** 78.96	35 **Br** 79.90	36 **Kr** 83.80
37 **Rb** 85.47	38 **Sr** 87.62	39 **Y** 88.91	40 **Zr** 91.22	41 **Nb** 92.91	42 **Mo** 95.94	43 **Tc** (98)	44 **Ru** 101.1	45 **Rh** 102.91	46 **Pd** 105.42	47 **Ag** 107.87	48 **Cd** 112.41	49 **In** 114.82	50 **Sn** 118.71	51 **Sb** 121.75	52 **Te** 127.60	53 **I** 126.91	54 **Xe** 131.29
55 **Cs** 132.91	56 **Ba** 137.33	57 ***La** 138.91	72 **Hf** 178.49	73 **Ta** 180.95	74 **W** 183.85	75 **Re** 186.21	76 **Os** 190.2	77 **Ir** 192.22	78 **Pt** 195.08	79 **Au** 196.97	80 **Hg** 200.59	81 **Tl** 204.38	82 **Pb** 207.2	83 **Bi** 208.98	84 **Po** (209)	85 **At** (210)	86 **Rn** (222)
87 **Fr** (223)	88 **Ra** 226.02	89 **†Ac** 227.03	104 **Rf** (261)	105 **Db** (262)	106 **Sg** (263)	107 **Bh** (262)	108 **Hs** (265)	109 **Mt** (266)	110 **§** (269)	111 **§** (272)	112 **§** (277)						

§ Not yet named

* Lanthanide Series

58 **Ce** 140.12	59 **Pr** 140.91	60 **Nd** 144.24	61 **Pm** (145)	62 **Sm** 150.4	63 **Eu** 151.97	64 **Gd** 157.25	65 **Tb** 158.93	66 **Dy** 162.50	67 **Ho** 164.93	68 **Er** 167.26	69 **Tm** 168.93	70 **Yb** 173.04	71 **Lu** 174.97

† Actinide Series

90 **Th** 232.04	91 **Pa** 231.04	92 **U** 238.03	93 **Np** 237.05	94 **Pu** (244)	95 **Am** (243)	96 **Cm** (247)	97 **Bk** (247)	98 **Cf** (251)	99 **Es** (252)	100 **Fm** (257)	101 **Md** (258)	102 **No** (259)	103 **Lr** (260)

1. What is the number of hydrogen molecules, H_2, in 12 grams of H_2 (gas)?

    A. 6.02×10^{23}
    B. 1.0×10^{23}
    C. 3.6×10^{23}
    D. 3.6×10^{24}
    E. 5.0×10^{22}

(D) There are 6 mols of hydrogen in 12 g H_2; 6 mols H_2 = 12 g (1 mol H_2 / 2 g H_2). Avogadro's number and the mols give the molecule count. (6 mols H_2)(6.02×10^{23} molecules H_2 / mol) = 3.6×10^{24}

2. How many mols of sulfuric acid will be formed when 24 mols of sulfur react according to the following pair of reactions? These following equations summarize how acid rain is formed in the atmosphere.

$$2\ S\ (s) + 3\ O_2\ (g) \rightarrow 2\ SO_3\ (g)$$
$$SO_3\ (g) + H_2O\ (l) \rightarrow H_2SO_4\ (aq)$$

    A. 24
    B. 48
    C. 12
    D. 6
    E. 3

(C) The mol ratio is 1 mol H_2SO_4 / 2 mol S. This gives mols H_2SO_4 = 24 mols S (1 mol H_2SO_4 / 2 mol S).

3. How many moles of CO_2 will be formed when 120 grams of carbon are burned according to the following equation?

$$C(s) + O_2\ (g) \rightarrow CO_2\ (g)$$

    A. 120
    B. 152
    C. 130
    D. 10
    E. 5

(D) The balanced equation gives a ratio of 1 mole CO_2 / 1 mole C. The molar mass of carbon is 1 mole C = 12 g C. This gives moles CO_2 = 120 g C (1 mole C / 12 g C) (1 mole CO_2 / 1 mole C) = 10 moles CO_2.

4. Which of the following compounds has the greatest percent hydrogen by mass?

    A. HF
    B. HCl
    C. HBr
    D. HAt
    E. HI

(A) The molar mass is smallest for HF. Hydrogen contributes more to the molar mass than in the other formulas.

5. Which of the following sets of coefficients is needed to balance this equation for the incomplete combustion of methane?

$$CH_4 (g) + O_2 (g) \rightarrow CO (g) + H_2O (g)$$

    A. 1, 2, 1, 1
    B. 2, 3, 2, 2
    C. 2, 3, 2, 4
    D. 1, 3, 1, 4
    E. 2, 3, 2, 3

(C) The balanced equation requires 2 molecules of methane. This immediately dictates 2 CO and 4 H_2O. The oxygen molecules are adjusted by using a multiplier of 3.

6. What is the new volume in liters for 34.0 L of $SO_2(g)$ initially at 17°C and 750 torr when the new temperature increases to17°C and the pressure decreases to 375 torr?

    A. 68.0 L
    B. 17.0 L
    C. 34.0 L
    D. 8.5 L
    E. L

(A) This is an example of Boyle's law: $P_2V_2 = P_1V_1$, $V_2 = V_1 [P_1 / P_2] = 34.0$ L [750 torr /375 torr] = 68.0 L.

7. Which of the following gases will have the highest density?

    A. H_2 (g)
    B. HI(g)
    C. HCl(g)
    D. HF(g)
    E. HBr(g)

(B) The density for HI is highest. The sequence of HF, HCl, HBr, HI has increasingly heavier halogen atoms. The H_2 is one of the smallest mass atoms in the periodic table with correspondingly low densities.

8. A gas mixture has the following gases and partial pressures. N_2 = 120 torr; H_2 = 300 torr; O_2 = 80 torr. What is the mole fraction of nitrogen in this mixture?

    A. 0.12
    B. 0.06
    C. 0.48
    D. 0.96
    E. 0.24

(E) Mole fractions are determined using Dalton's law of partial pressures. The ratio of partial pressure to total pressure ratio equals the mole fraction, χ. $\chi = P_{artial} / T_{otal}$ = 120 torr / 500 torr = 0.24.

9. Which of the following molecules has a tetrahedral shape?

    A. ammonia, NH_3
    B. carbon monoxide, CO
    C. carbon dioxide, CO_2
    D. silane, SiH_4
    E. water, H_2O

(D) A tetrahedral-shaped molecule must have four atoms attached to the central atom. Silane is tetrahedral.

10. What will happen to the pressure of an ideal gas in a sealed steel container when it is heated from 200°C to 400°C?

    A. The pressure will increase by a factor of two.
    B. The pressure will be cut in half.
    C. The pressure will increase by a factor of 673/473.
    D. The pressure will decrease by a factor of 473/673.
    E. The pressure will remain the same.

(C) Gay-Lussac's law $P_2/T_2 = P_1/T_1$ is the relation used. $P_2 = P_1(T_2/T_1) = P_1$ (673 Kelvin / 473 Kelvin)

11. Which of the following molecules is the most polar?

    A. HF
    B. SO_3
    C. HI
    D. H_2
    E. CO_2

(A) The polarity of the molecule depends on electronegativity differences between atoms and the molecular shape. Fluorine has the highest electronegativity of all elements. Molecules like CO_2 and SO_3 have polar bonds, but symmetry cancels out the polarity.

12. Which of the following molecules has a molar mass of 78 grams?

    A. H_2
    B. C_2H_2
    C. SO_3
    D. CH_2Cl_2
    E. C_6H_6

(E) Add the atomic masses for all atoms in the formula. $MM = 6 \times 12.0 + 6 \times 1.0 = 78$.

13. Which of the following metals is the most reactive with water?

    A. silver
    B. calcium
    C. sodium
    D. potassium
    E. gold

(D) Group 1A elements are the most reactive metals. Potassium is in Group 1A. The reactivity with water increases going down the group.

---

14. Which of the following elements has the electron configuration $1s^2\, 2s^2\, 2p^5$?

    A. hydrogen
    B. carbon
    C. lithium
    D. fluorine
    E. neon

(D) Fluorine has 9 electrons: $1s^2\, 2s^2\, 2p^5$.

---

15. Which of the following elements has exactly six valence electrons?

    A. carbon with atomic number 6
    B. nitrogen with atomic number 7
    C. oxygen with atomic number 8
    D. fluorine with atomic number 9
    E. neon with atomic number 10

(C) Oxygen has 8 electrons: $1s^2\, 2s^2\, 2p^4$. There are six electrons in the $n = 2$ outer shell.

---

16. Which one of these elements has the highest density in the following set?

    A. C
    B. Si
    C. Ge
    D. Sn
    E. Pb

(E) These are Group 4A elements. The density increases down the group.

---

17. Which of the following elements is a rare gas or noble gas?

    A. neon
    B. oxygen
    C. chlorine
    D. nitrogen
    E. hydrogen

(A) Neon, Ne, is in Group 8A. These are the rare or noble gases.

---

18. When the following weak acids are neutralized to form a sodium salt, which of the sodium salts will hydrolyze to give the highest pH?

    A. chlorous acid, $HClO_2$ $K_a = 1.1 \times 10^{-2}$
    B. acetic acid, $HC_2H_3O_2$ $K_a = 1.8 \times 10^{-5}$
    C. hydrocyanic acid, HCN $K_a = 4.0 \times 10^{-10}$
    D. formic acid, HCOOH $K_a = 6.0 \times 10^{-7}$
    E. nitrous acid, HNO_2 $K_a = 4.5 \times 10^{-3}$

(C) Hydrocyanic acid forms NaCN. The weakest acid of this set will yield the most basic solution with the biggest $K_b = K_w / K_a = (1.0 \times 10^{-14})/(4.0 \times 10^{-10}) = 2.5 \times 10^{-5}$ This is about the same base strength as aqueous ammonia.

19. A spontaneous reaction will always have a negative value for which property?

    A. internal energy

    B. enthalpy

    C. entropy

    D. reaction speed

    E. free energy

(E) Free energy is always negative for a spontaneous process: $\triangle G = \triangle H - T\triangle S$. The enthalpy change, $\triangle H$, can be positive where the $T\triangle S$ term can offset it.

20. Which of the following will have a negative enthalpy change?

    A. breaking a hydrogen bond

    B. breaking a carbon-carbon single bond

    C. breaking a carbon-carbon double bond

    D. forming a hydrogen-hydrogen single bond in H_2

    E. forming a sodium ion from a sodium atom

(D) All bond breaking processes are endothermic. All bond formation processes are exotyhermic with a negative enthalpy change.

21. How many electrons are there in a +2 cation formed from uranium-235 with Z = 92?

    A. 90

    B. 92

    C. 235

    D. 233

    E. 94

(A) Uranium has atomic number 92. There will be 90 electrons remaining in a uranium +2 cation.

22. Which of the following systems has the lowest entropy?

    A. sodium metal, Na(s)

    B. hydrogen gas, H_2(g)

    C. liquid mercury, Hg(l)

    D. neon gas, Ne(g)

    E. salt water, NaCl(aq)

(A) Sodium metal is the most organized of the materials listed.

23. Which of the following reactions requires the least energy?

    A. dissociation of O_2 molecules

    B. dissociation of F_2 molecules

    C. dissociation of Cl_2 molecules

    D. dissociation of Br_2 molecules

    E. dissociation of N_2 molecules

(B) Fluorine is the most reactive of the Group 7A elements. This reactivity is partly due to the weakest single bond.

24. Which of the following is true of nonmetals?

    A. high density
    B. usually poor conductors of electricity
    C. usually good conductors of electricity
    D. usually form positive ions
    E. typically solids at room temperature

(B) Nonmetals are typically poor conductors of electricity and heat. They usually form anions. Metals are typically solids.

25. For the reaction, $2 NO_2F (g) \longleftrightarrow N_2O_4 (g) + F_2 (g)$, at some given set of conditions, we find that at equilibrium the concentrations are $[NO_2F]=0.1$, $[N_2O_4]=0.2$ and $[F_2]=0.3$. What is the value of the equilibrium constant for this reaction at these conditions?

    A. 1.67
    B. 0.167
    C. 6.
    D. 0.6
    E. 0.00167

(C) The equilibrium expression is from = reactants / products = $[N_2O_4] [F_2]/ [NO_2F]^2= [0.2] [0.3]/ [0.1]^2 = 6$.

26. How many neutrons are in the nucleus of a U-238 isotope of uranium with atomic number 92?

    A. 238
    B. 146
    C. 92
    D. 328
    E. 148

(B) The number of neutrons equals the mass number, A, (238) minus Z, the atomic number, (92). Neutrons = A – Z = 238 – 92 = 146.

27. Which of the following best describes the electronic configuration $1s^22s^22p^53s^2$?

    A. forbidden state
    B. excited state
    C. triplet state
    D. unknown state
    E. ground state

(B) This is an excited state in which an electron is excited from the 2p orbital to a 3s orbital.

28. Where is silver being produced in the following reaction $Cu|Cu^{+2}||Ag^+|Ag$?

    A. anode
    B. cathode
    C. salt bridge
    D. voltmeter
    E. ampmeter

(B) Silver ions are reduced at the cathode from $Ag^+|$to Ag atoms. The formalism shows the species involved in the anode half reaction first (Cu and Cu^{+2}), then a symbol for a salt bridge ($\|$), and finally the species reacting in the cathode half reaction (Ag^+ and Ag).

---

29. What is the role of aluminum chloride in the reaction?

$$NH_3 + AlCl_3 \rightarrow NH_3AlCl_3$$

  A. Lewis acid
  B. Lewis base
  C. Brønsted-Lowry base
  D. Brønsted-Lowry acid
  E. Arrhenius base

(A) Aluminum chloride is a Lewis acid. Aluminum is electron deficient. It can accept an electron pair from ammonia.

---

30. What state of matter has the characteristics of definite shape and volume?

  A. liquid
  B. solid
  C. plasma
  D. gas
  E. ether

(B) Solids have definite shape and volume.

---

31. Which of the following would give a Normal concentration of 0.4 N for a molar concentration of 0.2 M concentration?

  A. all of these
  B. HCl(aq)
  C. H_2SO_4(aq)
  D. H_3PO_4(aq)
  E. NH_3(aq)

(C) Sulfuric acid can produce two equivalents of protons per formula unit. Normality = 0.2 M × 2 equivalents / mol.

---

32. Which of the following types of radiation is the most dangerous?

  A. beta
  B. gamma
  C. alpha
  D. neutrons
  E. ultraviolet

(B) Gamma radiation has the highest energy and is the most penetrating. Beta particles can be stopped by a sheet of aluminum. Alpha radiation can be stopped by a layer of paper.

33. What is the maximum number of electrons that can "fit" in a sigma bonding molecular orbital?

    A. 2
    B. 1
    C. 3
    D. 4
    E. 6

(A) Sigma bonding molecular orbitals can each hold a maximum of two electrons. This makes up a single bond.

34. What is the oxidizing agent in the following redox reaction?

$$2\,H^+ (aq) + 2\,Fe^{+2} (aq) + NO_3 (aq) \rightarrow 2\,Fe^{+3} (aq) + NO_2^- (aq) + H_2O\ (l)$$

    A. iron II ion
    B. nitrate ion
    C. iron III ion
    D. hydronium ion
    E. nitrite ion

(B) Nitrogen in nitrate ion is reduced from +5 to +3 in nitrite ion.

35. What does malleability relate to when describing iron?

    A. a physical property
    B. a chemical property
    C. a measurement
    D. a chemical change
    E. an exact number

(B) The ease of hammering a material into sheets is described as *malleability*.

36. When the Soviet nuclear power plant at Chernobyl went through a meltdown, radioactive strontium was released. Which of the following body organs is the most likely place for strontium to accumulate?

    A. liver
    B. heart
    C. spleen
    D. bone
    E. lungs

(D) Strontium is in Group 2A just like calcium. Strontium is incorporated in bone in the same fashion as calcium.

37. The relation $t_{1/2} = (\,1\,/\,ak[A]_o)$ predicts the half life for a second order decomposition reaction. The half-life time is 0.01 seconds when the initial concentration is 2.00 M for $[A]_o$. What is the value for ak? The general form for the reaction is a A $\rightarrow$ product.

    A. 0.02 $M^{-1}sec^{-1}$
    B. 500 $M^{-1}sec^{-1}$
    C. 0.2 $M^{-1}sec^{-1}$
    D. 50 $M^{-1}sec^{-1}$
    E. 200 $M^{-1}sec^{-1}$

(D) Solve the half-life equation for ak: ak = (1 / $t_{1/2}$ [A]$_o$) = (1 / (0.01) [2.00]) = 1 / 0.02 = 50 $M^{-1}sec^{-1}$.

---

38. Which of the following molecules has the strongest oxygen-oxygen bond based on the molecular orbital energy diagram?

A. O_2^{+}
B. O_2
C. O_2^{-2}
D. O_2^{+2}
E. O_2^{-1}

(D) There are 16 electrons in the O_2 molecule. The bond order for the O_2^{+2} cation is 3. The other structures have more anti-bonding electrons that yield a lower bond order.

---

39. Calcium hydroxide, $Ca(OH)_2$, forms a saturated solution with [Ca^{+2}] = 0.01 M. What is the solubility product for calcium hydroxide?

A. 2×10^{-4}
B. 1×10^{-4}
C. 4×10^{-6}
D. 8×10^{-6}
E. 2×10^{-6}

(C) Calcium hydroxide has the formula $Ca(OH)_2$. The solubility product expression is K_{sp}=[Ca^{+2}][OH^-]^2. If the concentration of calcium is 0.01, though, the concentration of hydroxide will be 0.02 because of the stoichiometric ratio, 2 hydroxides /1 calcium. Thus, K_{sp} = [0.01][0.02]^2 = 4×10^{-6}.

---

40. Which of the following acid-base theories is the only one that can be applied to non-aqueous systems?

A. Lewis
B. Arrhenius
C. Brønsted-Lowry
D. Dalton
E. Boyle

(A) The Lewis model is an electron pair acceptor. Dalton and Boyle never proposed acid-base models. Arrhenius and Brønsted-Lowry models involve proton (hydronium ion) ion transfer.

---

41. When a radioactive nucleus emits an alpha particle, the daughter nucleus will have a mass number that is

    A. lower by 2 mass units.
    B. higher by 4 mass units.
    C. lower by 4 mass units.
    D. higher by 2 mass units.
    E. unchanged.

(C) An alpha particle has a mass number of 4 units. The daughter nucleus will have a mass number lower by 4 units.

---

42. Which of the following is a decomposition reaction?

    A. $CH_4(g) + O_2(g) \rightarrow CO(g) + H_2O(g)$
    B. $C_6H_{10}(g) + H_2(g) \rightarrow C_6H_{12}(g)$
    C. $C_6H_{12}(g) + Cl_2(g) \rightarrow C_6H_{10}Cl_2(g) + 2\,HCl(g)$
    D. $HCl(aq) + NaOH(aq) \rightarrow NaCl(aq) + H_2O(aq)$
    E. $CaCO_3(s) \rightarrow CaO(s) + CO_2(g)$

(E) Decomposition reactions involve a single reactant that forms multiple products.

---

43. Which of the following salts will form a neutral aqueous solution?

    A. NaF
    B. NaCN
    C. $NaHSO_3$
    D. NaCl
    E. NaOH

(D) Sodium chloride is the salt formed by the reaction of a strong acid and a strong base. This type of salt forms a neutral solution.

---

44. Which of the following liquids has the fewest number of ions in solution?

    A. 0.1 M NaCl
    B. 0.1 M $CaCl_2$
    C. 0.1 M $FeCl_3$
    D. pure water
    E. rain water

(D) Pure water has the fewest number of dissolved ions. Rain water contains ions formed when atmospheric gases dissolve in the rain drops.

---

45. What is the correct IUPAC name for $FePO_4$?

    A. Iron (III) Phosphate
    B. Iron (II) Phosphate
    C. Iron (I) Phosphate
    D. Iron Phosphate
    E. Iron (III) Phosphite

(A) The ions in $FePO_4$ are iron (III), Fe^{+3}, and phosphate, PO_4^{-3}. The charge on the metal ion is written as a Roman numeral in the name of the compound.

46. If you neutralize the following solutions, which one will require the largest volume 0.10 N NaOH?

    A.   300 mL of 0.20 N HCl

    B.   30 mL of 1.00 N HCl

    C.   3 mL of 1.00 N HCl

    D.   2.00 L of 0.06 N HNO_3

    E.   3.00 L of 1.00 N HCl

(E) The 3.00 liters of 1.00 N HCl contains the greatest number of equivalents of acid and require the largest volume of base to neutralize the acid. Equivalents of acid = normality × liters of solution.

47. What type of atomic nucleus will form when ^{205}Pb with Z = 82 undergoes alpha decay?

    A. ^{204}Bi

    B. ^{205}Bi

    C. ^{201}Hg

    D. ^{203}Hg

    E. ^{201}Pb

(C) The daughter nucleus will have a mass number of 201 and an atomic number of 80. This matches mercury-201.

48. What is the reason for the term "a" in the Van der Waal's equation for gases, $(P + a\, n^2/V^2)(V - nb) = nRT$?

    A.   to correct for errors introduced by using temperature scales other than Kelvin

    B.   to correct for colligative properties of mixtures of gases

    C.   to correct for the volume occupied by real gas particles

    D.   to account for intermolecular forces that are present in real gases

    E.   to account for entropy differences due to molecular structure

(D) Real gas pressures are lower than the value needed to make PV = nRT. The *a* term is added to the pressure to account for intermolecular forces that produce a lower observed pressure.

49. For the reaction $2\, NO_2\, (g) \longleftrightarrow N_2O_4\, (g)$, what is the reaction quotient if $[NO_2] = 0.1$ and $[N_2O_4] = 1.0$?

    A.   0.1

    B.   10

    C.   100

    D.   0.01

    E.   1000

(D) The reaction quotient $Q = [N_2O_4] / [NO_2]^2 = 1.0 / 0.1^2 = 100$. This is not the equilibrium constant because the reaction is not at equilibrium.

50. If it were to dissociate completely, how many ions (total) would be produced by $Ca_3(PO_4)_2$?

    A.   3

    B.   13

    C.   4

    D.   5

    E.   16

(D) The salt forms three Ca^{+2} and two PO^{-3}_4 ions for a total of 5 ions.

51. Which of the following functional groups will yield the most partial positive carbon in the β position to the functional group?

    A. aldehyde
    B. alcohol
    C. alkene
    D. amine
    E. alkyl halide

(A) An aldehyde has a double-bonded oxygen in a carbonyl group, and with oxygen's strong electronegativity, the O atom draws electrons from nearby beta carbons (the inductive effect).

52. Formaldehyde has the formula CH_2O. How many pi bonds would be present in this compound according to Lewis structures?

    A. 0
    B. 1
    C. 3
    D. 2
    E. ½

(A) An aldehyde has a double-bonded oxygen in a carbonyl group. A double-bond has one pi bond and one sigma bond.

53. Which of the following will lead to the formation of a free radical in an organic reaction?

    A. hydrolysis
    B. rearrangement
    C. heterolytic cleavage
    D. homolytic cleavage
    E. dehydration

(D) Homolytic cleavage means that a single bond is split with one electron going to each of the atoms involved in the bond. This leaves an unpaired electron on each fragment producing two free radicals.

54. How many pi bonds are in a triple bond?

    A. 4
    B. 2
    C. 1
    D. 3
    E. 0

(B) A single bond consists of a sigma bond, a double-bond consists of one sigma and one pi bond, and a triple bond consists of one sigma and two pi bonds. Pi bonds are electron rich and important in organic reactions involving electrophilic agents that attack the electron rich and weaker pi bonds.

55. Of the following free radicals, which will be the most stable?

    A. methyl carbon

    B. primary carbon

    C. tertiary carbon

    D. secondary carbon

    E. hydrogen atom

(C) The more carbons and branched the free radical, the more stable the free radical will be. Radicals that have resonance possibilities are more stable.

56. The dehydration reaction of a carboxylic acid with an alcohol yields what functional group?

    A. acid anhydride

    B. ether

    C. amide

    D. ester

    E. alkene

(D) Esters are formed when RCOOH and R'OH react to eliminate water and form RCOOR'.

57. In the infra-red spectrum of an alcohol, the hydroxide functional group usually is shown how?

    A. a broad strong peak at 3200-3550 cm^{-1}

    B. a sharp peak at 1630-1780 cm^{-1}

    C. a medium peak at 2220-2260 cm^{-1}

    D. a medium-strong peak at 2853-2962 cm^{-1}

    E. a narrow strong band in the range 1200-800 cm^{-1}

(A) The broad strong hydroxyl (OH) band in an IR spectrum at 3200–3550 cm^{-1} is one of the most easily recognized functional groups in infra-red spectroscopy. A band at 1630–1780 cm^{-1} is a carbonyl; a band at 2220–2260 cm^{-1} is a nitrile; and a common band at 2853–2962 cm^{-1} is due to stretching the C–H bond.

58. Which of the following is a meta director for aromatic electrophilic substitution?

    A. $-CO_2H$

    B. $-NH_2$

    C. $-OH$

    D. $-X$

    E. $-CH_2CH_3$

(A) Meta directors help stabilize a positive charge on the benzene meta position and withdraw electrons from the ortho and para positions. A meta director typically has an atom with a relative positive charge or withdraws electrons from the aromatic ring.

59. Which of the following functional groups contains the most highly oxidized carbon atom?

    A. alkene
    B. ketone
    C. alcohol
    D. alkyne
    E. alkane

(B) The order of oxidation is alkyne, alkene, alkane, alcohol, ketone or aldehyde, carboxylic acid, carbon dioxide.

60. Which part of an organic compound is likely to give a peak at 30 AMU on a mass spectrograph?

    A. CH_2O^+
    B. OH^+
    C. CH_3^+
    D. $C_6H_5^+$
    E. CH_2^+

(A) A mass spectrograph breaks molecules into positively charged parts by impacting the molecules with high energy electrons. This creates positively charged species that are transient fragments (such as the hydroxide cation). Separation of these pieces is based simply on mass to charge ratios. The masses of the pieces are determined just like you would any molecule. The abundance of a fragment is related to its stability and the strength of the bonds broken to make it.

61. What will be the most likely product in the dehydrochlorination of 5,7,9-trichloro-1,3-nonadiene (shown below)?

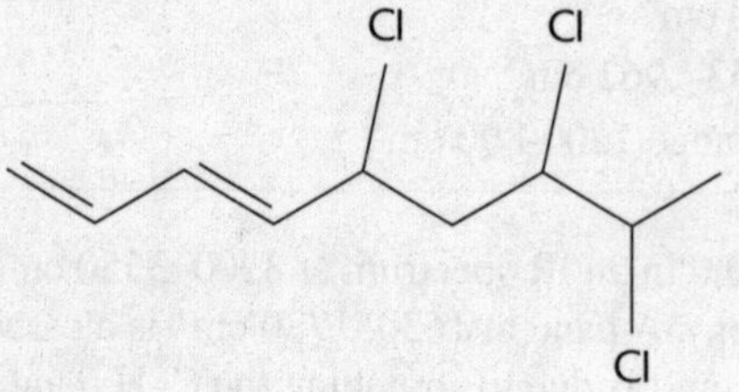

    A. 7,9-dichloror-1,3,5-nonatriene
    B. 5,9-dichloro-1,3,6-nonatriene
    C. 5,9-dichloro-1,3,5-nonatriene
    D. 5,7-dichloro-1,3,8-nonatriene
    E. 5,7-dichloro-1,3,6,8-nonatetraene

(A) The significance of this compound is the conjugated diene; this can help stabilize (through resonance) the cation formed in the loss of the chlorine at the 5 position. Because the cation will be stabilized, we are likely to lose that chlorine fastest, further propagating the conjugated pi system.

62. Which of the following does not contain a carbonyl group?

    A. ketones
    B. aldehydes
    C. alkynes
    D. carboxcylic acid anhydrides
    E. esters

(C) Alkynes are hydrocarbons with a triple bond., RC:::CR'. There are no carbonyl groups in alkynes.

63. Which of the following functional groups have an infrared spectrum with an intense band at 1630–1780 cm^{-1}?

    A. alkenes
    B. alcohol
    C. alkanes
    D. ketones
    E. alkyl halides

(D) Ketones contain a carbonyl group that has a strong absorption band in the range 1630–1780 cm^{-1}.

64. What type of isomer will rotate plane polarized light?

    A. Enantiomer
    B. Diastereomer
    C. Constitutional
    D. Hydration
    E. Cis-trans

(A) Enantimers are mirror images of one another.

65. What type of amine will be the most alkaline?

    A. primary
    B. secondary
    C. tertiary
    D. quaternary
    E. protonated

(C) The more substituted the amine the more alkaline; 1°< 2°< 3°. However, quaternary amines cannot be alkaline because no lone pair electrons are on the nitrogen in the amine.

66. "Reducing sugars" contain a carbonyl that can be further oxidized (without oxidizing completely to carbon dioxide). What functional group would reducing sugars have?

    A. carboxylic acid
    B. aldehyde
    C. alcohol
    D. ketone
    E. ester

(B) Aldehydes can be oxidized to a carboxylic acid. Alcohols have no carbonyl (C=O) group. Carboxylic acids are oxidized as far as possible short of carbon dioxide. Ketones cannot be further oxidized.

67. Which of the following is the reaction mechanism of an organic decomposition caused by the presence of another substance to get the reaction started?

    A. S_N1
    B. E1
    C. S_N2
    D. E2
    E. hydrogenation

(D) Decomposition is an elimination (for example the dehydration of alcohols to form alkenes). E2 involves a second species to facilitate the reaction.

---

68. What is the correct name for the compound in the figure?

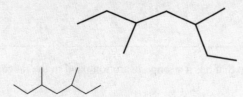

    A.   2-ethyl-4-methyl hexane
    B.   2-ethyl-5-methyl hexane
    C.   5-ethyl-3-methyl hexane
    D.   3,5-dimethyl heptane
    E.   3,5,6-trimethyl pentane

(D) The name is determined by the longest continuous carbon chain, in this case, seven carbons (heptane).

---

69. Which of the following types of carbon atoms will form the most stable carbocation intermediate?

    A.   primary
    B.   secondary
    C.   tertiary
    D.   quaternary
    E.   methyl

(C) The more carbons on the carbocation, the more stable the carbocation. A quaternary carbocation cannot exist.

---

70. Which of the following DOES NOT contain at least one sp^2 hybridized carbon atom?

    A.   formaldehyde
    B.   acetone
    C.   ethylene
    D.   acetic acid
    E.   methane

(E) Carbonyl carbon atoms are sp^2 hybridized. Alkenes have sp^2 hybridized carbons. Alkanes like methane only have sp^3 hybridized carbons.

---

71. Which of the following types of molecular orbitals is populated with the most energetic electrons?

    A.   LUMO
    B.   HOMO
    C.   sigma bonds
    D.   pi bonds
    E.   sigma antibonding

(B) "HOMO" is the "highest occupied molecular orbital". "LUMO" means "lowest unoccupied molecular orbital."

72. What is the most stable conformation of cyclohexane?

    A. chair
    B. boat
    C. twist
    D. conformational
    E. planar

(A) In the chair conformation, the atoms are as far apart from each other as possible, and as close to the angle of tetrahedral atoms, as possible.

73. Which of the following groups is a meta director in electrophilic aromatic substitution?

    A. –OH
    B. –NH$_2$
    C. –CH$_3$
    D. –NO$_2$
    E. –CH$_2$CH$_3$

(D) The nitro group withdraws electrons from the ortho and para positions, making them less susceptible to electrophilic attack.

74. Which of the following contains a chiral carbon atom?

    A. CH$_4$
    B. CH$_3$CH$_3$
    C. CH$_3$CH$_2$CHClCH$_3$
    D. C$_6$H$_6$
    E. CH$_2$Br$_2$

(C) A chiral carbon atom must have four different groups bonded to it.

75. Which of the following has a skeleton of eight carbon atoms?

    A. pentane
    B. butane
    C. hexane
    D. heptane
    E. octane

(E) An octane has eight carbon atoms in the longest chain.

76. In the nomenclature of alkenes, what means the two higher priority groups of four different groups are on the same side of the double bond?

    A. cis
    B. trans
    C. E
    D. Z
    E. ortho

(D) The labels cis and trans apply to two of the same type of group on the two different carbons at the ends of a double bond in an alkene.

77. Which of the following is the formula for propanoic acid?

    A. CH_3COOH

    B. CH_3CH_2COOH

    C. $CH_3CH_2CH_2COOH$

    D. C_6H_5COOH

    E. $HCOOH$

(B) The acid name is based on the number of carbons in the "skeleton" including the carbon in the carboxyl group.

78. Which of the following contains an sp^3 hybridized oxygen atom and no sp^2 hybridized oxygen?

    A. CO_2

    B. CH_3COOCH_3

    C. CH_3OCH_3

    D. CH_3COCH_3

    E. CH_3CH_2CHO

(C) Ethers have an oxygen in the same hybridization state as exists in water. The ether has alkyl groups in place of the hydrogen atoms in water.

79. The Huckel $4n + 2$ rule predicts that which of the following will be aromatic?

    A. cyclopropenyl cation, $C_3H_3^+$

    B. cyclopentadienyl anion, $C_5H_5^-$

    C. benzene, C_6H_6

    D. tropylium cation, $C_7H_7^+$

    E. all of these

(E) The rule applies to planar pi systems where n can have integer values from 0 to 5. The examples given all are planar with sp^2 hybridization at all the carbon atoms.

80. Acid hydrolysis of esters will yield which of the following pairs of compounds?

    A. ether and an alcohol

    B. ether and ketone

    C. carboxylic acid and alcohol

    D. carboxylic acid and water

    E. carboxylic acid and an amine

(C) Esters are formed from alcohols and carboxylic acids. Acid hydrolysis reverses the reaction.

81. The Tollen's test deposits a silver mirror on the clean glass wall of a test tube. What functional group is oxidized in the reaction?

    A. ketones

    B. alcohols

    C. carboxylic acids

    D. ethers

    E. aldehydes

(E) The RCHO group is oxidized to a carboxylic acid. Ketones and carboxylic acids cannot be oxidized further. Alcohols and ethers are not oxidized so easily.

82. The reaction of a carboxylic acid with an alcohol will produce which of the following types of compounds?

    A.   ether
    B.   ester
    C.   amide
    D.   water
    E.   amino acid

(B) The alcohol R'OH and acid RCOOH will form an ester, RCOOR'.

83. Friedel-Crafts alkylation of aromatics requires a Lewis acid. What carbon cation is formed when $AlCl_3$ and CH_3CH_2Cl are used in the reaction with benzene?

    A. $CH_3CH_2{}^+$
    B. $CH_3CH_2Cl^+$
    C. $C_6H_6{}^+$
    D. $C_6H_5{}^+$
    E. $CH_3{}^+$

(A) The alkylhalide, CH_3CH_2Cl, is converted to a carbon cation by the loss of Cl^- (halide) to the aluminum chloride.

84. What type of compound has two or more internal chiral carbons that cancel out the rotation of light?

    A.   meso
    B.   chiral
    C.   racemic
    D.   enantiomer
    E.   tautomer

(A) In a meso compound, there is always a plane of symmetry. A racemic mixture will also show no plane polarized light rotation, but this is because it is a mixture of equal amounts of two enantiomers.

85. Which of the following would not make a good leaving group?

    A.   iodide
    B.   hydroxide
    C.   halides
    D.   chloride
    E.   methyl

(E) A good leaving group would be stable in an ionic form in water; methyl does not form a stable cation or anion.

86. What functional group is represented by the formula RCH_2OOCH_2R?

    A.   ethers
    B.   acid anhydrides
    C.   peroxides
    D.   esters
    E.   carboxylic acids

(C) The structure has a single bond between two oxygen atoms. This is a peroxide analogous to H_2O_2.

87. Which of the following is expected to have the most acidic hydrogen atoms?

   A.   terminal alkenes
   B.   terminal alkynes
   C.   alkanes
   D.   non-terminal alkenes
   E.   aromatics

(B) Terminal alkynes are the most acidic. The triple-bond pi electron system in alkynes can stabilize the anion.

88. What kind of isomer has a non-superimposeable mirror image?

   A.   enantiomer
   B.   cis-trans isomer
   C.   achiral compound
   D.   constitutional isomer
   E.   diastereoisomers

(A) Enantiomers by definition are compounds whose mirror image is nonsuperimposeable. Diastereoisomers are not mirror images of one another. A constitutional isomer is not the mirror image of its isomers. This is not a stereoisomer.

89. What type of reaction mechanism produces a chiral center if the reactant begins with a chiral center?

   A. S_N1
   B.   E2
   C. S_N2
   D.   E1
   E.   dehydration

(C) Elimination reactions produce pi bonds, which cannot be connected to a chiral center. In S_N1 reactions, the chiral center is destroyed in the intermediate.

90. What type of spectroscopy destroys the sample in the analysis?

   A.   MS
   B.   NMR
   C.   FT-IR
   D.   UV-Vis
   E.   Polarimetry

(A) Mass spectrometers routinely destroy the sample. A high energy electron beam is used to break up the sample molecules and produce cation fragments. The other methods are nondestructive.

91. Which of the following is the type of reaction that follows the Saytzeff rule?

   A.   dehydration of alcohols
   B.   esterification
   C.   reduction of aldehydes
   D.   oxidation of aldehydes
   E.   electrophilic attack of aromatic compounds

(A) The Saytzeff rule applies to the dehydration and dehalogenation reactions. The rule says that an H atom is preferentially removed from 3o . 2o . 1o. This can be described as "the poor get poorer". The more Rs on a carbon, the more likely it will lose an H atom. The more Rs on the C=C group, the more stable the alkene.

---

92. Which of the following compounds is the least polar?

    A. cis-1,2-dichloroethylene

    B. trans-1,2-dichloroethylene

    C. 1,1-dichloroethylene

    D. 1,1-dibromoethylene

    E. 1,1-difluoroethylene

(B) The trans isomer of dichloroethylene is the least polar. The C-Cl bond moments are equal but are in opposite directions. They cancel one another.

---

93. Ultraviolet spectroscopy depends on molecules absorbing light to excite electrons from a low-energy molecular orbital to a higher one. These electrons are in σ bonds, π bonds and unshared electrons, n, in non-bonding MOs. Which of the following types of compounds cannot have an excitation from a π to a π^* molecular orbital?

    A. aldehydes

    B. ketones

    C. alkanes

    D. esters

    E. aromatics

(C) Alkanes only have single bonds. There are no molecular orbitals in alkanes so there can be no excitation from a π_to a π^* MO.

---

94. Proton magnetic resonance is used to identify different types of protons because the magnetic field surrounding a particular H atom depends on any external field and the bonding environment of the H in the molecule. The "chemical shift, δ" is used to identify H atoms in different functional groups and bonding environments. Which of the following has the smallest chemical shift?

    A. CH_3CH_3

    B. CH_4

    C. $(CH_3)_4Si$

    D. C_6H_6

    E. C_3H_3

(D) The reference for chemical shift values is TMS, tetramethylsilane, $(CH_3)_4Si$. The zero of the chemical shift scale is determined by the signal produced by the H's in TMS.

---

95. Proton magnetic resonance is useful to determine structures, partly because of spin-spin coupling. The groups of peaks clustered around a chemical shift result from this effect. The spectrum for $CH^a_3CH^bCl_2$ has two chemical shifts. What are the multiplets expected for the types of H atoms, H^a? and H^b?

    A. H^a singlet and H^b, doublet

    B. H^a singlet and H^b singlet

    C. H^a quartet and H^b doublet

    D. H^a doublet and H^b quartet

    E. H^a triplet and H^b singlet

(D) The $n + 1$ rule predicts the number of "lines" that a resonance is split into by neighboring H atoms. The H^a resonance is subject to two different magnetic fields, $n + 1 = 1 + 1 = 2$, exerted by the one H^b atom. The H^b resonance is split into a quartet by four magnetic fields, $n + 1 = 3 + 1 = 4$, produced by the three H^a atoms.

---

96. Electromagnetic energy is related to wavelength. Which of the following wavelength ranges matches the visible spectrum?

    A. 100–200 nm
    B. 200–350 nm
    C. 350–700 nm
    D. 1–300 μm
    E. 1 m

(C) The visible spectrum approximately matches the range 350–700 nm. The far uv matches 100–200 nm. Near uv matches 200–350–nm. Infrared matches 1–300 μm. Electron spin (ESR) and nuclear magnetic resonance match radio waves in the range cm to meters.

---

97. Which of the following has the greatest stability resulting from delocalization.

    A. cyclohexane
    B. cyclohexene
    C. 1,4-cyclohexadiene
    D. benzene
    E. 1,3-cyclohexadiene

(D) Benzene has the greatest delocalization energy for this set. The six electrons in the conjugated pi system are stabilized more than pi electrons in three isolated double bonds by 150.7 kJ/mol.

---

98. The reaction between sodium amide and acetylene yields which of the following compounds?

    A. HC:::CNa
    B. NaC:::CNa
    C. HC:::CNH_2
    D. NH_2C:::CNH_2
    E. CH_3CH_3C

(A) The acetylenic hydrogen is acidic. It will react with the amide anion, NH_2^- to form ammonia. The acetylide anion, HC:::C^-, forms a salt with sodium ion.

---

99. Which of the following is the only functional group that is alkaline?

    A. alcohol
    B. amine
    C. amide
    D. alkyne
    E. alkane

(B) Amines are alkaline. Amides are acidic in spite of the presence of the nitrogen. Resonance makes amides slightly acidic.

100. A Claisen Rearrangement will produce which of the following types of compounds?

    A. amine derivative

    B. phenol derivative

    C. carboxylic acid derivative

    D. alkyne derivative

    E. halide derivatives

(B) The Claisen Rearrangement tends to cause phenyl-ethers to internally rearrange to form o-substituted phenols.

Perceptual Ability Test

Aperture Passing

The first section of the Perceptual Ability Test is the Aperture Passing section. In this section you are given a drawing of a three-dimensional object and five apertures. Your task is to determine which of the apertures the object will pass through perfectly. The apertures are like keyholes, and the three-dimensional object is like a strangely shaped key that fits only one of the keyholes.

It is important to understand the rules of these problems so that you will be able to eliminate incorrect answers quickly and just as quickly choose the correct answer.

Rule #1

One of the primary purposes of the aperture passing test is to determine if the applicant has the ability to mentally rotate and flip an object just by looking at one perspective. This leads to the first rule for this set of problems:

Before inserting the object into the aperture or keyhole, the object may be turned and rotated in any direction. The object may be passed through the correct aperture using a side not even shown.

In general this means that the object will *have to be* rotated and twisted before passing through the aperture. Since the objects you see in this test will have top, bottom, right, left, front, and back sides, you might think that there are six possible correct answers. In actual fact, you have to account for only three directions. An object inserted from the front or the back will require the same size hole. Likewise, the same will be true of left/right insertions and top/bottom insertions.

Here is an example of a three-dimensional object that might be used in an aperture passing problem:

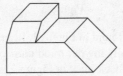

Figure 1

One of the difficulties of the Aperture Passing section of the PAT is that the three-dimensional objects are always *strange* in that you will have never quite seen an object just like that pictured. It is very easy, however, to mentally note certain attributes and determine that the shape is *like* something in your everyday life. Doing this might seem to be a useful exercise, but in most cases, this will result in your choosing the wrong aperture. You are likely to miss certain essential details that are unique to the test object and not found on the similar object you have conjured up in your mind.

The first thing you should do is note any protrusions on any of the six sides, any holes or indentations, any sides that have irregular heights and lengths compared with the rest.

The object in Figure 1 has three possible directions that it can pass through the aperture. If you extend the edges, you can find the following three correct apertures:

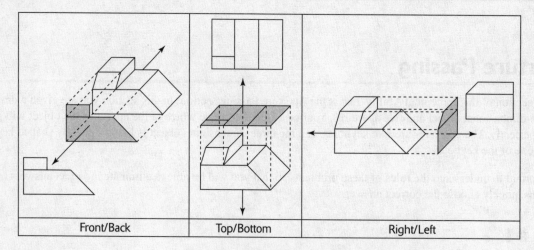

Figure 2

Figure 3 is a sample Aperture Passing problem. Using the three-dimensional figure at the left, determine which of the five apertures is correct.

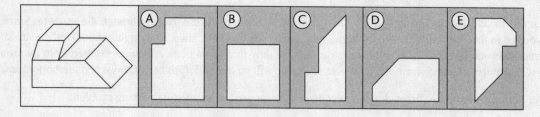

Figure 3

None of these apertures looks exactly like those found in Figure 2. Remember, the object might be twisted or turned, so look at each of the shapes and rotate them mentally in your mind until you find the correct answer. In this problem, the correct answer is C. The aperture from the front/back view in Figure 2 is rotated counter-clockwise 90°.

Rule #2

The second rule is critical to choosing the correct aperture:

Once the object is started through the aperture, it may not be twisted or turned. It must pass completely through the opening. The opening is always the exact shape of the appropriate external outline of the object.

In other words, the only aperture that the object can pass through is one that works with one single smooth motion.

Note that it is important that the object can pass entirely through the aperture. The keyholes are also the exact shape of the outline of the object with no extra indentations or room for nonexistent protrusions.

Rule #3

Both objects and apertures are drawn to the same scale. Thus, it is possible for an opening to be the correct shape but too small for the object. In all cases, however, differences are large enough to judge by eye.

This rule is very important. The appropriately *shaped* aperture is still an incorrect answer if it is too big or too small. The difference in size will, however, be obvious to the trained eye. It is important to train yourself to notice the size differences so that you are not misled. Examine Figure 4 to try to determine the correct aperture:

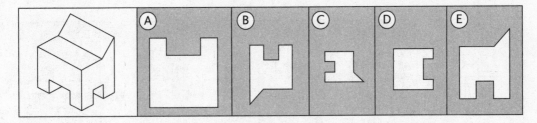

Figure 4

Notice that answers A and D are the same basic shape, as are answers B, C, and E. The only difference is in the size of the aperture. To determine which sized aperture is the correct one, focus on a single line on the original object in the left of the problem. Vertical lines are good to focus on. Which of the objects seems to have the same height as the back right edge of the object? Since A appears to be larger than the object, anything drawn to the same scale as answer A is eliminated. This leaves us with answers B, C, and D. Next notice which of the remaining objects appear to have the same dimensions as the original object. It becomes quite clear that answer B is the only answer with the correct dimensions.

Rule #4

The fourth rule is very important:

There are no irregularities in any hidden portion of the object. However, if the figure has symmetric indentations, the hidden portion is symmetric with the part shown.

This means that you are not expected to anticipate irregularities on that part of the object that you can't see. It also means that you can expect a certain level of symmetry with what you CAN see. Let's examine the object from Figure 4. There are two indentations that are visible. You should expect those indentations to continue through the object unless there is some visible stopping point. In the following figure, you can see the object from Figure 4, with the indentations marked, as well as two views of the object that show how the indentations continue through the object:

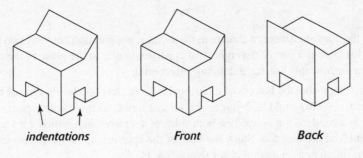

indentations   **Front**   **Back**

Figure 5

Rule #5

For each object there is only one correct aperture.

This may seem like an obvious statement that does not require a rule, but it is an important point. There is only one correct answer in each set of apertures. If you are working on this section and you find two answers that seem equally correct, then you have missed some detail, and it is important to re-examine the problem to find the differences in your two choices. If you can identify the differences, you will probably be able to determine the correct answer.

Understanding the Three-Dimensional Drawing

It is important to become familiar with the three-dimensional drawing so that you can interpret what the lengths and angles of the lines mean in terms of the apertures. The following is a sample problem with a very complex object:

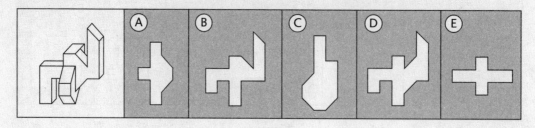

Figure 6

Figure 7 is the three-dimensional object. Understanding each of the lines on the drawing will help you to choose the correct aperture. After the drawing is an explanation of some of its key features.

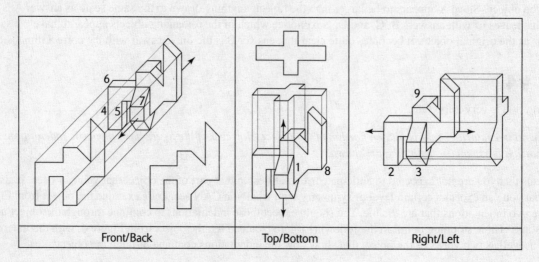

Figure 7

1. Each of the lines in the diagram denotes a change in the surface, a separation between two planes. In the top/bottom view, line 1 shows that there is a part of the object that is perpendicular to the plane of the paper. When you look at the aperture, you can see how this line has a dramatic effect on it.

2. Notice in the right/left view that the bottom of the irregular object has two bases. One of them comes to a point 2, and the other does not (3). This could lead you to choose aperture C as the correct aperture; however, in the case of aperture C, there is a gentle slope upward on both sides of a square base, which does not match the upward slope seen from point 3 on the diagram. Study the base of the aperture in the right/left view and compare it with the object to note the differences and similarities to aperture C.

3. Referring again to the right/left view, the two legs of the object at lines 2 and 3 are even with one another. If we look at apertures B and D, we see that the two legs are not even with one another. Therefore, these two apertures are not correct answers.

4. In the top/bottom view, lines 4 and 5 are parallel lines. It is important to note when lines are parallel and when they are not parallel. Parallel lines denote something the same width or thickness or height. Lines that are not parallel are a sure indicator that there is something different going on.

5. In the top/bottom view, lines 6 and 7 are *not* parallel, which demonstrates that something is different between these two lines. From the plane of the paper, 7 sticks out at a much more extreme angle than 6 to denote a slanted side. This is important when choosing the correct aperture.

6. It is important to note that the outer corners of the object, like 8 on the top/bottom view, will help you to determine the exterior shape of the object from all three directions. This will help you to eliminate some of the incorrect answers.

7. Line 9 in the right/left drawing extends into the plane of the paper, demonstrating that the object has a depth to it. This line could be one of the most misleading if it is overlooked.

When we take all of the hints from the drawing of the object into account, we have already eliminated 3 out of the 5 possible answers. The two remaining apertures are A and E. It looks like A could be the correct answer, but it doesn't appear to be long enough in some places and has a strange protuberance on one side. On the other hand, E looks like it could easily be the shape of the aperture when looking at it from the top/bottom. Therefore, E is the correct answer.

Practice Problem Set One

No matter how many tips and tricks you read about, there is nothing that will replace practice. The following practice problems help you to become more familiar with the intricacies of these three-dimensional drawings. For the first set of problems, you practice drawing the aperture from the top/bottom, right/left, and front/back perspectives. The following is an example using the object from Figure 6:

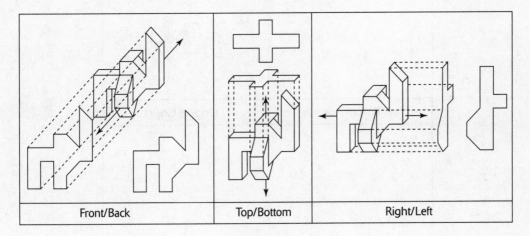

Figure 8

In the following problems, draw the front/back, top/bottom, and right/left apertures.

Example:

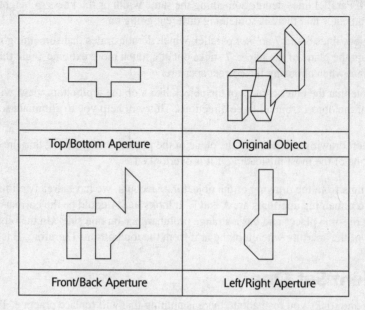

1.

2.

Top/Bottom Aperture	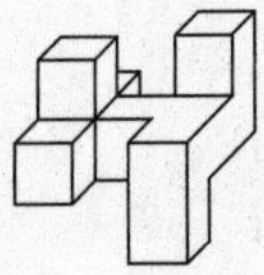 Original Object
Front/Back Aperture	Left/Right Aperture

3.

Top/Bottom Aperture	 Original Object
Front/Back Aperture	Left/Right Aperture

4.

	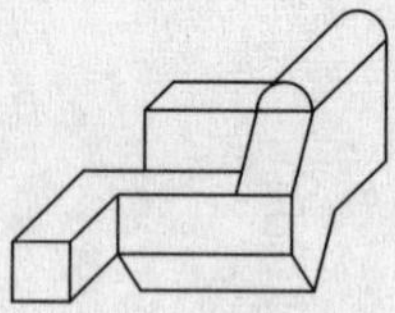
Top/Bottom Aperture	Original Object
Front/Back Aperture	Left/Right Aperture

5.

	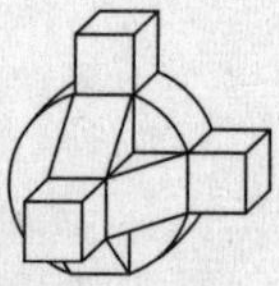
Top/Bottom Aperture	Original Object
Front/Back Aperture	Left/Right Aperture

6.

Top/Bottom Aperture	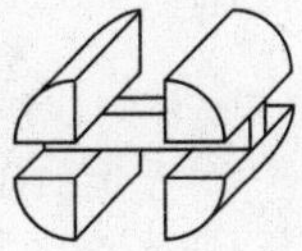 Original Object
Front/Back Aperture	Left/Right Aperture

7.

Top/Bottom Aperture	 Original Object
Front/Back Aperture	Left/Right Aperture

8.

Top/Bottom Aperture	 Original Object
Front/Back Aperture	Left/Right Aperture

9.

Top/Bottom Aperture	 Original Object
Front/Back Aperture	Left/Right Aperture

10.

Top/Bottom Aperture	Original Object
Front/Back Aperture	Left/Right Aperture

Answers for Problem Set One

1.

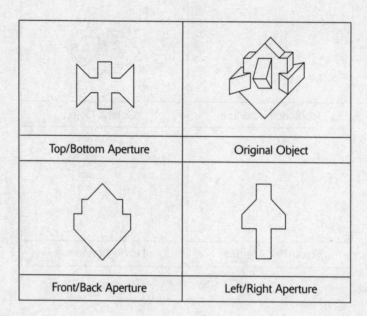

2.

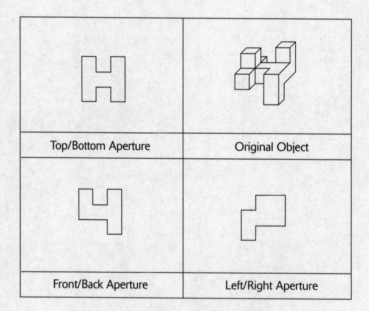

3.

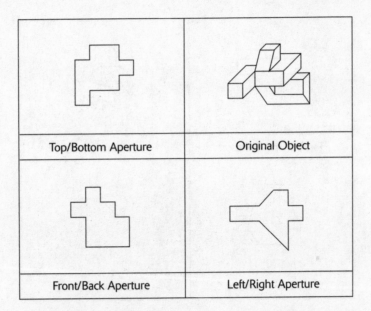

4.

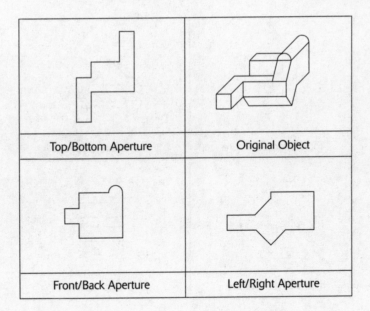

5.

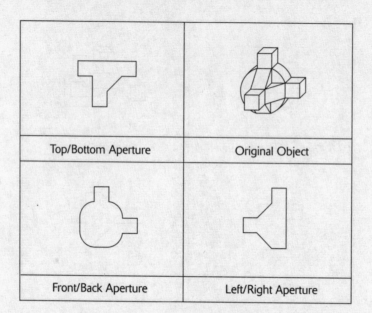

6.

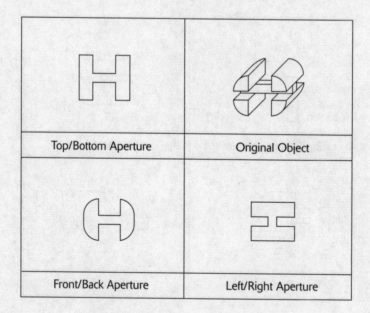

7.

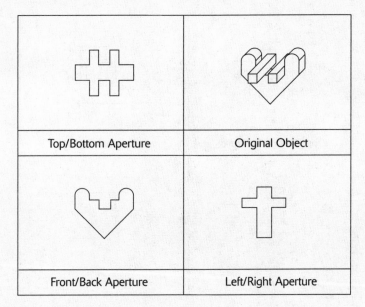

Top/Bottom Aperture	Original Object
Front/Back Aperture	Left/Right Aperture

8.

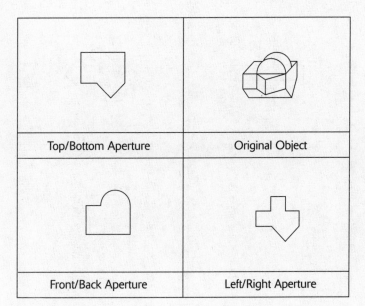

Top/Bottom Aperture	Original Object
Front/Back Aperture	Left/Right Aperture

9.

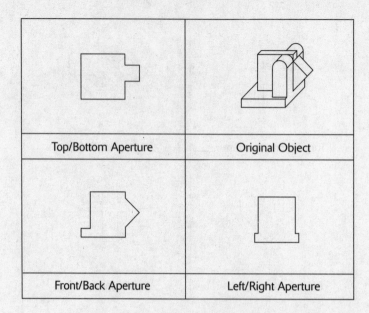

10.

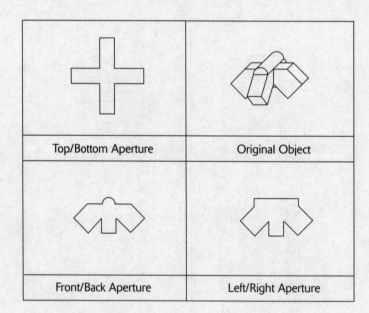

Practice Problem Set Two

For the following 10 problems, select the appropriate aperture for the object at the left.

1.

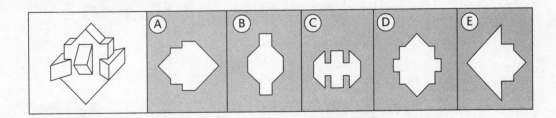

2.

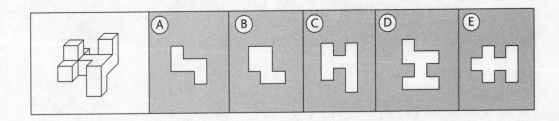

3.

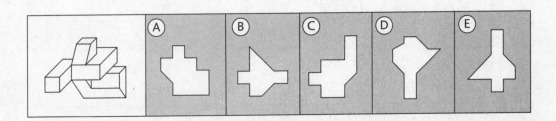

4.

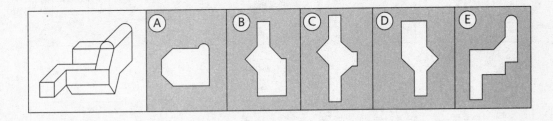

5.

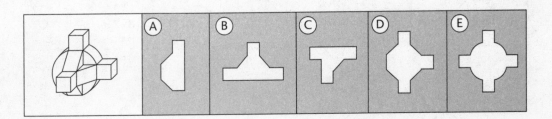

6.

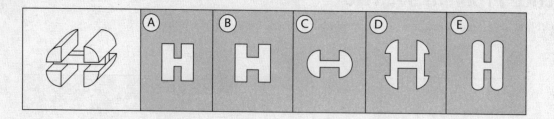

7.

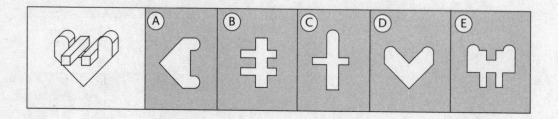

8.

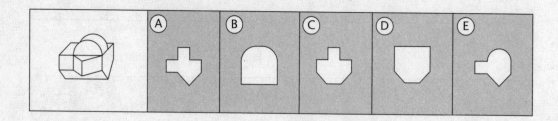

9.

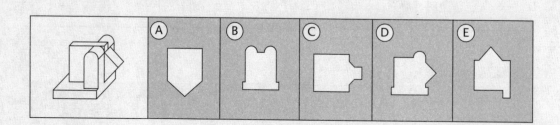

10.

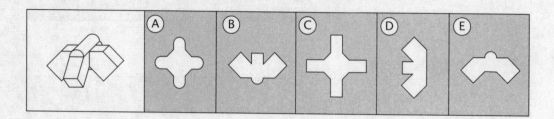

Answers for Problem Set Two

1. A
2. B
3. E
4. B
5. C
6. A
7. B
8. A
9. E
10. B

Orthographic Projections

Orthographic projections are the second section of the PAT. These are very similar to the aperture passing questions. In this section you are given two views of a three-dimensional object and asked to choose the third view of the object from four possible choices.

Orthographic projection is a means of representing a three-dimensional object in two dimensions. Engineers frequently use orthographic projections to create a series of descriptive drawings from a variety of perspectives.

Orthographic projections in the PAT are a series of three views of an object: top view, front view, and side view. On the test you will be given two of these views and asked to select the appropriate third view. The views have no perspective, which means that each view shows only one side of the object. Here is a very simple example. The three-dimensional object is inside this box, and the three views are *projected* onto the sides of the box:

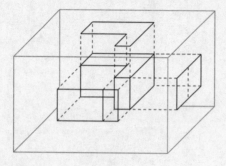

Figure 1

The three projections from Figure 1 are the important elements of this portion of the PAT. Following is the format you will see on the PAT using the object in Figure 1:

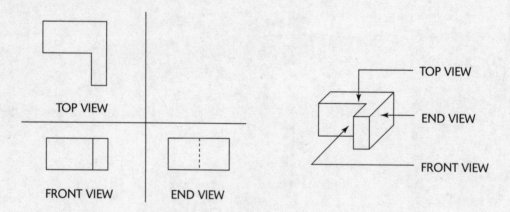

Figure 2

Notice in the front view that there is a solid vertical line inside the rectangle. The line represents a visible line that is seen from the front of the object. On the end view, however, there is a dotted vertical line. This denotes a hidden line that is not seen from the end, but that exists. When you look at the top view, you can see where the visible line comes from in the front view and where the hidden line comes from in the end view.

In the following example, you can see how the solid lines are constructed:

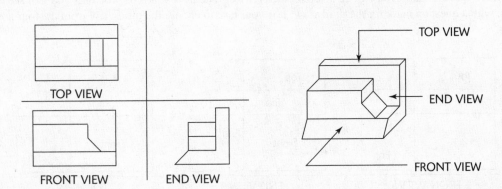

Figure 3

Notice how each of the lines that are visible from the front are solid lines. The same is true from the top and from the side. No hidden edges are in any of the three views, so there are no dotted lines. In the following example, there are some hidden edges:

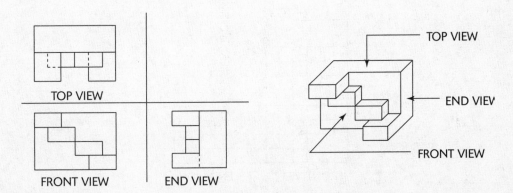

Figure 4

The front view shows four smaller rectangular solids that protrude from the larger solid in the background; two of them overlap with the rectangle above them, resulting in dotted lines in the top view. Examine Figure 4 and make certain that you understand the source of each line in the three figures. When a visible line overlaps with a hidden line, the line will be solid, and when two hidden lines overlap, it will remain dotted.

In the actual test, you will not have the advantage of the three-dimensional view of the object so it is important to correlate the three views and see how they relate to one another. There are some important facts to keep in mind when you are doing these problems. The first is that the end view is always the right side of the object. In fact, the alignment of all three sides will always follow the pattern in the following figure:

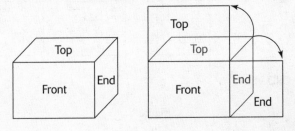

Figure 5

In Figure 5, on the left is the three-dimensional object, and on the right the top and end views have been folded forward to show the three specific views you will be given on the PAT test. The three kinds of problems you will see include two of the views, with a question mark for the third view; it is your task to choose the third view from the four possible correct answers.

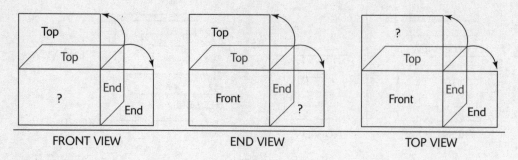

Figure 6

The way these three views line up is an important key to determining the correct answer from the possibilities presented. Notice how the three views line up in the following figure:

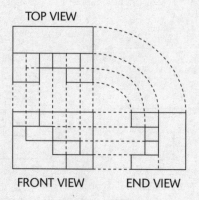

Figure 7

The vertical lines in the front view of Figure 7 line up with the vertical lines in the top view. The horizontal lines in the front view line up with the horizontal lines in the end view. And the vertical lines in the end view line up with the horizontal lines in the top view. Let's examine the following example and see if the lines in the four possible end views properly line up with the lines in the top and the front views:

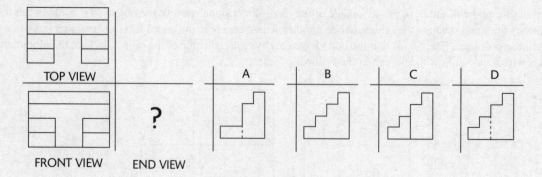

Figure 8

Notice that there are three horizontal lines in the front view between the top and the bottom horizontal lines. Answer A only has two horizontal lines, so it cannot be the correct answer. Next compare answers B, C, and D. All three answers are very similar in appearance. One has no internal vertical line; one has a dotted internal vertical line; and one has a solid internal vertical line. So determining the correct answer depends on that internal vertical line. To determine if there should be one, look at the horizontal lines in the top view. Notice how the top and the front view both show a gap in the center. This is an indication that there needs to be either a solid or a dotted internal vertical line. This excludes answer B. Since the gap is in the interior, it will be a hidden line, which leaves C as the only possible answer.

When you are taking this, and all other parts of the PAT, it is important to use the scratch paper you are provided to keep track of the answers that you eliminate. Using the scratch paper can be as simple as writing down the four choices and crossing off those answers you have eliminated as the incorrect:

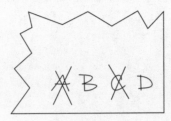

Figure 9

As with all of the other tasks on the PAT, it is important to become as familiar as possible with the types of questions you will be given in advance. The more you practice, the better you will be able to do on the actual test. Practice the following nine problems to see if you can begin to recognize the correct answer quickly.

Practice Problems

1. Choose the correct END VIEW.

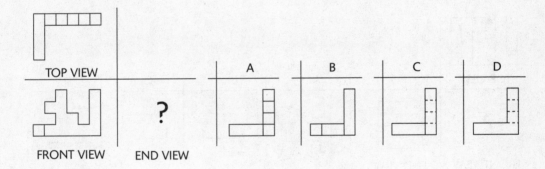

2. Choose the correct TOP VIEW.

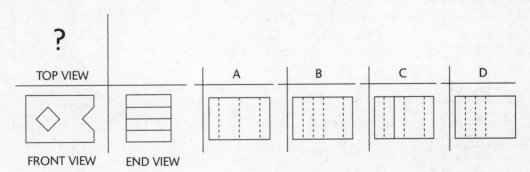

3. Choose the correct FRONT VIEW.

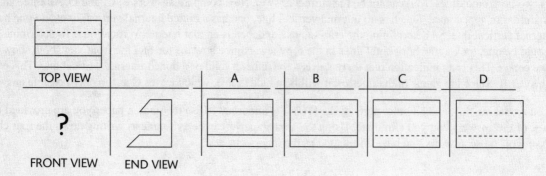

4. Choose the correct TOP VIEW.

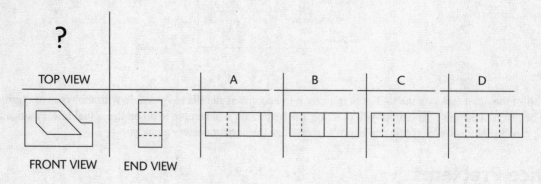

5. Choose the correct FRONT VIEW.

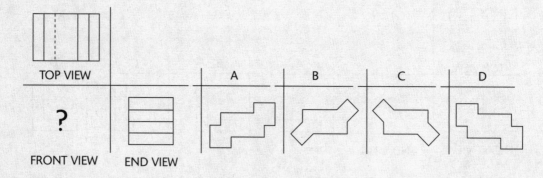

6. Choose the correct END VIEW.

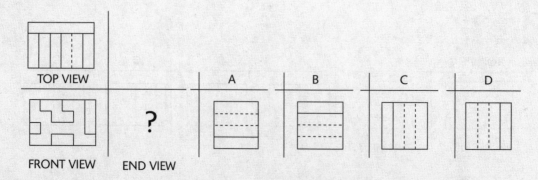

7. Choose the correct FRONT VIEW.

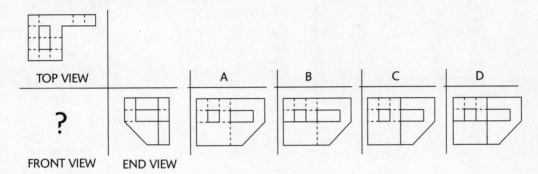

8. Choose the correct END VIEW.

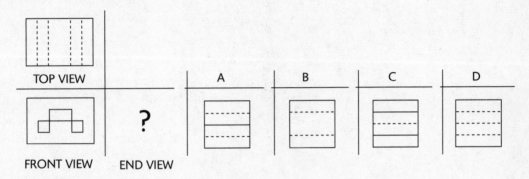

9. Choose the correct TOP VIEW.

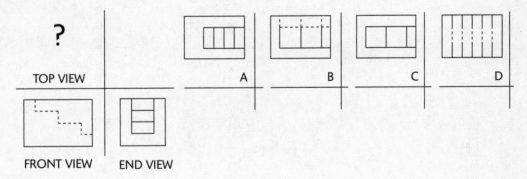

Answers

1. C
2. B
3. A
4. C
5. B
6. A
7. D
8. D
9. C

Angle Discrimination

Angle Discrimination is the third part of the Perceptual Ability Test, and it is the only part of the PAT that is two-dimensional in nature. These questions ask you to rank angles from the smallest angle up through the largest angle. Some of the questions will be very simple and easy, and some will be more difficult. The tricks you learn in this section will help you to make the correct decisions, and the more you practice, the sharper your ability will be.

The first important thing to understand is what makes an angle *larger* or *smaller*. All angles have two legs and a vertex:

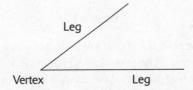

Smaller angles result in the legs being closer together, and larger angles result in the legs being farther away from each other:

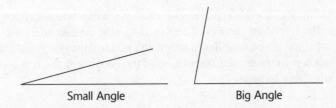

For the problems on the Angle Discrimination test, you will rank the angles in order from smallest to largest. For example, if you think that angle 1 is the smallest, and 4 is the largest, the two possible answers are 1, 2, 3, 4 or 1, 3, 2, 4.

To get an idea what the test questions are like, go ahead and try the next example problem by ranking the angles from smallest to largest:

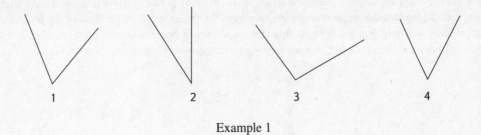

Example 1

The correct ranking is 2, 4, 1, 3. In this example, the two larger angles are fairly obvious, 1 and 3. In a similar manner, the two smaller angles are also quite obvious, 2 and 4. The key to being able to get these problems correct is to be able to determine the larger angles from the smaller angles and then to be able to rank the ones that are the closest to each other in size. If you did not get the correct ranking, look now at the angles you got wrong and try to see what the difference is between them. Remember, this will get easier with practice, and there are several tips and tricks that we go over in this section to help you to choose the correct angle.

Now let's try this again. Rank the following angles from smallest to largest:

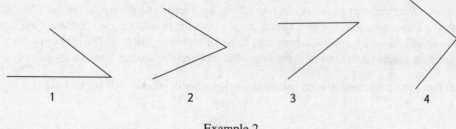

Example 2

The correct ranking is 1, 3, 2, 4. In this example, the largest angle is easily noted. In fact, the most difficult decision is choosing which of 1 and 3 is the smaller angle. When you note which angle is the largest, you can look at the answers given to you and eliminate all answers that disagree with your assessment. When you eliminate incorrect responses you increase your odds of getting the correct answer through guessing.

Nesting Strategy

One helpful method of determining which angle is larger and which is smaller when they appear almost the same is to use a technique called *nesting*. The important concept of nesting is that the smaller angle will always fit within the larger angle. You mentally nest the angle you consider to be smaller *inside* the angle you think must be larger. If you are correct about which angle is smaller, your mental manipulation of the image will result in something like the following image, which uses angles 1 and 3 from Example 2:

As you can see from the diagram, angle 1 nests within angle 3. This means that angle 1 is smaller than angle 3. Nesting angles will always work; the smaller angle will always fit within the larger angle, regardless of the length of the legs. Remember that practice will help you get better at this technique until it becomes second nature. Here are six examples of pairs of angles. Choose the larger angle using the nesting technique and then check your answers:

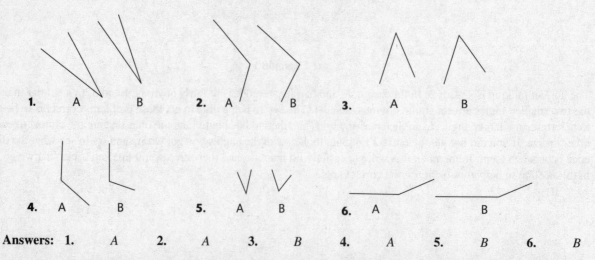

Answers: 1. *A* 2. *A* 3. *B* 4. *A* 5. *B* 6. *B*

Some test-takers believe that the people who design the test are trying to *trick* them into choosing the wrong answer. Although this is a somewhat paranoid belief, it is true that the makers of the test are writing it in such a way that if you don't know the correct answer, the incorrect answer will appear very appealing. That is the trick. And the way around the trick, in any testing environment, is knowing how to solve the problem so that you are not suckered into choosing the wrong answer.

Leg length is one of the ways that the test-makers will try to trick you. It is crucial that you remember and understand an important rule when you begin the Angle Discrimination part of the test:

The size of an angle is independent of the length of the angle's legs.

In the following example, try to rank the angles in order from smallest to largest. At least two angles are the same size.

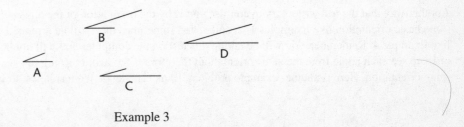

Example 3

This was a trick question. All four angles are the same size. If you did not see that, try to look back on your choices and see if your decision was based on the length of the legs. Remember, the length of the legs has nothing to do with the size of the angle.

The Angle Discrimination test would be a lot easier if you had any sort of measuring device, even just the ability to use your fingers or your test-taking materials. Without the ability to use those handy tools, you are forced to use only your visual acuity to determine relative sizes. For this reason, practicing before you take the test will sharpen your visual acuity and enable you to do well on this portion of the DAT.

Sameness Strategy

Angles are going to have different length legs on the test. One way to keep from being tricked like in Example 3 is to develop a method for looking only at the same part of each angle. If the part you are looking at ignores longer lengths of legs, you will be able to focus instead on the relative sizes of the angles. It is important that you concentrate on the same size portion of each angle in order for your comparisons to be valid.

If we look at Example 3, we can focus on those parts of the angles that are the same:

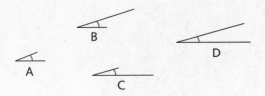

When you focus only on those parts of the angles that are the same, it is very easy to see that the four angles are identical. When using this method, it is very important that you focus on a distance from the vertex that is the same for each of the four angles. Let's try another example problem. Rank the angles from smallest to largest:

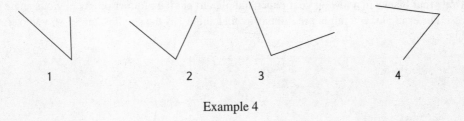

Example 4

The correct answer is 1, 4, 2, 3. When we draw a line that is the same distance from the vertex on each angle, the length of the line is an indicator of the size of each angle. Small angles have the shortest line, and large angles have longer lines:

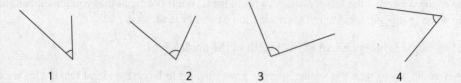

Another way that the test writers try to confuse you is by the orientation of the angles. Sometimes they will all be in the same basic orientation like Examples 1, 2, and 3, and sometimes they will be arranged in a more complicated manner, like Example 4. Remember, you will be taking this test on the computer and will not be able to rotate the computer in order to see each angle from the same orientation; therefore try to avoid turning this textbook to see the angles from the same orientation. Here is another example problem. Rank each angle from smallest to largest:

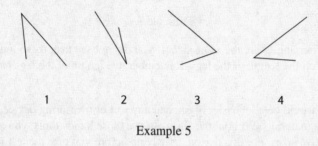

Example 5

The correct order is 2, 1, 4, 3.

Test-Taking Strategies

It is important to go into the test with some very specific test-taking strategies for each element of the DAT. Each of the 15 Angle Discrimination problems will be in the same format, just like the examples we've had in this section of the text. Develop a strategy to use the scratch paper and pencil you will be provided to write down decisions about obvious relationships between the angles in a specific problem. There is no one way that is better than others; you must choose a method that works for you and stick with that method. Here, we show you a couple of methods you might find useful when taking this portion of the test. Let's use the next example to discuss these strategies. Rank the angles from smallest to largest:

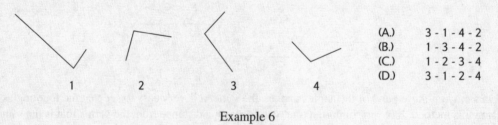

(A.)	3 - 1 - 4 - 2
(B.)	1 - 3 - 4 - 2
(C.)	1 - 2 - 3 - 4
(D.)	3 - 1 - 2 - 4

Example 6

The correct answer is C. Knowing that you are going to have these problems will enable you to be prepared with your scratch paper. Draw four blanks in a row on your paper and plan to put the number of any obvious angle in place, from smallest to largest. For example, you might see right away that angle 1 is the smallest angle, so your scratch paper might be like this:

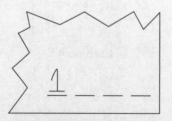

As soon as you've written down the smallest angle on your scratch paper, you can look at the possible answers and see that two of the answers, *A* and *D,* are eliminated. Now look at the two remaining answers, *B* and *C:* in answer *B* angle 2 is the largest angle; in answer *C,* the largest angle is 4. At this point the only decision you have to make is which is larger, 2 or 4, and you will know which one is the correct answer.

Another method of using your scratch paper to help you with these problems is to already have the four angle numbers written down. Circle the largest or the smallest angle and use that information to help guide your selection of the correct answer in the same way as the previous technique. It is important that you choose one technique that works for you and use that one technique exclusively. If you are selecting the largest angle as your best starting point, always work with the largest angle. If you want to identify the largest and the smallest angles, you might use a circle for the smallest angle and a square for the largest angle. Here is an example using a circle to indicate which angle is smallest.

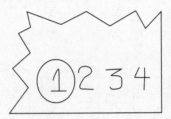

The two examples demonstrate that one of the first important steps in solving these problems is to note which angle is the largest or the smallest and then *write this down* on your scratch paper. Use this information to narrow down your choices and improve your chance of getting the correct answer.

Practice Problems

In the following sample problems, two of the angles are the same size, one is larger, and one is smaller. Identify the angles that are the same and the largest and the smallest angle in each grouping. Keep the following ideas in mind when working on these problems:

- First determine the largest or the smallest angle.
- Use the nesting technique to help determine which of two similar angles is larger.
- Concentrate on the same portion of each angle, ignoring longer legs.

1.

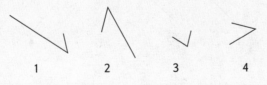

2.

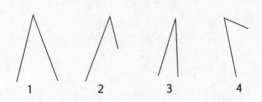

3.

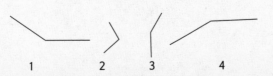

4.

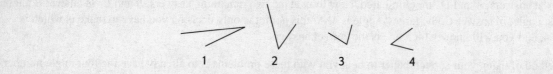

5.

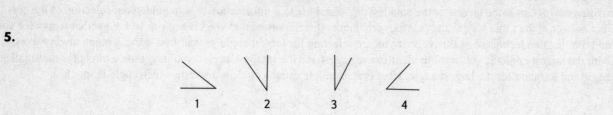

6.

7.

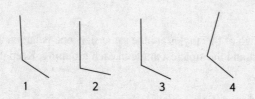

8.

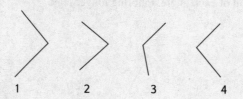

Answers

1. Largest: 3   Smallest: 1   Same: 2, 4

2. Largest: 4   Smallest: 3   Same: 1, 2

3. Largest: 4   Smallest: 2   Same: 1, 3

4. Largest: 3   Smallest: 1   Same: 2, 4

5. Largest: 4   Smallest: 3   Same: 1, 2

6. Largest: 3   Smallest: 2   Same: 1, 4

7. Largest: 1   Smallest: 2   Same: 3, 4

8. Largest: 3   Smallest: 2   Same: 1, 4

It is important when taking this portion of the PAT that you limit the amount of time you spend on these problems; some of the other sections will most likely require more time. Move quickly through this portion of the test but make sure to make your selections based on the strategies you have learned in this section. Use your scratch paper to make notes and eliminate answers you know are wrong quickly. If you had difficulty with the practice problems in this section, practice the problems some more and study the practice test items to try to determine what error you are consistently making. When you become adept at choosing the correct ranking, you will find that this portion of the test will go extremely quickly and efficiently. Make certain that you practice with scratch paper and make no notes on the actual practice test. The PAT is computerized, and it is essential that you practice in a manner consistent with the actual administration of the test.

Paper Folding

This is the fourth section of the Perceptual Ability Test. It involves a square piece of paper that is folded one or more times and then a hole is punched into it (more than one hole may be punched). Depending on where this hole is punched, there is a different pattern of holes exhibited on the paper when it is unfolded.

There are no tricks to this—it just involves your ability to visualize where these holes would be when the paper is unfolded. There are certain basic rules on this test.

1. The paper will always be square. If you want to practice, you can cut out the blank forms at the end of this chapter, or make your own squares, drawing in the circles that represent the grids.

2. The paper will never be turned. In other words, you won't have a hole punched in the lower right corner of a fold and expect to choose an answer with the unfolded holes on top.

3. Paper is shown as a solid line. When the paper is folded, dashed lines will represent the absence of the paper. In the following illustration, you can see the square in the left illustration, and the paper folded in half in the right one. The dashed lines represent where the paper was before it was folded. You should see that the paper was folded from right to left.

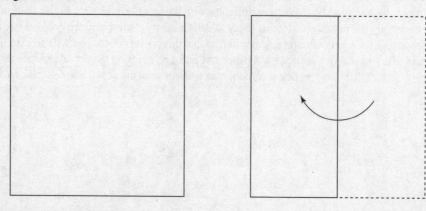

4. You will be given a folding sequence and five grids that show where the holes have been punched, but only one of these grids will have the correct sequence of holds.

To make it easier, you have to imagine the square looking like the grid. Here is what the grids will look like:

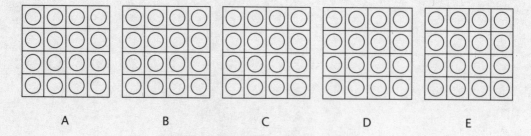

| A | B | C | D | E |

The next thing is to visualize the square, unfolded paper, looking like a grid:

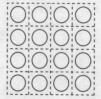

However, it actually will look like this on the page:

By visualizing an overlay of the grids, the punched holes will make much more sense to you. Let's see how this works with another basic example.

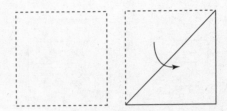

The left illustration shows the full square of paper (which will *not* be shown on the test). The right illustration shows that the paper has been folded diagonally in half, top left to bottom right. Now, let's visualize the folded page with the grid holes.

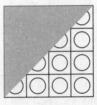

If we punch a hole in the bottom corner, you see this on the page:

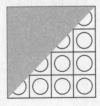 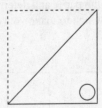

Can you visualize now what would happen? The hole is punched on the lower right side. Since the top left of the page is folded over, the holes appear on both the bottom right, where the hole was punched, and on the top-left corner when the paper is unfolded. The grid would then look like this:

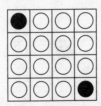

Here are several different types of folds. Fortunately, there are a finite number of folds that can be made. For example, all of the folds will remain within the original square. Here's one progression of folds:

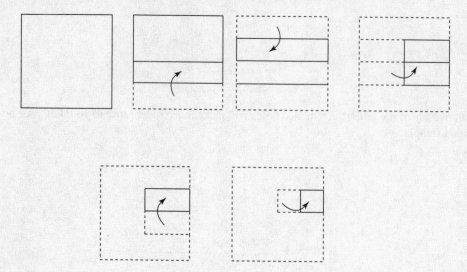

And, of course, there will be angles:

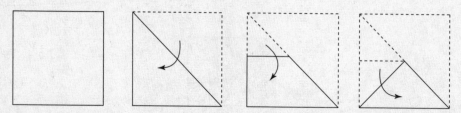

There will also be a combination of straight folds and angles. It just requires that you to keep your eye (and mind) on where the hole is and what it will look like when unfolding. Try a couple of these problems now.

Your task is to mentally unfold the paper and determine where the holes will be on the original square. You will be given five choices (A–E) from which to make your choice.

1.

2.

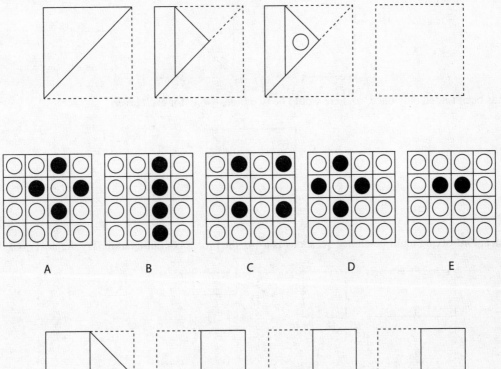

3.

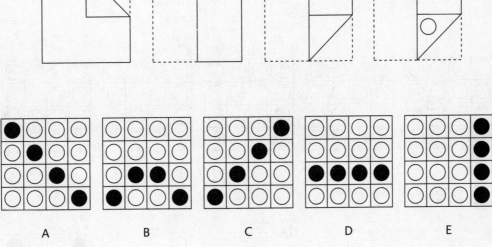

Answers

1. B

2. A

3. B

How did you do? Here is where it might be helpful to cut out some of the blank squares in the back and try folding them like the folds in the preceding problems.

The next step is to understand what lies behind the folding. Several basic concepts are at work here. First, the more folds (layers) of paper, the more holes you'll have in the final output. If the paper is folded only once, for example, you're likely to have only two holes—the more folds, the more holes. Knowing this can often help you eliminate those choices with more or less punched holes in the answer grids. To see how this works, let's look at one of the earlier illustrations:

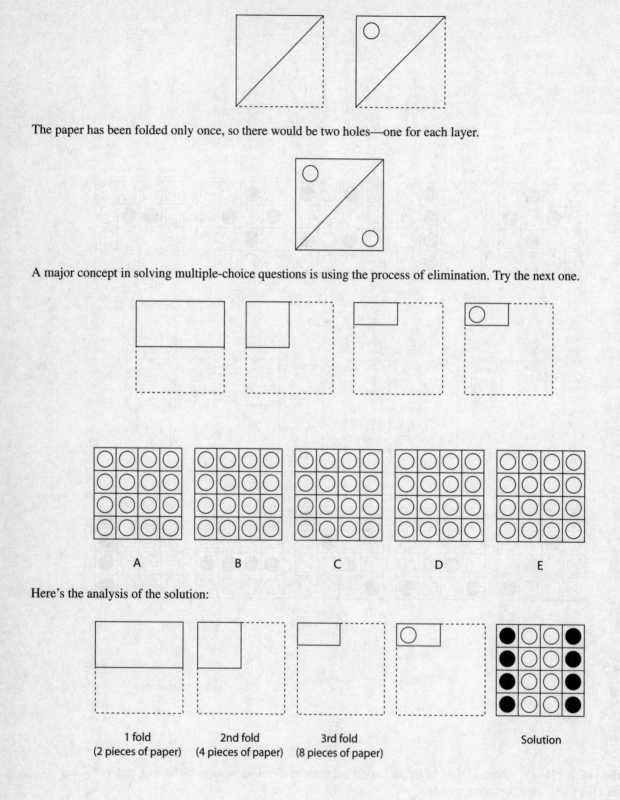

The paper has been folded only once, so there would be two holes—one for each layer.

A major concept in solving multiple-choice questions is using the process of elimination. Try the next one.

A	B	C	D	E

Here's the analysis of the solution:

1 fold
(2 pieces of paper)

2nd fold
(4 pieces of paper)

3rd fold
(8 pieces of paper)

Solution

The next step in analyzing the answers is to look at *where* are the holes. This will give you an idea as to which choice(s) you can eliminate. If the hole is in one of the center hole areas (inner four circles), you will have at least one of the holes in the center area. Look at the following:

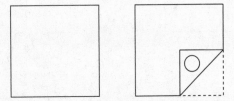

You can see that the hole is in one of the four center holes. So there must be at least one center hole punched. It is also obvious that if one corner is folded up, that corner should also have the hole.

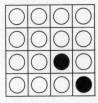

Remember what we said earlier about position—if the fold has been reversed, so would your answer.

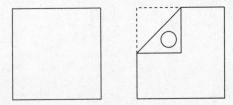

Which of the answer choices would you select?

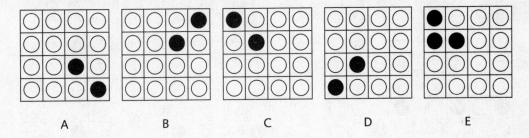

The correct answer is **C.** You should have noticed that Choice E had three holes and should have been eliminated immediately. At the same time, if the paper is folded in such a way that a hole is punched in the outer (perimeter) edge of the page, you will have a least one hole along the edge. They could still occur in the center area. Here are two different ones.

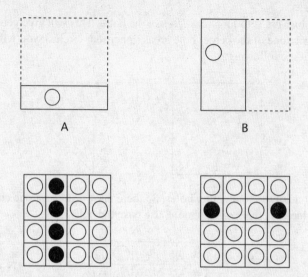

Two folds are in illustration A and, therefore, you'll find four holes. In illustration B there is only one fold, resulting in two holes, and these are only around the perimeter.

Now take the time to practice on the following problems. Check your answers at the end of this section.

Your task is to mentally unfold the paper and determine where the holes will be on the original square. You will be given five choices (A–E) from which to make your choice.

Practice Problems

1.

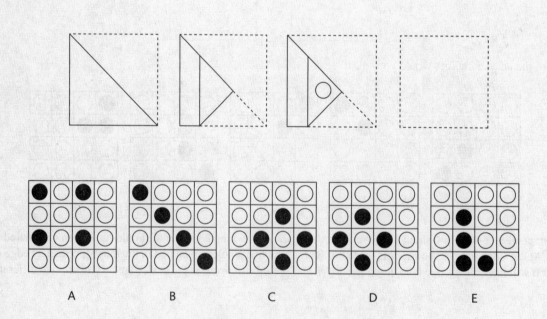

2.

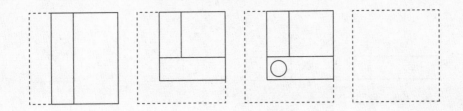

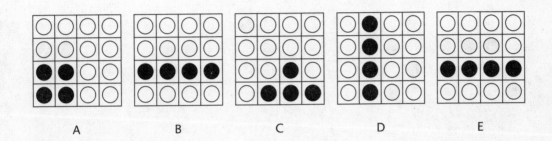

A   B   C   D   E

3.

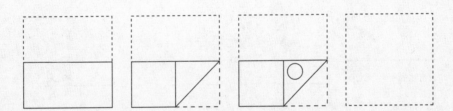

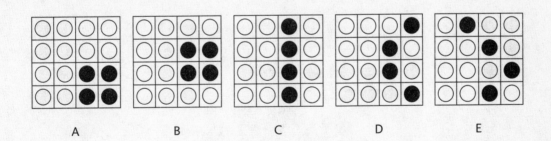

A   B   C   D   E

4.

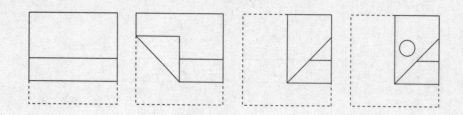

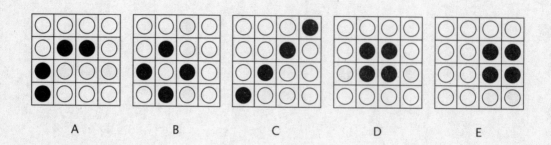

A   B   C   D   E

5.

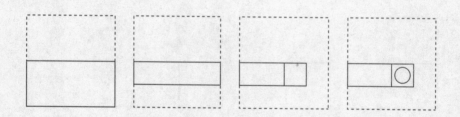

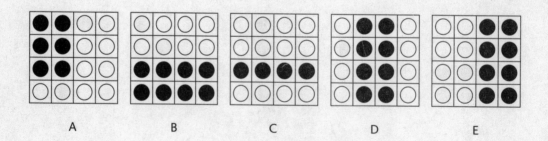

A   B   C   D   E

6.

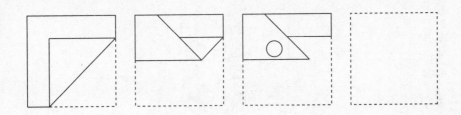

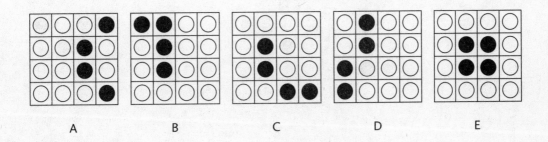

7.

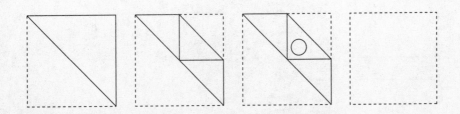

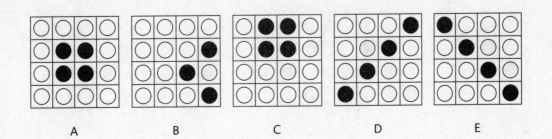

8.

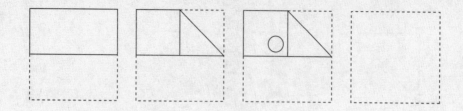

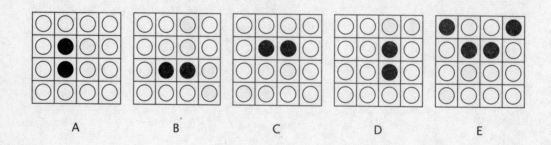

9.

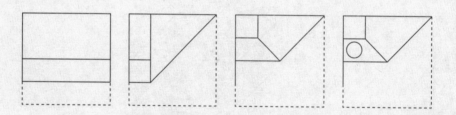

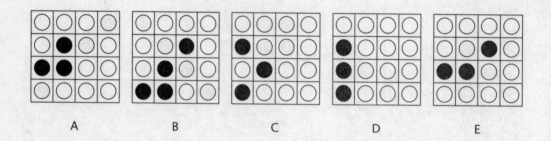

10.

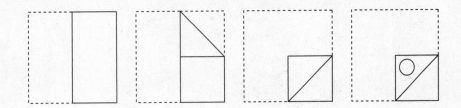

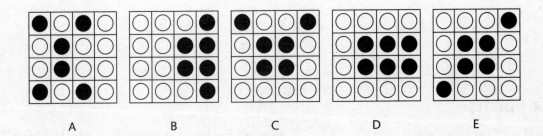

A   B   C   D   E

Answers

1. C
2. A
3. D
4. A
5. E
6. C
7. D
8. A
9. D
10. C

Blank Forms

On the next page, we've provided several sets of blank forms to use. Cut them out and practice with the folding. Use a hole-punch if you have one. Make copies if you wish.

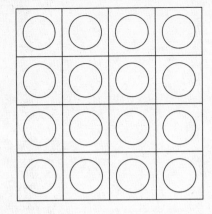 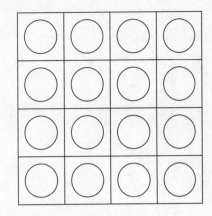

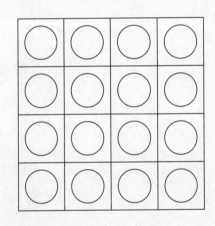 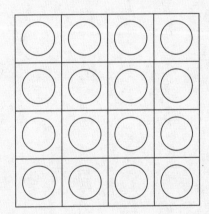

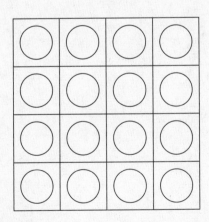 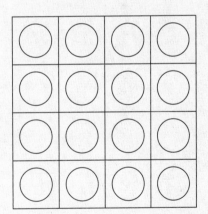

CUT HERE

Cubes

Part 5 of the Perceptual Ability Test involves counting the painted surfaces of cubes. Actually, it calls for you to determine which sides of the stacked cubes are exposed and assume that these are the painted sides. It is considered to be the easiest section of the PAT, but obviously, you shouldn't play down the importance of this section, since it counts the same as the other sections of this portion of the exam. Just do your best on this, which should help your other scores. The easier it is, the faster you can get to the next section, and you'll have more time to spend on that one.

Two steps are involved in the process. The first is being able to determine the *number of cubes,* and the second is determining *which sides are exposed.* Without knowledge of the first, you can't figure out the second.

Counting Cubes

How many cubes do you see?

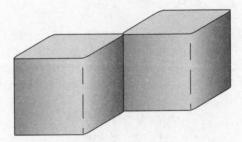

You should see 2 cubes, but now we add one more.

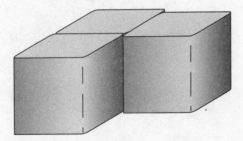

Now there are three cubes. Let's just jump ahead for a moment to give you an idea of what will be expected on the test. How many surfaces are exposed? You should have counted 11 surfaces. You have to remember to count the surfaces in the back also.

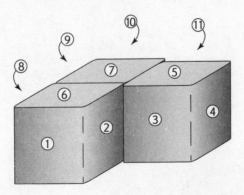

But this easy exercise indicates why it's important to be able to determine the number of cubes first. How many cubes are in the following diagram?

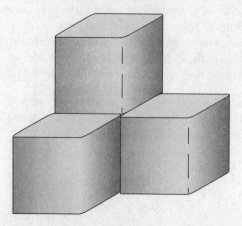

We've added one more cube on top of the earlier construction. There are four cubes now. You can't see it, but there is one cube beneath the one that is raised—otherwise, it would be able to stand on its own. Remember that for each level on which there is a cube, there must be one beneath it. There are no tricks here; each cube will have only one cube beneath it. A cube will not straddle the line between cubes. You won't see something like the following illustration:

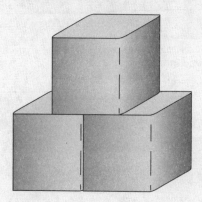

Let's start by practicing counting cubes.

1.

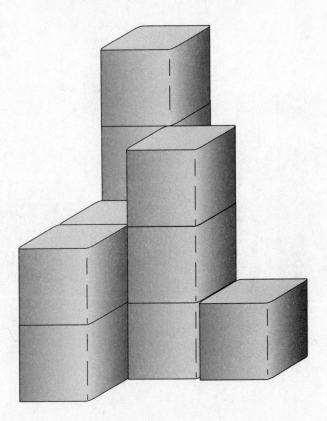

2.

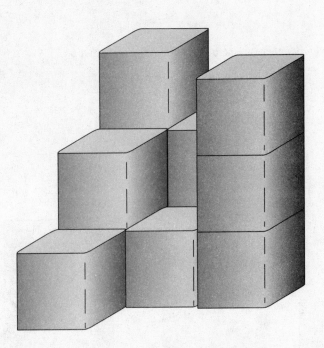

3.

Answers

  1. 12

  2. 12

  3. 15

You should also be able to tell when there are no cubes behind the construction:

  1.   **2.**

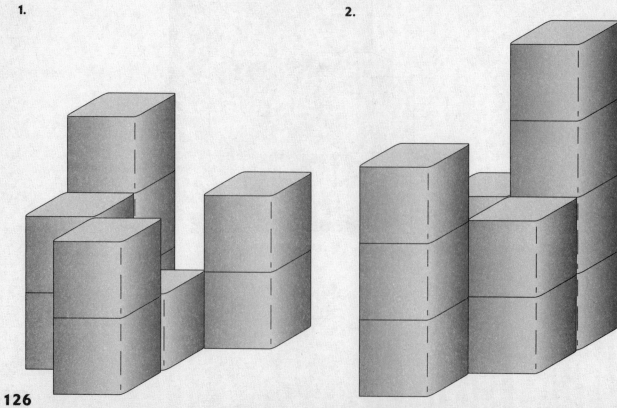

Answers

1. 10

2. 13

Practice Problems

1.

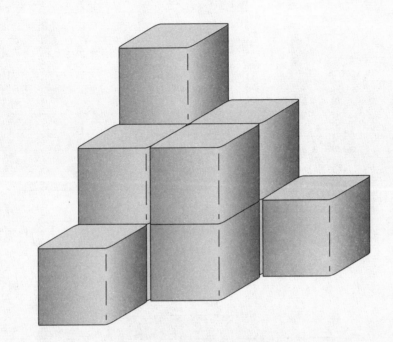

2.

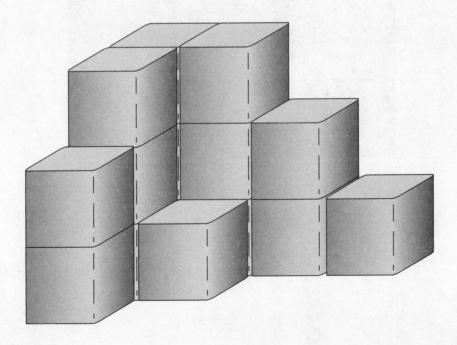

3.

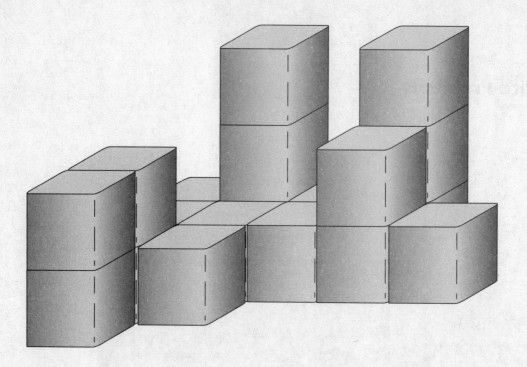

4.

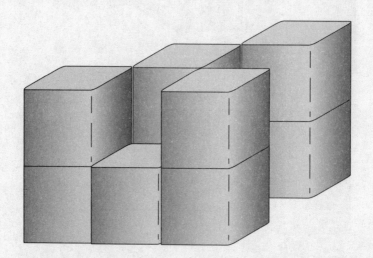

5.

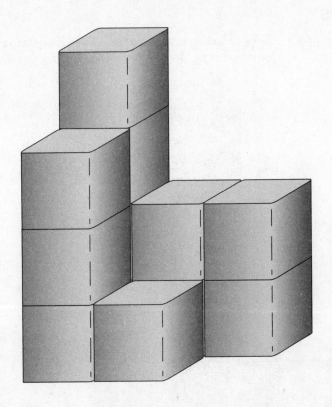

Answers

1. 11
2. 15
3. 19
4. 9
5. 12

Painted Surfaces

Now let's turn to the next part of this section—counting painted surfaces. Remember that you need to know how many cubes there are first, before you can figure the surfaces. Here's a typical construction that might appear on the test.

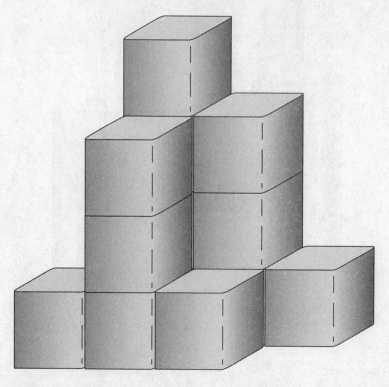

First of all, how many cubes are there? You can see that there are four levels, so you know that for each level there is a cube beneath it. We've labeled each top cube by the number of cubes beneath it.

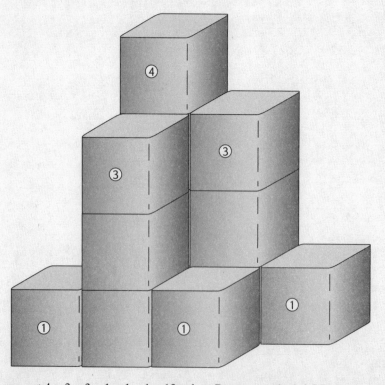

If you add them all up, you get 4 + 3 + 3 + 1 + 1 + 1 = 13 cubes. Pretty easy, isn't it? Let's try another one.

When you add these cubes you get $4 + 3 + 3 + 2 + 2 + 2 + 1 + 1 = 18$ cubes.

Painted Sides

We said earlier that you will be asked to determine which sides are exposed and painted. However, on the test, there are several sets of questions that are asked of you. You will be asked to determine various combinations of painted sides. For example, on the figure we just worked on, you may be asked how many cubes have only one of their sides painted. The questions will be asked as follows:

Figure A

1. In Figure A, how many cubes have one of their exposed sides painted?

    A. 1 cube
    B. 2 cubes
    C. 3 cubes
    D. 4 cubes
    E. 5 cubes

2. In Figure A, how many have two of their exposed sides painted?

    A. 1 cube
    B. 2 cubes
    C. 3 cubes
    D. 4 cubes
    E. 5 cubes

3. In Figure A, how many have three of their exposed sides painted?

    A. 1 cube
    B. 2 cubes
    C. 3 cubes
    D. 4 cubes
    E. 5 cubes

4. In Figure A, how many have four of their exposed sides painted?

   A. 1 cube
   B. 2 cubes
   C. 3 cubes
   D. 4 cubes
   E. 5 cubes

Answers

  1. B

  2. C

  3. C

  4. D

Calculating the Painted Sides

Each cube has a total of six sides (4 sides + 1 top + 1 bottom), but because each cube is sitting either on the surface or on another cube, the maximum number of exposed (painted) sides can be 5—you can't count the bottom.

As soon as there is another cube on top of it, you can then only see 4 sides. The one on top still has 5 sides exposed.

If another cube abuts the first one, you now only see three sides.

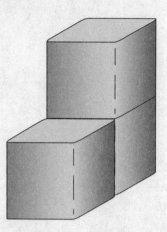

As a new cube is added, if it is touching the original cube, you are reducing the number of exposed sides by one. Add a cube to the back, and there will only be the front and one side exposed. Place a cube in front of the original cube, and you have only one side exposed. If another block is added to that last side, then there are no sides exposed. You can then ignore that cube in terms of counting painted sides.

2-sides exposed:

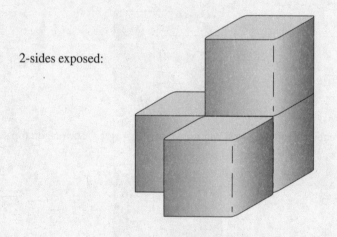

1-side exposed:

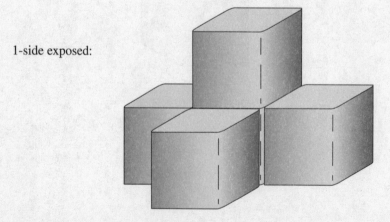

0 sides exposed:

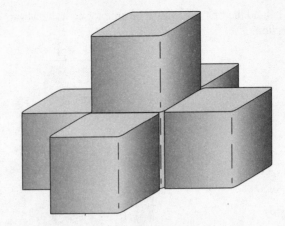

Is There a Strategy?

The answer is a definite maybe. You can create your own strategies based on your own way of looking at things. You can start by counting the number of cubes on each level; then add them up. For example, there are no tricks in working with the cubes, since you will see the construction at an angle that will reveal what's there—or not there. You *will not* see something like this on the test:

If there is another row behind the first row, you'll be able to see it. However, sometimes there will be a missing cube, as shown earlier in this section.

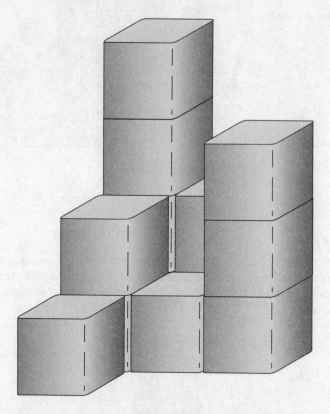

Let's use the preceding construction to practice a strategy counting the cubes and painted sides, starting from the top. Since there are four levels, label the top row, *Row 4,* and work your way down.

It is sometimes easier to begin with a diagram of the construction, looking down at it from the top and drawing columns, as follows. Indicate the number of blocks in that column, so that you'll have an exact count of the number of blocks. In the end, all of the numbers should add up.

```
 ┌───┬───┐
 │ 4 │ 2 │
 ├───┼───┼───┐
 │ 2 │ 1 │ 3 │
 ├───┼───┴───┘
 │ 1 │
 └───┘
   7   3   3   = 13 cubes
```

You can see that there are a total of 13 cubes.

Then count the exposed sides for each row, working your way down. List each row, and the number of cubes in the row. You then count the sides, row by row, block by block. You can see in the following chart that there is one cube on Row 4, two cubes on Row 3, four cubes on Row 2, and six cubes on the bottom row. We are working from top to bottom, although you might find it easier to work your way up.

Row 4	cube 1	5 sides
Row 3	cube 1	4 sides
	cube 2	5 sides
Row 2	cube 1	4 sides
	cube 2	4 sides
	cube 3	2 sides
	cube 4	4 sides
Row 1	cube 1	4 sides
	cube 2	1 side
	cube 3	2 sides
	cube 4	2 sides
	cube 5	3 sides
	cube 6	2 sides

Make sure that you've accounted for 13 cubes. Often a cube may be in the middle and have no sides exposed. Write that down also. This may seem tedious but it's a way to begin. You may create your own system, but it's a good way to teach yourself how to look at the number of cubes and then the painted sides. Just take this one more level. Count of the number of cubes with 5 painted sides, then 4 painted sides, and so on, and make a chart, crossing off the ones you've already counted to make sure that you've eliminated them all.

5 painted sides	2 cubes
4 painted sides	5 cubes
3 painted sides	1 cube
2 painted sides	4 cubes
1 painted sides	1 cube

Again, you have a total of 13 cubes.

Practice Problems

It's time to put all of these techniques to work. The first part of the exercise is to practice counting cubes. This part, of course, is not on the test. (Try to get in the habit of drawing a *top down* schematic of the cubes to help you remember how many blocks there are.) The second part is to answer the questions. If one strategy doesn't work, develop another one for yourself. That's the advantage of using this book. There are a lot of questions on which to practice and help you get ready for the final exam. Good luck on these.

137

Figure A

How many cubes are there? ___

1. In Figure A, how many cubes have one of their exposed sides painted?

    A. 1 cube
    B. 2 cubes
    C. 3 cubes
    D. 4 cubes
    E. 5 cubes

2. In Figure A, how many have two of their exposed sides painted?

    A. 1 cube
    B. 2 cubes
    C. 3 cubes
    D. 4 cubes
    E. 5 cubes

3. In Figure A, how many have four of their exposed sides painted?

    A. 1 cube
    B. 2 cubes
    C. 3 cubes
    D. 4 cubes
    E. 5 cubes

4. In Figure A, how many have five of their exposed sides painted?

    A.   1 cube
    B.   2 cubes
    C.   3 cubes
    D.   4 cubes
    E.   5 cubes

Figure B

How many cubes are there? ___

5. In Figure B, how many cubes have two of their exposed sides painted?

    A.   1 cube
    B.   2 cubes
    C.   3 cubes
    D.   4 cubes
    E.   5 cubes

6. In Figure B, how many have four of their exposed sides painted?

    A.   1 cube
    B.   2 cubes
    C.   3 cubes
    D.   4 cubes
    E.   5 cubes

7. In Figure B, how many have five of their exposed sides painted?

    A.   1 cube
    B.   2 cubes
    C.   3 cubes
    D.   4 cubes
    E.   5 cubes

Figure C

How many cubes are there? ___

8. In Figure C, how many cubes have three of their exposed sides painted?

    A.   1 cube
    B.   2 cubes
    C.   3 cubes
    D.   4 cubes
    E.   5 cubes

Figure D

How many cubes are there? ___

9. In Figure D, how many cubes have two of their exposed sides painted?

    A.   1 cube
    B.   2 cubes
    C.   3 cubes
    D.   4 cubes
    E.   5 cubes

10. In Figure D, how many have three of their exposed sides painted?

    A.   1 cube
    B.   2 cubes
    C.   3 cubes
    D.   4 cubes
    E.   5 cubes

11. In Figure D, how many have four of their exposed sides painted?

    A.   1 cube
    B.   2 cubes
    C.   3 cubes
    D.   4 cubes
    E.   5 cubes

Figure E

How many cubes are there? ___

12. In Figure E, how many cubes have two of their exposed sides painted?

    A.   1 cube
    B.   2 cubes
    C.   3 cubes
    D.   4 cubes
    E.   5 cubes

13. In Figure E, how many have five of their exposed sides painted?

    A.   1 cube
    B.   2 cubes
    C.   3 cubes
    D.   4 cubes
    E.   5 cubes

Answers

Figure A has 19 cubes.

1. B

2. E

3. C

4. C

Figure B has 20 cubes.

5. D

6. D

7. A

Figure C has 20 cubes.

8. E

Figure D has 14 cubes.

9. D

10. B

11. E

Figure E has 14 cubes.

12. D

13. C

If you had trouble with these, you need more practice. It's probably worth buying an inexpensive set of children's blocks and re-creating these constructions so you can see them better in three dimensions. For additional practice, go to the tests at the end of this book.

Form Development

Form development is the last section of the Perceptual Ability Test. In this section, you are given a two-dimensional flat pattern or *net*, and you are asked to select the three-dimensional drawing that would be the result if you were to fold the two-dimensional object into a three-dimensional figure.

One of the difficulties of form development is that it can take an inordinate amount of time to complete. Remember, you only have 60 minutes to complete all 90 questions. Under time pressure, it is important to remember the skills you learn from this section, as well as this important test-taking strategy: skip the difficult problems and come back to them later!

A net is a two-dimensional rendition of a three-dimensional object. A good way to grasp the meaning is to look at a cube and its net:

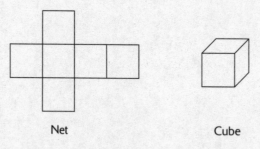

Net   Cube

Figure 1

Figure 1 illustrates one of the simplest concepts for a net. On the left is the two-dimensional representation. If the figure were folded at the lines, it would create the image on the right, which is a simple cube. One familiar cube you have probably encountered in your life is a die. Following is the net for a single die, along with six different three-dimensional representations of dice:

Figure 2

The form development questions begin with the two-dimensional representation, followed by four different three-dimensional representations. Of those four, only one will be correct. In Figure 2, the dice are all correct representations. To help your understanding, it would be useful to either find or purchase some dice. None of the following images of dice are correct; why? Compare the drawings to real dice to see the difference.

A.   B.   C.   D.

In answer *A,* the die is wrong since you would expect to see the four on top. In answer *B,* you would expect to see either a six or a one to the right of the three. In answer *C,* there should be a five to the right and a three on top, or a four on top and a two to the right. In answer *D,* there should be a six to the right. Are there any other ways that you can tell what the incorrect answers are? The opposite faces of dice always add up to seven. Does this obscure fact help you to rule out any of the preceding dice?

At the end of the Form Development section are several large nets that can be cut out and folded into three-dimensional figures. If necessary, use those to help you to understand the examples in this section.

Most of the nets you will encounter will be more complicated than a simple cube. Some of them will have geometric patterns and designs; some will be very complicated. Each line on the net will have a specific meaning: the outline, where you fold the object, or the edge of one of the shaded regions. Following is an example of a net:

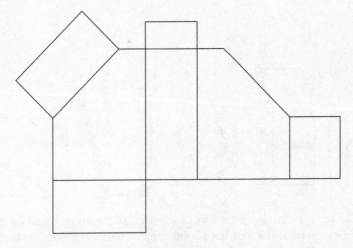

Figure 3

When the object is folded into its three-dimensional shape, it can be represented from many perspectives:

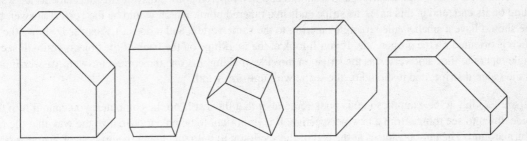

The Form Development section has problems that are made more difficult with the use of geometric figures and shading. For the following net, determine which of the five images is the correct three-dimensional representation.

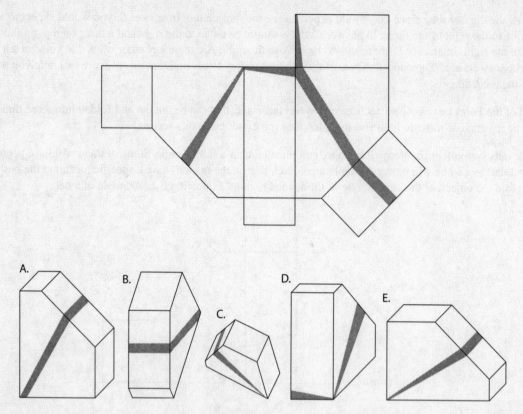

The correct answer is **D**. The key to determining the correct answer is in the stripes found on the two largest sides of the net. Looking at the net, the large panel to the right has a solid stripe of uniform width. The large panel to the left, on the other hand, starts in the bottom left as a broad stripe but tapers to a single point at the opposite vertex. In each of the three figures, there is either a broad stripe or a tapered stripe. In answer *A*, the stripe is uniform; however, it does not pass evenly on either side of the vertex. In addition, for answer *A*, the stripe on the side we are shown should end in a tapered point. Answer *B* has a broad stripe, and it should end in a tapered point. Answer *C* is the same as answer *A* only it is standing on its end, and in this case, the stripe ends in a tapered point, which would be the correct answer, but the back spine should have a small shaded triangle tapering to the same vertex, and it doesn't. Answer *D* shows the tapered point, which is oriented on the proper side. If you'll look at the markings on the back of the object, you will see that the gray triangle tapers to the same vertex as the stripe on the side, making this one the correct answer. Answer *E* once again has the tapered stripe, and it should be the stripe with uniform width.

When you are looking at the examples in this book remember that the test is on the computer; you cannot turn the computer upside down to see things from a new perspective. It is important to be able to visualize the way that the net will fold and turn around. The cut-out shapes at the end of the section will help you begin the process of visualization, but you need to eventually develop the skill of looking at the net and visualizing the correct three-dimensional form.

Shading and designs on the surfaces of the object, as in the examples, can help or hinder you in your quest to get these questions right. The designs and shading can actually do more toward helping you to get them correct if you learn how to use them to your advantage. We'll use the following net to illustrate the point:

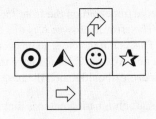

Figure 4

As you see a net like the preceding one, you might make note of certain things. The target symbol and the smiley face are on opposite sides of the cube. The straight arrow will point to the chin of the smiley face. The star is shaded on the side away from the smiley face. The bent arrow points to the star. The half-shaded arrowhead points toward and in the same direction as the bent arrow. Now look at the cubes that follow. Which one is a correct version of the preceding net, and why are the other three incorrect?

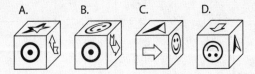

Answer A is not correct. If you look at the star and at the target symbol, you can see that the shaded part of the star should be toward the target symbol, and in this picture, the shade is to the left instead of to the bottom. Answer B has the bent arrow pointing away from the star, but looking at the net, you can see that the bent arrow is supposed to point directly toward the star. Answer **C** is the correct answer. The arrow and the arrow head are placed exactly the same as in Figure 4, and when you fold everything together, the arrow should be pointing to the chin of the smiley face. Answer D is incorrect because of the arrow head. It should be pointing away from the arrow, not toward it.

Shading can actually be easier than the designs on the faces of the cubes in the examples. Following is a net with the sides shaded. Pay close attention to the way that the sides are shaded to determine which of the answers are possible:

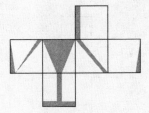

Figure 5

In Figure 5, there is shading on each of the six sides of the net. When you look at the samples that follow, focus on one face and see if you can find a flaw in the way that face looks in relation to the positioning of the other faces:

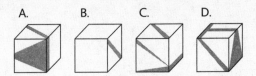

Answer *A* looks like it could be correct. The large trapezoid on the front face widens to the right. The face on the right should be a thin stripe on the left, just as it is. The error in answer A is that the top face should be a thin tapering stripe leading down to another marking at the back. This is not the case, so answer A is incorrect. Answer B should have the two tapered triangles on the right face but does not. Answer C should have the large trapezoid on the top face but doesn't. Answer **D** is correct. The small base of the trapezoid should match the base of the T-shaped face.

When you start with just one shaded face and start eliminating choices that are incorrect, you improve your chances of getting the correct answer. Try to practice eliminating incorrect answers as quickly as possible and see how many choices you have left. Usually this is a good way to improve your score on this portion of the test.

Sometimes the forms you see will be very complex and require you to look at the figure creatively. Often the most complex forms are the easiest to determine wrong answers. Let's look at the following figure:

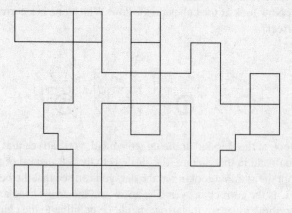

Figure 6

The first step in determining the correct answer for a problem like Figure 6 is to find the largest surface and compare it to all four choices. Any of the choices that does not have that precise shape would be incorrect. In Figure 7 that follows, you can see the largest surface from Figure 6.

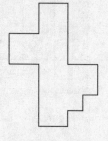

Figure 7

Now examine the following three-dimensional figures to determine which one is the correct rendition of Figure 6.

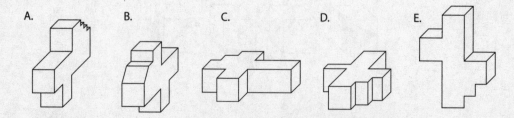

A.   B.   C.   D.   E.

None of the examples is correct. In all of the situations but E, the largest face has been subtly altered and the alteration hidden by the orientation of the object. Answer A has an extra step in the upper right. Answer B is missing a step and instead has a slope in the middle left. Answer C is like a religious cross; the lower leg is supposed to be offset with the upper leg. Answer D is incorrect because the leg that sticks out to the left is too slender. Figure E is incorrect because the lower step area is missing the three-dimensional effect. Each stair should have depth and does not.

Whenever you find a complex problem like in the previous example it is important to make sure that the largest face is represented correctly and the correct number of times. It is also important to make certain that the sides of the form are also properly represented. Eliminating obvious choices should improve your chances of getting the answer right if you are forced due to time constraints to guess.

You are allowed to use scratch paper while you are taking the PAT. Use your scratch paper wisely. Have a strategy for making a note of the answers you have eliminated. It might help to write down the letters A, B, C, and D on your scratch paper and cross out any that you have eliminated. This will enable you to improve your chances for a correct answer, even if you are running short of time and have to guess on the remaining possibilities:

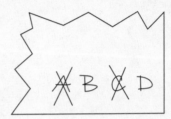

Practice Problems

The following problems are the exact format you will encounter in the Form Development section of the Perceptual Ability Test on the DAT. In each case, choose the correct three-dimensional representation of the flattened image shown in the center.

 1.

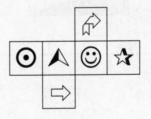

A.   B.   C.   D.

2.

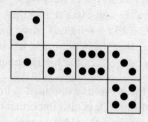

A.   B.   C.   D.

3.

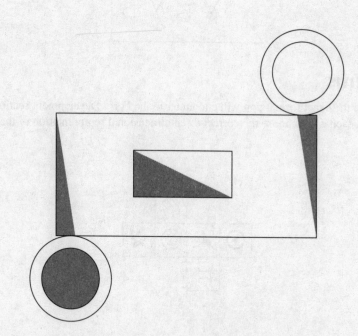

A.    B. 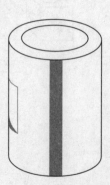   C.    D.

4.

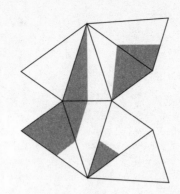

A.

B.

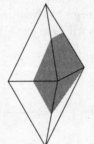

C.

D.

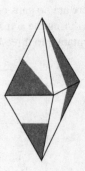

5.

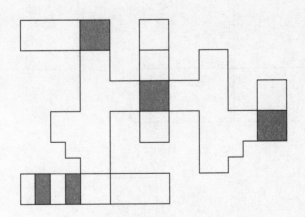

A.

B.

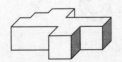

C.

D.

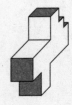

Answers

1. D
2. B
3. C
4. C
5. A

Cut-Out Section

The following nets can be removed from the book or, for best effect, photocopied onto cardstock paper. Cut out each net and fold at the lines, taping them together in a three-dimensional form. Be careful to tape them together properly so that there are no gaps or holes or extra flaps. Remember, you will not have the opportunity or the time to create these objects during the actual test. These objects are here to help you begin to visualize the transition from two-dimensional representation to three-dimensional object. The following objects will help you to master the material in this section.

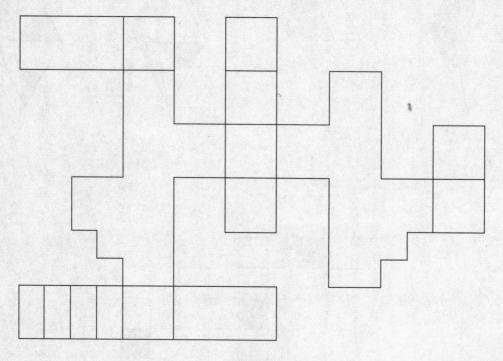

Figure 8

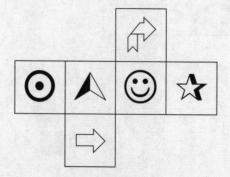

Figure 9

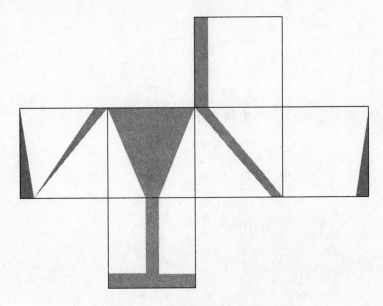

Figure 10

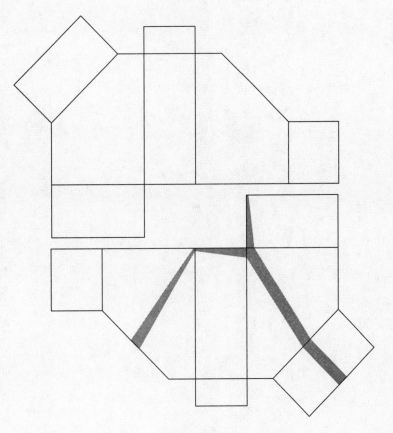

Figure 11

Reading Comprehension

The passages on the actual DAT will be somewhat longer than those presented in this book, in order to help you practice in a more controlled way. We've presented passages here with multiple-choice questions following each passage. The answers to these passages appear at the end of each set of questions in order for you to develop an understanding of why the specific answer is correct.

Directions: Read each of the following passages and answer the questions that follow.

Passage 1

With the cloning of Dolly, the sheep, in 1997, speculators believed that such scientific breakthroughs would soon apply to cells in the human body. Soon afterwards, investigators reported isolating for the first time, human embryonic cells that have the potential to develop into muscle, blood, nerves or any other tissue cell in the human body. In fact, these types of cells are called totipotent because of their multiple possibilities. With these mother cells, scientists may someday create many sorts of tissues to treat conditions such as spinal cord injuries, diabetes, leukemia, and even the neurodegenerative disorders like Parkinson's disease.

To understand the development of human embryos and to generate tissue for transplantation, several research teams had searched for human embryonic stem cells with no success. They initially tried to separate human blastocysts, clusters of 100 or so cells that constitute a stage of embryonic development. When this didn't work, the scientists collected primordial germ cells, the cells that give rise to sperm and eggs. Grown under certain conditions, these cells come to resemble stem cells derived from blastocysts. These cells were kept alive for more than seven months. These cells are shaped like embryonic stem cells, carry several of the same surface proteins and make telomerase, an enzyme thought to keep stem cells virtually immortal. They can spontaneously form embryoid bodies, clusters of differentiated cells also formed by embryonic stem cells.

Debate continues over whether primordial germ cells are the equivalent of blastocyst-derived stem cells. As germ cells develop into sperm or eggs, some genes receive a sex-specific chemical imprint that governs their activity during development. This imprinting may compromise the use of such cells as stem cells. However, if efforts prove successful with human embryonic stem cells that generate blood stem cells, they could eliminate the use of bone marrow tissues or umbilical cord blood to treat blood disorders such as leukemia.

---

1. The reason for calling the cells *totipotent* is

   A. they come from all parts of the body such as muscles, blood, and nerves.
   B. they are very powerful in regenerating diseased tissue.
   C. they can be used directly to treat many conditions and injuries.
   D. they become the mother cells, which can create tissues that have many possibilities.

(D) (A) They do not come from different parts of the body, and although they can help regenerate tissue (B), that is not the reason for this name. (C) These cells are not directly used to treat anything.

---

2. Blastocysts are

   A. cells that were kept alive for over seven months.
   B. another name for primordial germ cells.
   C. cells at a certain beginning stage of development.
   D. any group of more than 100 cells.

(C) (A) The length of time being kept alive does not categorize these cells nor does the number (D). (B) Primordial germ cells are a different type. The blactocysts are in an "embryonic" stage of development; hence, they are the "beginning" stage of development.

> **3.** Scientists became interested in primordial germ cells because
>
>   **A.** they give rise to sperm and eggs.
>   **B.** they can resemble blastocysts.
>   **C.** they will live for a long time.
>   **D.** it is easy to cultivate them.

(B) (A) It is irrelevant that they give rise to eggs and sperm; there is no textual evidence that they are easy to cultivate (D). There is no evidence that their living for seven months was the reason for interest (C).

> **4.** The most important aspect of the germ cells is
>
>   **A.** their shape.
>   **B.** their size.
>   **C.** the fact that they have proteins.
>   **D.** the fact that they have enzymes.

(D) Although there shape and proteins are interesting in connection with the other cells (A, C), it is the production of enzyme telomerase that is significant. (B) There is nothing said about their size.

> **5.** Germ cells and stem cells both
>
>   **A.** form embryoid bodies.
>   **B.** form clusters of differentiated cells.
>   **C.** form spontaneously.
>   **D.** all of the above.

(D) The last two sentences of the second paragraph contain all those facts.

> **6.** The use of the word *compromise* in the last paragraph best means
>
>   **A.** restrict.
>   **B.** enhance.
>   **C.** differentiate.
>   **D.** compliment.

(A) To compromise something means to give up a little to get something. Hence, (B) enhance and (D) compliment are positive words. To differentiate (C) means to be able to see the differences in something. The imprinting of the chemical would limit the use of the cells.

> **7.** The author's attitude about cloning can best be described as
>
>   **A.** optimistic about future discoveries.
>   **B.** skeptical about the application of this discovery.
>   **C.** curious about the ethics of the discovery.
>   **D.** cynical about testing on human cells.

(A) The last sentence indicates a positive feeling about this research. Therefore (B) and (D) are not appropriate. There is nothing mentioned about ethical concerns (C).

Passage 2

The old adage "Early to bed, early to rise, makes a man healthy, wealthy, and wise" may be more true than people think. Recent interest in the power and importance of sleep has revealed that a good night's sleep "wakes up" your mind and increases your brain power. Scientists have discovered that sleep deprivation causes changes in the brain that are almost identical to those that occur naturally in people in their seventies and eighties. These changes, which are in the hardworking frontal part of the brain's cortex, affect decision-making and the ability to absorb and adapt to new information. People who are affected tend to talk more in clichés and become more rigid in their thinking. A young intern in a hospital, after a long shift, could easily make a mistake if a patient comes in with unexpected symptoms that stretch and challenge his deductive powers.

Thus, it is important for employers to ensure that their staff does not work exhaustively long hours. Even a power nap in a workplace sleep zone could help in a crisis.

However, there is good news with this research for those worrying about the decline of brainpower. You don't have to spend time reading extremely weighty books or doing crossword puzzles in order to keep your mental acumen. It is more important to bombard your mind with information that is interesting to you—whether it be sightseeing, going to art galleries, surfing the Net, or window-shopping. The latest studies show that other parts of the brain take over from the declining frontal cortex during sleep to reorganize the fresh information gathered during the day. New neural connections are forged during the first hours of sleep.

Thus, for most people, a good night's sleep will restore their brains to full power.

---

8. It can be inferred from this passage, that as one grows older, one's brain

   A. has more power to connect to ideas that have accumulated over time.
   B. takes more time to hear the information that is being given.
   C. places new information into very specific categories.
   D. allows one to think creatively.

(C) When they talk about the elderly speaking in clichés and being rigid in their thinking, this eliminates creativity (D). There is nothing mentioned about the ability to hear (B) or the relationship of new ideas to previous ones (A)

---

9. A sleep-deprived intern might misdiagnose a patient's condition because the intern

   A. has fallen asleep.
   B. can't remember details of the symptoms.
   C. can't recognize and apply similar symptoms to ones in the medical textbook.
   D. is irritable and doesn't want to take extra time to figure out challenging solutions.

(C) The passage indicates that deductive reasoning powers are affected. It doesn't talk about irritability (D) or actually sleeping on the job (A), nor does it mention that the memory is affected (B).

---

10. The best reason for employers to have places for employees to rest on break is that

   A. even short naps can rejuvenate people.
   B. their snoring won't annoy those who are working.
   C. the brain can only rest if the person is lying down.
   D. quiet places help lower a person's heart rate.

(A) The last sentence of the first paragraph states the fact. (B), (C), and (D) are not even mentioned.

11. In the second paragraph, the term *mental acumen* most closely means

    A. memory.
    B. sharpness of intellect.
    C. good vocabulary.
    D. ability to do math problems.

(B) Acumen means mental sharpness and is not restricted to only math (D), vocabulary (C), or memory (A).

12. According to this passage, if you were a sports enthusiast, an effective way to maintain your mental acumen would be to

    A. read *Sports Illustrated.*
    B. read the *Wall Street Journal.*
    C. read *TV Guide.*
    D. do crossword puzzles.

(A) The passage directly states that acquiring knowledge about things that interest you is the best way to keep mentally sharp. Thus, a sports person would enjoy reading about sports in a magazine devoted to such.

13. Which of the following statements is NOT supported by the text?

    A. Other parts of the brain can take over the role of the front of the brain.
    B. The best sleep that you get is at the beginning of your cycle.
    C. Your frontal cortex is important to your daytime thinking.
    D. Once your brain is fatigued, those cells are never rejuvenated.

(D) (A), (B), and (C) are all found in the last paragraph. The last sentence of the passage is directly opposite of this statement (D).

14. The main idea of this passage is

    A. healthy brain function is dependent on your frontal cortex.
    B. active people have higher intelligence levels.
    C. rest is a medicinal activity.
    D. certain activities are better for your mental health than others.

(C) The word medicinal means acting like a remedy. The last sentence says that rest will restore people to full brain power much like a type of medicine. (A), (B), and (D) are not supported by the passage.

Passage 3

The Greeks believed that everything should be done in moderation. Thus, even exercise can be bad for your health. There is a pattern that is repeated every year after the holiday months of November and December. Overeating and excessive drinking during this period is followed by a nationwide fitness drive. Just examine the newspaper sales ads for all the diet and exercise aids. Slim-Fast and Atkins products are splashed across magazine pages with interim advertisements for those "ab-toners" and treadmills. However, health experts are warning people to avoid the trap of "binge exercising," which can lead to injury and disillusionment.

Over-exercising can damage muscles and bones that may heal in a matter of weeks, but the damaged self-confidence may last for years. One of the most common injuries is stress fractures, which are extremely painful hairline breaks. Bones need to be strengthened gradually over time. Ones that are too weak to take the strain of new, repetitive exercise can split in as little as two or three weeks of a new exercise regimen. Furthermore, sporadic exercise of any type might increase levels of bad cholesterol. Studies have shown that although regular exercise protects the body by increasing the number of cholesterol-fighting molecules, short bursts of activity either had no effect or made it rise.

The recommendation for introducing a new exercise program suggests moderate exercise for 30 consecutive minutes five times a week. Moderate exercise, which leaves you slightly breathless but not in discomfort, includes brisk walking, cycling, and even gardening. Although gym membership is expensive, it can be a good investment because it offers exercise in a controlled way. You cannot change the effects of overindulgence in a day. The secrets of success are patience and realistic expectations.

---

15. The reference to *moderation* in the first sentence implies

    A. that it is not good to be the champion of anything.

    B. that people waste their talents by trying to succeed and then fail.

    C. that too much of even a good thing can be bad.

    D. that it is healthy to drink only a little at a time.

(C) The next sentence supports the idea that even good things in excess can be bad. The text does not talk about competition (A), talents (B), or the idea of drinking and its solutions (D).

---

16. The purpose of mentioning Slim-Fast and Atkins is

    A. to compare effective weight loss plans.

    B. to advertise for the companies.

    C. to suggest ways to lose weight in moderation.

    D. to give examples of the yearly cycle.

(D) The author uses the information to help support the idea that the sudden concern for exercise is cyclical. There is no attempt to fully examine any type of dieting (A, C), and it is obviously not selling a product (B).

---

17. *Binge exercising* means

    A. only exercising in random bursts of energy.

    B. eating and then exercising immediately afterward.

    C. exercising during the month of January.

    D. exercising once a week.

(A) There are no textual examples of exercising immediately after eating (B). A certain month for exercise is not advocated (C), and evidence of exercising on a regular basis is not bad (D).

18. A *stress fracture* is

    A. a very small, hardly noticeable break in a bone.
    B. an emotional breakdown.
    C. a cut near your scalp.
    D. a laceration to your skin.

(A) The definition directly follows the word.

19. Gym membership is advocated because

    A. it helps the economy.
    B. it gives you more choices of types of exercises.
    C. it encourages a controlled approach to exercise.
    D. it provides you with company while you exercise.

(C) The third to the last sentence in the last paragraph states this fact.

20. The author's attitude about exercise in this article can best be described as

    A. guarded because not all exercise is good.
    B. enthusiastic because exercise makes you fit and healthy.
    C. objective because the type of exercise that is best is up to the individual.
    D. cautionary because people need to diet along with exercise.

(A) The main idea of the passage is that not all exercise is good. Thus, there is skepticism. Guarded means having doubts.

Passage 4

The movie *Jurassic Park* is science-fiction. DNA from animals over 50,000 years ago cannot be reliably recovered. However through the power of the computer and virtual reality, researchers have demonstrated that computers can reconstruct with 98% accuracy the DNA of a creature that was a contemporary of the dinosaurs—a small, furry, nocturnal animal. Knowing the mammal's complete genome—the sequence of As, Cs, Ts, and Gs in the DNA that made up its chromosomes—does not mean that scientists can bring the creature to life. It does mean, however, that this information can help scientists explore the evolution of human and other mammals at the molecular level. It can be called a kind of DNA-based archaeology of comparative genomics. Scientists believe that much more can be learned from this type of research than from the comparative studies of living species such as the mouse, the rat, or the chimpanzee. For instance, if a DNA sequence in the human genome is missing in the corresponding place in the mouse genome, it is uncertain whether that DNA was inserted in the evolution of humans from the mammalian ancestor or deleted in the evolution of mice. If an ancestral genome is available, the ambiguity disappears.

Based on a huge amount of data from research analysis of genomic sequences from any different vertebrate species, an artificial evolutionary tree was created with a massive software program. The software program was able to simulate mammalian evolution on the molecular level. This resulted in simulated modern DNA sequences for 20 different species. Then, the reconstruction procedure was used to create an ancestral sequence. This used no information from the simulated process. When the two were compared, there was a 98% accuracy. To do a complete reconstruction of the ancestral mammalian genome, there would have to be additional genome sequencing. However, if this were accomplished, there would be not only new insights into the core biology that all mammals share but also the unique traits that define each species.

---

21. The reference to *Jurassic Park* sets the tone

    A. that information about that period is highly speculative.
    B. that movies take liberties about scientific discoveries.
    C. that information about dinosaurs is very unreliable.
    D. that it is an important document about DNA retrieval.

(A) The phrase "highly unreliable" indicates that speculation is involved in determining information about dinosaurs. The passage is not focused on the quality of movies (B). The statement in the text says that the retrieval of DNA is unreliable (C, D).

---

22. Understanding and identifying an animal's complete genome

    A. does not mean that the creature can be replicated under similar circumstances.
    B. means that you have the effective blueprints for re-creation of that creature.
    C. is the basis of determining nocturnal animals of prehistoric times.
    D. does not mean that you have the sequence of the chromosomes.

(A) Although the knowledge of the genome provides a kind of pattern for the re-creation, it isn't necessarily possible to actually re-create it (B). The focus is not on only how to re-create nocturnal creatures (C). Chromosome are what make up the DNA (D).

---

23. The basic reason why scientists believe that computer-generated DNA archeology is better than comparative live species study is

    A. because computers can overcome human error.
    B. because missing elements could be contingent on an insertion of DNA in one species or the deletion of DNA in the other species along the evolutionary line.
    C. because even though there are similarities among rats, chimpanzees, and humans, they are not exactly alike.
    D. because computers are faster and more objective in their findings.

(B) The focus is not trying to convince you of the speed of the computer (D) or the ability of people making mistakes (A). The relationships between mammals is not relevant here (C).

24. The most important data in creating an artificial evolutionary tree is

    A. the genome sequences.
    B. understanding of mammalian ancestry.
    C. blood samples from ancient mammals.
    D. chromosome mapping.

(A) The first sentence of the second paragraph states this.

25. Statistics were used in this passage to

    A. present the effectiveness of a computer-generated study.
    B. show the averages of human error.
    C. explain how DNA typing works.
    D. convince you that *Jurassic Park* was a movie based on inaccuracy.

(A) This is not a persuasive essay on film (D), nor does it give examples of how they type DNA (C). The purpose is not to evaluate human error, as it is to show the advantages to using computers.

26. The end of this passage implies

    A. that this type of study can only be taken to a certain level before it no longer works.
    B. that this type of study can lead to changes in existing understandings of species.
    C. that it would take too long to bring this type of study up to date.
    D. that this type of study would be beneficial in supporting existing hypotheses.

(B) The last sentence says " there would be new insights into the core biology," which indicates that new information might challenge the existing ones.

27. The tone of this passage is

    A. critical of movies that misrepresent scientific facts.
    B. supportive of research done by computers.
    C. amazed at the extent to which genome sequencing has led to discoveries.
    D. relieved that a reliable source of study is available through DNA archeology.

(B) This is a basic expounding of information that demonstrates the worth of computer research. Hence, it is not critical of movies (A) nor amazed (C) at anything. There is no anxiety in the tone, so there is no need to be relieved (D).

Passage 5

In December of 2002, in Fort Meyers, Florida, over 3,000 people met in the convention center to protest federal restrictions on waterfront development. These people felt that their basic rights were being violated. They did not have the freedom to use land as they wished. Since land in Florida is at a premium, especially on the intercoastal waterway which is a superhighway for boats, these people wanted their voices to be heard. On the other hand, the government's concern is to safeguard the chubby, marine mammal known as the manatee. These sea cows inhabit the many bays, canals and rivers of Florida. Their primary cause of death of these slow-moving creatures is accidents with boats. They were placed on the endangered species list in 1967. Boaters and developers argue that these mammals have rebounded in numbers, but their protectors maintain that they are just holding their own.

These creatures are certainly not beautiful yet they endear themselves to many, Their body looks like a dumpling with a paddlelike tail and a squint like Mr. Magoo's. An average adult is about ten feet long and weighs 1,000 pounds. The animals tend to be solitary, except when mating or when cold weather prompts them to huddle near the warm springs or power plant discharge pipes. Like seals and walruses, manatees breathe through their snouts. They surface to take breathes every three or four minutes. Manatees eat mostly aquatic vegetation and have even been seen hauling themselves onto lawns to munch the grass. Because of this grazing, they have been given the bovine nickname. They usually swim no faster then five miles an hour although they can sprint nearly three times as fast.

Although manatees once ranged from the Carolinas to the west coast of Africa, now they stay in the warmer waters. People once killed the manatees for their succulent meat, but even as early as the 1700's, there was recognition of their decreasing numbers. One of Florida's founding fathers, Frederick Morse, put a ban on the hunting of these mammals in 1893. Then, the major threat to their lives was the increase of boating accidents. Boat hulls and keels crack manatee's skulls and their ribs. The many scars on the animal's hide are nearly as distinctive as a fingerprint and constitute a way of identifying each individual creature. Even though these creatures are not vicious, because of man's encroachment on the waterways, their existence is constantly in peril. Proponents of expansion feel that these animals are no longer in danger and in fact, are encroaching upon man's territory. Thus, the solution to the problem would be the development of a symbiotic relationship between man and mammal.

---

28. The purpose of the 3,000 people at the convention center was

    A. to protest the endangerment of the manatees.

    B. to voice their concern about the inability to develop land.

    C. to complain about the intrusion of government on local politics.

    D. to encourage people to get out and vote.

(B) The purpose of the people was to " protest federal restrictions" so they would not be supporting the manatees (A) nor did it have anything to do with voting (D). There was no mention of a clash between federal and local politics. (C).

---

29. The biggest threat to manatees is

    A. dwindling food supplies.

    B. polluted waterways.

    C. accidents from boats.

    D. human diseases carried in the water.

(C) Disease, pollution and feeding grounds were never included in the passage.

---

30. Manatees are most like

    A. whales because of their enormous size.

    B. seals because they are cute.

    C. walruses because they breathe air.

    D. sharks because they swim slowly.

(C) Both creatures needs to surface in order to breathe.

31. They are nicknamed sea cows because of

    A. how they look.
    B. how they eat.
    C. how they swim.
    D. how they reproduce.

(B) It states that sea cows graze on vegetation and can be seen munching on people's lawns.

32. The scars on their backs indicate

    A. how old they are.
    B. how aggressive they have been.
    C. what diseases they have had.
    D. how many injuries from boats have happened.

(D) The passage never talks about age (A) temperament (B) or disease (C) in the animals.

33. Scientists can best label individual manatees through

    A. their feeding habits.
    B. their scar patterns.
    C. their dorsal fins.
    D. their swimming style.

(B) The unique scar patterns are like fingerprints.

34. The author's purpose of this passage was to

    A. present a compelling reason for outlawing boats on the waterway.
    B. criticize developers for their avarice.
    C. propose solutions to the dilemma.
    D. explain the information behind a heated issue.

(D) The purpose is not to outlaw boats (A) nor to put value judgments on the developers (B). There is no concrete solution. (C). It purely talks about the different perspectives on the problem.

Passage 6

Most people get up in the morning and immediately turn on the radio or television to see what the temperature is and what the weather will be. This is how we plan our day. Likewise, the U.S. military relies on the scientists and programmers at the Navy's Fleet Numerical Meteorology and Oceanography Center (FNMOC) for timely, accurate weather data and maps to facilitate their missions. This is a very tall order for this group. Faced with having to create about 2.6 million oceanic and atmospheric charts, analyses, forecasts and related data sets daily, the center is in need of improving their processes. The task of keeping data in some sort of order is one challenge. To be able to retrieve and analyze it provides another challenge. Furthermore, having the space that such paper documentation uses is a further issue. To try and rectify this, the Naval center has turned to a collaborative approach where there is an online forum. This cyberspace chat room is where scientists can communicate about their projects. The software, specially developed for this purpose allows military and civilian scientists, meteorologists and developers who discuss their objectives, strategies and deadlines within the firewall. Users exchange open-source or proprietary codes within their own repositories. Unlike using e-mail, people can communicate in a single location which facilitates project tracking. This increases efficiency for the meteorology and oceanography centers where the number of teams of programmers has dwindled due to budget cuts. Currently, there are 64 Navy projects and up to 200 registered users who are spread out across multiple locations.

It is too early to quantify how much this computer service has improved application-development process, but there is evidence of fewer meetings and exchanges of e-mails. Furthermore, all the documentation can be stored on the hard drive to eliminate the space problem. The retrieval of information is immediate and organized. The Navy is optimistic about transferring over 170 applications that were done manually to computer-generated activities.

---

35. The U.S. military relies on the FNMOC for

    A. only maps for indication of ocean currents.

    B. weather data for ground conditions of troop removal.

    C. maps and weather for military missions.

    D. help in deciding the next move in an important project.

(C) (A) and (B) are too narrow. (D) has no evidence in the text.

---

36. The biggest challenge for the FNMOC is

    A. creating 2.6 million oceanic and atmospheric charts.

    B. keeping data in one place.

    C. being able to retrieve the information.

    D. all of the above.

(D) All those details are found in the first paragraph.

---

37. Their cyberspace chatroom is where

    A. scientists can exchange ideas about their project.

    B. naval officers can get good suggestions about maneuvers.

    C. weather reports are found.

    D. maps of ocean currents are available.

(A) The sentence which states this fact is in the middle of the first paragraph.

38. The new software is

    A.   useful to all different groups of people.
    B.   has complicated security codes.
    C.   allows only the most important data to be stored easily.
    D.   allows only the military to access the important information.

(A) The text states that military and civilian scientists, meteorologists and developers all can use the system. Thus it is useful to all people.

39. What helps facilitate project tracking is

    A.   meteorology and oceanography centers located near each other.
    B.   the software that allows people to communicate in a single location.
    C.   the dwindling number of teams of programmers.
    D.   the 200 users are spread out across multiple locations.

(B) This statement is found at the end of the first paragraph.

40. The word *quantify* in the first sentence of the last paragraph most closely means

    A.   looking for positive data.
    B.   determining how much something costs.
    C.   examining the program for its bugs.
    D.   predicting its future success.

(D) Although looking for positive data (A) and examining for bugs (C) might be incorporated in analyzing its effectiveness, the word quantify suggests predicting its future success.

41. Success will be measured by

    A.   the number of e-mails and meetings that have to have happen.
    B.   the positive questionnaire that they receive.
    C.   the success of Naval missions.
    D.   the happiness of 170 applications of the Navy workers.

(A) No questionnaires were mentioned (B). there is no specific information about successes (C) and the reference to 170 applications is talking about something else (D).

Passage 7

Most people believe that mental illness is some form of psychological weakness or hereditary trait. However, some scientists at the National Institute of Mental Health have extracted protein from spinal fluid of both healthy and schizophrenic people that indicate patterns that might identify viruses linked to some cases of the disease. Theories about the possible role of viral infections in schizophrenia have circulated in the psychiatric community for more than a century. Because there has only been indirect evidence, there is much controversy about this issue.

The term schizophrenia encompasses a number of disorders that are caused by genes, stress, early family interactions, chemical imbalance, infections, nutrition, or some combination of them. Symptoms include social withdrawal, incoherent speech, blunted emotions, delusions, and hallucinations. At least 2 million people in the United States are estimated to have some form of this mental disease.

In the past few years, other ailments like multiple sclerosis and Alzheimer's disease are brain diseases which are being examined for evidence of viral infections. Researchers believe that this form of mental disease might also be related to viruses because incidents may remain inactive for 20 years and then flare-up.

One way to check for evidence of viruses is to examine the spinal fluid, which closely reflects brain proteins. More than 300 proteins have now been separated and identified by advanced staining and computer analysis processes. Since one third of the patients had a pair of proteins that always surfaced together, and these proteins are also present in those suffering from herpes encephalitis or creutzfeldt-Jakob disease, there is speculation that there might be a connection to schizophrenia. However, the problem remains as to whether the proteins represent a viral infection that precedes the disease or whether they are a result of the nervous system and immune system changes caused by the disease.

Continued research could unlock more information about the connections that might present medication that could help or prevent the onslaught of this mental illness. What has to happen is the collaboration between immunologists and biological psychiatrists so that theories can be more rigorously studied and tested.

---

42. The following statement is true:

    A. Mental illness is a hereditary trait.
    B. Bacterial infections cause schizophrenia.
    C. Protein in spinal fluid might be used as a determinant to causes of mental illness.
    D. There are no recognizable patterns in types of mental illnesses.

(A) It is stated in the first sentence.

---

43. Schizophrenia is a disorder that

    A. could be linked to early family interactions.
    B. is not a major illness in the United States.
    C. only causes delusions and hallucinations.
    D. is definitely caused by a chemical imbalance.

(A) The first sentence in the second paragraph states this.

---

44. The reason why doctors are examining spinal fluid is

    A. because it is easy to reach and cultivate in labs.
    B. it resembles brain proteins.
    C. it has over 200 proteins.
    D. it can be easily stained and analyzed by a computer.

(B) This is stated in the first sentence of the fourth paragraph.

45. The commonality between herpes encephalitis and creutzfeldt-Jakob disease is

    A.   people who have either disease possess similar blood proteins.

    B.   they are also suffering from schizophrenia.

    C.   they might have caught a bacteria infection.

    D.   they are immune to certain antibiotics.

(A) Evidence is found in paragraph four.

46. The major problem with the results of this study is

    A.   whether the proteins are a result of an infection that precedes the disease or if it is the result of changes in the immune system before the disease.

    B.   whether the proteins are a result of an infection the proceeds with the disease or if the result if caused by nervous system infections.

    C.   whether the proteins are a result of an infection that precedes the disease if it is the result of changes in the immune system due to the disease.

    D.   whether the proteins are a result of immunization or whether they are the result of post disease syndrome.

(C) Evidence is found in paragraph four. Be careful of the difference between "precedes" (C) and "proceeds"(B).

47. The results of the research hope to be able to

    A.   find medications that could help or prevent the onslaught of the disease.

    B.   predict when the onslaught of the disease will happen.

    C.   unlock connections between medications and infections.

    D.   rebuild the nervous system after the onslaught of the disease.

(A) (B) and (C) are too narrow and (D) has no evidence to support that idea.

48. The attitude of the author of this article is:

    A.   angry with the lack of money given for this type of research.

    B.   annoyed that research is happening so slowly.

    C.   encouraged that connections will help with a breakthrough in the next year or so.

    D.   adamant that immunologists and biological psychiatrists need to work together for progress to be made.

(D) The wording of the last sentence indicates a firm belief (adamant) about the need for collaboration. There is no evidence of anger (A), annoyance (B), or the encouragement (C) are due to the collaboration that is necessary.

Passage 8

Prostate cancer is the most common form of cancer in men. Although the causes of this disease are not truly understood, there is evidence that it is associated with age. The way to test for this disease is to take a biopsy, a microscopic examination of a tiny sample of prostate tissue. However, even if the results come back negative, as they do for the majority of the tests, this is not the end of the potential problem. As men age, they continue to be at risk. If there is history of this disease, then they are at higher risk. Furthermore, some of the symptoms of the disease continue even if the cancer is not there.

The existing treatment of this cancer can include hormonal therapy, radiation treatment and surgery. All three conventional treatments are accepted widely. However, because there are significant side effects to each of the treatments, people are also turning to herbal remedies and nutritional supplements to alleviate symptoms or promote prostate health. The challenge to the consumer is to keep careful watch on the evidence of effectiveness of this ever-growing list of vitamins, herbs and minerals.

While widely used drugs have gone through rigorous tests, many of the "natural" remedies have not. Thus, the need for appropriate lab tests and research is an expanding area of science. Pre-clinical tests include test tube procedures, followed by cell-based assays and end with animal-based studies. For natural based compounds, the primary question is whether these substances exhibit toxicity and to what extent. Studies on these elements will determine the effect the substance has for cell proliferation and whether their effect is tissue specific. As more and more of these tests are taken, the cost of these "natural" remedies are going to increase, making them less appealing to patients and more of a concern to the insurance companies who will have to determine if they will pay for them.

---

49. In the third sentence, the word *biopsy* most closely indicates

   A. a type of minor, investigative surgery.
   B. a type of lab test on rat cells to figure out rate of tissue growth.
   C. a major type of surgery to correct the problem.
   D. an aggressive use of medication to cure the problem.

(A) It states that it is microscopic and uses only a tiny bit of tissue.

---

50. Which of the following statements is correct?

   A. As men age, they are less likely to need to be tested as often.
   B. Even a negative test does not indicate the lack of cancer.
   C. These tests are easily done and completely accurate.
   D. Past history does not affect the possibilities of getting the cancer.

(B) This is stated in the third sentence of the first paragraph.

---

51. Because of the negative side effects of traditional treatments of prostate cancer, patients are

   A. dying faster because patients are not following the regimen.
   B. seeking alternatives that might be less invasive.
   C. asking insurance companies to pay for their over-the-counter medication.
   D. watching TV for advice on how to treat the disease.

(B) (A)(C)(D) have no support within the article.

52. The danger with *natural remedies* is that

    A. they haven't had assays done.
    B. they are very expensive.
    C. their effectiveness is entirely false.
    D. their test tube results are spurious.

(A) Tests include three steps and doing assays is one of them. Natural remedies have not gone through the extensive tests that the pharmaceuticals have.

53. Two areas of importance in determining the effectiveness of natural remedies are

    A. pre-clinical tests and cost.
    B. cell proliferation and tissue specificity.
    C. taste and toxicity.
    D. how they are marketing and who will market them.

(B) This is stated at the end of the third paragraph. Cost (A) is not mentioned. (C) Taste is not mentioned nor is marketing (D).

54. What might make these remedies less appealing is

    A. the cost when more tests require higher prices.
    B. the availability because more people will want them.
    C. the taste because they are all natural.
    D. the lack of studies in comparison to the other treatments.

(A) The second to the last sentence of the article states this.

55. There is the suggestion that alternate treatments to diseases is partially controlled by

    A. news reports on TV.
    B. doctors and pharmacists.
    C. insurance companies.
    D. researchers and scientists.

(C) This is stated in the last sentence.

Quantitative Reasoning

Numerical Calculations

---

1. A bread recipe calls for $3\frac{1}{4}$ cups of flour. If you only have $2\frac{1}{8}$ cups, how much more flour is needed?

  A. $1\frac{1}{8}$

  B. $1\frac{1}{4}$

  C. $1\frac{3}{8}$

  D. $1\frac{3}{4}$

  E. $5\frac{3}{4}$

(A) $3\frac{1}{4} - 2\frac{1}{8} = \frac{13}{4} - \frac{17}{8} = \frac{26}{8} - \frac{17}{8} = \frac{9}{8} = 1\frac{1}{8}$ more cups of flour.

---

2. Jack lives $6\frac{1}{2}$ miles from the library. If he walks $\frac{1}{3}$ of the way and takes a break, what is the remaining distance to the library?

  A. $2\frac{1}{6}$ miles

  B. 4 miles

  C. $4\frac{1}{3}$ miles

  D. $5\frac{5}{6}$ miles

  E. $6\frac{1}{6}$ miles

(C) $\frac{1}{3}$ of $6\frac{1}{2}$ miles is $\frac{1}{3} \times 6\frac{1}{2} = \frac{1}{3} \times \frac{13}{2} = \frac{13}{6}$ miles walked. The remaining distance is

$6\frac{1}{2} - \frac{13}{6} = \frac{13}{2} - \frac{13}{6} = \frac{39}{6} - \frac{13}{6} = \frac{26}{6} = 4\frac{1}{3}$ miles.

---

3. The sum of 2 feet $2\frac{1}{2}$ inches, 4 feet $3\frac{3}{8}$ inches, and 3 feet $9\frac{3}{4}$ inches is

  A. 9 feet $\frac{7}{8}$ inches.

  B. 9 feet $9\frac{5}{8}$ inches.

  C. 10 feet $\frac{5}{8}$ inches.

  D. 10 feet $2\frac{5}{8}$ inches.

  E. 10 feet $3\frac{5}{8}$ inches.

(E) First, add the number of feet together and then add the number of inches: 2 ft + 4 ft + 3 ft = 9 ft. Then,

$$2\frac{1}{2} \text{ in} + 3\frac{3}{8} \text{ in} + 9\frac{3}{4} \text{ in} = \frac{5}{2} + \frac{27}{8} + \frac{39}{4} = \frac{20}{8} + \frac{27}{8} + \frac{78}{8} = \frac{125}{8} = 15\frac{5}{8} \text{ in.}$$

$$15\frac{5}{8} \text{ in} = 1 \text{ ft } 3\frac{5}{8} \text{ in, so, all together, } 9 \text{ ft} + 1 \text{ ft } 3\frac{5}{8} \text{ in} = 10 \text{ ft } 3\frac{5}{8} \text{ in.}$$

---

4. A 10-foot rope is to be cut into equal segments measuring 8 inches each. The total number of segments is

    A. 1.

    B. 8.

    C. 15.

    D. 20.

    E. 40.

(C) The total number of inches in a 10-foot rope is $10 \times 12 = 120$ inches. The number of 8-inch segments that can be cut is $\frac{120}{8} = 15$.

---

5. A piece of wood measuring 16.5 inches long is cut into 2.75-inch pieces. How many smaller pieces of wood are there?

    A. 3

    B. 4

    C. 5

    D. 6

    E. 7

(D) The number of smaller pieces is $\frac{16.5}{2.75} = 6$.

---

6. The least common multiple of 8, 12, and 20 is

    A. 4.

    B. 24.

    C. 60.

    D. 90.

    E. 120.

(E) Factors of 8 are $2 \times 2 \times 2$; factors of 12 are $2 \times 2 \times 3$; factors of 20 are $2 \times 2 \times 5$. The least common multiple of 8, 12, and 20 is $2 \times 2 \times 2 \times 3 \times 5$ or 120.

---

7. A recipe calls for 3 cups of wheat and white flour combined. If $\frac{3}{8}$ of this is wheat flour, how many cups of white flour are needed?

    A. $1\frac{1}{8}$

    B. $1\frac{7}{8}$

    C. $2\frac{3}{8}$

    D. $2\frac{5}{8}$

    E. $3\frac{3}{8}$

(B) If $\frac{3}{8}$ is wheat flour, then $1 - \frac{3}{8}$ or $\frac{5}{8}$ is white flour. So $3 \times \frac{5}{8} = \frac{15}{8} = 1\frac{7}{8}$ cups of white flour is needed.

---

8. Felix buys 3 books for $8.95 each. How much does he owe if he uses a $12.73 credit toward his purchase?

    A. $39.58
    B. $26.85
    C. $21.68
    D. $18.24
    E. $14.12

(E) The total cost of the purchase is $8.95 \times 3 = $26.85. With a $12.73 credit, the amount owed is $26.85 − $12.73 = $14.12.

---

9. 12 is 15% of what number?

    A. 1.8
    B. 8
    C. 18
    D. 36
    E. 80

(E) Let n represent the number. If 12 is 15% of n, then $12 = 0.15n$. Divide both sides by 0.15. Therefore, $n = 80$.

---

10. How many distinct prime factors are there in 120?

    A. 2
    B. 3
    C. 4
    D. 5
    E. 6

(B) Prime factors of 120 are $2 \times 2 \times 2 \times 3 \times 5$. Distinct factors are 2, 3, and 5. Therefore, there are 3 distinct prime factors.

---

11. The greatest common factor of 24 and 36 is

    A. 6.
    B. 8.
    C. 12.
    D. 36.
    E. 60.

(C) Factors of 24 are $2 \times 2 \times 2 \times 3$. Factors of 36 are $2 \times 2 \times 3 \times 3$. The greatest common factor is $2 \times 2 \times 3 = 12$.

---

12. There are 800 employees at a company. If 60% drive to work and 30% take the train, how many employees arrive to work by car?

    A. 240
    B. 360
    C. 480
    D. 540
    E. 600

(C) 60% arrive to work by car, so $800 \times 60\% = 480$.

---

13. Melodi eats $\frac{3}{8}$ of a pizza and divides the rest between her two friends. What percent of the pizza do her friends each receive?

    A. 62.50%

    B. 37.50%

    C. 31.25%

    D. 20.83%

    E. 18.75%

(C) If $\frac{3}{8}$ of the pizza is eaten, then $1 - \frac{3}{8} = \frac{5}{8}$ remains. If that is divided by 2, then each receives $\frac{5}{8} \div 2 = \frac{5}{8} \times \frac{1}{2} = \frac{5}{16} = 0.3125 = 31.25\%$.

---

14. There are 72 freshmen in the band. If freshmen make up $\frac{1}{3}$ of the entire band, the total number of students in the band is

    A. 24.

    B. 72.

    C. 144.

    D. 216.

    E. 288.

(D) Let n represent the number of students in the band. Then $\frac{1}{3} n = 72$, so $n = 72 \times 3 = 216$.

---

15. What percent of $\frac{3}{4}$ is $\frac{1}{8}$?

    A. $9\frac{3}{8}\%$

    B. 12%

    C. $16\frac{2}{3}\%$

    D. 20%

    E. 60%

(C) Let p represent the unknown percent. Then $p \times \frac{3}{4} = \frac{1}{8}$. Solve for p by multiplying by the reciprocal of $\frac{3}{4} \cdot p \times \frac{3}{4} \times \frac{4}{3} = \frac{1}{8} \times \frac{4}{3} = \frac{4}{24} = \frac{1}{6}$. As a percent, $\frac{1}{6}$ is % $16\frac{2}{3}\%$.

Algebra

---

16. If $a = \frac{5}{2}$, then $\frac{1}{a}$ is

    A. $\frac{2}{5}$.

    B. 2.

    C. $\frac{5}{2}$.

    D. 5.

    E. 10.

(A) Substitute $\frac{5}{2}$ for a. $\frac{1}{a} = \frac{1}{\frac{5}{2}} = 1 \div \frac{5}{2} = 1 \cdot \frac{2}{5} = \frac{2}{5}$.

---

17. Evaluate $3r^3 - 2s^2 + t$ if $r = -1$, $s = -2$, and $t = -3$.

   A. −14
   B. −8
   C. 2
   D. 4
   E. 14

(C) Substituting the given values for r, s, and t into $3r^3 - 2s^2 + t$ gives $3(-1) - 2(-2) + (-3) = 3(-1) - 2(4) - 3 = -3 + 8 - 3 = 2$.

---

18. The scale on a map shows 500 feet for every $\frac{1}{4}$ inch. If two cities are 6 inches apart on the map, what is the actual distance they are apart?

   A. 125 feet
   B. 750 feet
   C. 2,000 feet
   D. 6,000 feet
   E. 12,000 feet

(E) The proportion $\frac{500 \text{ ft}}{\frac{1}{4} \text{ in}} = \frac{x \text{ ft}}{6 \text{ in}}$ can be used to find the actual distance. Cross multiply. $500 \times 6 = \frac{1}{4}x$ so $3,000 = \frac{1}{4}x$ and $x = 3,000 \times 4 = 12,000$ ft.

---

19. $(3 - 1) \times 7 - 12 \div 2 =$

   A. −2.
   B. 1.
   C. 2.
   D. 4.
   E. 8.

(E) Following the correct order of operations produces: $(3 - 1) \times 7 - 12 \div 2 = 2 \times 7 - (12 \div 2) = 14 - 6 = 8$.

---

20. Evaluate $3x + 7$ when $x = -3$.

   A. −16
   B. −2
   C. 10
   D. 16
   E. 21

(B) Substitute −3 for x. Then $3(-3) + 7 = -9 + 7 = -2$.

---

21. Subtract $(2x^3 - 3x + 1) - (x^2 - 3x - 2)$.

    A. $\quad 2x^2 + x + 1$

    B. $\quad 2x^3 - x^2 - 6x - 1$

    C. $\quad x^3 - 6x - 1$

    D. $\quad x^2 + 3$

    E. $\quad 3x^2 + x + 1$

(A) Subtraction can be changed to addition by changing the signs in the entire term being subtracted. $(2x^3 - 3x + 1) - (x^2 - 3x - 2) = (2x^3 - 3x + 1) + (x^2 - 3x - 2)$.

Combine like terms. $2x^3 - x^2 - 3x + 3x + 1 + 2 = 2x^3 - x^2 + 3$.

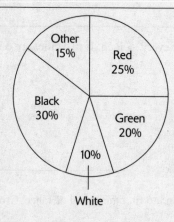

22. Heidi tallied the different car colors in the parking lot and summarized her results in a pie chart. There are 260 cars in the lot. How many cars are either red or black?

    A. $\quad$ 65

    B. $\quad$ 78

    C. $\quad$ 117

    D. $\quad$ 130

    E. $\quad$ 143

(E) The percent of cars that are either red or black is $25\% + 30\% = 55\%$. The total cars that are either red or black is $260 \times 55\% = 143$.

---

23. Simplify $5(a - 2) - (4a - 6)$.

    A. $\quad 9a - 4$

    B. $\quad a - 4$

    C. $\quad a - 8$

    D. $\quad a - 10$

    E. $\quad a + 4$

(B) $5(a - 2) - (4a - 6) = 5a - 10 - 4a + 6 = a - 4$.

24. The product of the square of x and three less than x is

    A. $\sqrt{x}(x-3)$.

    B. $\sqrt{x}(3-x)$.

    C. $x^2(x-3)$.

    D. $x^2(3-x)$.

    E. $-x^2(x-3)$.

(C) The square of x is x^2. Three less than x is $x-3$. Their product is $x^2(x-3)$.

25. Factor $2a^2 - 4ab + ab - 2b^2$.

    A. $(a+2b)(2a-b)$

    B. $(a-2b)(2a+b)$

    C. $(2a-b)(a+2b)$

    D. $(2a+b)(a-b)$

    E. $(a+2b)(a-2b)$

(B) Group the first two terms and the last two terms together: $(2a^2 - 4ab) + (ab - 2b^2)$. Factoring out common terms from each group gives $2a(a-2b)\ b(a-2b)$. Common to both terms is $(a-2b)$. Factoring this out results in $(a-2b)(2a+b)$.

26. If b represents the cost of a book and m represents the cost of a magazine, which of the following expressions represents the cost of 5 books and 3 magazines if books cost twice as much as magazines?

    A. $13m$

    B. $8m$

    C. $11b$

    D. $8b$

    E. $13b$

(A) If books are twice as much as magazines, then $b = 2m$. 5 books + 3 magazines $= 5b + 3m$. Substituting $2m$ for b gives $5(2m) + 3m = 10m + 3m = 13m$.

27. Rachel ran $\frac{1}{2}$ mile in 4 minutes. At this rate, how many miles can she run in 15 minutes?

    A. $1\frac{7}{8}$

    B. $2\frac{1}{8}$

    C. 4

    D. 30

    E. 60

(A) The proportion $\dfrac{\frac{1}{2} \text{ mile}}{4 \text{ minutes}} = \dfrac{x \text{ miles}}{15 \text{ minutes}}$ models this situation. Cross multiply. $\frac{1}{2} \times 15 = 4x$ so $\frac{15}{2} = 4x$ and $x = \frac{15}{2} \cdot \frac{1}{4} = \frac{15}{8} = 1\frac{7}{8}$ miles.

28. What is the value of $(-8)^{\frac{2}{3}}$?

    A. -4

    B. -2

    C. 2

    D. 4

    E. 16

(D) $(-8)^{\frac{2}{3}} = \left(\sqrt[3]{-8}\right)^2 = (-2)^2 = 4$.

29. If $2^{b+3} = \frac{1}{8}$, then $b =$

    A. -6.

    B. -5.

    C. -3.

    D. 0.

    E. 2.

(A) $\frac{1}{8} = \frac{1}{2^3} = 2^{-3}$ so $2^{b+3} = 2^{-3}$ and $b + 3 = -3$. Therefore, $b + 3 - 3 = -3 - 3 = -6$.

30. Three boxes are needed to hold 18 reams of paper. How many boxes are needed for 90 reams?

    A. 5

    B. 6

    C. 9

    D. 15

    E. 30

(D) The proportion $\frac{3 \text{ boxes}}{18 \text{ reams}} = \frac{x \text{ boxes}}{90 \text{ reams}}$ can be used to find the number of boxes. Cross multiply. $3 \times 90 = 18x$

so $270 = 18x$ and $x = \frac{270}{18} = 15$ boxes.

31. Multiply $(5a^3bc^2)(-3a^2c)$.

    A. $-15a^5bc^3$

    B. $15a^5bc^3$

    C. $-15a^6bc^2$

    D. $2abc$

    E. $2a^5bc^3$

(A) $(5a^3bc^2)(-3a^2c) = 5 \cdot -3 \; a^{3+2}bc^{2+1} = -15a^5bc^3$.

32. The cube root of 512 is

    A. 6.

    B. 8.

    C. 56.

    D. $170\frac{2}{3}$.

    E. 1,536.

(B) The cube root of 512 is $\sqrt[3]{512} = \sqrt[3]{8 \times 8 \times 8} = 8$.

---

33. Simplify $\left(\dfrac{a^{-3}b^2}{2ab^{-1}}\right)^{-3}$.

    A. $\dfrac{2a^6}{b}$

    B. $\dfrac{8a^{12}}{b^9}$

    C. $\dfrac{a^8}{8b^3}$

    D. $\dfrac{a^{12}}{8b^9}$

    E. $\dfrac{8a^8}{b}$

(B) $\left(\dfrac{a^{-3}b^2}{2ab^{-1}}\right) = \dfrac{a^9 b^{-6}}{2^{-3}a^{-3}b^3} = 2^3 a^{9-(-3)} b^{-6-3} = 8a^{12}b^{-9} = \dfrac{8a^{12}}{b^9}$.

---

34. Simplify $\dfrac{9x^2 y^3 z - 12xy^2 z^2}{3yz}$.

    A. $3xy^2z - 4xyz$

    B. $3x^2y^2 - 12xyz$

    C. $3x^2y^2 - 4xyz$

    D. $3y^2 - 4xy^2z^2$

    E. $9x^2y^3z - 4xyz$

(C) $\dfrac{9x^2 y^3 z - 12xy^2 z^2}{3yz} = \dfrac{9x^2 y^3 z}{3yz} - \dfrac{12xy^2 z^2}{3yz} = 3x^2 y^2 - 4xyz$.

---

35. What is the value of $\left(\dfrac{9}{4}\right)^{-\frac{1}{2}}$?

    A. $-\dfrac{2}{3}$

    B. $-\dfrac{16}{81}$

    C. $\dfrac{16}{81}$

    D. $\dfrac{2}{3}$

    E. $\dfrac{3}{2}$

(D) $\left(\dfrac{9}{4}\right)^{-\frac{1}{2}} = \left(\dfrac{4}{9}\right)^{\frac{1}{2}} = \sqrt{\dfrac{4}{9}} = \dfrac{2}{3}$.

36. What is the value of $-27^{\frac{2}{3}}$?

    A. -9
    B. -6
    C. -3
    D. 3
    E. 9

(A) $-27^{\frac{2}{3}} = -\left(27^{\frac{2}{3}}\right) = -\left(\sqrt[3]{27}\right)^2 = -(3)^2 = -9$.

37. If $w - 3 = 3 - w$, what is the value of w^2?

    A. 0
    B. 1
    C. 3
    D. 6
    E. 9

(E) Solve for w by adding w to both sides. $w - 3 + w = 3 - w + w$ so $2w - 3 = 3$. Adding 3 to both sides gives $2w = 6$. So $\frac{2w}{2} = \frac{6}{2}$ and $w = 3$. Therefore, $w^2 = 3^2 = 9$.

38. If $\frac{m}{n} = \frac{3}{5}$, what is the value of $m + n$?

    A. 2
    B. 8
    C. $\frac{6}{5}$
    D. $\frac{9}{25}$
    E.   It cannot be determined.

(E) The values of m and n can be anything as long as they are in the proportion $\frac{m}{n} = \frac{3}{5}$. For example, it could be that $m = 3$ and $n = 5$. However, it is also possible that $m = 6$ and $n = 10$. Therefore, it is not possible to determine the sum.

39. Simplify $\frac{x^2 - 25}{5 - x}$.

    A. $x + 5$
    B. $x - 5$
    C. $-(x + 5)$
    D. $5 - x$
    E. $x - 20$

(C) $\frac{x^2 - 25}{5 - x} = \frac{(x+5)(x-5)}{5-x} = \frac{(x+5)(x-5)}{-(x-5)} = \frac{(x+5)}{-1} = -(x+5)$.

40. If $3^{4x+2} = 9^{x-1}$, then what is the value of x?

    A. −2
    B. −1
    C. 0
    D. 1
    E. 2

(A) Begin by rewriting 9 as 3^2, so that $3^{4x+2} = 9^{x-1}$ becomes $3^{4x+2} = 3^{2(x-1)}$. The only way this can be true is if $4x + 2 = 2(x-1)$. This equation is true if $x = -2$.

Geometry

41. Which expression represents the volume of a cylinder whose height is equivalent to the length of the radius?

    A. πr^2
    B. πr^3
    C. $(\pi r)^2$
    D. $(\pi r)^3$
    E. $\dfrac{\pi r^3}{2}$

(B) The volume of a cylinder is given by the formula $V = \pi r^2 h$, where r is the radius of the circular base and h is the height. Since $h = r$, $V = \pi r^2 r = \pi r^3$.

42. The length of a rectangle is three times its width. If the perimeter of the rectangle is 48, what is its area?

    A. 144
    B. 108
    C. 96
    D. 54
    E. 48

(D) The perimeter of a rectangle is $l + w + l + w = 48$. Since $l = 3w$, the perimeter is $3w + w + 3w + w = 48$, so $8w = 48$ and $w = 6$. Therefore, the length is 3×6 or 18, and the area of the rectangle is $l \times w = 18 \times 3 = 54$.

43. Find the length of the radius in the following figure.

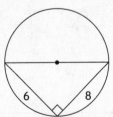

    A. 3
    B. 4
    C. 5
    D. 8
    E. 10

(C) The hypotenuse of the triangle is the diameter of the circle. By the Pythagorean Theorem, $d^2 = 6^2 + 8^2 = 36 + 64 + 100$. So $d = \sqrt{100} = 10$, and the radius is $\frac{10}{2} = 5$.

---

44. Find the value of x in the figure:

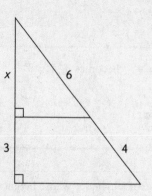

    A. 4.5
    B. 4.6
    C. 4.8
    D. 5
    E. 5.2

(A) The proportion $\frac{x}{6} = \frac{x+3}{10}$ can be used to find x. Cross multiply. $10x = 6(x + 3)$ and $10x = 6x + 18$. Bring all x terms to one side by subtracting $6x$ from each side. Then, $4x = 18$ and $x = \frac{18}{4} = 4.5$.

---

45. What is the measure of $\angle A$?

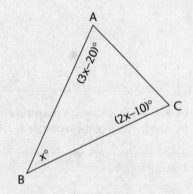

    A. 35°
    B. 60°
    C. 65°
    D. 75°
    E. 85°

(E) The sum of all angles in a triangle equal 180°. So $(3x - 20)° + x° + (2x - 10)° = 180°$. $3x + x + 2x - 20 - 10 = 180$ and $6x - 30 = 180$. Then $6x = 210$ and $x = \frac{210}{6} = 35$. Therefore, $\angle A$ is $3(35) - 20$ or 85°.

46. Find the area of a regular hexagon whose sides measure 6 cm.

    A. $9\sqrt{2}$

    B. 36

    C. $54\sqrt{3}$

    D. 108

    E. 216

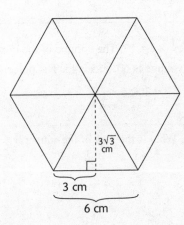

3√3 cm

3 cm

6 cm

(C) A regular hexagon is made up of six equilateral triangles. Find the area of one equilateral triangle and multiply that by 6 to find the area of the hexagon. The height, or altitude, of a triangle can be found by the Pythagorean Theorem. The right triangle formed by the altitude has a hypotenuse of 6 and a shorter leg of $\frac{6}{2}$ or 3. So $3^2 + h^2 = 6^2$ so $9 = h^2 = 36$ and $h^2 = 27$. Therefore, $h = \sqrt{27} = 3\sqrt{3}$. The area of one equilateral triangle is $\frac{1}{2}bh = \frac{1}{2} \cdot 6 \cdot 3\sqrt{3} = 9\sqrt{3}$, and the area of the hexagon is $6 \cdot 9\sqrt{3} = 54\sqrt{3}$.

47. What is the slope of the line $x = -3y + 9$?

    A. -3

    B. $-\frac{1}{3}$

    C. $\frac{1}{3}$

    D. 3

    E. 9

(B) Begin by rewriting $x = -3y + 9$ in slope-intercept form as $y = -\frac{1}{3}x + 3$. The slope of the line is the coefficient of x, that is, $-\frac{1}{3}$.

48. The angles of a triangle are in the ratio 3:4:5. What is the measure of the smallest angle?

    A. 15°

    B. 30°

    C. 45°

    D. 60°

    E. 75°

(C) Angles in a triangle add to 180°. So $3x + 4x + 5x = 180°$ and $12x = 180°$. Dividing both sides by 12 results in $x = 15°$. The smallest angle is represented by $3x = 3(15°) = 45°$.

49. A cardboard box has a length of 3 feet, height of $2\frac{1}{2}$ feet, and a depth of 2 feet. If the length and depth are doubled, by what percent does the volume of the box change?

    A. 200%

    B. 300%

    C. 400%

    D. 500%

    E. 600%

(B) The volume of the original box is $3 \times 2\frac{1}{2} \times 2 = 15$. The volume of the box with the length and depth doubled is $6 \times 2\frac{1}{2} \times 4 = 60$. The amount of change in volume is $60 - 15 = 45$. The percent change is the amount of change in volume divided by the original volume. $\frac{45}{15} = 3 = 300\%$.

50. The diagonal of a square is 10 inches. What is the area of the square?

    A. 40 in^2

    B. 50 in^2

    C. 80 in^2

    D. 100 in^2

    E. 150 in^2

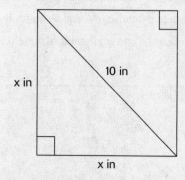

(B) Let x represent a side of the square. The area of the square is x^2. To find the value of x^2, use the Pythagorean Theorem. $x^2 + x^2 = 10^2$ so $2x^2 = 100$ and $x^2 = \frac{100}{2}$ or 50 in^2.

51. The slope of the line shown is

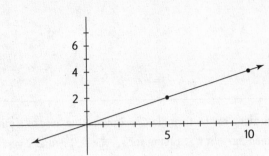

    A. $-\frac{2}{5}$.

    B. $-\frac{5}{2}$.

    C. $\frac{2}{5}$.

    D. $\frac{2}{3}$.

    E. $\frac{5}{2}$.

(C) Slope is found by identifying two points on the line and finding the $\frac{\text{change in } y}{\text{change in } x}$. The points $(0, 0)$ and $(5, 2)$ form the slope $\frac{2-0}{5-0} = \frac{2}{5}$.

52. The figure contains 5 equal squares. If the area is 405, what is the perimeter?

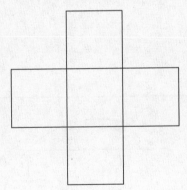

    A. 81

    B. 90

    C. 108

    D. 144

    E. 216

(C) The area of one square is $\frac{405}{5} = 81$. So the length of each side is $\sqrt{81} = 9$. The total number of sides in the figure is 12, so the perimeter is $9 \times 12 = 108$.

53. What is the diameter of a circle whose circumference is equivalent to its area?

    A. 1

    B. 2

    C. 3

    D. 4

    E. 6

(D) The circumference of a circle is given by the formula $C = 2\pi r$, and the area of a circle is given by $A = \pi r^2$. If the circumference is equal to the area, then $2\pi r = \pi r^2$. Solving for r, $\frac{2\pi r}{\pi r} = \frac{\pi r^2}{\pi r}$ and $2 = r$. The diameter is $2r$, or 4.

54. A line parallel to the line $y = 5x + 9$ has a slope of

    A. -5.

    B. $-\frac{1}{5}$.

    C. $\frac{1}{5}$.

    D. $\frac{9}{5}$.

    E. 5.

(E) Parallel lines have the same slope. Since the given line is in the slope-intercept form, the slope is the coefficient of the x term, which is 5. This must also be the slope of a parallel line.

55. A square garden is to be built inside a circular area. Each corner of the square touches the circle. If the radius of the circle is 2, how much greater is the area of the circle than the square?

    A. $4 - 4\pi$

    B. $4 - 8\pi$

    C. $4\pi - 4$

    D. $4\pi - 8$

    E. $8\pi - 8$

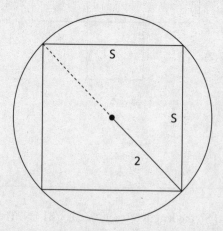

(D) Find the difference between the area of the circle and the area of the square. The area of the circle is $\pi r^2 = \pi \cdot 2^2 = 4\pi$. The area of the square is s^2, where s represents the length of the square. The radius is half the length of the square's diagonal, so the diagonal is 4. By the Pythagorean Theorem, $s^2 + s^2 = 4^2$. $2s^2 = 16$, so $s^2 = 8$. The difference in area is $4\pi - 8$.

56. What is the slope of the line $2x + y = 7$?

    A. -2

    B. 1

    C. 2

    D. $\frac{7}{2}$

    E. 7

(A) Re-write the equation in slope-intercept form as $y = -2x + 7$. The slope is the coefficient of x, which is -2.

57. The volume of a cube is 343 cm^3. The surface area of the cube is

    A. 7 cm^2.

    B. 49 cm^2.

    C. 294 cm^2.

    D. 588 cm^2.

    E. 2401 cm^2.

(C) The volume of a cube is s^3, where s represents the length of an edge. Surface area is $6s^2$. If the volume $= 343$ cm^3, then $s = \sqrt[3]{343} = \sqrt[3]{7 \cdot 7 \cdot 7} = 7$. So the surface area is $6 \cdot 7^2 = 294$ cm^2.

58. A cylinder whose height is 8 inches has a volume of 128πcm^3. If the radius is doubled and its height is cut in half, the volume of the resulting cylinder is

    A. 64π cm^3.

    B. 128π cm^3.

    C. 256π cm^3.

    D. 512π cm^3.

    E. $1,024\pi$ cm^2.

(C) The volume of a cylinder is $\pi r^2 h$. In the original cylinder, $\pi r^2 8 = 128\pi$, so $r^2 = \frac{128\pi}{8\pi} = 16$, and the radius, r, equals $\sqrt{16} = 4$. In the new cylinder, the radius is doubled to 8, and the height is cut in half to 4. The resulting volume is $\pi \cdot 8^2 \cdot 4 = 256\pi$ cm^3.

59. The value of x is

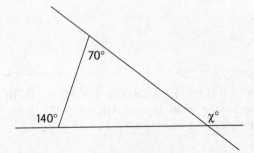

    A. $30°$.

    B. $70°$.

    C. $110°$.

    D. $140°$.

    E. $180°$.

(C)

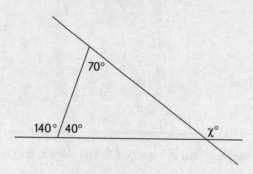

The angle adjacent to the 140° angle is 40° since supplementary angles add to 180°. The angles of a triangle add to 180°, so the angle adjacent to angle x is $180° - 70° - 40° = 70°$. Angle x and 70° are supplementary, so $x = 180° - 70° = 110°$.

---

60. Squares ADEC, BCFG, and ABHI are shown. If the area of ADEC is 81 and the area of BCFG is 144, what is the perimeter of △ABC?

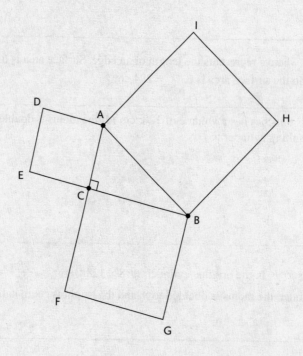

    A. 36
    B. 54
    C. 72
    D. 225
    E. 450

(A) Since the area of ADEC is 81, AC = $\sqrt{81}$ = 9. Since the area of BCFG is 144, BC = $\sqrt{144}$ = 12. Use the Pythagorean Theorem to find the length of the remaining side AB. $AB^2 + 12^2$, so $AB^2 = 81 + 144 = 225$ and AB = $\sqrt{225}$ = 15. Therefore, the perimeter of the triangle = 9 + 12 + 15 = 36.

Conversions

---

61. Yan can read 2 pages in 3 minutes. At this rate, how long will it take him to read a 360 page book?

    A. 30 minutes
    B. 2 hours
    C. 6 hours
    D. 9 hours
    E. 12 hours

(D) Using the ratio $\frac{\text{pages}}{\text{minutes}}$, the proportion $\frac{2}{3} = \frac{360}{x}$ can be used to find the time. Cross multiply. $2x = 3 \times 360$, so $2x = 1080$ and $x = \frac{1080}{2} = 540$ minutes. Convert minutes to hours. There are 60 minutes in 1 hour, so $\frac{540}{60} = 9$ hours.

---

62. How many omelets can be made from 2 dozen eggs if an omelet contains 3 eggs?

    A. 1
    B. 3
    C. 4
    D. 6
    E. 8

(E) There are 24 eggs in 2 dozen eggs. If 3 eggs are in an omelet, then $24 \div 3$, or 8 omelets can be made.

---

63. A blueprint has a scale of 3 feet per $\frac{1}{2}$ inch. If a bathroom is $1\frac{1}{2}$ inches $\times$ 2 inches, what are its actual dimensions?

    A. $4\frac{1}{2}$ feet $\times$ 6 feet
    B. 6 feet $\times$ $7\frac{1}{2}$ feet
    C. $7\frac{1}{2}$ feet $\times$ 9 feet
    D. 6 feet $\times$ 9 feet
    E. 9 feet $\times$ 12 feet

(E) If the blueprint shows $\frac{1}{2}$ inch for every 3 feet, then 1 inch represents 6 feet. The actual dimensions of a room $1\frac{1}{2}$ inches $\times$ 2 inches would be $(1\frac{1}{2} \times 6)$ by (2×6) or 9 feet by 12 feet.

---

64. Tiling costs $2.89 per square foot. What is the cost to tile a kitchen whose dimensions are 4 yards by 5 yards?

    A. $57.80
    B. $62.28
    C. $173.40
    D. $289.00
    E. $520.20

(E) There are 3 feet in a yard, so a kitchen 4 yards by 5 yards is equivalent to (4×3) feet by (5×3) feet, or 12 feet by 15 feet. The area of the kitchen is $12 \times 15 = 180$ square feet. The cost to tile is $2.89 \times 180 = \$520.20$.

65. A machine can produce 8,000 widgets in 3 hours. How many widgets are produced in one day?

    A. 96,000
    B. 64,000
    C. 48,000
    D. 32,000
    E. 8,000

(B) If a machine produces 8,000 widgets in 3 hours, it produces $\frac{8000}{3}$ widgets in one hour. There are 24 hours in a day, so $\frac{8000}{3} \times 24$ or 64,000 widgets are produced in one day.

66. Dennis ran a race in 2.2 minutes. Kayla ran the same race in 124 seconds. What is the difference between these two times?

    A. 2 seconds
    B. 8 seconds
    C. 12 seconds
    D. 14 seconds
    E. 22 seconds

(B) Convert 2.2 minutes to seconds. $2.2 \times 60 = 132$ seconds. The difference in the two times is $132 - 124 = 8$ seconds.

67. Stanley can type 35 words per minute. If it takes him a half hour to type a document, about how many words are in the document?

    A. 525
    B. 900
    C. 1,050
    D. 1,500
    E. 2,100

(C) There are 30 minutes in a half hour. $30 \times 35 = 1,050$ words.

68. Floor tiling costs $13.50 per square yard. What would it cost to tile a room 15 feet long by 18 feet wide?

    A. $20
    B. $405
    C. $425
    D. $1,350
    E. $3,645

(B) The area of a room 15 feet wide by 18 feet long is $15 \times 18 = 270$ square feet. Since there are 3 feet in a yard, there are 3×3 or 9 feet in a square yard. Convert 270 square feet to square yards. $\frac{270}{9} = 30$ square yards. Since the cost is $13.50 per square yard, the total cost is 13.50×30 or $405.

69. A car travels 20 miles in 30 minutes. At this rate, how far will the car travel in 2 hours?

    A. 40 miles
    B. 60 miles
    C. 80 miles
    D. 100 miles
    E. 120 miles

(C) There are 120 minutes in 2 hours. Setting up a proportion yields $\frac{20 \text{ miles}}{30 \text{ minutes}} = \frac{x \text{ miles}}{120 \text{ minutes}}$. Cross multiplying results in $30x = 20 \times 120$ or $30x = 2400$. Dividing both sides by 30 gives $x = \frac{2400}{30} = 80$ miles.

---

70. How many blocks 6" × 4" × 4" can fit in a box 8' × 6' × 4'?

    A. 2
    B. 48
    C. 288
    D. 576
    E. 3,456

(E) Convert the dimensions of the box from feet to inches. 8' × 6' × 4' is equivalent to $(8 \times 12 \text{ in}) \times (6 \times 12 \text{ in}) \times (4 \times 12 \text{ in}) = 96 \text{ in} \times 72 \text{ in} \times 48 \text{ in}$. The volume $= 96 \times 72 \times 48 = 331{,}776$. The volume of each block is $6 \times 4 \times 4 = 96$. The number of blocks that fit in the box is $\frac{331{,}776}{96} = 3{,}456$.

Trigonometry and Applied Mathworks

71. If $\sin a > 0$ and $\cos a < 0$, then $-a$ must lie in which quadrant?

    A. I
    B. II
    C. III
    D. IV
    E. Either I or II

(B) The sine function is positive in the first and second quadrants. The cosine function is negative in the second and third quadrants. Overall, then, $-a$ must lie in the second quadrant.

---

72. Which of the following values of x is a solution of the equation $\cos x = -1$?

    A. $x = 0°$
    B. $x = 45°$
    C. $x = 90°$
    D. $x = 180°$
    E. $x = 270°$

(D) The only one of the given angles for which $\cos x = -1$ is $x = 180°$.

---

73. The expression $\tan\theta \cos\theta \csc\theta$ is equivalent to

    A. 1.
    B. $\sin \theta$.
    C. $\tan \theta$.
    D. $\sec \theta$.
    E. $\cos \theta$.

(A) $\tan\theta \cos\theta \csc\theta = \frac{\sin\theta}{\cos\theta} \times \cos\theta \times \frac{1}{\sin\theta} = 1$.

---

74. What is the period of the function $g(x) = 6\sin 2x$?

    A. 2

    B. π

    C. 4

    D. 2π

    E. 6π

(B) To find the period, set $2x$ equal to 2π, and solve for x. It is easy to see that $x = \pi$ is the period.

---

75. If $\sin b < 0$ and $\cos b < 0$, then $\angle b$ must lie in which quadrant?

    A. I

    B. II

    C. III

    D. IV

    E. Either III or IV

(C) The sine function is negative in quadrants III and IV, while the cosine function is negative in quadrants II and III. Therefore, they are both negative in the third quadrant.

---

76. For which of the following values of x is the function $h(x) = \tan 2x$ undefined?

    A. 0

    B. $\dfrac{\pi}{4}$

    C. $\dfrac{\pi}{2}$

    D. π

    E. 2π

(B) A good way to think about this problem is to recall that $\tan 2x = \dfrac{\sin 2x}{\cos 2x}$. Therefore, $\tan 2x$ will be undefined when $\cos 2x = 0$. Note that $\cos\left(\dfrac{\pi}{2}\right) = 0$, and, at $\dfrac{\pi}{4}$, $\cos 2x = \cos\left(\dfrac{\pi}{2}\right) = 0$. Thus, $\tan 2x$ is undefined at $\dfrac{\pi}{4}$.

---

77. The expression $\tan\theta \cos\theta \sec\theta$ is equivalent to

    A. $\cot\theta$.

    B. $\sec\theta$.

    C. $\sin\theta$.

    D. $\tan\theta$.

    E. $\cos\theta$.

(D) $\tan\theta \cos\theta \sec\theta = \dfrac{\sin\theta}{\cos\theta} \times \cos\theta \times \dfrac{1}{\cos\theta} = \tan\theta$.

---

78. Which of the following values of x is a solution to the equation $\csc x = 2$?

    A. $x = 0°$

    B. $x = 30°$

    C. $x = 45°$

    D. $x = 60°$

    E. $x = 90°$

(B) Recall that the cosecant function is the reciprocal of the sine function. Thus, $\csc x = 2$ is the same as $\sin x = \frac{1}{2}$, which is true when $x = 30°$.

---

79. The expression $\sec^2\theta - 1$ is equivalent to

  A. $\tan^2\theta$.
  B. $\csc^2\theta$.
  C. $\sin^2\theta$.
  D. $\cos^2\theta$.
  E. $\sec^2\theta$.

(A) One of the Pythagorean identities in trigonometry is $\tan^2\theta + 1 = \sec^2\theta$. Thus, $\tan^2\theta = \sec^2\theta. - 1$.

---

80. If $\csc\theta > 0$ and $\cos\theta < 0$, then what quadrant is the angle θ in?

  A. I
  B. II
  C. III
  D. IV
  E. Either I or II

(B) The cosecant function is positive in quadrants I and II. The cosine function is negative in quadrants II and III. Thus, the angle must be in the second quadrant.

---

81. Rae earns \$8.40 an hour plus an overtime rate equal to $1\frac{1}{2}$ times her regular pay for each hour worked beyond 40 hours. What are her total earnings for a 45 hour work week?

  A. \$336
  B. \$341
  C. \$370
  D. \$399
  E. \$567

(D) The overtime rate is $\$8.40 \times 1.5 = \$12.60$. Five hours of overtime were completed, so the total earnings are $(\$8.40 \times 40) + (\$12.60 \times 5) = \$336 + \$63 = \$399$.

---

82. Davis donates $\frac{4}{13}$ of his paycheck to his favorite charity. If he donates \$26.80, what is the amount of his paycheck?

  A. \$8.25
  B. \$82.50
  C. \$87.10
  D. \$92.25
  E. \$348.40

(C) Let p represent the amount of the paycheck. $\frac{4}{13} p = \$26.80$, so $p = \$26.80 \cdot \frac{13}{4} = \$87.10$.

193

83. One phone plan charges a $20 monthly fee and $0.08 per minute on every phone call made. Another phone plan charges a $12 monthly fee and $0.12 per minute for each call. After how many minutes would the charge be the same for both plans?

    A. 60 minutes
    B. 90 minutes
    C. 120 minutes
    D. 180 minutes
    E. 200 minutes

(E) Let m represent the minutes of the phone calls. The monthly charge for the first plan is $20 + 0.08m$. The monthly charge for the second plan is $12 + 0.12m$. When the monthly charges are the same, $20 + 0.08m = 12 + 0.12m$. Solve for m to find the number of minutes both plans have the same rate.

$20 + 0.08m - 0.08m = 12 + 0.12m - 0.08m$

$20 = 12 + 0.04m$

$20 - 12 = 12 + 0.04m - 12$

$8 = 0.04m$ so $m = \dfrac{8}{0.04} = \dfrac{800}{4} = 200$ minutes.

84. A sweater originally priced at $40 is on sale for $30. What percent has the sweater been discounted?

    A. 20%
    B. 25%
    C. 33%
    D. 70%
    E. 75%

(B) The amount of discount is $40 - $30 = $10. The percent of discount is the amount of discount divided by the original price. $\dfrac{10}{40} = \dfrac{1}{4} = 25\%$.

85. Staci earns $9.50 an hour plus 3% commission on all sales made. If her total sales during a 30-hour work week were $500, how much did she earn?

    A. $15
    B. $250
    C. $285
    D. $300
    E. $435

(D) For a 30-hour week with $500 in sales, total earnings are $(30 \times \$9.50) + (3\% \times \$500) = \$285 + \$15 = \$300$.

86. One-fourth of the cars purchased at a dealership are luxury models. If 360 luxury models were purchased last year, how many total cars were purchased?

    A. 90
    B. 250
    C. 1,440
    D. 2,880
    E. 3,600

(C) $\frac{1}{4}$ of the total cars, t, sold are luxury. Luxury cars sold = 360, so $\frac{1}{4}t = 360$ and $t = 360, \times 4 = 1,440$ total cars sold.

---

87. A television is on sale for 20% off. If the sale price is $800, what was the original price?

    A. $160
    B. $640
    C. $960
    D. $980
    E. $1,000

(E) If an item is discount 20%, the sale price is 80% of the original price. Let p represent the original price. Then $\$800 = 80\% \times p$ and $p = \frac{800}{80\%} = \frac{800}{.80} = \$1,000$.

---

88. A barrel holds 60 gallons of water. If a crack in the barrel causes $\frac{1}{2}$ a gallon to leak out each day, how many gallons of water remain after 2 weeks?

    A. 30
    B. 53
    C. $56\frac{1}{2}$
    D. 58
    E. 59

(B) In 2 weeks, or 14 days, $\frac{1}{2} \times 14 = 7$ gallons leak out, leaving $60 - 7 = 53$ gallons.

---

89. A restaurant bill without tax and tip comes to $38.40. If a 15% tip is included after a 6% tax is added to the amount, how much is the tip?

    A. $6.11
    B. $6.05
    C. $5.76
    D. $5.15
    E. $2.30

(A) The tax on the bill is $\$38.40 \times 6\% = \$2.30$. The amount, including tax, is $\$38.40 + \$2.30 = \$40.70$. The tip is $\$40.70 \times 15\% = \$6.11$.

---

90. A savings account earns $2\frac{1}{4}\%$ interest each year. How much interest is earned on a $1,000 deposit after a 5-year period?

    A. $22.50
    B. $100.00
    C. $112.50
    D. $124.00
    E. $150.00

(C) Interest = Principle × Rate × Time. Thus, Interest = $\$1,000 \times 2\frac{1}{4}\% \times 5 = \$1,000 \times 0.0225 \times 5 = \$112.50$.

Probability and Statistics

91. Kyle ran 3 miles in $17\frac{1}{2}$ minutes on Saturday, $4\frac{1}{2}$ miles in 22 minutes on Sunday, and 2 miles in 9 minutes on Monday. What was Kyle's average rate of speed while running?

    A.   1.6 minutes per mile
    B.   5.1 minutes per mile
    C.   5.6 minutes per mile
    D.   16.2 minutes per mile
    E.   17.8 minutes per mile

(B) Average is the total time divided by the total miles run. The total time is $17.5 + 22 + 9 = 48.5$ minutes. The total number of miles run is $3 + 4.5 + 2 = 9.5$. The average is $\frac{48.5}{9.5} = 5.1$ minutes per mile.

92. Tanya's bowling scores this week were 112, 156, 179, and 165. Last week, her average score was 140. How many points did her average improve?

    A.   18
    B.   13
    C.   11
    D.   10
    E.   8

(B) The average is found by adding up all the scores and dividing by the total number of scores. The average this week is $\frac{112 + 156 + 179 + 165}{4} = \frac{612}{4} = 153$. The amount of improvement is $153 - 140 = 13$.

93. For which of the following sets of numbers is the median the same as the arithmetic mean?

    A. $\{-2, -1, 0, 2, 3\}$
    B. $\{0, 2, 3, 4, 5\}$
    C. $\{-1, 1, 4\}$
    D. $\{0, 2, 4, 6, 10\}$
    E. $\{-2, -1, 0, 1, 2\}$

(E) The median of an odd amount of numbers is the value in the middle when the numbers are put in numerical order. Note, then, that the median of this set is 0, which is also the mean.

94. What is the probability of rolling a sum of 9 using two dice?

    A. $\frac{1}{9}$

    B. $\frac{1}{6}$

    C. $\frac{7}{36}$

    D. $\frac{1}{4}$

    E. $\frac{5}{12}$

(A) There are 4 possible ways to roll a 9 using 2 dice: 3 and 6, 4 and 5, 5 and 4, 6 and 3. The total number of possible outcomes when rolling 2 dice is 6^2 or 36. Therefore, the probability of rolling a 9 is $\frac{4}{36} = \frac{1}{9}$.

95. Two runners finished a race in 80 seconds; another runner finished the race in 72 seconds; and the final runner finished in 68 seconds. The average of these times is

- **A.** 73 seconds.
- **B.** 74 seconds.
- **C.** 75 seconds.
- **D.** 76 seconds.
- **E.** 77 seconds.

(C) Since two runners finished in 80 seconds, the average of 80, 80, 72, and 68 must be found. This average is $\frac{80 + 80 + 72 + 68}{4} = \frac{300}{4} = 75$ seconds.

96. What is the mode of the set of numbers {1, 1, 1, 2, 2, 3, 3, 3, 3, 4, 4, 4, 5, 6, 6, 6}?

- **A.** 1
- **B.** 3
- **C.** 4
- **D.** 5
- **E.** 6

(B) The mode is the number that occurs the most often, which is, in the this case, 3.

97. In a standard deck of playing cards, a king of hearts is drawn and not replaced. What is the probability of drawing another king from the deck?

- **A.** $\frac{3}{52}$
- **B.** $\frac{1}{17}$
- **C.** $\frac{1}{13}$
- **D.** $\frac{1}{4}$
- **E.** $\frac{3}{13}$

(B) Probability is $\frac{\text{number of expected outcomes}}{\text{number of possible outcomes}}$. Since one king was drawn and not replaced, three kings remain in the deck of 51 cards. So the probability of drawing another king is $\frac{3}{51} = \frac{1}{17}$.

98. If a 4-digit number is formed at random from the digits 3, 5, 7, and 8, and each digit is used once, what is the probability that the number is even?

- **A.** $\frac{1}{16}$
- **B.** $\frac{1}{8}$
- **C.** $\frac{1}{4}$
- **D.** $\frac{1}{3}$
- **E.** $\frac{1}{2}$

(C) The only even digit is 8, so for the 4-digit number to be even, 8 must be the last digit. If the number is formed at random, there is a one in four chance that the last digit will be 8.

---

99. What is the probability of flipping 3 heads in a row using a fair coin?

    A. $\frac{1}{8}$

    B. $\frac{1}{4}$

    C. $\frac{3}{8}$

    D. $\frac{1}{2}$

    E. $\frac{2}{3}$

(A) The probability of flipping one head is $\frac{1}{2}$. The probability of flipping three heads in a row is $\frac{1}{2} \times \frac{1}{2} \times \frac{1}{2}$ or $\frac{1}{8}$.

---

100. A 4-digit number is formed at random from the digits 1, 2, 3, and 4. If digits *can* be repeated in the number, what is the probability that the number is greater than 2,500?

    A. $\frac{1}{16}$

    B. $\frac{1}{8}$

    C. $\frac{1}{4}$

    D. $\frac{1}{3}$

    E. $\frac{1}{2}$

(E) The number will be larger than 2,500 if the first digit is either 3 or 4. Since all digits are selected at random, the probability that a 3 or a 4 is selected for the first digit is $\frac{1}{2}$.

PART III

DAT PRACTICE TESTS

Answer Sheets for Practice Test 1

Remove these sheets and use to mark your answers.

Natural Sciences

1 Ⓐ Ⓑ Ⓒ Ⓓ Ⓔ	26 Ⓐ Ⓑ Ⓒ Ⓓ Ⓔ
2 Ⓐ Ⓑ Ⓒ Ⓓ Ⓔ	27 Ⓐ Ⓑ Ⓒ Ⓓ Ⓔ
3 Ⓐ Ⓑ Ⓒ Ⓓ Ⓔ	28 Ⓐ Ⓑ Ⓒ Ⓓ Ⓔ
4 Ⓐ Ⓑ Ⓒ Ⓓ Ⓔ	29 Ⓐ Ⓑ Ⓒ Ⓓ Ⓔ
5 Ⓐ Ⓑ Ⓒ Ⓓ Ⓔ	30 Ⓐ Ⓑ Ⓒ Ⓓ Ⓔ
6 Ⓐ Ⓑ Ⓒ Ⓓ Ⓔ	31 Ⓐ Ⓑ Ⓒ Ⓓ Ⓔ
7 Ⓐ Ⓑ Ⓒ Ⓓ Ⓔ	32 Ⓐ Ⓑ Ⓒ Ⓓ Ⓔ
8 Ⓐ Ⓑ Ⓒ Ⓓ Ⓔ	33 Ⓐ Ⓑ Ⓒ Ⓓ Ⓔ
9 Ⓐ Ⓑ Ⓒ Ⓓ Ⓔ	34 Ⓐ Ⓑ Ⓒ Ⓓ Ⓔ
10 Ⓐ Ⓑ Ⓒ Ⓓ Ⓔ	35 Ⓐ Ⓑ Ⓒ Ⓓ Ⓔ
11 Ⓐ Ⓑ Ⓒ Ⓓ Ⓔ	36 Ⓐ Ⓑ Ⓒ Ⓓ Ⓔ
12 Ⓐ Ⓑ Ⓒ Ⓓ Ⓔ	37 Ⓐ Ⓑ Ⓒ Ⓓ Ⓔ
13 Ⓐ Ⓑ Ⓒ Ⓓ Ⓔ	38 Ⓐ Ⓑ Ⓒ Ⓓ Ⓔ
14 Ⓐ Ⓑ Ⓒ Ⓓ Ⓔ	39 Ⓐ Ⓑ Ⓒ Ⓓ Ⓔ
15 Ⓐ Ⓑ Ⓒ Ⓓ Ⓔ	40 Ⓐ Ⓑ Ⓒ Ⓓ Ⓔ
16 Ⓐ Ⓑ Ⓒ Ⓓ Ⓔ	41 Ⓐ Ⓑ Ⓒ Ⓓ Ⓔ
17 Ⓐ Ⓑ Ⓒ Ⓓ Ⓔ	42 Ⓐ Ⓑ Ⓒ Ⓓ Ⓔ
18 Ⓐ Ⓑ Ⓒ Ⓓ Ⓔ	43 Ⓐ Ⓑ Ⓒ Ⓓ Ⓔ
19 Ⓐ Ⓑ Ⓒ Ⓓ Ⓔ	44 Ⓐ Ⓑ Ⓒ Ⓓ Ⓔ
20 Ⓐ Ⓑ Ⓒ Ⓓ Ⓔ	45 Ⓐ Ⓑ Ⓒ Ⓓ Ⓔ
21 Ⓐ Ⓑ Ⓒ Ⓓ Ⓔ	46 Ⓐ Ⓑ Ⓒ Ⓓ Ⓔ
22 Ⓐ Ⓑ Ⓒ Ⓓ Ⓔ	47 Ⓐ Ⓑ Ⓒ Ⓓ Ⓔ
23 Ⓐ Ⓑ Ⓒ Ⓓ Ⓔ	48 Ⓐ Ⓑ Ⓒ Ⓓ Ⓔ
24 Ⓐ Ⓑ Ⓒ Ⓓ Ⓔ	49 Ⓐ Ⓑ Ⓒ Ⓓ Ⓔ
25 Ⓐ Ⓑ Ⓒ Ⓓ Ⓔ	50 Ⓐ Ⓑ Ⓒ Ⓓ Ⓔ

51 Ⓐ Ⓑ Ⓒ Ⓓ Ⓔ	76 Ⓐ Ⓑ Ⓒ Ⓓ Ⓔ
52 Ⓐ Ⓑ Ⓒ Ⓓ Ⓔ	77 Ⓐ Ⓑ Ⓒ Ⓓ Ⓔ
53 Ⓐ Ⓑ Ⓒ Ⓓ Ⓔ	78 Ⓐ Ⓑ Ⓒ Ⓓ Ⓔ
54 Ⓐ Ⓑ Ⓒ Ⓓ Ⓔ	79 Ⓐ Ⓑ Ⓒ Ⓓ Ⓔ
55 Ⓐ Ⓑ Ⓒ Ⓓ Ⓔ	80 Ⓐ Ⓑ Ⓒ Ⓓ Ⓔ
56 Ⓐ Ⓑ Ⓒ Ⓓ Ⓔ	81 Ⓐ Ⓑ Ⓒ Ⓓ Ⓔ
57 Ⓐ Ⓑ Ⓒ Ⓓ Ⓔ	82 Ⓐ Ⓑ Ⓒ Ⓓ Ⓔ
58 Ⓐ Ⓑ Ⓒ Ⓓ Ⓔ	83 Ⓐ Ⓑ Ⓒ Ⓓ Ⓔ
59 Ⓐ Ⓑ Ⓒ Ⓓ Ⓔ	84 Ⓐ Ⓑ Ⓒ Ⓓ Ⓔ
60 Ⓐ Ⓑ Ⓒ Ⓓ Ⓔ	85 Ⓐ Ⓑ Ⓒ Ⓓ Ⓔ
61 Ⓐ Ⓑ Ⓒ Ⓓ Ⓔ	86 Ⓐ Ⓑ Ⓒ Ⓓ Ⓔ
62 Ⓐ Ⓑ Ⓒ Ⓓ Ⓔ	87 Ⓐ Ⓑ Ⓒ Ⓓ Ⓔ
63 Ⓐ Ⓑ Ⓒ Ⓓ Ⓔ	88 Ⓐ Ⓑ Ⓒ Ⓓ Ⓔ
64 Ⓐ Ⓑ Ⓒ Ⓓ Ⓔ	89 Ⓐ Ⓑ Ⓒ Ⓓ Ⓔ
65 Ⓐ Ⓑ Ⓒ Ⓓ Ⓔ	90 Ⓐ Ⓑ Ⓒ Ⓓ Ⓔ
66 Ⓐ Ⓑ Ⓒ Ⓓ Ⓔ	91 Ⓐ Ⓑ Ⓒ Ⓓ Ⓔ
67 Ⓐ Ⓑ Ⓒ Ⓓ Ⓔ	92 Ⓐ Ⓑ Ⓒ Ⓓ Ⓔ
68 Ⓐ Ⓑ Ⓒ Ⓓ Ⓔ	93 Ⓐ Ⓑ Ⓒ Ⓓ Ⓔ
69 Ⓐ Ⓑ Ⓒ Ⓓ Ⓔ	94 Ⓐ Ⓑ Ⓒ Ⓓ Ⓔ
70 Ⓐ Ⓑ Ⓒ Ⓓ Ⓔ	95 Ⓐ Ⓑ Ⓒ Ⓓ Ⓔ
71 Ⓐ Ⓑ Ⓒ Ⓓ Ⓔ	96 Ⓐ Ⓑ Ⓒ Ⓓ Ⓔ
72 Ⓐ Ⓑ Ⓒ Ⓓ Ⓔ	97 Ⓐ Ⓑ Ⓒ Ⓓ Ⓔ
73 Ⓐ Ⓑ Ⓒ Ⓓ Ⓔ	98 Ⓐ Ⓑ Ⓒ Ⓓ Ⓔ
74 Ⓐ Ⓑ Ⓒ Ⓓ Ⓔ	99 Ⓐ Ⓑ Ⓒ Ⓓ Ⓔ
75 Ⓐ Ⓑ Ⓒ Ⓓ Ⓔ	100 Ⓐ Ⓑ Ⓒ Ⓓ Ⓔ

Perceptual Ability Test

Part 1

1 (A) (B) (C) (D) (E)
2 (A) (B) (C) (D) (E)
3 (A) (B) (C) (D) (E)
4 (A) (B) (C) (D) (E)
5 (A) (B) (C) (D) (E)
6 (A) (B) (C) (D) (E)
7 (A) (B) (C) (D) (E)
8 (A) (B) (C) (D) (E)
9 (A) (B) (C) (D) (E)
10 (A) (B) (C) (D) (E)
11 (A) (B) (C) (D) (E)
12 (A) (B) (C) (D) (E)
13 (A) (B) (C) (D) (E)
14 (A) (B) (C) (D) (E)
15 (A) (B) (C) (D) (E)

Part 2

16 (A) (B) (C) (D)
17 (A) (B) (C) (D)
18 (A) (B) (C) (D)
19 (A) (B) (C) (D)
20 (A) (B) (C) (D)
21 (A) (B) (C) (D)
22 (A) (B) (C) (D)
23 (A) (B) (C) (D)
24 (A) (B) (C) (D)
25 (A) (B) (C) (D)
26 (A) (B) (C) (D)
27 (A) (B) (C) (D)
28 (A) (B) (C) (D)
29 (A) (B) (C) (D)
30 (A) (B) (C) (D)

Part 3

31 (A) (B) (C) (D)
32 (A) (B) (C) (D)
33 (A) (B) (C) (D)
34 (A) (B) (C) (D)
35 (A) (B) (C) (D)
36 (A) (B) (C) (D)
37 (A) (B) (C) (D)
38 (A) (B) (C) (D)
39 (A) (B) (C) (D)
40 (A) (B) (C) (D)
41 (A) (B) (C) (D)
42 (A) (B) (C) (D)
43 (A) (B) (C) (D)
44 (A) (B) (C) (D)
45 (A) (B) (C) (D)

Part 4

46 (A) (B) (C) (D) (E)
47 (A) (B) (C) (D) (E)
48 (A) (B) (C) (D) (E)
49 (A) (B) (C) (D) (E)
50 (A) (B) (C) (D) (E)
51 (A) (B) (C) (D) (E)
52 (A) (B) (C) (D) (E)
53 (A) (B) (C) (D) (E)
54 (A) (B) (C) (D) (E)
55 (A) (B) (C) (D) (E)
56 (A) (B) (C) (D) (E)
57 (A) (B) (C) (D) (E)
58 (A) (B) (C) (D) (E)
59 (A) (B) (C) (D) (E)
60 (A) (B) (C) (D) (E)

Part 5

61 (A) (B) (C) (D) (E)
62 (A) (B) (C) (D) (E)
63 (A) (B) (C) (D) (E)
64 (A) (B) (C) (D) (E)
65 (A) (B) (C) (D) (E)
66 (A) (B) (C) (D) (E)
67 (A) (B) (C) (D) (E)
68 (A) (B) (C) (D) (E)
69 (A) (B) (C) (D) (E)
70 (A) (B) (C) (D) (E)
71 (A) (B) (C) (D) (E)
72 (A) (B) (C) (D) (E)
73 (A) (B) (C) (D) (E)
74 (A) (B) (C) (D) (E)
75 (A) (B) (C) (D) (E)

Part 6

76 (A) (B) (C) (D)
77 (A) (B) (C) (D)
78 (A) (B) (C) (D)
79 (A) (B) (C) (D)
80 (A) (B) (C) (D)
81 (A) (B) (C) (D)
82 (A) (B) (C) (D)
83 (A) (B) (C) (D)
84 (A) (B) (C) (D)
85 (A) (B) (C) (D)
86 (A) (B) (C) (D)
87 (A) (B) (C) (D)
88 (A) (B) (C) (D)
89 (A) (B) (C) (D)
90 (A) (B) (C) (D)

Reading Comprehension

1 Ⓐ Ⓑ Ⓒ Ⓓ	26 Ⓐ Ⓑ Ⓒ Ⓓ
2 Ⓐ Ⓑ Ⓒ Ⓓ	27 Ⓐ Ⓑ Ⓒ Ⓓ
3 Ⓐ Ⓑ Ⓒ Ⓓ	28 Ⓐ Ⓑ Ⓒ Ⓓ
4 Ⓐ Ⓑ Ⓒ Ⓓ	29 Ⓐ Ⓑ Ⓒ Ⓓ
5 Ⓐ Ⓑ Ⓒ Ⓓ	30 Ⓐ Ⓑ Ⓒ Ⓓ
6 Ⓐ Ⓑ Ⓒ Ⓓ	31 Ⓐ Ⓑ Ⓒ Ⓓ
7 Ⓐ Ⓑ Ⓒ Ⓓ	32 Ⓐ Ⓑ Ⓒ Ⓓ
8 Ⓐ Ⓑ Ⓒ Ⓓ	33 Ⓐ Ⓑ Ⓒ Ⓓ
9 Ⓐ Ⓑ Ⓒ Ⓓ	34 Ⓐ Ⓑ Ⓒ Ⓓ
10 Ⓐ Ⓑ Ⓒ Ⓓ	35 Ⓐ Ⓑ Ⓒ Ⓓ
11 Ⓐ Ⓑ Ⓒ Ⓓ	36 Ⓐ Ⓑ Ⓒ Ⓓ
12 Ⓐ Ⓑ Ⓒ Ⓓ	37 Ⓐ Ⓑ Ⓒ Ⓓ
13 Ⓐ Ⓑ Ⓒ Ⓓ	38 Ⓐ Ⓑ Ⓒ Ⓓ
14 Ⓐ Ⓑ Ⓒ Ⓓ	39 Ⓐ Ⓑ Ⓒ Ⓓ
15 Ⓐ Ⓑ Ⓒ Ⓓ	40 Ⓐ Ⓑ Ⓒ Ⓓ
16 Ⓐ Ⓑ Ⓒ Ⓓ	41 Ⓐ Ⓑ Ⓒ Ⓓ
17 Ⓐ Ⓑ Ⓒ Ⓓ	42 Ⓐ Ⓑ Ⓒ Ⓓ
18 Ⓐ Ⓑ Ⓒ Ⓓ	43 Ⓐ Ⓑ Ⓒ Ⓓ
19 Ⓐ Ⓑ Ⓒ Ⓓ	44 Ⓐ Ⓑ Ⓒ Ⓓ
20 Ⓐ Ⓑ Ⓒ Ⓓ	45 Ⓐ Ⓑ Ⓒ Ⓓ
21 Ⓐ Ⓑ Ⓒ Ⓓ	46 Ⓐ Ⓑ Ⓒ Ⓓ
22 Ⓐ Ⓑ Ⓒ Ⓓ	47 Ⓐ Ⓑ Ⓒ Ⓓ
23 Ⓐ Ⓑ Ⓒ Ⓓ	48 Ⓐ Ⓑ Ⓒ Ⓓ
24 Ⓐ Ⓑ Ⓒ Ⓓ	49 Ⓐ Ⓑ Ⓒ Ⓓ
25 Ⓐ Ⓑ Ⓒ Ⓓ	50 Ⓐ Ⓑ Ⓒ Ⓓ

CUT HERE

Quantitative Reasoning

1 Ⓐ Ⓑ Ⓒ Ⓓ Ⓔ		21 Ⓐ Ⓑ Ⓒ Ⓓ Ⓔ
2 Ⓐ Ⓑ Ⓒ Ⓓ Ⓔ		22 Ⓐ Ⓑ Ⓒ Ⓓ Ⓔ
3 Ⓐ Ⓑ Ⓒ Ⓓ Ⓔ		23 Ⓐ Ⓑ Ⓒ Ⓓ Ⓔ
4 Ⓐ Ⓑ Ⓒ Ⓓ Ⓔ		24 Ⓐ Ⓑ Ⓒ Ⓓ Ⓔ
5 Ⓐ Ⓑ Ⓒ Ⓓ Ⓔ		25 Ⓐ Ⓑ Ⓒ Ⓓ Ⓔ
6 Ⓐ Ⓑ Ⓒ Ⓓ Ⓔ		26 Ⓐ Ⓑ Ⓒ Ⓓ Ⓔ
7 Ⓐ Ⓑ Ⓒ Ⓓ Ⓔ		27 Ⓐ Ⓑ Ⓒ Ⓓ Ⓔ
8 Ⓐ Ⓑ Ⓒ Ⓓ Ⓔ		28 Ⓐ Ⓑ Ⓒ Ⓓ Ⓔ
9 Ⓐ Ⓑ Ⓒ Ⓓ Ⓔ		29 Ⓐ Ⓑ Ⓒ Ⓓ Ⓔ
10 Ⓐ Ⓑ Ⓒ Ⓓ Ⓔ		30 Ⓐ Ⓑ Ⓒ Ⓓ Ⓔ
11 Ⓐ Ⓑ Ⓒ Ⓓ Ⓔ		31 Ⓐ Ⓑ Ⓒ Ⓓ Ⓔ
12 Ⓐ Ⓑ Ⓒ Ⓓ Ⓔ		32 Ⓐ Ⓑ Ⓒ Ⓓ Ⓔ
13 Ⓐ Ⓑ Ⓒ Ⓓ Ⓔ		33 Ⓐ Ⓑ Ⓒ Ⓓ Ⓔ
14 Ⓐ Ⓑ Ⓒ Ⓓ Ⓔ		34 Ⓐ Ⓑ Ⓒ Ⓓ Ⓔ
15 Ⓐ Ⓑ Ⓒ Ⓓ Ⓔ		35 Ⓐ Ⓑ Ⓒ Ⓓ Ⓔ
16 Ⓐ Ⓑ Ⓒ Ⓓ Ⓔ		36 Ⓐ Ⓑ Ⓒ Ⓓ Ⓔ
17 Ⓐ Ⓑ Ⓒ Ⓓ Ⓔ		37 Ⓐ Ⓑ Ⓒ Ⓓ Ⓔ
18 Ⓐ Ⓑ Ⓒ Ⓓ Ⓔ		38 Ⓐ Ⓑ Ⓒ Ⓓ Ⓔ
19 Ⓐ Ⓑ Ⓒ Ⓓ Ⓔ		39 Ⓐ Ⓑ Ⓒ Ⓓ Ⓔ
20 Ⓐ Ⓑ Ⓒ Ⓓ Ⓔ		40 Ⓐ Ⓑ Ⓒ Ⓓ Ⓔ

CUT HERE

PERIODIC TABLE OF THE ELEMENTS

1																	2
H 1.0079																	**He** 4.0026
3 **Li** 6.941	4 **Be** 9.012											5 **B** 10.811	6 **C** 12.011	7 **N** 14.007	8 **O** 16.00	9 **F** 19.00	10 **Ne** 20.179
11 **Na** 22.99	12 **Mg** 24.30											13 **Al** 26.98	14 **Si** 28.09	15 **P** 30.974	16 **S** 32.06	17 **Cl** 35.453	18 **Ar** 39.948
19 **K** 39.10	20 **Ca** 40.08	21 **Sc** 44.96	22 **Ti** 47.90	23 **V** 50.94	24 **Cr** 51.00	25 **Mn** 54.93	26 **Fe** 55.85	27 **Co** 58.93	28 **Ni** 58.69	29 **Cu** 63.55	30 **Zn** 65.39	31 **Ga** 69.72	32 **Ge** 72.59	33 **As** 74.92	34 **Se** 78.96	35 **Br** 79.90	36 **Kr** 83.80
37 **Rb** 85.47	38 **Sr** 87.62	39 **Y** 88.91	40 **Zr** 91.22	41 **Nb** 92.91	42 **Mo** 95.94	43 **Tc** (98)	44 **Ru** 101.1	45 **Rh** 102.91	46 **Pd** 105.42	47 **Ag** 107.87	48 **Cd** 112.41	49 **In** 114.82	50 **Sn** 118.71	51 **Sb** 121.75	52 **Te** 127.60	53 **I** 126.91	54 **Xe** 131.29
55 **Cs** 132.91	56 **Ba** 137.33	57 *****La** 138.91	72 **Hf** 178.49	73 **Ta** 180.95	74 **W** 183.85	75 **Re** 186.21	76 **Os** 190.2	77 **Ir** 192.22	78 **Pt** 195.08	79 **Au** 196.97	80 **Hg** 200.59	81 **Tl** 204.38	82 **Pb** 207.2	83 **Bi** 208.98	84 **Po** (209)	85 **At** (210)	86 **Rn** (222)
87 **Fr** (223)	88 **Ra** 226.02	89 †**Ac** 227.03	104 **Rf** (261)	105 **Db** (262)	106 **Sg** (263)	107 **Bh** (262)	108 **Hs** (265)	109 **Mt** (266)	110 **§** (269)	111 **§** (272)	112 **§** (277)						

§ Not yet named

***** Lanthanide Series

58 **Ce** 140.12	59 **Pr** 140.91	60 **Nd** 144.24	61 **Pm** (145)	62 **Sm** 150.4	63 **Eu** 151.97	64 **Gd** 157.25	65 **Tb** 158.93	66 **Dy** 162.50	67 **Ho** 164.93	68 **Er** 167.26	69 **Tm** 168.93	70 **Yb** 173.04	71 **Lu** 174.97

† Actinide Series

90 **Th** 232.04	91 **Pa** 231.04	92 **U** 238.03	93 **Np** 237.05	94 **Pu** (244)	95 **Am** (243)	96 **Cm** (247)	97 **Bk** (247)	98 **Cf** (251)	99 **Es** (252)	100 **Fm** (257)	101 **Md** (258)	102 **No** (259)	103 **Lr** (260)

DAT Practice Test 1

Natural Sciences

Time: 90 Minutes

100 Questions: Biology (1–40), General Chemistry (41–70), and Organic Chemistry (71–100)

1. The primary function of the mitochondria found in eukaryotic cells is to

   A. carry out protein synthesis.
   B. control the physical properties of the cell.
   C. control the biochemical properties of the cell.
   D. produce energy for cellular functions.
   E. manufacture glucose.

2. Which of the following statements regarding cellular respiration is INCORRECT?

   A. Cellular respiration occurs only in animal cells, whereas plant cells carry out photosynthesis.
   B. Aerobic respiration tends to be more efficient in terms of energy production than anaerobic respiration (fermentation).
   C. Cellular respiration produces energy for the cell through the process of breaking down glucose molecules into carbon dioxide and water.
   D. Cellular respiration takes place in the mitochondria of both plant and animal cells.
   E. The process of fermentation occasionally takes place in human cells.

3. Which of the following components is not necessary for the process of photosynthesis to take place?

   A. carbon dioxide
   B. oxygen
   C. chlorophyll
   D. light energy
   E. water

4. Proteins that act as catalysts to speed up the rate of a reaction by lowering the activation energy required for the reaction to take place are referred to as

   A. cofactors.
   B. substrates.
   C. enzymes.
   D. polypeptides.
   E. promoters.

5. The passive movement of substances across cell membranes occurs primarily through

   A. plasmolysis.
   B. ion pumping channels.
   C. active transport.
   D. diffusion and osmosis.
   E. eletrochemical gradients.

6. An organism with a chromosome number of 24 in each of its somatic cells would give rise to gametes (eggs or sperm) with a chromosome number of

   A. 24.
   B. 12.
   C. 6.
   D. 48.
   E. 36.

7. Yeast, used in the fermentation process to make ethanol, is classified as a member of which of the following groups of organisms?

   A. prokaryotes
   B. protists
   C. fungi
   D. bacteria
   E. slime molds

GO ON TO THE NEXT PAGE

8. Which of the following features separates angiosperms (flowering plants) from the other plant groups?

   A. the production of seeds
   B. the presence of vascular tissue
   C. reproduction by spores
   D. the presence of nutritive tissue in the seed
   E. the production of fruit

9. Which of the following animal phyla includes both invertebrate and vertebrate organisms?

   A. Arthropoda
   B. Annelida
   C. Mollusca
   D. Chordata
   E. Echinodermata

10. Which of the following features is NOT considered a defining characteristic of vertebrate organisms?

    A. notochord
    B. dorsal, hollow nerve cord
    C. segmented body plan
    D. pharyngeal slits
    E. muscular, postanal tail

11. Which of the following represents the vertebrate system responsible for eliminating metabolic waste products from the body and maintaining the osmotic balance of the blood?

    A. excretory system
    B. endocrine system
    C. digestive system
    D. circulatory system
    E. respiratory system

12. Which of the following represents the correct order in which food travels through the human digestive system?

    A. mouth → esophagus → pharynx → stomach → small intestine
    B. mouth → pharynx → esophagus → stomach → small intestine
    C. mouth → esophagus → pharynx → small intestine → stomach
    D. mouth → pharynx → esophagus → small intestine → stomach
    E. mouth → esophagus → stomach → pharynx → small intestine

13. When taking your blood pressure, you are actually measuring

    A. your heart rate.
    B. the number of times your heart beats per minute.
    C. the force that blood exerts against the walls of the blood vessels.
    D. your pulse.
    E. the rate at which blood is flowing through your blood vessels.

14. Which of the following is NOT a function of the human dermal system?

    A. gas exchange
    B. sensory organ
    C. protection against invading microorganisms
    D. outer body covering
    E. protection of internal organs

15. The primary function of the red blood cells in the human circulatory system is to

    A. produce antibodies against invading microorganisms.
    B. initiate the blood clotting process.
    C. stimulate the immune response.
    D. transport oxygen and carbon dioxide throughout the body.
    E. provide a liquid matrix within which the white blood cells are suspended.

16. Mucous membranes, phagocytic white blood cells, and the inflammatory response are all examples of

    A. specific immune responses.
    B. non-specific immune responses.
    C. barrier defense mechanisms.
    D. initial immune responses.
    E. primary defense mechanisms.

17. The transfer of antibodies from a mother to her fetus is an example of

    A. passive immunity.
    B. active immunity.
    C. maternal immunity.
    D. fetal immunity.
    E. prenatal immunity.

18. Which of the following hormones is NOT produced by the pituitary gland?

    A. oxytocin
    B. growth hormone
    C. prolactin
    D. thyroid stimulating hormone
    E. epinephrine

19. Intercellular chemical messengers released at synapses are referred to as

    A. axons.
    B. dendrites.
    C. neurons.
    D. neurotransmitters.
    E. membrane potentials.

20. The system responsible for conveying signals that regulate involuntary control of the cardiac muscles and the smooth muscles of the digestive, cardiovascular, excretory, and endocrine systems in humans is the

    A. central nervous system.
    B. autonomic nervous system.
    C. peripheral nervous system.
    D. somatic nervous system.
    E. sensory nervous system.

21. In the human males, sperm are formed in the

    A. penis.
    B. seminal vesicles.
    C. vas deferens.
    D. epididymis.
    E. seminiferous tubules.

22. Which of the following represents the correct order of development in vertebrate embryos?

    A. fertilization → cleavage → gastrulation → organogenesis
    B. fertilization → gastrulation → cleavage → organogenesis
    C. fertilization → cleavage → organogenesis → gastrulation
    D. fertilization → organogenesis → cleavage → gastrulation
    E. fertilization → gastrulation → organogenesis → cleavage

23. The three tissue layers that form during gastrulation in vertebrate embryo development each give rise to a variety of tissues and organs in the adult organism. Which of the following embryonic tissue layers is MISmatched with one of the adult tissues or organs it gives rise to?

    A. ectoderm   skin
    B. endoderm   lining of the digestive tract
    C. mesoderm   skeletal system
    D. endoderm   circulatory system
    E. ectoderm   cornea and lens of the eye

24. Which of the following represents the possible gametes that could be produced by an individual with the genotype AABbcc, assuming that no crossing over takes place during meiosis?

    A. AA, Bb, or cc
    B. A, B, b, or c
    C. ABc, or Abc
    D. AB, Ab, Ac, Bc, or bc
    E. AB, or bc

25. If straight body form is completely dominant to spiral body form in earthworms, which of the following represents the correct ratio of offspring that would be produced by a cross between a worm that was heterozygous for straight body type (Bb) and a worm that was homozygous recessive for spiral body type (bb)?

    A. All offspring would have straight bodies.
    B. All offspring would have spiral body types.
    C. 3:1, with 3 straight bodies : 1 spiral body
    D. 3:1, with 3 spiral bodies : 1 straight body
    E. 1:1, with half the offspring having straight bodies and half the offspring having spiral bodies

26. Sex-linked traits refer to those traits that

    A. are carried on the sex chromosomes (X and Y).
    B. determine the sex of an individual during embryo development.
    C. are responsible for the development of primary sexual characteristics during development.
    D. are responsible for the development of secondary sexual characteristics during development.
    E. are responsible for the production of gametes during meiosis.

GO ON TO THE NEXT PAGE

27. Mistakes that take place during meiosis can result in nondisjunction of entire sets of chromosomes, such that the resulting gamete (egg or sperm) is diploid instead of haploid. If a diploid gamete unites with a normal haploid gamete, the resulting zygote would be

    A. aneuploid.
    B. alloploid.
    C. autoploid.
    D. triploid.
    E. tetraploid.

28. Which of the following represents the correct order of events that takes place in the conversion of the genetic code into a polypeptide?

    A. DNA → (translation) → mRNA → (transcription) → polypeptide
    B. DNA → (transcription) → mRNA → (translation) → polypeptide
    C. mRNA → (translation) → DNA → (transcription) → polypeptide
    D. mRNA → (transcription) → DNA → (translation) → polypeptide
    E. mRNA → (transcription) → tRNA → (translation) → polypeptide

29. DNA is composed of

    A. chains of nucleotides arranged to form a double helix held together by hydrogen bonds between pairs of deoxyribose sugar molecules.
    B. chains of nucleotides arranged to form a double helix held together by hydrogen bonds between pairs of phosphate groups.
    C. chains of nucleotides arranged to form a double helix held together by hydrogen bonds between deoxyibose sugars and nitrogenous bases.
    D. chains of nucleotides arranged to form a double helix held together by hydrogen bonds between nitrogenous bases and phosphate groups.
    E. chains of nucleotides arranged to form a double helix held together by hydrogen bonds between pairs of nitrogenous bases.

30. Which of the following techniques is frequently used in forensic science to produce sufficient copies of cloned DNA for testing from a small sample of blood found at a crime scene?

    A. transformation
    B. genetic engineering
    C. DNA fingerprinting
    D. polymerase chain reaction
    E. transduction

31. An organism that contains segments of DNA from another organism is referred to as being

    A. cloned.
    B. transgenic.
    C. restricted.
    D. amplified.
    E. fingerprinted.

32. Differences among individuals in a population in the ability to survive and successfully reproduce is referred to as

    A. evolution.
    B. descent with modification.
    C. adaptation.
    D. natural selection.
    E. inheritance.

33. Genetic drift, one of the mechanisms that prevents a population from maintaining Hardy-Weinberg equilibrium, is primarily due to

    A. migration into or out of the population.
    B. random mating.
    C. small population size.
    D. natural selection.
    E. mutations.

34. If two organisms belong to the same order, they must also belong to the same

    A. class.
    B. family.
    C. genus.
    D. phylum.
    E. species.

35. All of the species that live in a given geographic area and have the potential to interact with each other is referred to as a(n)

A. geographic unit.
B. gene pool.
C. ecosystem.
D. population.
E. community.

36. A type of interspecific interaction in which both individuals benefit from the relationship is referred to as

A. commensalism.
B. mutualism.
C. predation.
D. competition.
E. parasitism.

37. In a typical food chain, the primary consumers are often referred to as

A. decomposers.
B. producers.
C. carnivores.
D. herbivores.
E. predators.

38. Movement of water, carbon, and nutrients through an ecosystem occurs

A. in one direction, with a loss of water, carbon, or nutrients at each trohpic level in the food chain.
B. in one direction, with a gain of water, carbon, or nutrients at each trophic level.
C. in a cyclical manner through the living organisms only.
D. in a cyclical manner through the abiotic elements only.
E. in a cyclical manner through both the living organisms and abiotic elements.

39. The rapid increase in atmospheric carbon dioxide in recent years is primarily due to

A. an increase in photosynthesis by primary producers.
B. an increase in respiration by living organisms.
C. an increase in decomposition of organic matter.
D. an increase in fertilizer run-off from agricultural and urban areas.
E. an increase in the burning of fossil fuels and wood.

40. The nature vs. nurture controversy is concerned with

A. the relative importance of genes and the environment in shaping behavior.
B. the various forms of learning behavior.
C. the roles of learning and maturation in behavior.
D. the evolution of social behavior.
E. interspecific versus intraspecific behavior.

41. What type of element is arsenic?

A. metal
B. nonmetal
C. noble gas
D. metalloid
E. transition metal

42. Which of the following pairs of elements will most likely form an ionic substance?

A. copper and chlorine
B. sulfur and chlorine
C. hydrogen and chlorine
D. carbon and chlorine
E. silicon and chlorine

43. What is the name for the polyatomic ion NO_3^-?

A. nitrite ion
B. nitrous ion
C. nitrate ion
D. nitride ion
E. nitrogen trioxide ion

GO ON TO THE NEXT PAGE

44. Complete the following chemical equation for the complete combustion reaction. Include the correct coefficients.

$$2\,CH_3OH(l) + 3\,O_2(g) \rightarrow$$

   A. $CO_2(g) + H_2O(g)$
   B. $2\,CO_2(g) + 3\,H_2O(g)$
   C. $CO_2(g) + 4\,H_2O(g)$
   D. $2\,C(s) + O_2(g) + 4\,H_2(g)$
   E. $2\,CO_2(g) + 4\,H_2O(g)$

45. How many mols of NH_3 will be equal to 1.0×10^{22} molecules of ammonia?

   A. 17
   B. 60
   C. 0.017
   D. 1.0×10^{22}
   E. 6.0×10^{45}

46. Which of the following is the nuclear decay equation for beta emission by carbon-14?

   A. $^{12}_{20}Ca \rightarrow\, ^{0}_{-1}e + ^{12}_{19}Ca$
   B. $^{12}_{20}Ca \rightarrow\, ^{0}_{1}e + ^{12}_{19}Ca$
   C. $^{14}_{6}C \rightarrow\, ^{0}_{-1}e + ^{14}_{7}N$
   D. $^{14}_{6}C \rightarrow\, ^{0}_{1}e + ^{14}_{5}B$
   E. $^{14}_{6}C \rightarrow\, ^{1}_{0}e + ^{13}_{6}C$

47. Iodine-131 has a half-life of 8.1 days. How many grams of iodine-131 will remain after 16.2 days if the initial sample had a mass of 3.00 grams?

   A. 0.750 g
   B. 1.50 g
   C. 1.00 g
   D. 2.00 g
   E. 0.375 g

48. What is the name for the process in which a solid changes into a gas?

   A. vaporization
   B. evaporation
   C. decomposition
   D. fusion
   E. sublimation

49. How does the rate of disappearance of H_2 compare with the rate of production of NH_3 for the gas phase reaction shown here?

$$3\,H_2 + N_2 \rightarrow 2\,NH_3$$

   A. The initial rates are equal.
   B. The rate of disappearance of H_2 is 1/2 the rate of production of NH_3.
   C. The rate of disappearance of H_2 is 3/2 the rate of production of NH_3.
   D. The rate of disappearance of H_2 is 2/3 the rate of production of NH_3.
   E. The rate of disappearance of H_2 is 1/3 the rate of production of NH_3.

50. Which of the following quantities when plotted versus time will give a straight line plot for a first order reaction?

   A. $1/[A]$
   B. $\ln [A]$
   C. $\ln [1/A]$
   D. $[A]$
   E. $\ln k$

51. In general which of the following statements is true about the chemical reaction rate when temperature increases?

   A. increases due to greater number of effective collisions
   B. increases due to an increase in the activation energy
   C. increases because bonds are weakened
   D. increases only for an endothermic reaction
   E. is the same regardless of temperature increases

52. Hydrofluoric acid has a $K_a = 7.2 \times 10^{-4}$. What is the value for the K_b for the fluoride ion, $F-$?

   A. approximately 1×10^{-14}
   B. approximately 1.4×10^{-11}
   C. approximately 7.2×10^{-4}
   D. approximately 7.2×10^{-15}
   E. approximately 7.2×10^{10}

53. Which of the following chlorine containing acids is the strongest?

   A. HCl
   B. HClO
   C. $HClO_2$
   D. $HClO_c$
   E. $HClO_4$

54. Ammonia is produced commercially by the Haber process. In this reaction H_2 and N_2 react according to this formula: $N_2(g) + 3 H_2(g) \leftrightarrow 2 NH_3(g)$ $\Delta H = -92{,}200$ joules

    Which of the following changes at equilibrium will cause the reaction to shift and increase production of ammonia?

    A. removal of nitrogen
    B. removal of hydrogen
    C. addition of a catalyst
    D. decreasing the size of the reaction vessel
    E. increasing the temperature from 200°C to 300°C

55. What is the approximate pH for the solution produced when CH_3COOH is reacted with an equal number of mols of NaOH? **Note:** $K_a = 1.8 \times 10^{-5}$

    A. 9
    B. 0
    C. 7
    D. 14
    E. 1

56. Which of the following is the solubility product expression for iron (III) sulfide, Fe_2S_3?

    A. $K_{sp} = [Fe^{3+}][S^{2-}]$
    B. $K_{sp} = [Fe^{2+}]^2[S^{3-}]^3$
    C. $K_{sp} = [Fe^{2+}][S^{3-}]$
    D. $K_{sp} = [Fe^{3+}]^2[S^{2-}]^3$
    E. $K_{sp} = [Fe^{2+}][S^{2-}]^3$

57. Which of the following gas molecules effuses at the highest rate?

    A. N_2
    B. He
    C. Ne
    D. CO
    E. O_2

58. Which of the following gases will have the lowest density at STP?

    A. He
    B. CO_2
    C. CO
    D. CH_4
    E. H_2

59. Which of the following substances contains cations bonded together by mobile electrons?

    A. $Br_2(l)$
    B. KBr(s)
    C. Ag(s)
    D. $MgCl_2(s)$
    E. $S_8(s)$

60. What is the hybridization on the carbon atoms in CH_4 and CO_2, respectively?

    A. sp, sp
    B. sp^3, sp^2
    C. sp^2, sp^2
    D. sp^3, sp
    E. sp^3, sp^3

61. How many pi electrons are in $CH_3C{:::}N$?

    A. 0
    B. 2
    C. 3
    D. 6
    E. 4

62. What type of orbital, if any, is designated by the quantum numbers $n = 2$, $\ell = 1$, $m\ell = -1$?

    A. 1s
    B. 2p
    C. 2s
    D. 3s
    E. 3p

63. Which of the following is a non-metal?

    A. Cl
    B. Cr
    C. Cs
    D. Ca
    E. Cu

GO ON TO THE NEXT PAGE

64. What is the net enthalpy for the reaction H_2O (l) + CO_2 (g) → H_2CO_3 (aq) based on the following reactions?

$2 H_2$ (g) + O_2 (g) → $2 H_2O$ (l) $\Delta H = -285.8$ kJ/mol

C (s) + O_2 (g) → CO_2 (g) $\Delta H = -393.5$ kJ/mol

H_2 (g) + C (s) + O_2 (g) → H_2CO_3 (aq) $\Delta H = -691.1$ kJ/mol

- **A.** +11.8 kJ/mol
- **B.** +1307.4 kJ/mol
- **C.** −1307.4 kJ/mol
- **D.** −11.8 kJ/mol
- **E.** +679.3 kJ/mol

65. Based on the following standard electrode potentials for the two half reactions, what is the standard electrode potential for the reaction $I^-|I_2||Ag^+|Ag$?

$I_2 + 2 e^- → 2 I^-$ $E° = 0.535$ V

$Ag^+ + e^- → Ag$ $E° = 0.7994$ V

- **A.** +0.2644 V
- **B.** +1.3344 V
- **C.** −0.2706 V
- **D.** +1.0638 V
- **E.** 2.1338 V

66. In a chemical reaction, which of the following will "stop" the reaction by running out first?

- **A.** the products
- **B.** the activation energy
- **C.** the limiting reagent
- **D.** the percent yield
- **E.** the theoretical yield

67. What do we know about a reaction mixture when the reaction quotient, Q, is smaller than the equilibrium constant for a reversible reaction, $Q < K_{eq}$?

- **A.** Reactant concentrations are higher than equilibrium values.
- **B.** Reactant concentrations are lower than equilibrium values.
- **C.** Product concentrations are higher than equilibrium values.
- **D.** Reactant and product concentrations are equal to equilibrium values.
- **E.** The reaction is at equilibrium.

68. What hybridization exists on the central atom in the molecule, PF_5?

- **A.** sp^2
- **B.** sp^3
- **C.** sp^3d
- **D.** sp^3d^2
- **E.** sp^4

69. What is the enthalpy change for the reaction between CH_4 and Cl_2? The reaction is $CH_4 + Cl_2 →$ $CH_4 + HCl$. Use these bond energies. The C–H bond energy is 414 kJ/mol; Cl–Cl is 244 kJ/mol; C–Cl is 326 kJ/mol; and H–Cl is 432 kJ/mol.

- **A.** 758 kJ/mol
- **B.** −758 kJ/mol
- **C.** 658 kJ/mol
- **D.** −100 kJ/mol
- **E.** +100 kJ/mol

70. What is the name used to label a compound that can act as either an acid or a base?

- **A.** amorphous
- **B.** amphoteric
- **C.** anomers
- **D.** allotropes
- **E.** Arrhenius

71. What is the product from the reaction of Br_2(g) with 2-butene?

- **A.** 1,4-dibromobutene
- **B.** 2,3-dibromobutene
- **C.** 1,1-dibromobutene
- **D.** 2,3-dibromobutane
- **E.** 1,3-dibromobutane

72. What is the name for the molecule shown here?

- **A.** p-dichlorobenzene
- **B.** m-dichlorobenzene
- **C.** o-dichlorobenzene
- **D.** o-chlorotoluene
- **E.** 1,4-dichlorocyclohexane

73. Why is the Diels-Alder reaction important?

    A. It is an inexpensive way to do halogen addition.

    B. It converts alkane compounds to more reactive forms.

    C. It extends the length of the parent chain.

    D. It produces ring closure and structures.

    E. It introduces a carbonyl group.

74. What is the name for this conformation of cyclohexane?

    A. chair

    B. boat

    C. twist

    D. conforming

    E. linear

75. What functional group is in this molecule?

    A. halogen

    B. aldehyde

    C. ketone

    D. ether

    E. ester

76. What is the proper name for the compound shown in the following figure?

$$Br \quad F$$
$$H \diagdown \diagup CH_3$$

    A. E-1-bromo-2-fluoro propene

    B. Z-1-bromo-2-fluoro propene

    C. Z-3-bromo-2-fluoro propene

    D. E-3-bromo-2-fluoro propene

    E. trans-3-bromo-2-fluoro propene

77. Which of the following types of alcohols will undergo dehydration the fastest?

    A. methanol

    B. primary

    C. tertiary

    D. secondary

    E. quaternary

78. What type of reaction mechanism will be favored if the intermediate is very stable?

    A. E2

    B. E1

    C. S_N2

    D. S_N1

    E. TSA

79. What step in the formation of a polymer ends the growth of the polymer?

    A. propagation

    B. initiation

    C. termination

    D. elimination

    E. dissociation

80. The reaction product of CO_2 and CH_3CH_2MgCl is hydrolyzed. What functional group will result?

    A. ester

    B. ether

    C. aldehyde

    D. carboxylic acid

    E. ketone

81. Which of the following is the correct order for the reactivity of alkyl halides in nucleophilic displacement reactions?

    A. RF > RCl > RBr > RI

    B. RF > RBr > RCl > RI

    C. RI > RBr > RF > RCl

    D. RBr > RI > RCl > RF

    E. RI > RBr > RCl > RF

82. What is the reaction product for the reaction

$ICH_2CH_2I + Mg(ether)$

    A. $(ICH_2CH_2I)_2Mg_2$

    B. CH_2CH_2

    C. $CH_3CH_2CH_2CH_3$

    D. CHCH

    E. ICH_2CH_2IMg

GO ON TO THE NEXT PAGE

83. What is the correct sequence in decreasing S_N1 reactivity for the following halides?

I   II   III

A.   I > II > III
B.   III > II > I
C.   I > III > II
D.   III > I > II
E.   I = II = III

84. Which of the following is a CORRECT pairing of class of compound and general formula?

A.   ether, R–O–O–R
B.   aldehyde, ROH
C.   thiol, R–S–S–R
D.   ketone, $R_2C=O$
E.   acid anhydride, $R_2C=O$

85. Which of the following types of reactant is most likely to react with an aromatic compound?

A.   electrophile
B.   nucleophile
C.   base
D.   hydrophobe
E.   enzyme

86. Which of the following functional groups involves nitrogen?

A.   carboxylic acid
B.   alcohol
C.   amine
D.   phenol
E.   ether

87. What peak pattern in the proton magnetic resonance spectrum will be observed for the "a" hydrogen (as written) in 1,1,2-trichloroethane, $CH^aCl_2CH_2^bCl$?

A.   singlet
B.   doublet
C.   triplet
D.   quartet
E.   higher than quartet

88. Which of the following compounds will have a CMR decoupled spectrum with only two peaks?

A. CH_4
B. CH_3CH_3
C. CH_3CHO
D. H_2CO
E. $CH:::CH$

89. Which of the following compounds will have a mass spectrum with a cation-radical peak of a mass to charge ratio m / e of 43?

A. $C_3H_7^+$
B. $C_3H_8^+$
C. $C_3H_6^+$
D. $C_3H_6^+$
E. $C_3H_8^+$

90. Which of the following combinations of functional groups and IR absorption band stretching frequencies is NOT correct?

A.   C–H, in alkanes, 2800–3000 cm^{-1}
B.   C=O, in carbonyls, 1690–1750 cm^{-1}
C.   O–H, in alcohols, 3600–3650 cm^{-1}
D.   C–O, in ethers, 2800–3000 cm^{-1}
E.   C=O, in carbonyls, 2900–3000 cm^{-1}

91. Which of the following bond types will have the highest infrared stretching frequency?

    A. C-C single bond

    B. C::C double bond

    C. C:::C triple bond

    D. all are the same

    E. carbon carbon bonds do not undergo stretching in the IR range

92. Which of the following has the largest delocalization energy?

    A. benzene

    B. cyclohexene

    C. 1,4-cyclohexadiene

    D. 1,3-cyclohexadiene

    E. cyclohexane

93. What is the principle type of intermolecular force acting between alkanes?

    A. dipole-dipole

    B. van der Waals (or London)

    C. hydrogen bonding

    D. metallic

    E. ionic

94. What type of reaction mechanism produces a chiral center if the reactant begins with a chiral center?

    A. S_N1

    B. E2

    C. S_N2

    D. E1

    E. all of these

95. In the following figure, which site is most likely to be attacked by the amine?

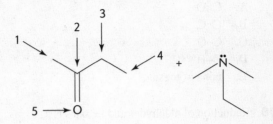

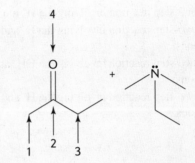

    A. 1

    B. 2

    C. 3

    D. 4

    E. 5

96. How many chiral carbon atoms are in this figure?

    A. 0

    B. 1

    C. 2

    D. 3

    E. 4

GO ON TO THE NEXT PAGE

97. Which of the following bonds is NOT present in a carboxylic acid functional group?

    A. C::O

    B. C::C

    C. C–O

    D. O–H

    E. none of these

98. Reduction of aldehydes and ketones is a

    A. one-step reaction involving the hydride ion.

    B. one-step reaction involving the H^+ ion.

    C. two-step reaction involving the H^- and H^+ ions.

    D. two-step reaction involving the OH^- and H^+ ions.

    E. two-step reaction involving the H^- and OH^- ions.

99. Which of the following compounds will give a positive Tollen's test?

    A. 2-pentanone

    B. 3-pentanone

    C. pentanoic acid

    D. pentane

    E. pentanal

100. What is the major product resulting from the dehydration of the following molecule?

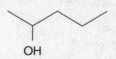

    A. 1-pentene

    B. 2-pentene

    C. n-pentane

    D. 1,2-pentadiol

    E. 1,3-pentanediol

IF YOU FINISH BEFORE TIME IS CALLED, CHECK YOUR WORK ON THIS SECTION ONLY. DO NOT WORK ON ANY OTHER SECTION IN THE TEST.

Perceptual Ability Test

Time: 60 Minutes

90 Questions

Part 1

For Questions 1–15, this visualization test consists of a number of items similar to the sample below. A three-dimensional object is shown at the left. This is followed by outlines of five apertures or openings.

All of the tasks throughout this test are identical. The first step is to look at the object and imagine how it looks from every viewpoint. Then select the appropriate aperture from the five choices that will accommodate the object passing through it, if the object is inserted from the correct side. Then mark your choice on the answer sheet.

Here are the rules:

1. Prior to passing through the aperture, the irregular solid object may be turned in any direction. It may be started through the aperture on a side not shown.

2. Once the object is started through the aperture, it may not be twisted or turned. It must pass completely through the opening. The opening is always the exact shape of the appropriate external outline of the object.

3. Both objects and apertures are drawn to the same scale. Thus it is possible for an opening to be the correct shape but too small for the object. In all cases, however, differences are large enough to judge by eye.

4. There are no irregularities in any hidden portion of the object. However, if the figure has symmetric indentations, the hidden portion is symmetric with the part shown.

5. For each object there is only one correct aperture.

Example:

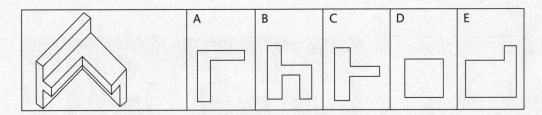

The correct answer is E since the object would pass through this aperture if the side at the left were introduced first.

Proceed to Questions 1–15.

GO ON TO THE NEXT PAGE

1.

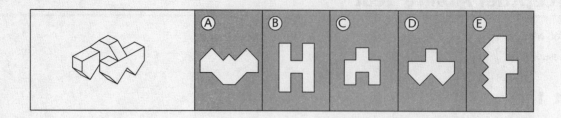

2.

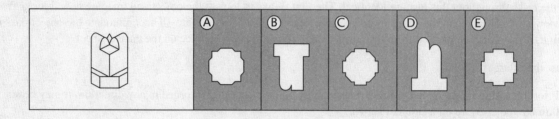

3.

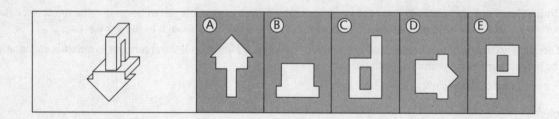

4.

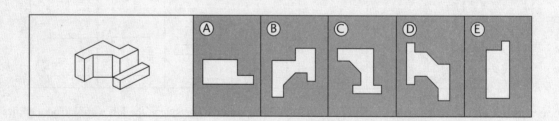

5.

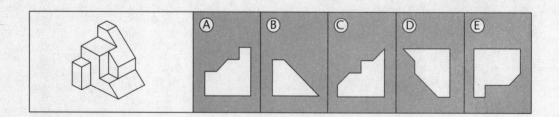

6.

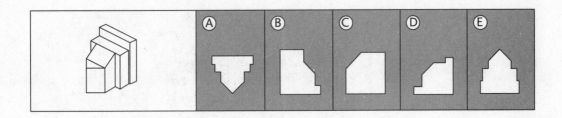

7.

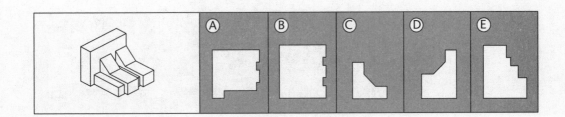

8.

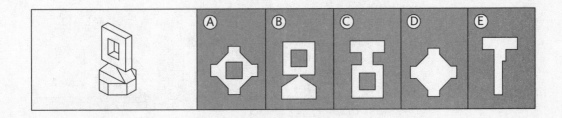

9.

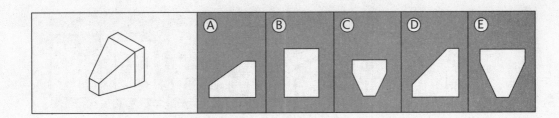

10.

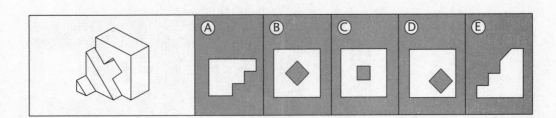

GO ON TO THE NEXT PAGE

11.

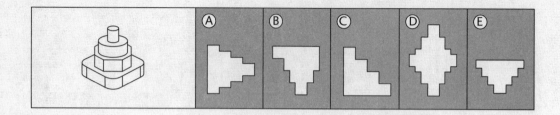

12.

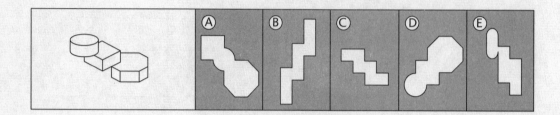

13.

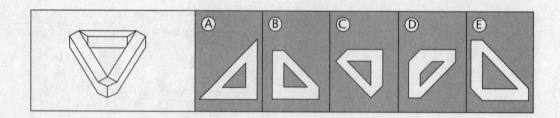

14.

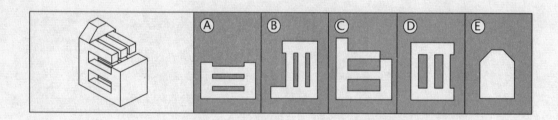

15.

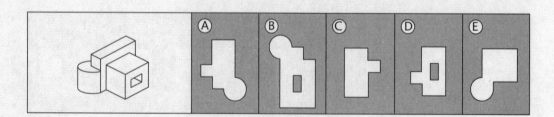

Part 2

For Questions 16–30, the following pictures illustrate top, front, and end views of various solid objects. The views are flat—without perspective, which means that the points in the viewed surface are viewed along parallel lines of vision. In the upper-left corner is the top view and the projection is looking down on it. In the lower-left corner is the front view, and the projection is looking at the object from the front. In the lower-right corner is the projection looking at the object from the end, which is labeled end view. These views are always in the same positions and are labeled accordingly.

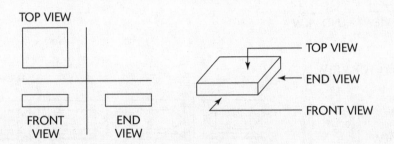

If there were a hole in the block, the views would look like this:

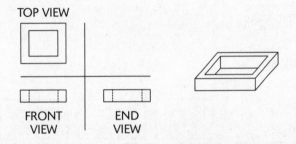

Note that lines that cannot be seen on the surface in some particular view are dotted in that view.

In the problems that follow, two views will be shown, with four alternatives to complete the set. You are to select the correct one and mark it on the answer sheet.

Example: Choose the correct end view.

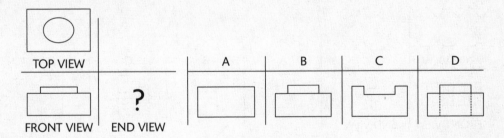

The front view shows that there is a smaller block on the base and that there is no hole. The top view shows that the block is round and in the center of the base. The answer, therefore, must be B.

In the problems that follow, it is not always the end view that must be selected; sometimes it is the top view or front view that is missing.

Proceed to Questions 16–30.

GO ON TO THE NEXT PAGE

16. Choose the correct TOP VIEW.

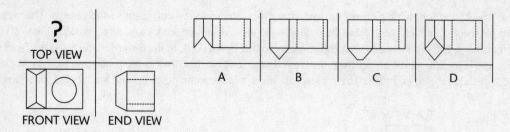

17. Choose the correct TOP VIEW.

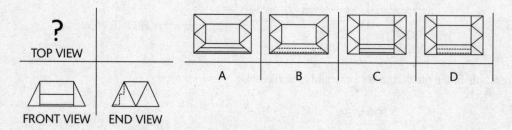

18. Choose the correct TOP VIEW.

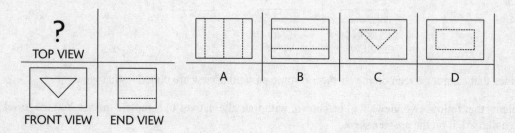

19. Choose the correct END VIEW.

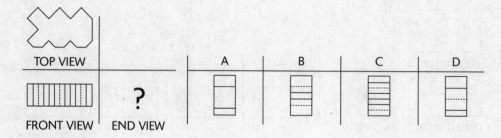

20. Choose the correct FRONT VIEW.

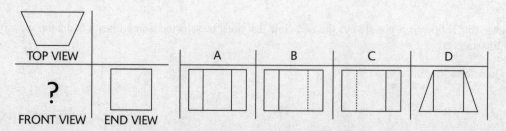

21. Choose the correct END VIEW.

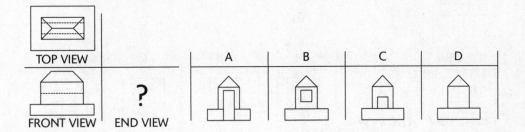

22. Choose the correct END VIEW.

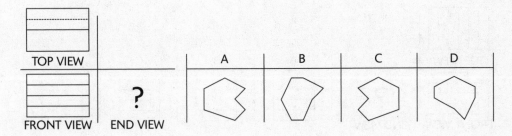

23. Choose the correct END VIEW.

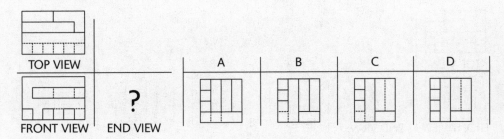

24. Choose the correct TOP VIEW.

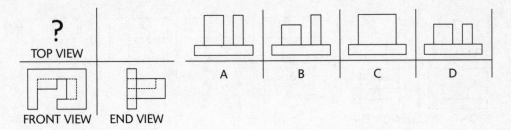

GO ON TO THE NEXT PAGE

25. Choose the correct END VIEW.

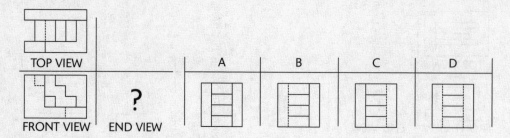

26. Choose the correct END VIEW.

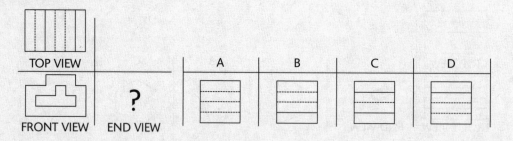

27. Choose the correct END VIEW.

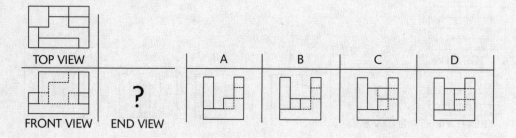

28. Choose the correct TOP VIEW.

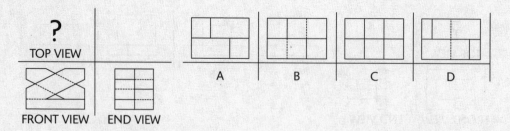

29. Choose the correct FRONT VIEW.

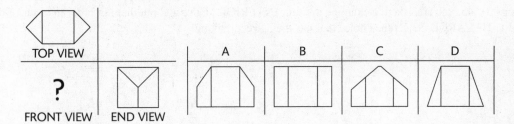

30. Choose the correct TOP VIEW.

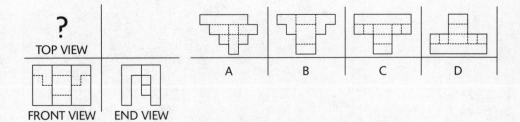

GO ON TO THE NEXT PAGE

Part 3

For Questions 31–45, you are asked to examine the four INTERIOR angles and put them in order in terms of degrees from SMALL TO LARGE. Select the choice that has the correct ranking.

Example:

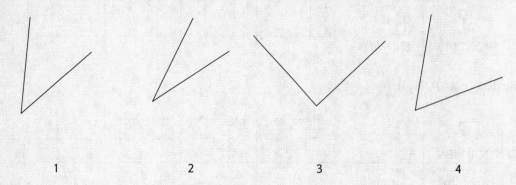

| 1 | 2 | 3 | 4 |

    A. 1 – 2 – 3 – 4
    B. 2 – 1 – 4 – 3
    C. 1 – 3 – 2 – 4
    D. 3 – 4 – 1 – 2

The correct ranking of the angles from small to large is 2 – 1 – 4 – 3; therefore, B is correct.

Proceed to Questions 31–45.

31.

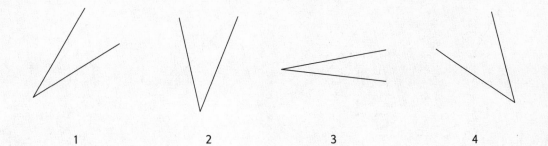

        1   2   3   4

A. 3 – 1 – 2 – 4
B. 3 – 1 – 4 – 2
C. 1 – 3 – 2 – 4
D. 1 – 2 – 3 – 4

32.

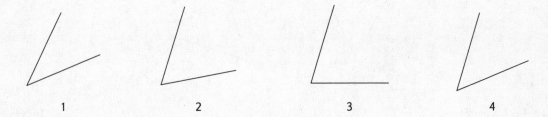

        1   2   3   4

A. 4 – 1 – 2 – 3
B. 1 – 2 – 4 – 3
C. 1 – 4 – 2 – 3
D. 4 – 1 – 3 – 2

33.

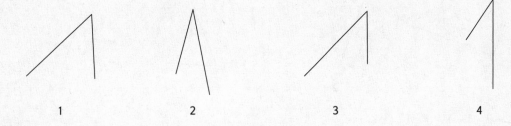

        1   2   3   4

A. 4 – 2 – 3 – 1
B. 2 – 4 – 3 – 1
C. 4 – 2 – 1 – 3
D. 2 – 4 – 1 – 3

GO ON TO THE NEXT PAGE

34.

1   2   3   4

A. 4 – 1 – 3 – 2
B. 1 – 4 – 2 – 3
C. 1 – 4 – 3 – 2
D. 4 – 1 – 2 – 3

35.

1   2   3   4

A. 4 – 1 – 3 – 2
B. 1 – 4 – 3 – 2
C. 4 – 1 – 2 – 3
D. 4 – 3 – 1 – 2

36.

1   2   3   4

A. 2 – 3 – 1 – 4
B. 1 – 2 – 3 – 4
C. 1 – 3 – 2 – 4
D. 3 – 2 – 1 – 4

37.

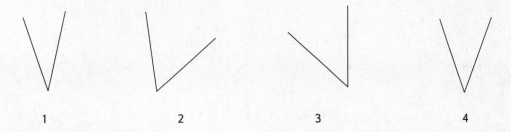

1   2   3   4

A.   1 – 4 – 2 – 3
B.   4 – 1 – 3 – 2
C.   4 – 1 – 2 – 3
D.   1 – 4 – 3 – 2

38.

1   2   3   4

A.   3 – 2 – 4 – 1
B.   2 – 3 – 4 – 1
C.   2 – 4 – 3 – 1
D.   3 – 4 – 2 – 1

39.

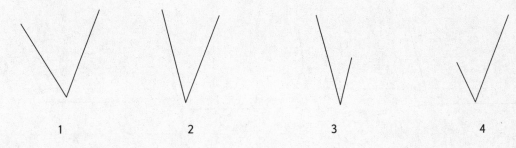

1   2   3   4

A.   3 – 4 – 2 – 1
B.   3 – 2 – 4 – 1
C.   2 – 3 – 4 – 1
D.   2 – 4 – 3 – 1

GO ON TO THE NEXT PAGE

40.

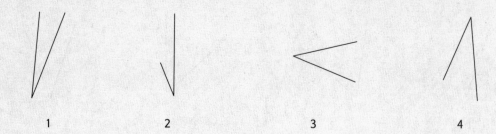

A. 2 – 1 – 4 – 3
B. 2 – 1 – 3 – 4
C. 1 – 2 – 3 – 4
D. 1 – 2 – 4 – 3

41.

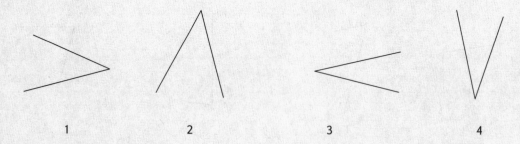

A. 3 – 4 – 1 – 2
B. 4 – 3 – 1 – 2
C. 3 – 4 – 2 – 1
D. 4 – 1 – 3 – 2

42.

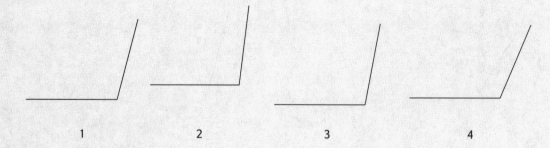

A. 2 – 1 – 3 – 4
B. 2 – 3 – 4 – 1
C. 2 – 3 – 1 – 4
D. 2 – 4 – 1 – 3

43.

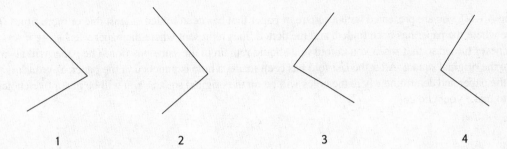

1 2 3 4

A. 3 – 1 – 2 – 4
B. 3 – 1 – 4 – 2
C. 1 – 3 – 2 – 4
D. 1 – 3 – 4 – 2

44.

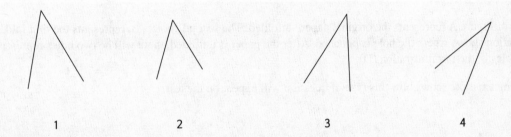

1 2 3 4

A. 2 – 4 – 3 – 1
B. 4 – 3 – 2 – 1
C. 4 – 3 – 1 – 2
D. 2 – 4 – 1 – 3

45.

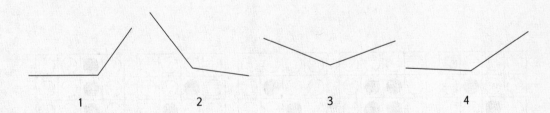

1 2 3 4

A. 1 – 4 – 3 – 2
B. 1 – 2 – 3 – 4
C. 1 – 2 – 4 – 3
D. 1 – 3 – 2 – 4

GO ON TO THE NEXT PAGE

Part 4

For Questions 46–60, you are presented with a square of paper that has been folded at least one or more times. The solid lines indicate where the paper has been folded, and the dotted lines represent where the paper was before it was folded. The paper is never turned so that when you unfold it, it should remain in the same position. The paper will always be folded within the original square. After the last fold has been made, a hole is punched in the paper. Your task is to mentally unfold the paper and determine where the holes will be on the original square. You will be given five choices (A–E) from which to make your choice.

Example 1:

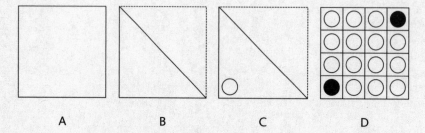

| A | B | C | D |

In Example 1, Figure A represents the original paper, unfolded. The second choice, B, represents the first fold. The third illustration shows where the hole is punched. After the paper is unfolded, there will be two holes represented by the dark circles in the last illustration (D).

The following example shows how this type of question will appear on the test.

Example 2:

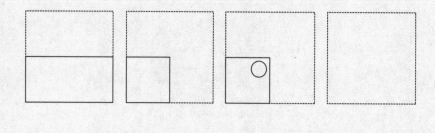

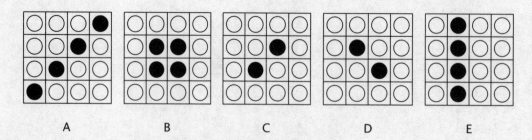

| A | B | C | D | E |

The correct answer to this example is B. With one fold, you would have two holes punched. With two folds, you will have four holes punched.

Proceed to Questions 46–60

46.

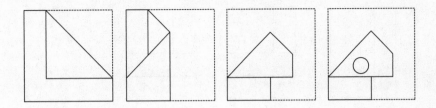

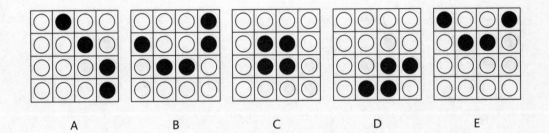

A   B   C   D   E

47.

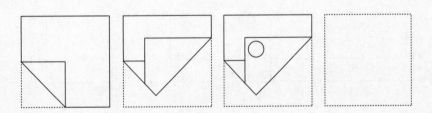

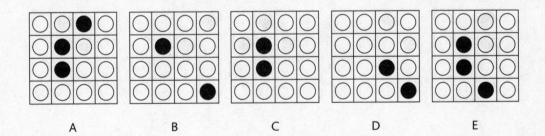

A   B   C   D   E

GO ON TO THE NEXT PAGE

48.

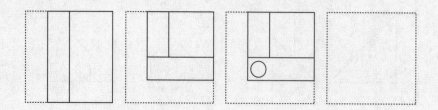

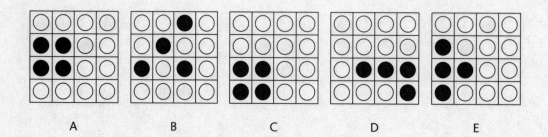

A   B   C   D   E

49.

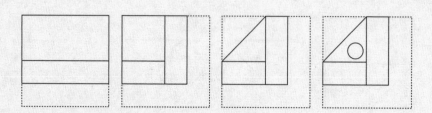

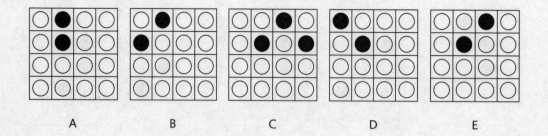

A   B   C   D   E

50.

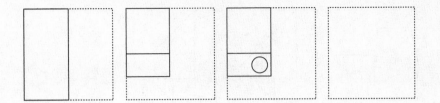

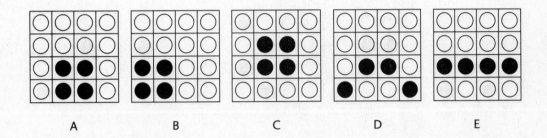

A   B   C   D   E

51.

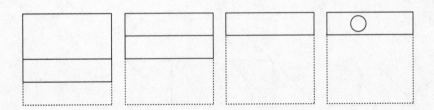

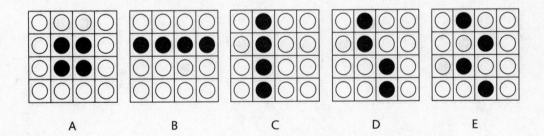

A   B   C   D   E

GO ON TO THE NEXT PAGE

52.

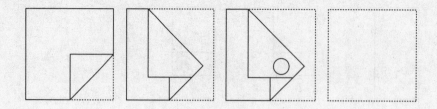

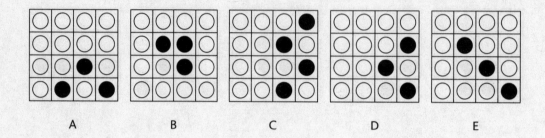

A   B   C   D   E

53.

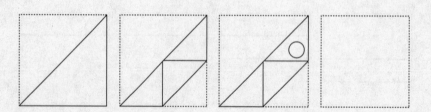

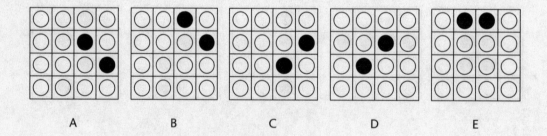

A   B   C   D   E

GO ON TO THE NEXT PAGE

54.

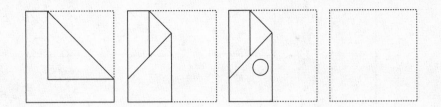

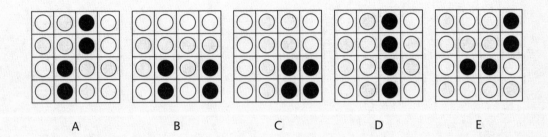

A   B   C   D   E

55.

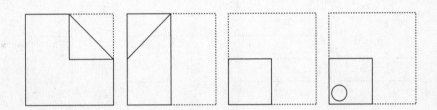

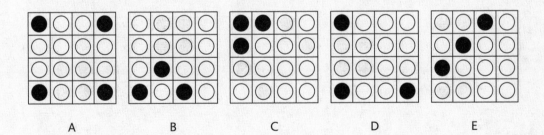

A   B   C   D   E

GO ON TO THE NEXT PAGE

56.

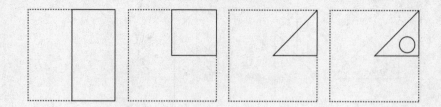

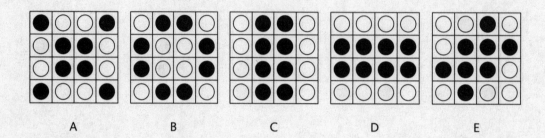

A   B   C   D   E

57.

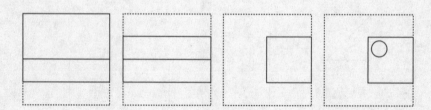

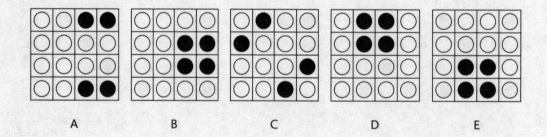

A   B   C   D   E

58.

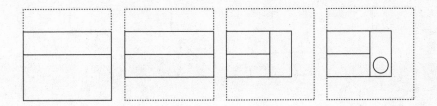

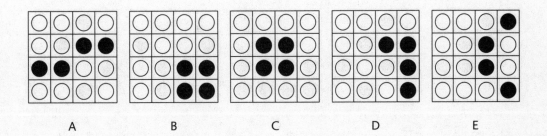

A   B   C   D   E

59.

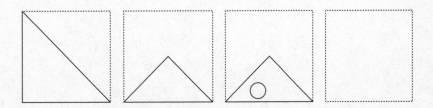

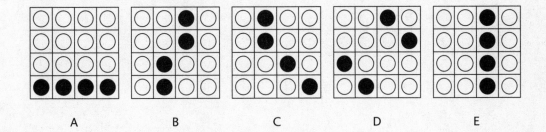

A   B   C   D   E

GO ON TO THE NEXT PAGE

60.

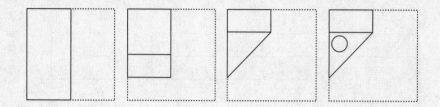

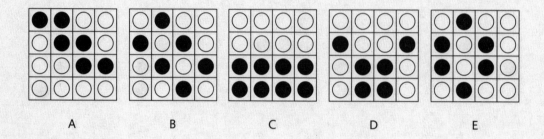

Part 5

Each figure has been made by attaching cubes of an identical size. After being attached, each group was painted on all sides. Only the bottom sides on which each cube rests were not painted. Hidden cubes are those that support other cubes.

For Questions 61–75, you are asked to answer the following questions based on the related figure:

- How many cubes have only one of their sides painted?
- How many cubes have only two of their sides painted?
- How many cubes have only three of their sides painted?
- How many cubes have only four of their sides painted?
- How many cubes have all five of there sides painted?

There will be no problems for which zero (0) is the correct answer.

In the following figures, how many cubes have two of their exposed sides painted?

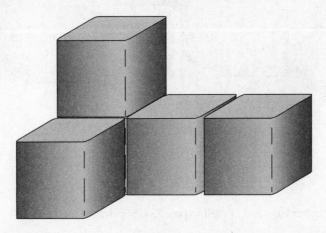

Figure 1

- **A.** 1 cube
- **B.** 2 cubes
- **C.** 3 cubes
- **D.** 4 cubes
- **E.** 5 cubes

There are five cubes in Figure 1. Four cubes are visible and one is hidden, which supports the cube on the top row. The hidden cube has only two sides painted. The top cube has five sides painted. The front cube and the cube on the right each have four sides painted, and the middle cube has three sides painted. The correct answer is A.

Remember that after the cubes have been attached, each figure was painted on all exposed sides, except the bottom.

Proceed to Questions 61–75.

GO ON TO THE NEXT PAGE

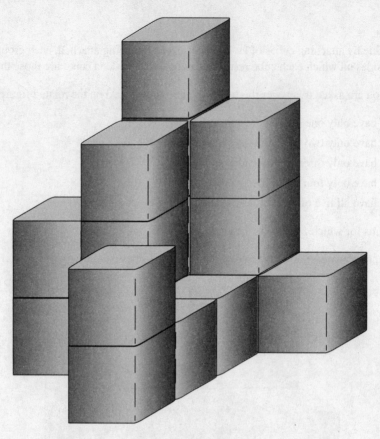

Figure A

61. In Figure A, how many cubes have two of their exposed sides painted?

    A. 1 cube

    B. 2 cubes

    C. 3 cubes

    D. 4 cubes

    E. 5 cubes

62. In Figure A, how many cubes have three of their exposed sides painted?

    A. 1 cube

    B. 2 cubes

    C. 3 cubes

    D. 4 cubes

    E. 5 cubes

63. In Figure A, how many cubes have four of their exposed sides painted?

    A. 1 cube

    B. 2 cubes

    C. 3 cubes

    D. 4 cubes

    E. 5 cubes

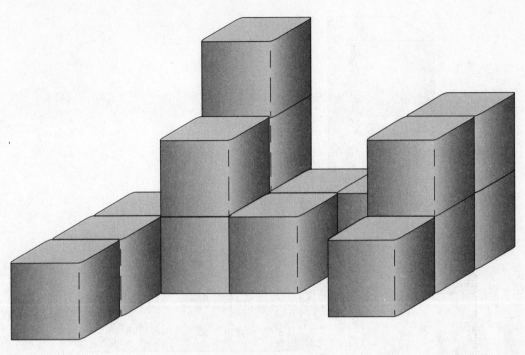

Figure B

64. In Figure B, how many cubes have two of their exposed sides painted?

    A. 1 cube
    B. 2 cubes
    C. 3 cubes
    D. 4 cubes
    E. 5 cubes

65. In Figure B, how many cubes have three of their exposed sides painted?

    A. 1 cube
    B. 2 cubes
    C. 3 cubes
    D. 4 cubes
    E. 5 cubes

GO ON TO THE NEXT PAGE

Figure C

66. In Figure C, how many cubes have two of their exposed sides painted?

    A. 1 cube
    B. 2 cubes
    C. 3 cubes
    D. 4 cubes
    E. 5 cubes

67. In Figure C, how many cubes have three of their exposed sides painted?

    A. 1 cube
    B. 2 cubes
    C. 3 cubes
    D. 4 cubes
    E. 5 cubes

68. In Figure C, how many cubes have four of their exposed sides painted?

    A. 1 cube
    B. 2 cubes
    C. 3 cubes
    D. 4 cubes
    E. 5 cubes

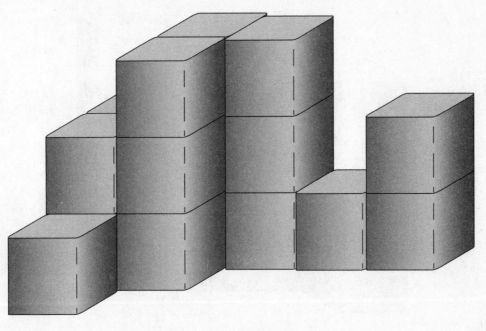

Figure D

69. In Figure D, how many cubes have one of their exposed sides painted?

    A. 1 cube
    B. 2 cubes
    C. 3 cubes
    D. 4 cubes
    E. 5 cubes

70. In Figure D, how many cubes have two of their exposed sides painted?

    A. 1 cube
    B. 2 cubes
    C. 3 cubes
    D. 4 cubes
    E. 5 cubes

71. In Figure D, how many cubes have four of their exposed sides painted?

    A. 1 cube
    B. 2 cubes
    C. 3 cubes
    D. 4 cubes
    E. 5 cubes

72. In Figure D, how many cubes have five of their exposed sides painted?

    A. 1 cube
    B. 2 cubes
    C. 3 cubes
    D. 4 cubes
    E. 5 cubes

GO ON TO THE NEXT PAGE

Figure E

73. In Figure E, how many cubes have one of their exposed sides painted?

    A.   1 cube
    B.   2 cubes
    C.   3 cubes
    D.   4 cubes
    E.   5 cubes

74. In Figure E, how many cubes have four of their exposed sides painted?

    A.   1 cube
    B.   2 cubes
    C.   3 cubes
    D.   4 cubes
    E.   5 cubes

75. In Figure E, how many cubes have five of their exposed sides painted?

    A.   1 cube
    B.   2 cubes
    C.   3 cubes
    D.   4 cubes
    E.   5 cubes

Part 6

In Questions 76–90, a flat pattern is presented. Based on your perception of this pattern, you must visualize what it will look like when it is folded into a three-dimensional figure. You are given four choices but only one will be the correct answer. There is only one correct figure in each set. The outside of the pattern is what is seen in the center.

Example:

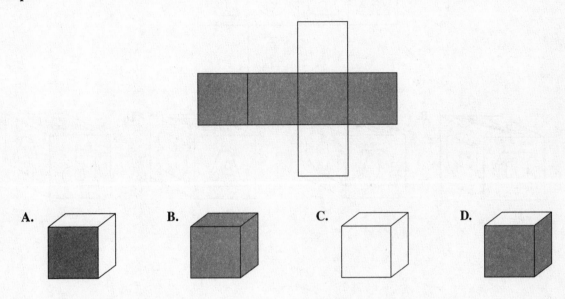

A.   B.   C.   D.

One of the preceding figures (A, B, C, or D) can be formed from the flat pattern in the center. The only figure that corresponds to the pattern is D. If the shaded surfaces are looked at as the sides of the box, then all four sides must be shaded, while the top and the bottom are white.

Proceed to Questions 76–90.

GO ON TO THE NEXT PAGE

76.

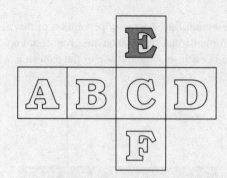

A.    B.    C.    D.

77.

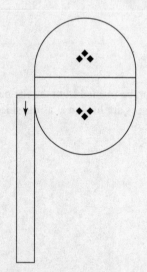

A. 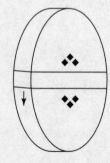   B. 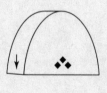   C. 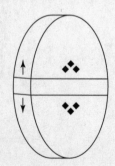   D.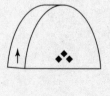

78.

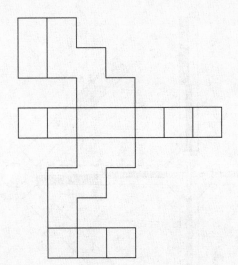

A.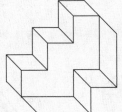

B.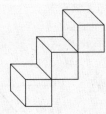

C.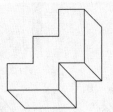

D.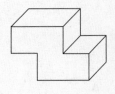

GO ON TO THE NEXT PAGE

79.

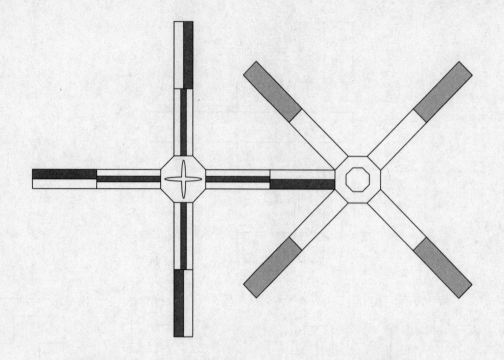

A.   B.   C.   D.

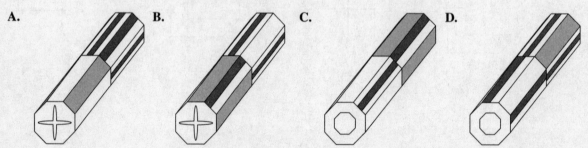

80.

A.   B.   C.   D.

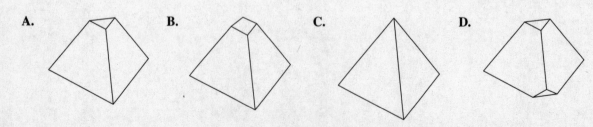

81.

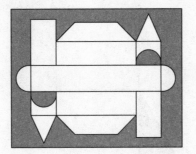

A.   B.   C.   D.

82.

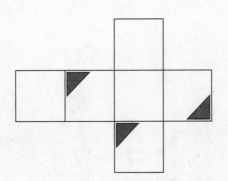

A.   B.   C.   D.

GO ON TO THE NEXT PAGE

83.

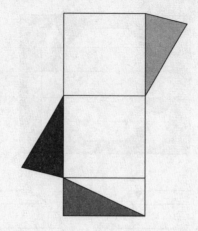

A. 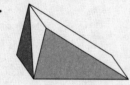 B.  C.  D.

84.

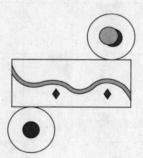

A.   B.   C.   D.

85.

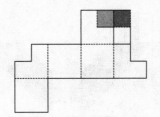

A.   B.   C.   D.

86.

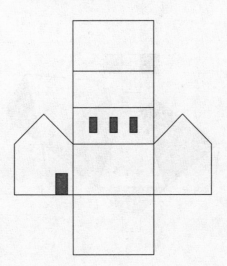

A. 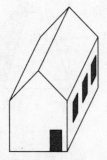   B. 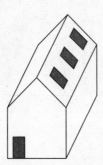   C. 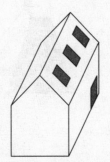   D.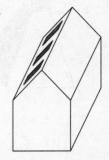

GO ON TO THE NEXT PAGE

87.

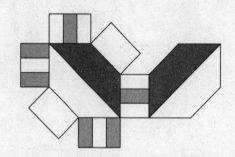

A.    B. 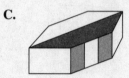   C. 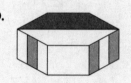   D.

88.

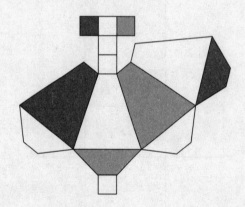

A. 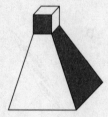   B. 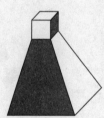   C. 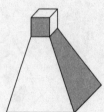   D.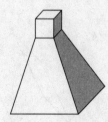

89.

A.   B. 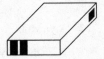 C.   D.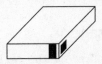

90.

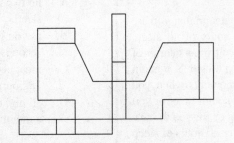

A.   B. 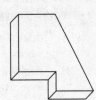 C. 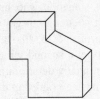 D.

IF YOU FINISH BEFORE TIME IS CALLED, CHECK YOUR WORK ON THIS SECTION ONLY. DO NOT WORK ON ANY OTHER SECTION IN THE TEST.

Reading Comprehension

Time: 60 Minutes

50 Questions

Directions: This section measures your ability to read and understand written English similar to what one may expect in a college or university setting. Read each passage and answer the questions based on what is stated or implied in the passage.

Passage 1

College students are known for pulling "all nighters" before exams. Business executives, preparing reports, might stay up all night before a crucial presentation. A truck driver might push through the night so that he can get his cargo to the destination on time. You might have a caffeine drink to keep you awake or loud music to help those eyelids from drooping. But you cannot stifle a yawn, and that is the first sign that your brain is checking out for the night!

The yawn is the body's first external sign that you are losing your concentration. After 18 hours of no sleep, your reaction time begins to slow down from a quarter of a second to a half of a second and then longer. You begin to experience bouts of microsleep, moments when you zone out for 2 to 20 seconds. This is enough time for you to drift into another lane while driving or for you to have to reread a passage a second time. After 20 hours of sleep deprivation, you actually begin to nod off. Your reaction time is now equivalent to that of someone who has a blood alcohol level of 0.08, which is enough to get you arrested for driving under the influence in 49 states! Although you might feel that you get a second wind as the sun rises, your condition is continually deteriorating.

All through the animal kingdom, sleep ranks up there among the other necessities like food, water, shelter, and air for survival. Yet scientists still don't know precisely what sleep is for. We immediately think of rejuvenation. However, except for the muscles, which need periodic relaxation not necessarily sleep, the rest of our internal organs continue to chug along regardless of whether we are awake or asleep. Most researchers will agree that the part of the body that benefits us the most from sleep is our brain. Yet, scientists do not agree on what these benefits are. Some feel that sleep is the time that the brain reviews and consolidates all the streams of information it has gathered while awake. Others suggest that it is a time which allows the brain to refuel and slush out wastes. A third theory suggests that in some mysterious way, sleep helps the brain master various skills, such as how to play the piano and ride a bike.

1. A yawn is
   A. the way to indicate how much sleep you need.
   B. a sign that you are bored with the lecture.
   C. an indication that your brain needs rest.
   D. a rude thing to do in public.

2. The research shows that
   A. no two people need the same amount of sleep.
   B. as you get tired, it takes your reflexes two seconds to respond to stimuli.
   C. most people will be affected negatively after 18 hours of no sleep.
   D. all nighters are not harmful if done only once a month.

3. The word *microsleep* in the third sentence of the second paragraph most closely means
   A. that computer jargon is affecting medical words.
   B. that automatically, your brain will zone out to rejuvenate itself.
   C. that the word is the same as cat naps.
   D. that you are not dreaming.

4. The comparison between sleep deprivation and drinking alcohol is done to show
   A. that drinking and driving is dangerous.
   B. that drinking will just speed up the need to sleep.
   C. that both situations severely impair your judgment.
   D. that there should be a law against sleepy people driving.

5. When you get your *second wind,* it means

- **A.** that you are now ready to continue work because you are awake again.
- **B.** that your condition is still deteriorating, even though you don't know it.
- **C.** that your body is able to work harder now because you have gotten over the tiredness.
- **D.** that you can drive long distances now.

6. A contradictory fact to the concept of rejuvenation is

- **A.** that only your muscles sleep.
- **B.** that sometimes you don't feel rested when you wake up.
- **C.** that none of your organs rest when you sleep.
- **D.** that all creatures, animals, and humans need sleep.

7. The article ends with three theories that

- **A.** all focus on sleep's affects on the brain.
- **B.** indicate that sleep will help you perform better.
- **C.** completely contradict each other in scope and depth.
- **D.** are restatements of the basic tenet, sleep is necessary.

GO ON TO THE NEXT PAGE

Passage 2

A slimy lump of green is clumped at the bottom of a plastic bucket, the contents of which are hardly distinguishable. This jellied mass is actually a dozen bullfrogs, which have traveled thousands of miles to New York City's Chinatown to await their fate. Although they are native to North America, these particularly suspicious specimens have been raised in South America and imported to America. The trafficking of bullfrogs is big business. The U.S. Fish and Wildlife Service has reported that in 2002, nearly 49 million amphibians were imported for trade. Although most of the creatures were brought in to be pets, many found their place on people's dinner tables. Their skins are discarded in the trash and become vehicles for the communication of disease.

Chytridiomycosis, an amphibious fungal plague has cropped up throughout the world. These outbreaks have often led to the extinction of a species. Yet, not a single bullfrog or any other type of amphibian has been inspected at the U.S. border. Since September 11, our concern about biosecurity has been heightened. Tens of millions of dollars have been spent to try to protect the U.S., all the while, foreign pathogens sail into the country hidden in the bodies of exotic wildlife and their accompanying fleas and ticks. There is an estimated $1.5 million dollars spent in the legal business of U.S. wildlife imports, but there is an equally large illegal pet trade. However, there are fewer than 100 inspectors to investigate over 32 points of entry into the United States.

The Wildlife Services' aim is to protect endangered species and to ensure humane transport of animals. The Department of Agriculture inspects only for diseases that threaten livestock and poultry. The Center for Disease Control mandates public health issues so the idea of wildlife diseases falls through the cracks.

The result is that diseases spread easily among animals and through feeding stations that breed infection. Two-thirds of known human pathogens are zoonotic, able to pass from animals to humans and vice versa. West Nile virus, the bird flu, and Hendra-Nipah are recent examples of human diseases that started out in animals and birds. The problem is compounded by the fact that scientists have discovered that many of these animals host bacteria which is resistant to antibiotics. Thus, the germs are not just cycling between wildlife, livestock, and humans, but they are becoming more dangerous with each pass. Salmonella enterica variant Typhimurium DT104, was a fairly common serotype first seen about 15 years ago. Now it is resistant to eight drugs. So even though there are fewer incidents of food-borne salmonella outbreaks, there are more instances of multi-drug resistant bacteria. For most pathogens, there are no boundaries between animals and people, so the globe-trotting frogs are literally drops in the bucket when it comes to the modern spread of disease.

8. Bullfrogs are imported because

   A. they are not native to North America.
   B. they are needed for laboratory tests.
   C. they are part of the import trade business.
   D. they are easy to transport.

9. These frogs are mostly used for

   A. food.
   B. experiments.
   C. pets.
   D. high school science labs.

10. In paragraph two, the word *chytridiomycosis* means

   A. a disease of the frogs.
   B. a chemical taken from the frogs.
   C. a medicine used for the frogs.
   D. a medicine made from the frogs.

11. The effect that September 11 had on our country has

   A. effectively made the infiltration of foreign pathogens less.
   B. has made inspectors look more closely at the import of frogs.
   C. has increased the concern for biosecurity and, thus, uncovered numerous pathogens.
   D. has had no effect on the import of amphibious creatures.

12. The purpose of the third paragraph is to show

   A. how despite all the agencies, things still fall through the cracks.
   B. that the United States has many agencies that overlap their responsibilities.
   C. that the United States cares greatly for wildlife.
   D. that terrorists cannot infiltrate our livestock.

13. In the second sentence of the fourth paragraph, the word *zoonotic* most closely means

   A. able to pass from humans to animals.
   B. able to pass from animals to humans.
   C. able to pass back and forth between animals and humans.
   D. able to only affect human or animals but not both.

14. The inclusion of information about salmonella was to

    A. tell people to be careful of what they eat.

    B. make people more comfortable to know that it is less frequently found.

    C. alert people to the fact that bacteria can become resistant to drugs.

    D. Compare it to West Nile virus and Hendrah-Nipah.

GO ON TO THE NEXT PAGE

Passage 3

The winter of 2005 in the Northern Hemisphere has provided much excitement to those who enjoy gazing at the heavens. Visible to the naked eye under a dark sky have been a string of comets. Comet c/2004 Q2, Machholz, can be seen during February in the northern sky as it slowly slides toward the North Star, Polaris. At the 5th magnitude, it is fainter than the Beehive star cluster, which at this time is beginning to rise in the east. If you are in the city, you will need binoculars to locate them. Like a pop fly in a baseball rounding the top of its arc, Machholz appears to slow this month. Thus, from the Earth's perspective, it lies almost straight up from the North Pole. This gives us a good sight line of its tail, which points away from the Sun. In fact, one can see two tails: one that is slightly bluish in color due to the ionized gas blowing straight out in the solar wind of charged particles and a yellow-white tail as ejected motes of dust begin tracing their own orbital paths. As these tails leave the brighter background of the Milky Way, they can become more distinguishable.

Another glorious sight is Saturn with its rings. It can easily be located because it is the steady, pale-yellow "star" that is halfway up in the east as the sky grows dark. If the Earth's atmosphere is not too turbulent, you can detect the shadow of the planet on its rings. A couple of months ago, the shadow would have been seen on the opposite side, and in the afternoon, it appears longer.

Jupiter has been seen the previous October and is always full of intrigue. As the planet rises before midnight, its view becomes very clear. Will the Great Red Spot begin a comeback? Are there any white ovals? Even though the Moon lies closer to the Earth than Jupiter, the perspective makes it seem much closer to Jupiter. Thus, at a time during the winter cycle, Jupiter will obscure the red super giant, Antares. In truth, what meets the eye in the sky can be deceiving but also exciting.

15. Machholz is

    A. a planet.

    B. a moon.

    C. a comet.

    D. a beehive cluster.

16. The Macholtz and the Beehive star cluster

    A. can be seen at the same time.

    B. are moving away from each other.

    C. can never be seen at the same time.

    D. are names for the same comet.

17. The use of the baseball metaphor is

    A. to pique the reader's attention.

    B. to illustrate the placement and movement of the comet.

    C. to talk about its brightness and speed.

    D. to appeal to American sport's fans.

18. The blue comet tail is due to

    A. the weather conditions.

    B. the type of binoculars you use.

    C. the time of night you see the comet.

    D. the amount of ions in the gas.

19. Jupiter's rings

    A. never change their placement to the viewer.

    B. never change their shape to the viewer.

    C. only change size in the afternoon.

    D. can only be seen at night.

20. The Red Spot and white ovals are

    A. part of cosmic mythology.

    B. characteristics of Mars.

    C. variable unexplained characteristics.

    D. traits of comets and stars.

21. Antares is

    A. a planet near Jupiter.

    B. a red superstar.

    C. a large comet.

    D. a Greek giant.

Passage 4

The spirit of adventure has always been basic to human nature both in the imagination and in reality. Jules Verne wrote about traveling the world in 180 days, a magical concept in a balloon. Captain Joshua Slocum, 100 years ago, sailed a vessel around the world alone. Now, a small ocean glider named Spray is the first autonomous underwater vehicle, or AUV, to cross the Gulf Stream underwater. This voyage has proven the viability of self-propelled gliders for long-distance scientific missions and providing new possibilities for the studies of the oceans.

The Spray was launched on Sept. 11, 2004, about 100 miles south of Nantucket Island, MA. Looking like a model airplane, it is six feet long with a four-foot wing span and no visible moving parts. It journeyed between Cape Cod and Bermuda, traveling at one-half a knot, or 12 miles a day. It would surface three times a day to measure various properties of the ocean and then submerge to 1,000 meters in depth. During its 15-minute surfacing, the position in the ocean and conditions such as temperature and salinity are relayed back to Woods Hole, MA, and California via satellite.

The journey was not without its setbacks. Two malfunctions brought the Spray back to Woods Hole before its third successful venture. Even then, there were challenges. When it began to cross the Gulf Stream, the surface currents exceeded six mph across the width of the glider, catapulting it on a fast ride north. In just two days, they lost two weeks' of progress. However, the excellent communication with the vehicle from the command post allowed the glider to get back on track. Since the Spray has a range of 6,000 miles, it could probably cross the entire Atlantic Ocean. The major concern is whether the Spray can stay at sea for months at a relatively low cost. If so, this would allow observations of large-scale changes under the ocean that usually go unobserved.

The potential for the wide-spread use of gliders in all bodies of water are astounding. Spray gliders can look at entire sections of ocean basins like the Atlantic or serve as moorings for a keeping station at a single point. Unlike humans who need to stop for breaks, gliders can carry out missions from several weeks to as long as six months. Oceanographic gliders are now at the stage similar to the start of aviation. Within a few years, they will be as commonplace as air travel is now.

22. AUV is

    A.   a new type of military submarine.

    B.   a new type of four wheel drive car.

    C.   a new type of unmanned water vehicle.

    D.   a type of unexplained phenomenon.

23. Which statement is true?

    A.   There are no moving parts.

    B.   The vehicle looks a bit like a plane.

    C.   It is about the size of a super jet.

    D.   It is considered a nuclear powered glider.

24. The purpose of this vehicle is to

    A.   take sightseeing trips between Cape Cod and Bermuda.

    B.   examine fish underwater.

    C.   measure the saltiness of the water.

    D.   explore underwater places to moor submarine.

25. The reason why the Spray is successful

    A.   is because it has excellent communication with the ground crew.

    B.   is because it can travel across the Atlantic Ocean.

    C.   is because it is easy to maneuver.

    D.   is because it can ride the waves easily.

26. The only drawback about this invention is

    A.   keeping the cost down.

    B.   making enough vehicles so that they can be everywhere.

    C.   not competing against regular submarines.

    D.   convincing people of their worth.

27. The comparison to aviation is to

    A.   choose that vehicle because it looks like a plane.

    B.   go along with the term *glider* because it travels that way.

    C.   show that although they are sparse now, they can become very common.

    D.   show they will soon be used instead of planes.

28. The tone in the article is

    A.   skeptical about non-manned research.

    B.   excited about the global implications.

    C.   afraid that money will be wasted in this venture.

    D.   angry that it was not more commonly used.

GO ON TO THE NEXT PAGE

Passage 5

Cholera, a highly infectious disease, has resulted in millions of deaths time after time over centuries. It is caused by the bacterium *Vibrio cholerae,* first isolated by Robert Koch in 1883.

The organism enters the body through the digestive tract when contaminated food or water is ingested. The bacteria multiply in the digestive tract and establish infection. As they die, they release a potent toxin that leads to severe diarrhea and vomiting. This results in extreme dehydration, muscle cramps, kidney failure, collapse, and sometimes death. If the disease is treated promptly, death is less likely.

In many countries, a common source of the organism is raw or poorly cooked seafood taken from contaminated waters. The disease is especially prevalent after a natural disaster or other destruction that results in a lack of fresh water. Sewer systems fail, and waste travels into rivers or streams; piped water is not available, so people must take their drinking and cooking water from rivers or streams. Because people frequently develop communities along waterways, the disease can be spread easily from one community to the next community downstream, resulting in serious epidemics.

29. The word *infectious* in the first sentence is closest in meaning to

    A. communicable.
    B. severe.
    C. isolated.
    D. common.

30. According to the passage, cholera is caused by

    A. a virus.
    B. a bacterium.
    C. kidney failure.
    D. dehydration.

31. All of the following are probable causes of infection except

    A. eating food cooked with contaminated water.
    B. eating undercooked seafood.
    C. eating overcooked pork.
    D. eating raw oysters.

32. What is the logical order of the events leading to the illness?

    A. Sanitary system fails, so fresh water is unavailable; disaster occurs; people drink the water; contaminated water flows into waterways.
    B. Disaster occurs; sanitary system fails, so fresh water is unavailable; people drink the water; contaminated water flows into waterways.
    C. Disaster occurs; contaminated water flows into waterways; sanitary system fails, so fresh water is unavailable; people drink the water.
    D. Contaminated water flows into waterways; disaster occurs; sanitary system fails, so fresh water is unavailable; people drink the water.

33. According to the passage, what is a symptom of the infection?

    A. release of a toxin by the bacteria
    B. regurgitation
    C. overeating
    D. epidemics

34. Which of the following would be an appropriate title for this passage?

    A. Dysentery and Its Effects
    B. Water Purification Systems and Their Importance
    C. Results of War and Natural Disasters
    D. The Causes and Effects of Cholera

35. The word *prevalent* in the third paragraph is closest in meaning to

    A. dangerous.
    B. commonplace.
    C. unusual.
    D. organized.

36. The word *lack* in the third paragraph is closest in meaning to

- **A.** contamination.
- **B.** multitude.
- **C.** shortage.
- **D.** well.

37. According to the passage, cholera

- **A.** is easily passed from one person to another.
- **B.** is not a real threat.
- **C.** is no more dangerous than the common cold.
- **D.** cannot be passed from one to another by casual contact.

38. What can you infer from the passage?

- **A.** Careful cooking and hygiene practices can reduce the chance of getting the disease.
- **B.** Water mixed with other substances will not pass the disease.
- **C.** The respiratory system is the most common area of entrance.
- **D.** Kidney disease is the most common cause of the illness.

39. The word *epidemics* at the end of the passage is closest in meaning to

- **A.** studies.
- **B.** vaccines.
- **C.** bacteria.
- **D.** plagues.

GO ON TO THE NEXT PAGE

Passage 6

The ubiquitous bar code, developed more than 20 years ago, is not a stagnant product. On the contrary, the technology has been improved so that it can be used more efficiently. Much less expensive than a computer chip, the bar code can hold more information than it has in the past by adding a second dimension to the structure.

The bar code consists of a series of parallel vertical bars or lines of two different widths, although sometimes four widths are used, printed in black on a white background. Barcodes are used for entering data into a computer system. The bars represent the binary digits 0 and 1, just like basic computer language, and sequences of these digits can indicate the numbers from 0 to 9, which can then be read by an optical laser scanner and processed by a digital computer. Arabic numbers appear below the code.

The traditional bar code has been used to monitor skiers at ski lifts and to determine price and perform inventory control on groceries, drugs, medical supplies, manufactured parts, and library books to name a few. The bar code used on grocery products, introduced in the 1970s, is called a universal product code (or UPC) and assigns each type of food or grocery product a unique code. The five digits on the left are assigned to a particular manufacturer or maker, and the five digits on the right are used by that manufacturer to identify a specific type or make of product. Traditional single dimension bar codes are not readily customizable because there is little extra space.

The two-dimensional bar code, with an information density of 1,100 bytes, allows a considerably greater amount of information to be coded than does the traditional bar code, including customized information. It also has built-in redundancy, meaning that the identical information is duplicated on the same code. Therefore, if the code is damaged, it can still be read. The technology even allows pictures or text to be contained within the code, as well as barcode encryption. The new technology dramatically reduces the errors of the single dimensional bar code and reduces the enormous costs that some companies have reported in the past.

40. The word *ubiquitous* in the first sentence is closest in meaning to

- **A.** outdated.
- **B.** ever-present.
- **C.** new.
- **D.** complicated.

41. The word *stagnant* in the first sentence is closest in meaning to

- **A.** ever-changing.
- **B.** useful.
- **C.** stale.
- **D.** useless.

42. The author implies that the bar code

- **A.** has only recently become popular.
- **B.** will never change.
- **C.** is not useful.
- **D.** has existed in one-dimensional form for years.

43. The author's main purpose is to describe

- **A.** the current technology and newest innovation of bar codes.
- **B.** problems with the bar code.
- **C.** the UPC used in grocery stores.
- **D.** why the bar code is no longer viable.

44. Where in the final paragraph could the following sentence be logically placed?

"Thus, the manufacturer is able to add additional information on the bar code that it finds useful for its own tracking purposes."

The two-dimensional bar code, with an information density of 1,100 bytes, allows a considerably greater amount of information to be coded than does the traditional bar code, including customized information. (**A**) It also has built-in redundancy, meaning that the identical information is duplicated on the same code. (**B**) Therefore, if the code is damaged, it can still be read. (**C**) The technology even allows pictures or text to be contained within the code, as well as bar code encryption. (**D**) The new technology dramatically reduces the errors of the single dimensional bar code and reduces the enormous costs that some companies have reported in the past.

- **A.** (A)
- **B.** (B)
- **C.** (C)
- **D.** (D)

45. Which of the following can be a UPC symbol?

A. A code with five digits on the left, five on the right, two different widths, and one number under each

B. A code with six digits on the left, four on the right, two different widths, and one Roman numeral under each

C. A code with five digits on the left, five digits on the right, five or six different widths, and one number under each

D. A code with five digits on the left, five digits on the right, reverse form (white text on black background), and no numbers underneath

46. A UPC is a type of

A. computer program.

B. bar code.

C. grocery item.

D. scanner.

47. The word *widths* in the second paragraph refers to

A. its size.

B. its direction.

C. its location.

D. its content.

48. The word *traditional* in the third paragraph is closest in meaning to

A. conventional.

B. new.

C. logical.

D. technological.

49. In the past, a common use of the bar code was

A. to encrypt pictures.

B. to keep track of products stocked and sold.

C. to act as a computer.

D. to hide text.

50. The word *considerably* in the final paragraph is closest in meaning to

A. slightly.

B. technologically.

C. interestingly.

D. far.

IF YOU FINISH BEFORE TIME IS CALLED, CHECK YOUR WORK ON THIS SECTION ONLY. DO NOT WORK ON ANY OTHER SECTION IN THE TEST.

Quantitative Reasoning

Time: 45 Minutes

40 Questions

1. An employee earns $8.25 an hour. In 30 hours, what earnings are made?

   A. 240.00
   B. 247.50
   C. 250.00
   D. 255.75
   E. 260.00

2. $\frac{5}{16} + \frac{9}{24} =$

   A. $\frac{1}{4}$.
   B. $\frac{14}{48}$.
   C. $\frac{14}{40}$.
   D. $\frac{7}{20}$.
   E. $\frac{11}{16}$.

3. Seven more than 3 times a number is equal to 70. Find the number.

   A. 10
   B. 17
   C. 21
   D. 30
   E. 63

4. The area of one circle is 4 times as large as a smaller circle with a radius of 3 inches. The radius of the larger circle is

   A. 12 inches.
   B. 9 inches.
   C. 8 inches.
   D. 6 inches.
   E. 4 inches.

5. Which mathematical statement best represents the following?

   Six less a number is four.

   A. $4 < n + 6$
   B. $6 = n - 4$
   C. $6 < n + 4$
   D. $6 - n = 4$
   E. $n - 6 = 4$

6. How much change would you get back from a $20 bill if you purchased 8 CD covers costing $1.59 each?

   A. $7.28
   B. $10.41
   C. $12.00
   D. $12.72
   E. $18.41

7. If $a + b = 6$, what is the value of $3a + 3b$?

   A. 9
   B. 12
   C. 18
   D. 24
   E. It cannot be determined.

8. In a nut mixture, there are $1\frac{1}{8}$ pounds of almonds, $2\frac{3}{4}$ pounds of cashews, and $3\frac{1}{3}$ pounds of peanuts. The total weight of the mixture is

   A. $6\frac{1}{3}$ pounds.
   B. $6\frac{23}{24}$ pounds.
   C. $7\frac{5}{24}$ pounds.
   D. $7\frac{7}{12}$ pounds.
   E. $7\frac{3}{4}$ pounds.

9. Find the area of a triangle whose base is 3 inches less than its height, h.

   A. $\frac{1}{2}h^2 - 3h$
   B. $\frac{1}{2}h^2 - \frac{3}{2}h$
   C. $\frac{1}{2}h - \frac{3}{2}$
   D. $\frac{1}{2}h^2 - 3$
   E. $\frac{1}{2}h^2 + 3h$

10. Round $(2.5)^4$ to the nearest tenth.

   A. 10.0
   B. 25.4
   C. 38.9
   D. 39.0
   E. 39.1

11. Find the diagonal of a square whose area is 36.

   A. 6
   B. $6\sqrt{2}$
   C. 9
   D. $9\sqrt{2}$
   E. 18

12. Simplify $(3x^2 + 2x - 5) - (2x^2 - 5) + (4x - 7)$.

   A. $x^2 + 6x - 17$
   B. $x^2 + 4x - 7$
   C. $x^2 + 6x - 2$
   D. $x^2 + 6x - 7$
   E. $5x^2 + 6x - 7$

13. Joann ate $\frac{1}{4}$ of a peach pie and divides the remainder of the pie among her four friends. What fraction of the pie does each of her friends receive?

   A. $\frac{1}{8}$
   B. $\frac{3}{16}$
   C. $\frac{1}{4}$
   D. $\frac{1}{3}$
   E. $\frac{7}{12}$

14. The line perpendicular to the line $y = -\frac{1}{8}x + 7$ has a slope equal to what number?

   A. -8
   B. $-\frac{7}{8}$
   C. $-\frac{1}{8}$
   D. $\frac{1}{8}$
   E. 8

15. Roxanne deposited $300 into a savings account earning $5\frac{1}{4}$% annually. What is her balance after one year?

   A. $15.75
   B. $315
   C. $315.25
   D. $315.75
   E. $316.25

16. If $2y + 6 = 3y - 2$, then $y =$

   A. -2.
   B. 2.
   C. 4.
   D. 8.
   E. 12.

17. Cards normally sell for $3.00 each. How much was saved if 5 cards were purchased on sale for 2 for $5.00?

   A. $2.50
   B. $3.50
   C. $5.00
   D. $12.50
   E. $15.00

18. The area of the figure is

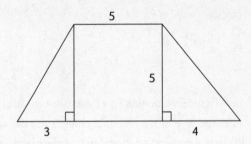

   A. 42.5
   B. 47
   C. 52.5
   D. 60
   E. 85

GO ON TO THE NEXT PAGE

19. If cos *y* > 0 and tan *y* < 0, then ∠*y* must lie in which quadrant?

   A. I
   B. II
   C. III
   D. IV
   E. I or IV

20. A winter coat is on sale for $150. If the original price was $200, what percent has the coat been discounted?

   A. 50%
   B. 40%
   C. 33%
   D. 25%
   E. 20%

21. How many minutes are there in one week?

   A. 10,080
   B. 5,760
   C. 1,440
   D. 420
   E. 168

22. What is the amplitude of the function $k(x) = 5 - 3\cos 8x$?

   A. 2
   B. 3
   C. 5
   D. 8
   E. 16

23. One-eighth of a bookstore's magazines are sold on a Friday. If $\frac{1}{4}$ of the remaining magazines are sold the next day, what fractional part of the magazines remains at the end of the second day?

   A. $\frac{1}{32}$
   B. $\frac{1}{8}$
   C. $\frac{7}{32}$
   D. $\frac{7}{16}$
   E. $\frac{21}{32}$

24. Standing by a pole, a boy $3\frac{1}{2}$ feet tall casts a 6-foot shadow. The pole casts a 24-foot shadow. How tall is the pole?

   A. 14 feet
   B. 18 feet
   C. 28 feet
   D. 41 feet
   E. 73.5 feet

25. The area of the shaded region is

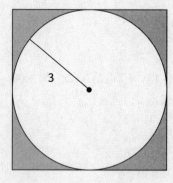

   A. $9 - 3\pi$.
   B. $36 - 3\pi^2$.
   C. $36 - 9\pi$.
   D. $81 - 9\pi$.
   E. 27π.

26. How many blocks with sides 4 inches in length can fit into a crate 3' × 2' × 2'?

   A. 3
   B. 32
   C. 196
   D. 324
   E. 392

27. What is the probability of rolling 2 even numbers in a row with a fair pair of dice?

   A. $\frac{1}{12}$
   B. $\frac{1}{8}$
   C. $\frac{1}{6}$
   D. $\frac{1}{4}$
   E. $\frac{1}{2}$

28. If x is a positive integer, solve $x^2 + 6x = 16$.

    A. 2

    B. 4

    C. 6

    D. 8

    E. 10

29. What is the product of the median and the mode of the following set:

$\{1, 2, 2, 5, 7, 7, 7\}$?

    A. 2

    B. 4

    C. 10

    D. 35

    E. 49

30. A rope is made by linking beads that are $\frac{1}{2}$" in diameter. How many feet long is a rope made from 60 beads?

    A. $2\frac{1}{2}$ ft

    B. $3\frac{1}{2}$ ft

    C. 10 ft

    D. 30 ft

    E. 120 ft

31. If $7p + 5q = -3$, find q when $p = 1$.

    A. -2

    B. $-\frac{8}{7}$

    C. -1

    D. $-\frac{2}{7}$

    E. 2

32. The radius of the smaller circle is $\frac{1}{4}$ as long as the larger circle. What percent of the figure shown is shaded?

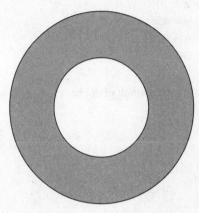

    A. $6\frac{1}{4}\%$

    B. 25%

    C. 75%

    D. 85%

    E. $93\frac{3}{4}\%$

33. Find the length of x in the figure.

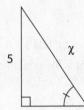

    A. $\frac{15}{4}$

    B. $6\frac{2}{3}$

    C. $7\frac{1}{3}$

    D. $8\frac{1}{4}$

    E. $8\frac{3}{4}$

GO ON TO THE NEXT PAGE

34. Which of the following values of x is a solution to the equation $\tan x = 0$?

    A. $x = 0°$
    B. $x = 30°$
    C. $x = 45°$
    D. $x = 60°$
    E. $90°$

35. What is the median of the set $\{1, 2, 2, 4, 4, 4\}$?

    A. 2
    B. 2.83
    C. 3
    D. 3.17
    E. 4

36. A Fahrenheit temperature can be changed to a Celsius temperature by using the formula $C = \frac{5}{9}(F - 32)$. If the temperature in Fahrenheit is $77°$, what is the temperature in Celsius?

    A. $20°$
    B. $22°$
    C. $24°$
    D. $25°$
    E. $26°$

37. Interest earned on an account totals $100. If the interest rate is $7\frac{1}{4}\%$, what is the principle amount?

    A. $725
    B. $1,333
    C. $1,379
    D. $1,428
    E. $1,456

38. What is the value of $8^{\frac{4}{3}}$?

    A. 4
    B. 8
    C. 16
    D. 32
    E. 64

39. The expression $1 - \cos^2 \theta$ is equivalent to

    A. $\tan^2\theta$
    B. $\cot^2\theta$
    C. $\sin^2\theta$
    D. $\csc^2\theta$
    E. $\sec^2\theta$

40. If $b^{-\frac{1}{4}}$, then what is the value of b?

    A. -16
    B. $-\frac{1}{16}$
    C. $\frac{1}{16}$
    D. $\frac{1}{8}$
    E. 16

IF YOU FINISH BEFORE TIME IS CALLED, CHECK YOUR WORK ON THIS SECTION ONLY. DO NOT WORK ON ANY OTHER SECTION IN THE TEST.

Answer Key for Practice Test 1

Natural Sciences

Biology

1. D	11. A	21. E	31. B
2. A	12. B	22. A	32. D
3. B	13. C	23. D	33. C
4. C	14. A	24. C	34. A
5. D	15. D	25. E	35. E
6. B	16. B	26. A	36. B
7. C	17. A	27. D	37. D
8. E	18. E	28. B	38. E
9. D	19. D	29. E	39. E
10. C	20. B	30. D	40. A

Chemistry

41. D	56. D	71. D	86. C
42. A	57. B	72. C	87. C
43. C	58. E	73. D	88. B
44. E	59. C	74. A	89. A
45. C	60. D	75. E	90. E
46. C	61. E	76. B	91. C
47. A	62. B	77. C	92. A
48. E	63. A	78. B	93. B
49. C	64. D	79. C	94. C
50. B	65. A	80. D	95. B
51. A	66. C	81. E	96. A
52. B	67. A	82. B	97. B
53. E	68. C	83. A	98. C
54. D	69. D	84. D	99. E
55. A	70. B	85. A	100. B

Perceptual Ability Test

Part 1

1. E	5. D	9. A	13. B
2. B	6. B	10. B	14. A
3. B	7. A	11. A	15. C
4. E	8. E	12. D	

Part 2

16. B	20. A	24. B	28. B
17. C	21. C	25. A	29. A
18. A	22. D	26. D	30. C
19. D	23. B	27. A	

Part 3

31. A	35. A	39. B	43. C
32. C	36. D	40. D	44. C
33. B	37. D	41. A	45. B
34. B	38. C	42. C	

Part 4

46. B	50. A	54. E	58. B
47. B	51. C	55. D	59. D
48. C	52. D	56. B	60. D
49. D	53. B	57. D	

Part 5

61. A	65. A	69. D	73. A
62. C	66. D	70. C	74. A
63. A	67. B	71. C	75. C
64. D	68. A	72. A	

Part 6

76. C	**80.** A	**84.** B	**88.** D
77. D	**81.** C	**85.** A	**89.** C
78. C	**82.** D	**86.** D	**90.** C
79. D	**83.** A	**87.** A	

Reading Comprehension

1. C	**14.** C	**27.** C	**40.** B
2. C	**15.** C	**28.** B	**41.** C
3. B	**16.** B	**29.** A	**42.** D
4. C	**17.** B	**30.** B	**43.** A
5. B	**18.** D	**31.** C	**44.** A
6. C	**19.** C	**32.** C	**45.** A
7. A	**20.** C	**33.** B	**46.** B
8. C	**21.** B	**34.** D	**47.** A
9. C	**22.** C	**35.** B	**48.** A
10. A	**23.** A	**36.** C	**49.** B
11. D	**24.** C	**37.** A	**50.** D
12. A	**25.** A	**38.** A	
13. C	**26.** A	**39.** D	

Quantitative Reasoning

1. B	**11.** B	**21.** A	**31.** B
2. E	**12.** B	**22.** B	**32.** E
3. C	**13.** B	**23.** E	**33.** B
4. D	**14.** E	**24.** A	**34.** A
5. E	**15.** D	**25.** C	**35.** C
6. A	**16.** D	**26.** D	**36.** D
7. C	**17.** A	**27.** D	**37.** C
8. C	**18.** A	**28.** A	**38.** C
9. B	**19.** D	**29.** D	**39.** C
10. E	**20.** D	**30.** A	**40.** C

Answers and Explanations for Practice Test 1

Natural Sciences

Biology

1. **D.** Mitochondria are organelles found within eukaryotic cells that function to produce energy for cellular processes through the breakdown of glucose to form carbon dioxide, water, and ATP (energy) through a process known as cellular respiration. Protein synthesis (A) is carried by at the ribosomes of eukaryotic cells, and the physical (B) and biochemical (C) properties of eukaryotic cells are controlled by DNA contained in chromosomes found in the nucleus. Glucose is manufactured from carbon dioxide and water in the chloroplasts of plant cells through the process of photosynthesis.

2. **A.** Cellular respiration involves the breakdown of glucose, in the presence of oxygen, to produce carbon dioxide, water, and ATP (energy), which can be used for cellular processes. It takes place in the mitochondria of eukaryotic cells. Fermentation takes place in the absence of oxygen and is sometimes referred to as anaerobic respiration. Fermentation is less efficient at energy production than cellular (aerobic) respiration, with fermentation resulting in the net production of 2 ATP molecules per glucose molecule broken down compared to a net of 36 ATP molecules for each glucose molecule broken down in cellular respiration. Alcoholic fermentation takes place in yeast and results in the production of ethanol from the anaerobic breakdown of glucose. Lactic acid fermentation takes place in human muscle cells when conditions become anaerobic, such as during heavy exercise. The result is the formation of lactic acid from the breakdown of glucose, which often leads to cramping in the muscle cells.

3. **B.** Oxygen is not necessary for photosynthesis to take place. In fact, the first photosynthetic organisms evolved in an anaerobic environment. The process of photosynthesis involves the use of light energy, in the presence of chlorophyll, to produce glucose from a combination of carbon dioxide and water. Oxygen is given off as a by-product of the reactions.

4. **C.** Enzymes are special types of proteins that speed up the rate of reactions by lowering the activation energy necessary for the reaction to take place. The enzymes themselves are not altered or consumed during the reaction. Cofactors (A) are nonprotein molecules or ions that are required for proper functioning of an enzyme. Substrates (B) are substances on which enzymes act to produce a product or products. Polypeptides (D) are chains of amino acids linked together by peptide bonds that serve as components of proteins. Promoters (E) are specific nucleotide sequences on DNA molecules in which RNA polymerase binds to initiate the transcription of mRNA from the DNA molecule.

5. **D.** Substances can move across cell membranes by means of passive transport, which does not require energy expenditure, or active transport, which requires an input of energy for movement of a substance across the membrane. Passive forms of transport include diffusion, the movement of substances across a semi-permeable membrane from a region of higher concentration to a region of lower concentration; osmosis, the movement of water across a semi-permeable membrane from a region of higher concentration to a region of lower concentration; and facilitated diffusion, the diffusion of substances across a semi-permeable membrane with the assistance of a transport protein. Active transport across cell membranes involves the pumping of substances across a membrane against their concentration gradient (from a region of lower concentration to a region of higher concentration). Some active transport mechanisms involve embedded proteins, and others involve the use of ion pumps, which generate voltage across the membrane. Both chemical forces (the ion concentration gradient) and electrical forces (the effect of the membrane potential on the movement of ions) act on the diffusion of ions across a membrane by establishing an electrochemical gradient.

6. **B.** Gametes are produced through a form of cell division referred to as meiosis, which results in the production of daughter cells with half the number of chromosomes as the parent cell. Thus, an organism with a somatic chromosome number of 24 would produce gametes containing 12 chromosomes. By halving the chromosome number in the gametes, the original somatic chromosome number of an organism is re-established at fertilization when two gametes unite to form a zygote.

7. **C.** Yeast are single-celled members of the Kingdom Fungi.

8. **E.** Angiosperms (flowering plants) are unique among the plant groups in that they produce a fruit that surrounds the seed(s). The production of fruit is considered an evolutionary advantage over the production of naked seeds (not enclosed in a fruit), as occurs in the gymnosperms. The fruit serves as both a protective structure for the seeds and a dispersal mechanism.

9. **D.** Phylum Chordata includes two invertebrate groups, subphylum Urochordata (tunicates) and subphylum Cephalochordata (lancelets), as well as all vertebrate organisms.

10. **C.** Vertebrate organisms, which are members of phylum Chordata, all possess a notochord, a dorsal, hollow nerve cord, pharyngeal slits, and a postanal tail at some point during development. In some cases, one or more features are present only during the embryo stage.

11. **A.** In vertebrate organisms, the excretory system (which includes the ureters, urethra, kidneys, and bladder) is responsible for eliminating metabolic waste from the body, as well as maintaining the osmotic balance of the blood. The endocrine system (B) functions to regulate internal body systems, primarily through the production of various hormones. The digestive system (C) is responsible for the ingestion, digestion, and absorption of nutrients by the body. The circulatory system (D) is responsible for the distribution of oxygen, carbon dioxide, nutrients, and metabolic wastes throughout the body. The respiratory system (E) is responsible for gas exchange (uptake of oxygen and elimination of carbon dioxide) in the body.

12. **B.** When food is ingested and begins to make its way down the human digestive system, it is first processed into small pieces in the mouth, and limited digestion of carbohydrates begins through the action of salivary amylase produced in saliva. With the aid of the tongue, the food is shaped into a ball, called a bolus, and pushed into the pharynx, which leads to both the esophagus and the trachea (windpipe). The act of swallowing pushes the trachea upward so that its opening, the glottis, is blocked by a cartilaginous flap called the epiglottis, thus ensuring that the bolus moves down into the esophagus instead of the windpipe. Muscular contractions, referred to as peristalsis, moves the bolus down the esophagus and into the stomach, where food is stored and preliminary digestion begins. As the bolus is mixed and processed by enzymes and acids produced in the stomach, it turns into a broth-like substance called chyme, which moves through the pyloric sphincter connecting the stomach to the small intestine. The small intestine is the site in which most digestion occurs and most nutrients are absorbed into the body. The pancreas, liver, and gall bladder participate in digestion by producing enzymes that are secreted into the top portion of the small intestine (the duodenum) that help break down the chyme. When digestion is complete, unabsorbed fluids and waste products pass into the large intestine and are eliminated as feces.

13. **C.** Blood pressure is a measurement of how much force the blood is exerting against the walls of the blood vessels. Systolic blood pressure measures the force exerted during the contraction phase of the cardiac cycle, while diastolic blood pressure measures the force exerted during the relaxation phase of the cardiac cycle.

14. **A.** The human dermal system (skin, hair, nails) serves as an outer covering for the body, protects the internal organs, helps protect the body against invading microorganisms, and serves as an important sensory organ. Although some organisms (for example, certain amphibians) carry out gas exchange at least partly through their skin; gas exchange in humans occurs through the respiratory system.

15. **D.** In the human circulatory system, the primary function of the red blood cells is to transport oxygen and carbon dioxide throughout the body. The various types of white blood cells function in defense and immunity against invading microorganisms and other foreign cells. Platelets are fragments of cells that function in the process of blood clotting. Plasma is the liquid medium within which the various blood cells and platelets are suspended and is responsible for the movement of nutrients and metabolic wastes throughout the body. The plasma also helps to maintain the osmotic balance of the blood.

16. **B.** Mucous membranes, phagocytic white blood cells, and the inflammatory response are all examples of nonspecific immune responses, meaning they act on any foreign invader. Conversely, the production of antibodies by exposure to various antigens is considered a specific immune response because each antigen encountered stimulates the production of antibodies specific to that antigen.

17. **A.** The transfer of antibodies from a pregnant woman to her fetus is considered a type of passive immunity, which only lasts as long as the antibodies last (typically, a few weeks to a few months). Although passive immunity is temporary, it usually lasts long enough to protect the baby until its own immune system matures.

18. E. Epinephrine is produced by the adrenal glands.

19. D. Neurotransmitters are chemical messengers that are released by the terminal end of an axon at a synapse and diffuses across the synaptic cleft to stimulate a response in a postsynaptic neuron.

20. B. The autonomic nervous system is responsible for conveying signals that regulate involuntary control of the cardiac muscles and the smooth muscles of the digestive, cardiovascular, excretory, and endocrine systems in humans. The autonomic nervous system is divided into two divisions: the parasympathetic division controls activities that conserve energy, such as digestion and a slowing of the heart rate; the sympathetic division controls activities that consume energy, such as increasing heart rate or metabolic function, preparing the body for action. The brain and spinal cord make up the central nervous system (A) of vertebrate organisms. The peripheral nervous system (C) is composed of the nerves and ganglia leading from the central nervous system to the rest of the body. The peripheral nervous system is divided into two divisions: the sensory division (E) conveys information to the central nervous system from sensory receptors; the motor division conveys signals from the central nervous system to effector cells. The somatic nervous system (D) carries signals to skeletal muscles, usually in response to an external stimulus.

21. E. In human males, sperm are formed in the seminiferous tubules—a series of highly coiled tubes surrounded by connective tissue, which together make up the testes. From the seminiferous tubules, the sperm move into the epididymis (D), where they mature and become motile. During ejaculation, the sperm move from the epididymis through the vas deferens (C) into an ejaculatory duct that opens up into the urethra. The urethra runs through the penis (A) and opens to the outside at the tip of the penis. Several glands add secretions to the semen, with approximately 60 percent of the total volume of semen produced in the seminal vesicles (B).

22. A. After fertilization, the uniting of an egg and a sperm to form a zygote, a special form of cell division referred to as cleavage takes place. Cleavage involves a rapid succession of cell divisions in which the cells undergo DNA synthesis and mitosis, but not the two growth stages of the cell cycle. The result is a partitioning of the zygote (a single large cell) into several smaller cells, called blastomeres, without an overall increase in the size of the developing embryo. This multicellular embryo is called a blastula. Different parts of the cytoplasm are partitioned into different blastomeres during cleavage, setting up the cells for future developmental events. Following cleavage, gastrulation occurs, resulting in the formation of a three-layered embryo called a gastrula. The next stage of development, organogenesis, results in the production of rudimentary organs in the embryo.

23. D. The circulatory system arises from the mesoderm tissue layer in vertebrate organisms.

24. C. The process of meiosis results in the production of gametes with one copy of each chromosome present in the parent cell. Assuming that no crossing over has occurred, the gametes produced by an individual with a genotype of AABbcc must each have one allele of each of the three genes. Because the parent is homozygous for the A and c alleles and heterozygous for the B allele, there are two possible combinations of alleles that could be present in the gametes: ABc and Abc. All gametes would get a dominant A allele and a recessive c allele, and half the gametes would receive a dominant B allele and half would receive a recessive b allele.

25. E. A cross between a heterozygous individual and a homozygous recessive individual would produce offspring with a ratio of 1:1, with half having straight bodies and half having spiral bodies. The heterozygous individual would produce two types of gametes with approximately equal frequency, with half the gametes containing the dominant allele coding for straight body type (B) and half having the recessive allele for spiral body type (b). The homozygous recessive parent would produce gametes carrying only the recessive allele (b). Thus, two combinations of gametes are possible from a cross between these two individuals: B + b (Bb) and b + b (bb), resulting in half the offspring (the heterozygous individuals, Bb) having a straight body type and half the offspring (the homozygous recessive individuals, bb) having a spiral body type.

26. A. Sex-linked traits refer to those traits that are carried on the sex chromosomes. In humans, most sex-linked traits are carried on the X chromosome; very few traits are carried on the Y chromosome.

27. D. If a diplod gamete, formed by nondisjunction during meiosis, unites with a normal haploid gamete, the resulting zygote would have three copies of each chromosome and, therefore, be triploid—which is a form of polyploidy.

28. B. Each gene on a molecule of DNA codes for one polypeptide, a component of proteins. DNA in the nucleus is read and copied onto a complementary mRNA (messenger RNA) molecule through the process of transcription. Following transcription, the noncoding regions of the mRNA molecule (introns), which lie between the coding regions (exons), are excised, and the exons are spliced together through RNA processing. The processed mRNA molecule moves out of the nucleus and into the cytoplasm and attaches to a ribosome, where the synthesis of polypeptides takes place through the process of translation.

29. E. DNA (deoxyribonucleic acid) is a polynucleotide composed of a chain of nucleotide units. Each nucleotide unit consists of the sugar deoxyribose, a phosphate group, and one of four nitrogenous bases (adenine, thymine, cytosine, guanine). The phosphate group of one nucleotide is attached to the sugar of the next nucleotide, forming a double backbone of alternating sugar and phosphate molecules with the nitrogenous bases projecting inward and held together by hydrogen bonds. The entire structure is twisted upon itself into the form of a double helix.

30. D. The polymerase chain reaction (PCR) allows for the amplification (making of hundreds or thousands of copies or "clones") of a DNA segment without using plasmids and bacterial cells. This technique is especially useful when small quantities of DNA are available to work with, such as the case with evidence (blood or semen) found at a crime scene. The amplification of the DNA allows for the production of a large quantity of DNA from a small sample relatively quickly. Transformation (A) refers to the uptake of DNA from the surrounding environment. Transduction (E) refers to the uptake of DNA by bacterial cells through infection of the cells with a bacteriophage (bacterial virus). DNA fingerprinting (C) involves the use of restriction fragment length polymorphism (RFLP) technology to characterize the DNA of an individual. Genetic engineering (B) refers to any direct manipulation of genes for research or practical purposes.

31. B. An organism that contains segments of DNA from another organism, inserted into it through genetic engineering technology, is referred to as being *transgenic*.

32. D. The differential success in reproduction among individuals in a population, in which the most fit or best adapted individuals are most likely to survive and reproduce, is, by definition, the process of natural selection. The process of natural selection is influenced by an interaction between the genetic make-up of an individual and environmental conditions and is based in part on the presence of heritable variation. Natural selection allows for the adaptation (C) of populations of organisms to their environment (E). The process of evolution (A) is often defined as *descent with modification* (B).

33. C. If a population is very small, its gene pool might not reflect the gene pool represented in the entire species. In addition, the existing gene pool of a small population may not be accurately represented in the next generation, due to random chance or sampling error, if all of the alleles are not passed on. This force of microevolution is referred to as genetic drift—changes to the gene pool of a small population due to random chance.

34. A. Classification of organisms follows a hierarchical approach, with the highest level being the domain and the lowest level being the species. The hierarchical classification proceeds as follows: domain, kingdom, phylum (or division, for plants), subphylum, class, order, family, genus, species.

35. E. A population (D) refers to a group of individuals of the same species that share a common geographic area. A community (E) refers to all of the populations of different species that share a common geographic area and have the potential to interact with each other. An ecosystem (C) refers to a community of organisms along with all of the abiotic factors with which the organisms in the community may interact. A gene pool (B) refers to the total complement of genes in a population at any given time.

36. B. Mutualism (B) describes an interspecific interaction in which both species benefit from the relationship. An example of mutualism can be found in lichens, which are composed of a fungal organism and a green alga or cyanobacteria living symbiotically, in which the green alga or cyanobacteria provides energy (carbohydrates) to both organisms through photosynthesis, while the fungus provides shelter from the elements, as well as a source of water and dissolved nutrients through absorption of broken down organic matter from the soil. Commensalism (A) refers to an interspecific relationship in which one species benefits from the relationship while the other species neither benefits nor is harmed by the relationship. An example of commensalism would be the presence of an epiphytic orchid living on a tree. This relationship benefits the orchid because the tree braches provide a place for the orchid to rest while absorbing water and nutrients from the atmosphere, whereas, the tree is neither helped nor harmed by the orchid. Predation (C) involves one organism (the predator) benefiting by capturing and eating another organism (prey), for example a mountain lion catching and consuming a deer. Competition (D) involves two (or more) species competing for limited resources (food, water, shelter, space) and usually results in detrimental effects on the populations of both species. Parasitism (E) involves one organism (the parasite) living on or in another organism (the host). While the parasite usually doesn't kill its host outright, it usually weakens it, leading to a reduction in fitness and reproductive potential of the host. An example would be mistletoe living on a tree host. Unlike epiphytic plants (such as the orchid in the preceding example), mistletoe puts down root-like projections into the living tissue of its host tree, absorbing water and nutrients at the expense of the host.

37. D. Primary consumers are those organisms that feed on the producers in a food chain. Because the producers are plants, algae, or photosynthetic bacteria, the primary consumers are considered herbivores—organisms that feed on plant material.

38. E. Water, nutrients, and carbon are cycled through an ecosystem, moving from nonliving (abiotic) components to living (biotic) components, and back to nonliving components. Conversely, energy moves through an ecosystem in one direction, with a loss of energy at each trophic level.

39. E. The processes of photosynthesis and cellular respiration account for the majority of transformations and movement of carbon through an ecosystem. Theoretically, on a global scale, the return of carbon dioxide to the atmosphere through cellular respiration should be approximately balanced by the removal of carbon dioxide from the atmosphere through photosynthesis. Globally, the amount of atmospheric carbon dioxide is steadily increasing due to the burning of wood and fossil fuels, which adds more carbon dioxide to the atmosphere than can be taken back out of the atmosphere through photosynthesis, disrupting the balance of the carbon cycle.

40. A. There are still common myths being perpetuated in society that behavior is controlled either entirely by the genetic make-up of the individual (nature) or entirely by environmental influences (nurture). Today, most geneticists, behavioral scientists, and social scientists agree that behavior is controlled by both the genetic make-up of an individual and by environmental influences. The degree of genetic versus environmental influence varies among individuals for different behaviors.

Chemistry

41. D. Arsenic is a metalloid. It is in Group 5A.

42. A. Copper and chlorine are a metal and nonmetal, respectively. Normally this type of combination will form an ionic substance. The other combinations all have pairs of nonmetals.

43. C. The nitrate ion, NO_3^-, is derived from nitric acid, HNO_3.

44. E. The complete combustion always yields $CO_2(g)$ and $H_2O(g)$. The coefficients must be "2" for $CO_2(g)$ to balance the carbons and a "4" for water to balance the 8 hydrogen atoms.

45. C. The mols of ammonia are determined by Avogadro's number and the count of ammonia molecules. Convert the molecules to mols # mols = (1 mol / 6.02×10^{23} molecules) (1.0×10^{22} molecules).

46. C. The carbon-14 isotope will emit a beta particle to form a nitrogen-14 daughter.

47. A. The 16.2 days equals two half-life periods. The amount left after time t can be determined this way.

$$A = A_0[1/2]^{t/t_{1/2}} = A_0[1/2]^{16.2 \text{ days}/8.1 \text{ days}} = A_0[1/2]^2 = A_0 1/4 =$$

48. E. *Sublimation* is the name for the conversion of a solid to a gas.

49. C. The stoichiometric ratio of 3/2 gives the ratio for the reaction rates.

50. B. The first order rate law for concentration versus time has the form, ln [A] = –kt + C.

51. A. Temperature increases normally increase reaction rates because there are more effective collisions between reactants. This is partially due to the fact that "hotter" molecules have more energy on average.

52. B. The conjugate base of weak acid has a K_b defined by $K_b = K_w / K_a = 1 \times 10^{-14} / 7.2 \times 10^{-4} = 1.4 \times 10^{-11}$.

53. E. The strongest acid is the oxyacid, $HClO_4$, which contain the most oxygen atoms on the central atom.

54. D. The decrease in container size will shift the mixture toward the side with fewer gas molecules.

55. A. Acetic acid is a weak acid. The acid neutralized with NaOH will give a basic solution with a pH near 9.

56. D. The solubility equilibrium expression has only the products in the expression. Iron (III) sulfide dissolves to form Fe^{3+} and S^{2-} ions.

57. B. The smallest mass molecule will have the highest effusion rate.

58. E. The density of a gas at STP is controlled by the molar mass. The lowest molar mass will have the lowest density.

59. C. Metallic solids consist of cations held together by a mobile sea of electrons.

60. D. Methane has four single bonds between the central C atom and the four hydrogen atoms. The carbon atom in carbon dioxide has two double bonds to the oxygen atoms.

61. E. There are two pi bonds and one sigma bond in $-C:::N:$ group. There are four pi electrons in these pi bonds.

62. B. The 2p atomic orbital has $n = 2$, $\ell = 1$ (true for all p orbitals) and allowed values for $m\ell = 1, 0, -1$.

63. A. The halogens, Group 7A, are non-metals.

64. D. Hess' Law tells us that the heat of reaction is independent of pathway. Reversing the first two reactions changes the sign for the enthalpy changes. The third reaction is added to the sum of the reversed first two.

65. A. We have to reverse the iodine reaction, which will change the sign. We have to multiply the iodine half reaction by $\frac{1}{2}$, but we do not change the potential. $E° = 0.7994 - 0.535 = 0.2644$ V.

66. C. A reaction runs until one of the reactants is exhausted. This is the limiting reagent.

67. A. The reaction quotient is smaller than the equilibrium constant when the reactant concentrations are higher than equilibrium values. The reaction mixture has not reached equilibrium concentrations. Remember Q depends on products/reactants.

68. C. The phosphorus central atom has sp^3d hybridization. There are five single bonds between the central atom and the five fluorine atoms. These single bonds are formed between the five sp^3d orbitals on the phosphorus atom and the fluorine atomic orbitals.

69. D. $\Delta E = \Sigma$ BE Bonds broken $- \Sigma$ BE Bonds formed $=$ BEH-H + BECl-Cl $-$ BEC-Cl $-$ BEH-Cl; $\Delta E = 414$ kJ/mol $+ 244$ kJ/mol -326 kJ/mol $- 432$ kJ/mol $= +658$ kJ/mol $- 758$ kJ/mol $= - 100$ kJ/mol

70. B. Amphoteric substances can act as both acids and bases.

71. D. Bromine adds symmetrically to the double bond in this alkene. The bromine atoms add to the number 2 and 3 carbon atoms in the butene.

72. C. Benzene substituents on adjacent carbon atoms in benzene are in the ortho positions.

73. D. The Diels-Alder reaction is an excellent synthetic tool for producing ring structures.

74. A. The chair form is the lowest energy conformer.

75. E. This is an ester: RCOOR".

76. B. The numbering of carbon is always such that the pi bond starts at the lowest number carbon as possible. The higher priority elements are on the same side (hence Z).

77. C. Tertiary alcohols form the most stable carbocation intermediate. The order is $3° > 2° > 1°$.

78. B. The E1 mechanism requires the reactant undergo a unimolecular elimination to form a cation.

79. C. The first step in polymerization is initiation. This is done by using an initiator that can easily dissociate into free radicals, such as benzoyl peroxide. The propagation step is the chain lengthening step, where monomer units are added. The termination step occurs when the polymer meets with something that can absorb the free radical without forming a new one (such as another strand of the polymer, radical, or oxygen).

80. D. A Grignard reagent reacting with CO_2 produces a carboxylate salt, $RCOO^-(MgX)^+$. The hydrolysis of this salt will produce a carboxylic acid, RCOOH.

81. E. The larger more polarizable species are soft bases (I^-, Br^-) and are more reactive than the less polarizable hard bases (F^-).

82. B. This is an E2 β-elimination via an alkyl magnesium iodide.

83. A. The reactivity for the S_N1 mechanism is 3° > 2° > 1°.

84. D. Symmetric ketones have the same carbon chains bonded to a carbonyl group, C=O.

85. A. Aromatic compounds have a lot of electrons and are subject to attack by electrophilic reagents.

86. C. Amine is $R-NH_2$. Amine compounds often display physiological activity and are used in pharmaceuticals.

87. C. The adjacent carbon has two hydrogen atoms that will generate $n + 1$ magnetic fields on the "a" hydrogen. This will produce a triplet peak pattern.

88. B. The decoupled spectrum will not show the spin-spin coupling with protons. Only the aldehyde has two types of carbon atoms. All the other compounds have only one type of carbon atom.

89. A. The m/e ratio for the cation is the molecular weight. Only $C_3H_7^+$ has a mass of 43.

90. E. The carbonyl C=O stretching frequency is in the range $1600–1750 \text{ cm}^{-1}$.

91. C. Stretching frequencies parallel bond strengths. Bond strengths increase with the number of bonds. Absorption frequencies increase with bond order for two given atoms.

92. A. Benzene has the most delocalization. The six pi electrons in benzene are delocalized around the six carbon ring. There is less and less delocalization with more isolation of the double bonds.

93. B. London forces are the weakest intermolecular forces, which is why alkanes have very high vapor pressure, low melting point, and boiling point.

94. C. Elimination reactions will produce pi bonds, which cannot be present in chiral compounds. In S_N1 reactions, the chiral center is destroyed in the intermediate.

95. B. The nitrogen in amines has a partial negative charge and has a lone pair of electrons; this makes amines nucleophilic. Carbon 2 will have the largest partial positive charge. The pi bond between this carbon and oxygen will make this carbon more reactive as well.

96. A. There are no chiral carbon atoms. The two sides of the ring –CH2CH2– joining the carbon atoms to the Cl atoms are the same.

97. B. There are no carbon-carbon double bonds in a carboxylic acid group.

98. C. Reduction of aldehydes and ketones is a two-step process. A hydride is used first, and then acid is used to hydrolyze the initial reduction product.

99. E. Aldehydes are oxidized in the Tollen's test.

100. B. Dehydration of alcohols produces the most branched or substituted alkene.

Reading Comprehension

1. C. This is stated in the last sentence of the first paragraph.

2. C. (A) There is no comparison between people. (B) The reflexes slow down at a quarter of a second. (D) There is no support for this idea.

3. B. This is stated in the third sentence of the second paragraph.

4. C. Although you might agree with (A) and (D), the article is not about this. There is no evidence of (B).

5. B. This is stated in the last sentence of the second paragraph.

6. C. Contradictory means opposite of what you expect. When you sleep, your organs don't sleep!

7. A. There is no contradiction (C), and the information goes beyond the fact that sleep is necessary (D). All statements include the affect of sleep on the brain.

8. C. This is stated in the first paragraph.

9. C. This is stated in the second to the last sentence of the first paragraph.

10. A. The first sentence of the second paragraph defines it as an amphibious fungal plague.

11. D. (A) This is contradicted by the information in the text. (B) The point of the articles is that there is no inspection. (C) The first part is true, but the second part of the statement is false.

12. A. The third paragraph explains the duties of various departments, but none deal with the examination of imported creatures.

13. C. The second sentence of the last paragraph defines the word.

14. C. There is the statement that this disease is resistant to eight drugs in the last paragraph.

15. C. It is defined in the third sentence of the first paragraph.

16. B. In the first paragraph, there is the description of one comet moving north and the other one moving east.

17. B. The description of a fly ball allows us to think about the comet's motion.

18. D. At the end of the first paragraph, they state that the bluish color is from ionized gas.

19. C. The second paragraph discusses the movement and shape of the rings.

20. C. The third paragraph raises these questions about changes in the planet Jupiter.

21. B. The last sentence of the last paragraph defines Antares as a red super giant.

22. C. The definition is given in the first paragraph, and the name is the abbreviation of autonomous underwater vehicle.

23. A. This is stated in the second sentence of the second paragraph.

24. C. The last sentence of the second paragraph states that it measure salinity, which means the amount of salt in the water.

25. A. This is stated in the middle of the third paragraph.

26. A. This is stated at the end of the fourth paragraph.

27. C. The last sentence mentions that it will become commonplace like the airplane did, but it takes time.

28. B. The use of the word astounding in the first sentence of the last paragraph indicates excitement.

29. A. Infectious means communicable, or easy to pass along to others. The passage makes it clear that one person can pass the disease on to another. Notice the word "infect," which means to transmit an illness, and the suffix indicates this is an adjective.

30. B. The second sentence of the first paragraph specifically states that cholera is caused by a *Vibrio cholerae* bacterium.

31. C. The second paragraph indicates that contaminated food and water carry the organism and that certain raw or poorly cooked foods cause infection. However, nothing indicates that food cooked too much (overcooked) causes cholera.

32. C. The order of events leading to the illness is: Disaster occurs; contaminated water flows into waterways; sanitary system fails, and fresh water becomes unavailable; and people drink the water.

33. B. Regurgitation, which means the same as vomiting.

34. D. "The Causes and Effects of Cholera" is the most general description of the passage. The entire passage is about cholera. Dysentery, in the first answer choice, is another illness that causes some of the same symptoms. Contaminated water is a cause of the disease, but the second choice is not a good title for the passage. The third answer choice relates to only a portion of the topic. Although war and natural disaster may cause cholera, the passage is about the disease, not the cause.

35. B. The context of the sentence leads you to understand that prevalent means very common.

36. C. Shortage is nearest in meaning to lack. Both words mean "to be without."

37. A. Cholera is easily passed from one person to another.

38. A. Careful cooking and hygiene practices can reduce the chance of getting the disease.

39. D. The sentence states that the epidemics have resulted in millions of deaths, so it's clear that epidemic is not a positive thing, which helps you eliminate the first two answer choices. Bacteria makes no sense because it means that cholera "has been responsible for" bacteria.

40. B. Ubiquitous means "omni-present" or "existing everywhere."

41. C. The word stagnant means stale, "out-of-date," or "not changing." This passage states that the bar code concept is still being changed.

42. D. The passage indicates that the bar code has been used in various ways since the 1970s.

43. A. The passage covers both a review of existing technology and the new two-dimensional code.

44. A. The two-dimensional bar code, with an information density of 1,100 bytes, allows a considerably greater amount of information to be coded than the traditional bar code, including customized information. Thus, the manufacturer is able to add additional information on the bar code that it finds useful for its own tracking purposes. It also has built-in redundancy, meaning that the identical information is duplicated on the same code. Therefore, if the code is damaged. it can still be read. The technology even allows pictures or text to be contained within the code, as well as bar code encryption. The new technology dramatically reduces the errors of the single dimensional bar code and reduces the enormous costs that some companies have reported in the past.

45. A. The reading states that the code consists of horizontal lines, black print on a white background, with two and sometimes four different widths, and Arabic numerals underneath.

46. B. The passage states: The bar code used on grocery products, introduced in the 1970s, is called a universal product code (or UPC), and assigns each type of food or grocery product a unique code.

47. A. Width is a noun related to the noun wide. It describes the size from left to right.

48. A. Traditional refers to a long-standing tradition or convention.

49. B. Keeping track of products stocked and sold means the same thing as inventory control. The other uses mentioned are potential uses of the new two-dimensional bar code.

50. D. In this context, considerably means "far" or "much."

Quantitative Reasoning

1. B. The earnings for 30 hours are $\$8.25 \times 30 = \$247.50$.

2. E. The least common multiple of the divisors 16 and 24 is 48. $\frac{5}{16} + \frac{9}{24} = \frac{15}{48} + \frac{18}{48} = \frac{33}{48} = \frac{11}{16}$.

3. C. Translate to a mathematical expression and solve. $3x + 7 = 70$ so $3x + 7 - 7 = 70 - 7$ and $3x = 63$. Divide both sides by 3. Therefore, $x = 21$.

4. D. The area of the circle with a radius of 3 is $\pi r^2 = \pi \cdot 3^2 = 9\pi$. The area of the larger circle is $4 \times 9\pi = 36\pi$. Therefore, $r^2 = 36$ so $r = \sqrt{36} = 6$. The radius of the larger circle is 6.

5. E. Six less a number is shown by $n - 6$. So six less a number is four is represented by $n - 6 = 4$.

6. A. The cost of the 8 CD covers is $8 \times \$1.59 = \$12.72$. The change received back is $\$20.00 - \$12.72 = \$7.28$.

7. C. $3a + 3b = 3(a + b)$. Since $a + b = 6$, $3a + 3b = 3(6) = 18$.

8. C. $1\frac{1}{8} + 2\frac{3}{4} + 3\frac{1}{3} = \frac{9}{8} + \frac{11}{4} + \frac{10}{3} = \frac{27}{24} + \frac{66}{24} + \frac{80}{24} = \frac{173}{24} = 7\frac{5}{24}$ pounds.

9. B. The area of a triangle is $A = \frac{1}{2}bh$. If the base is 3 inches less than the height, then $b = h - 3$. Substituting this value in for b gives $A = \frac{1}{2}(h-3)h = \frac{1}{2}h^2 - \frac{3}{2}h$.

10. E. $(2.5)^4 = 2.5 \times 2.5 \times 2.5 \times 2.5 = 39.0625$. Rounded to the nearest tenth is 39.1.

11. B. The area of a square is s^2 where s is a side of the square. If $s^2 = 36$, then $s = 6$. The diagonal of a square forms two right triangles; d is the hypotenuse, and the two legs are 6 units long.

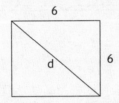

Using the Pythagorean Theorem, $d^2 = 6^2 + 6^2 = 36 + 36 = 72$. Therefore, $d = d = \sqrt{72} = 6\sqrt{2}$.

12. B. $(3x^2 + 2x - 5) - (2x^2 - 5) + (4x - 7) = 3x^2 + 2x - 5 - 2x^2 + 5 + 4x - 7 = 3x^2 - 2x^2 + 2x + 4x - 5 + 5 - 7 = x^2 + 6x - 7$.

13. B. After eating $\frac{1}{4}$ of a pie, what remains is $1 - \frac{1}{4} = \frac{3}{4}$. If 4 friends share the remainder, then each received $\frac{3}{4} \div 4 = \frac{3}{4} \times \frac{1}{4} = \frac{3}{16}$.

14. E. The line $y = -\frac{1}{8}x + 7$ has a slope of $-\frac{1}{8}$. A line perpendicular would have a slope equal to the negative reciprocal of $-\frac{1}{8}$, which is 8.

15. D. Interest earned in one year is $\$300 \times 5\frac{1}{4}\% = \$15.75$. The total amount of the account after one year is $\$300 + \$15.75 = \$315.75$.

16. B. Subtracting $2y$ from both sides leads to the equation $6 = y - 2$. Next, add 2 to both sides to get $y = 8$.

17. A. Five cards at \$3.00 each cost $5 \times \$3.00 = \$15.00$. If cards are 2 for \$5.00, the cost per cards is $\frac{\$5.00}{2} = \$2.50$ so 5 cards would cost $\$2.50 \times 5 = \$12.50$. The amount saved is $\$15.00 - \$12.50 = \$2.50$.

18. A. Add the areas of the two triangles and the square to find the total area. The area of the square is $5^2 = 25$. Both triangles have a height of 5. The area of one triangle is $\frac{1}{2}bh = \frac{1}{2} \cdot 3 \cdot 5 = \frac{15}{2} = 7.5$. The area of the other triangle is $\frac{1}{2}bh = \frac{1}{2} \cdot 4 \cdot 5 = \frac{20}{2} = 10$. The total area is $25 + 7.5 + 10 = 42.5$.

19. D. The cosine function is positive in the first and fourth quadrants. The tangent function is negative in the second and fourth quadrants. Thus, $\angle y$ must lie in the fourth quadrant.

20. D. The percent discounted is the amount discounted divided by the original price. The amount discounted is $\$200 - \$150 = \$50$. The percent discounted is $\frac{50}{200} = 0.25 = 25\%$.

21. A. There are 60 minutes in an hour, 24 hours in one day, and 7 days in one week. So 1 week = $\frac{7 \text{ days}}{1 \text{ week}} \times \frac{24 \text{ hours}}{1 \text{ day}} \times \frac{60 \text{ minutes}}{1 \text{ hour}} = 7 \times 24 \times 60 = 10,080$ minutes.

22. B. The amplitude of the function is the absolute value of the coefficient of the cosine term, that is, 3.

23. E. At the end of the first day, there are $1 - \frac{1}{8} = \frac{7}{8}$ of the magazines remaining. $\frac{7}{8} \times \frac{1}{4} = \frac{7}{32}$ sold the next day. So at the end of the second day, there are $\frac{7}{8} - \frac{7}{32} = \frac{28}{32} - \frac{7}{32} = \frac{21}{32}$ of the magazines remaining.

24. A. Using the ratio $\frac{\text{height}}{\text{shadow}}$, the proportion $\frac{3\frac{1}{2}}{6} = \frac{x}{24}$ models this situation, where x represents the height of the pole. Cross multiply. $3\frac{1}{2} \times 24 = 6x$ so $84 = 6x$ and $x =$ feet $\frac{84}{6} = 14$.

25. C.

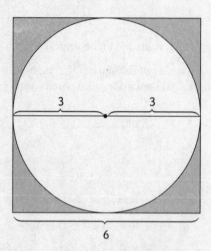

The area of the shaded region equals the area of the square minus the area of the circle. Since the radius of the circle is 3, the square has a side length of 6. The area of the square is 6^2 or 36. The area of the circle is $\pi r^2 = \pi \cdot 3^2 = 9\pi$. The shaded region, therefore, is $36 - 9\pi$.

26. D. The volume of each cube is $4 \times 4 \times 4 = 64$ in^3. The volume of the crate, in inches, is $(3 \times 12) \times (2 \times 12) \times (2 \times 12) = 20{,}736$ in^3. The number of blocks that can fit in the crate is $\frac{20736}{64} = 324$.

27. D. If a pair of dice are rolled one time, the probability of getting an even number is $\frac{18}{36} = \frac{1}{2}$. Thus, if rolled twice, the probability is $\frac{1}{2} \times \frac{1}{2} = \frac{1}{4}$.

28. A. Set the equation equal to 0 and factor. $x^2 + 6x - 16 = 0$ and $(x + 8)(x - 2) = 0$. Then, either $x + 8 = 0$ or $x - 2 = 0$, so $x = -8$ or $x = 2$. Since x is positive, $x = 2$ only.

29. D. The mode is the most frequently occurring number, which is 7. The median is the number in the middle, which is 5. The product is $5 \times 7 = 35$.

30. A. 60 beads $\times$ feet $\frac{1}{2} = 30$ inches. Converting this to feet gives 30 inches $\times \frac{1 \text{ foot}}{12 \text{ inches}} =$ feet $\frac{30}{12} = 2\frac{1}{2}$.

31. B. Substitute 1 for p and solve for q. $7(1) + 5q = -3$ and $7 + 5q = -3$.

$7 + 5q - 7 = -3 - 7$ and $5q = -10$. Dividing both sides by 5 results in $q = -2$.

32. E. Let the radius of the smaller circle $= 1$. Then the radius of the larger circle is 4. The shaded region is found by subtracting the area of the smaller circle from the area of the larger circle. The area of the smaller circle is $\pi(1)^2$ or π. The area of the larger circle is $\pi(4)^2$or 16π. The shaded region is $16\pi - \pi$ or 15π. The percent of the whole figure that is shaded is $\frac{15\pi}{16\pi} = 0.9375 = 93\frac{3}{4}\%$.

33. B. The proportion $\frac{5}{3} = \frac{x}{4}$ can be used to find x. Cross multiply. $5 \times 4 = 3x$ so $20 = 3x$ and $x = \frac{20}{3} = 6\frac{2}{3}$.

34. A. Since $\tan x = \frac{\sin x}{\cos x}$, $\tan x = 0$ whenever $\sin x = 0$. Of the choices, $\sin x = 0$ only at $0°$.

35. C. The set contains an even number of numbers, so the median of the numbers is the arithmetic mean of the two numbers in the middle. The numbers in the middle are 2 and 4, and the arithmetic mean of these numbers is 3.

36. D. Substituting $F = 77$ into the conversion formula yields $C = \frac{5}{9}(F - 32) = \frac{5}{9}(77 - 32) = \frac{5}{9}(45) = 5(5) = 25$.

37. C. Interest = principle × rate. Let p represent the principle. Then $\$100 = p \times 7\frac{1}{4}\%$ so $p = \frac{\$100}{7\frac{1}{4}\%} = \frac{\$100}{0.0725} = \$1,379$.

38. C. $8^{\frac{4}{3}} = \left(\sqrt[3]{8}\right)^4 = 2^4 = 16$.

39. C. One of the Pythagorean identities is $\sin^2\theta + \cos^2\theta = 1$, so $1 - \cos^2\theta = \sin^2\theta$.

40. C. To solve this equation, raise both sides to the power of –4. Thus, $\left(b^{-\frac{1}{4}}\right)^{-4} = 2^{-4}$ or $b = 2^{-4} = \left(\frac{1}{2}\right)^4 = \frac{1}{16}$.

Answer Sheets for Practice Test 2

Remove these sheets and use to mark your answers.

Natural Sciences

1 Ⓐ Ⓑ Ⓒ Ⓓ Ⓔ	26 Ⓐ Ⓑ Ⓒ Ⓓ Ⓔ
2 Ⓐ Ⓑ Ⓒ Ⓓ Ⓔ	27 Ⓐ Ⓑ Ⓒ Ⓓ Ⓔ
3 Ⓐ Ⓑ Ⓒ Ⓓ Ⓔ	28 Ⓐ Ⓑ Ⓒ Ⓓ Ⓔ
4 Ⓐ Ⓑ Ⓒ Ⓓ Ⓔ	29 Ⓐ Ⓑ Ⓒ Ⓓ Ⓔ
5 Ⓐ Ⓑ Ⓒ Ⓓ Ⓔ	30 Ⓐ Ⓑ Ⓒ Ⓓ Ⓔ
6 Ⓐ Ⓑ Ⓒ Ⓓ Ⓔ	31 Ⓐ Ⓑ Ⓒ Ⓓ Ⓔ
7 Ⓐ Ⓑ Ⓒ Ⓓ Ⓔ	32 Ⓐ Ⓑ Ⓒ Ⓓ Ⓔ
8 Ⓐ Ⓑ Ⓒ Ⓓ Ⓔ	33 Ⓐ Ⓑ Ⓒ Ⓓ Ⓔ
9 Ⓐ Ⓑ Ⓒ Ⓓ Ⓔ	34 Ⓐ Ⓑ Ⓒ Ⓓ Ⓔ
10 Ⓐ Ⓑ Ⓒ Ⓓ Ⓔ	35 Ⓐ Ⓑ Ⓒ Ⓓ Ⓔ
11 Ⓐ Ⓑ Ⓒ Ⓓ Ⓔ	36 Ⓐ Ⓑ Ⓒ Ⓓ Ⓔ
12 Ⓐ Ⓑ Ⓒ Ⓓ Ⓔ	37 Ⓐ Ⓑ Ⓒ Ⓓ Ⓔ
13 Ⓐ Ⓑ Ⓒ Ⓓ Ⓔ	38 Ⓐ Ⓑ Ⓒ Ⓓ Ⓔ
14 Ⓐ Ⓑ Ⓒ Ⓓ Ⓔ	39 Ⓐ Ⓑ Ⓒ Ⓓ Ⓔ
15 Ⓐ Ⓑ Ⓒ Ⓓ Ⓔ	40 Ⓐ Ⓑ Ⓒ Ⓓ Ⓔ
16 Ⓐ Ⓑ Ⓒ Ⓓ Ⓔ	41 Ⓐ Ⓑ Ⓒ Ⓓ Ⓔ
17 Ⓐ Ⓑ Ⓒ Ⓓ Ⓔ	42 Ⓐ Ⓑ Ⓒ Ⓓ Ⓔ
18 Ⓐ Ⓑ Ⓒ Ⓓ Ⓔ	43 Ⓐ Ⓑ Ⓒ Ⓓ Ⓔ
19 Ⓐ Ⓑ Ⓒ Ⓓ Ⓔ	44 Ⓐ Ⓑ Ⓒ Ⓓ Ⓔ
20 Ⓐ Ⓑ Ⓒ Ⓓ Ⓔ	45 Ⓐ Ⓑ Ⓒ Ⓓ Ⓔ
21 Ⓐ Ⓑ Ⓒ Ⓓ Ⓔ	46 Ⓐ Ⓑ Ⓒ Ⓓ Ⓔ
22 Ⓐ Ⓑ Ⓒ Ⓓ Ⓔ	47 Ⓐ Ⓑ Ⓒ Ⓓ Ⓔ
23 Ⓐ Ⓑ Ⓒ Ⓓ Ⓔ	48 Ⓐ Ⓑ Ⓒ Ⓓ Ⓔ
24 Ⓐ Ⓑ Ⓒ Ⓓ Ⓔ	49 Ⓐ Ⓑ Ⓒ Ⓓ Ⓔ
25 Ⓐ Ⓑ Ⓒ Ⓓ Ⓔ	50 Ⓐ Ⓑ Ⓒ Ⓓ Ⓔ

51 Ⓐ Ⓑ Ⓒ Ⓓ Ⓔ	76 Ⓐ Ⓑ Ⓒ Ⓓ Ⓔ
52 Ⓐ Ⓑ Ⓒ Ⓓ Ⓔ	77 Ⓐ Ⓑ Ⓒ Ⓓ Ⓔ
53 Ⓐ Ⓑ Ⓒ Ⓓ Ⓔ	78 Ⓐ Ⓑ Ⓒ Ⓓ Ⓔ
54 Ⓐ Ⓑ Ⓒ Ⓓ Ⓔ	79 Ⓐ Ⓑ Ⓒ Ⓓ Ⓔ
55 Ⓐ Ⓑ Ⓒ Ⓓ Ⓔ	80 Ⓐ Ⓑ Ⓒ Ⓓ Ⓔ
56 Ⓐ Ⓑ Ⓒ Ⓓ Ⓔ	81 Ⓐ Ⓑ Ⓒ Ⓓ Ⓔ
57 Ⓐ Ⓑ Ⓒ Ⓓ Ⓔ	82 Ⓐ Ⓑ Ⓒ Ⓓ Ⓔ
58 Ⓐ Ⓑ Ⓒ Ⓓ Ⓔ	83 Ⓐ Ⓑ Ⓒ Ⓓ Ⓔ
59 Ⓐ Ⓑ Ⓒ Ⓓ Ⓔ	84 Ⓐ Ⓑ Ⓒ Ⓓ Ⓔ
60 Ⓐ Ⓑ Ⓒ Ⓓ Ⓔ	85 Ⓐ Ⓑ Ⓒ Ⓓ Ⓔ
61 Ⓐ Ⓑ Ⓒ Ⓓ Ⓔ	86 Ⓐ Ⓑ Ⓒ Ⓓ Ⓔ
62 Ⓐ Ⓑ Ⓒ Ⓓ Ⓔ	87 Ⓐ Ⓑ Ⓒ Ⓓ Ⓔ
63 Ⓐ Ⓑ Ⓒ Ⓓ Ⓔ	88 Ⓐ Ⓑ Ⓒ Ⓓ Ⓔ
64 Ⓐ Ⓑ Ⓒ Ⓓ Ⓔ	89 Ⓐ Ⓑ Ⓒ Ⓓ Ⓔ
65 Ⓐ Ⓑ Ⓒ Ⓓ Ⓔ	90 Ⓐ Ⓑ Ⓒ Ⓓ Ⓔ
66 Ⓐ Ⓑ Ⓒ Ⓓ Ⓔ	91 Ⓐ Ⓑ Ⓒ Ⓓ Ⓔ
67 Ⓐ Ⓑ Ⓒ Ⓓ Ⓔ	92 Ⓐ Ⓑ Ⓒ Ⓓ Ⓔ
68 Ⓐ Ⓑ Ⓒ Ⓓ Ⓔ	93 Ⓐ Ⓑ Ⓒ Ⓓ Ⓔ
69 Ⓐ Ⓑ Ⓒ Ⓓ Ⓔ	94 Ⓐ Ⓑ Ⓒ Ⓓ Ⓔ
70 Ⓐ Ⓑ Ⓒ Ⓓ Ⓔ	95 Ⓐ Ⓑ Ⓒ Ⓓ Ⓔ
71 Ⓐ Ⓑ Ⓒ Ⓓ Ⓔ	96 Ⓐ Ⓑ Ⓒ Ⓓ Ⓔ
72 Ⓐ Ⓑ Ⓒ Ⓓ Ⓔ	97 Ⓐ Ⓑ Ⓒ Ⓓ Ⓔ
73 Ⓐ Ⓑ Ⓒ Ⓓ Ⓔ	98 Ⓐ Ⓑ Ⓒ Ⓓ Ⓔ
74 Ⓐ Ⓑ Ⓒ Ⓓ Ⓔ	99 Ⓐ Ⓑ Ⓒ Ⓓ Ⓔ
75 Ⓐ Ⓑ Ⓒ Ⓓ Ⓔ	100 Ⓐ Ⓑ Ⓒ Ⓓ Ⓔ

Perceptual Ability Test

Part 1

1	Ⓐ Ⓑ Ⓒ Ⓓ Ⓔ
2	Ⓐ Ⓑ Ⓒ Ⓓ Ⓔ
3	Ⓐ Ⓑ Ⓒ Ⓓ Ⓔ
4	Ⓐ Ⓑ Ⓒ Ⓓ Ⓔ
5	Ⓐ Ⓑ Ⓒ Ⓓ Ⓔ
6	Ⓐ Ⓑ Ⓒ Ⓓ Ⓔ
7	Ⓐ Ⓑ Ⓒ Ⓓ Ⓔ
8	Ⓐ Ⓑ Ⓒ Ⓓ Ⓔ
9	Ⓐ Ⓑ Ⓒ Ⓓ Ⓔ
10	Ⓐ Ⓑ Ⓒ Ⓓ Ⓔ
11	Ⓐ Ⓑ Ⓒ Ⓓ Ⓔ
12	Ⓐ Ⓑ Ⓒ Ⓓ Ⓔ
13	Ⓐ Ⓑ Ⓒ Ⓓ Ⓔ
14	Ⓐ Ⓑ Ⓒ Ⓓ Ⓔ
15	Ⓐ Ⓑ Ⓒ Ⓓ Ⓔ

Part 2

16	Ⓐ Ⓑ Ⓒ Ⓓ
17	Ⓐ Ⓑ Ⓒ Ⓓ
18	Ⓐ Ⓑ Ⓒ Ⓓ
19	Ⓐ Ⓑ Ⓒ Ⓓ
20	Ⓐ Ⓑ Ⓒ Ⓓ
21	Ⓐ Ⓑ Ⓒ Ⓓ
22	Ⓐ Ⓑ Ⓒ Ⓓ
23	Ⓐ Ⓑ Ⓒ Ⓓ
24	Ⓐ Ⓑ Ⓒ Ⓓ
25	Ⓐ Ⓑ Ⓒ Ⓓ
26	Ⓐ Ⓑ Ⓒ Ⓓ
27	Ⓐ Ⓑ Ⓒ Ⓓ
28	Ⓐ Ⓑ Ⓒ Ⓓ
29	Ⓐ Ⓑ Ⓒ Ⓓ
30	Ⓐ Ⓑ Ⓒ Ⓓ

Part 3

31	Ⓐ Ⓑ Ⓒ Ⓓ
32	Ⓐ Ⓑ Ⓒ Ⓓ
33	Ⓐ Ⓑ Ⓒ Ⓓ
34	Ⓐ Ⓑ Ⓒ Ⓓ
35	Ⓐ Ⓑ Ⓒ Ⓓ
36	Ⓐ Ⓑ Ⓒ Ⓓ
37	Ⓐ Ⓑ Ⓒ Ⓓ
38	Ⓐ Ⓑ Ⓒ Ⓓ
39	Ⓐ Ⓑ Ⓒ Ⓓ
40	Ⓐ Ⓑ Ⓒ Ⓓ
41	Ⓐ Ⓑ Ⓒ Ⓓ
42	Ⓐ Ⓑ Ⓒ Ⓓ
43	Ⓐ Ⓑ Ⓒ Ⓓ
44	Ⓐ Ⓑ Ⓒ Ⓓ
45	Ⓐ Ⓑ Ⓒ Ⓓ

Part 4

46	Ⓐ Ⓑ Ⓒ Ⓓ Ⓔ
47	Ⓐ Ⓑ Ⓒ Ⓓ Ⓔ
48	Ⓐ Ⓑ Ⓒ Ⓓ Ⓔ
49	Ⓐ Ⓑ Ⓒ Ⓓ Ⓔ
50	Ⓐ Ⓑ Ⓒ Ⓓ Ⓔ
51	Ⓐ Ⓑ Ⓒ Ⓓ Ⓔ
52	Ⓐ Ⓑ Ⓒ Ⓓ Ⓔ
53	Ⓐ Ⓑ Ⓒ Ⓓ Ⓔ
54	Ⓐ Ⓑ Ⓒ Ⓓ Ⓔ
55	Ⓐ Ⓑ Ⓒ Ⓓ Ⓔ
56	Ⓐ Ⓑ Ⓒ Ⓓ Ⓔ
57	Ⓐ Ⓑ Ⓒ Ⓓ Ⓔ
58	Ⓐ Ⓑ Ⓒ Ⓓ Ⓔ
59	Ⓐ Ⓑ Ⓒ Ⓓ Ⓔ
60	Ⓐ Ⓑ Ⓒ Ⓓ Ⓔ

Part 5

61	Ⓐ Ⓑ Ⓒ Ⓓ Ⓔ
62	Ⓐ Ⓑ Ⓒ Ⓓ Ⓔ
63	Ⓐ Ⓑ Ⓒ Ⓓ Ⓔ
64	Ⓐ Ⓑ Ⓒ Ⓓ Ⓔ
65	Ⓐ Ⓑ Ⓒ Ⓓ Ⓔ
66	Ⓐ Ⓑ Ⓒ Ⓓ Ⓔ
67	Ⓐ Ⓑ Ⓒ Ⓓ Ⓔ
68	Ⓐ Ⓑ Ⓒ Ⓓ Ⓔ
69	Ⓐ Ⓑ Ⓒ Ⓓ Ⓔ
70	Ⓐ Ⓑ Ⓒ Ⓓ Ⓔ
71	Ⓐ Ⓑ Ⓒ Ⓓ Ⓔ
72	Ⓐ Ⓑ Ⓒ Ⓓ Ⓔ
73	Ⓐ Ⓑ Ⓒ Ⓓ Ⓔ
74	Ⓐ Ⓑ Ⓒ Ⓓ Ⓔ
75	Ⓐ Ⓑ Ⓒ Ⓓ Ⓔ

Part 6

76	Ⓐ Ⓑ Ⓒ Ⓓ
77	Ⓐ Ⓑ Ⓒ Ⓓ
78	Ⓐ Ⓑ Ⓒ Ⓓ
79	Ⓐ Ⓑ Ⓒ Ⓓ
80	Ⓐ Ⓑ Ⓒ Ⓓ
81	Ⓐ Ⓑ Ⓒ Ⓓ
82	Ⓐ Ⓑ Ⓒ Ⓓ
83	Ⓐ Ⓑ Ⓒ Ⓓ
84	Ⓐ Ⓑ Ⓒ Ⓓ
85	Ⓐ Ⓑ Ⓒ Ⓓ
86	Ⓐ Ⓑ Ⓒ Ⓓ
87	Ⓐ Ⓑ Ⓒ Ⓓ
88	Ⓐ Ⓑ Ⓒ Ⓓ
89	Ⓐ Ⓑ Ⓒ Ⓓ
90	Ⓐ Ⓑ Ⓒ Ⓓ

CUT HERE

Reading Comprehension

1 Ⓐ Ⓑ Ⓒ Ⓓ		26 Ⓐ Ⓑ Ⓒ Ⓓ	
2 Ⓐ Ⓑ Ⓒ Ⓓ		27 Ⓐ Ⓑ Ⓒ Ⓓ	
3 Ⓐ Ⓑ Ⓒ Ⓓ		28 Ⓐ Ⓑ Ⓒ Ⓓ	
4 Ⓐ Ⓑ Ⓒ Ⓓ		29 Ⓐ Ⓑ Ⓒ Ⓓ	
5 Ⓐ Ⓑ Ⓒ Ⓓ		30 Ⓐ Ⓑ Ⓒ Ⓓ	
6 Ⓐ Ⓑ Ⓒ Ⓓ		31 Ⓐ Ⓑ Ⓒ Ⓓ	
7 Ⓐ Ⓑ Ⓒ Ⓓ		32 Ⓐ Ⓑ Ⓒ Ⓓ	
8 Ⓐ Ⓑ Ⓒ Ⓓ		33 Ⓐ Ⓑ Ⓒ Ⓓ	
9 Ⓐ Ⓑ Ⓒ Ⓓ		34 Ⓐ Ⓑ Ⓒ Ⓓ	
10 Ⓐ Ⓑ Ⓒ Ⓓ		35 Ⓐ Ⓑ Ⓒ Ⓓ	
11 Ⓐ Ⓑ Ⓒ Ⓓ		36 Ⓐ Ⓑ Ⓒ Ⓓ	
12 Ⓐ Ⓑ Ⓒ Ⓓ		37 Ⓐ Ⓑ Ⓒ Ⓓ	
13 Ⓐ Ⓑ Ⓒ Ⓓ		38 Ⓐ Ⓑ Ⓒ Ⓓ	
14 Ⓐ Ⓑ Ⓒ Ⓓ		39 Ⓐ Ⓑ Ⓒ Ⓓ	
15 Ⓐ Ⓑ Ⓒ Ⓓ		40 Ⓐ Ⓑ Ⓒ Ⓓ	
16 Ⓐ Ⓑ Ⓒ Ⓓ		41 Ⓐ Ⓑ Ⓒ Ⓓ	
17 Ⓐ Ⓑ Ⓒ Ⓓ		42 Ⓐ Ⓑ Ⓒ Ⓓ	
18 Ⓐ Ⓑ Ⓒ Ⓓ		43 Ⓐ Ⓑ Ⓒ Ⓓ	
19 Ⓐ Ⓑ Ⓒ Ⓓ		44 Ⓐ Ⓑ Ⓒ Ⓓ	
20 Ⓐ Ⓑ Ⓒ Ⓓ		45 Ⓐ Ⓑ Ⓒ Ⓓ	
21 Ⓐ Ⓑ Ⓒ Ⓓ		46 Ⓐ Ⓑ Ⓒ Ⓓ	
22 Ⓐ Ⓑ Ⓒ Ⓓ		47 Ⓐ Ⓑ Ⓒ Ⓓ	
23 Ⓐ Ⓑ Ⓒ Ⓓ		48 Ⓐ Ⓑ Ⓒ Ⓓ	
24 Ⓐ Ⓑ Ⓒ Ⓓ		49 Ⓐ Ⓑ Ⓒ Ⓓ	
25 Ⓐ Ⓑ Ⓒ Ⓓ		50 Ⓐ Ⓑ Ⓒ Ⓓ	

Quantitative Reasoning

1 Ⓐ Ⓑ Ⓒ Ⓓ Ⓔ		21 Ⓐ Ⓑ Ⓒ Ⓓ Ⓔ
2 Ⓐ Ⓑ Ⓒ Ⓓ Ⓔ		22 Ⓐ Ⓑ Ⓒ Ⓓ Ⓔ
3 Ⓐ Ⓑ Ⓒ Ⓓ Ⓔ		23 Ⓐ Ⓑ Ⓒ Ⓓ Ⓔ
4 Ⓐ Ⓑ Ⓒ Ⓓ Ⓔ		24 Ⓐ Ⓑ Ⓒ Ⓓ Ⓔ
5 Ⓐ Ⓑ Ⓒ Ⓓ Ⓔ		25 Ⓐ Ⓑ Ⓒ Ⓓ Ⓔ
6 Ⓐ Ⓑ Ⓒ Ⓓ Ⓔ		26 Ⓐ Ⓑ Ⓒ Ⓓ Ⓔ
7 Ⓐ Ⓑ Ⓒ Ⓓ Ⓔ		27 Ⓐ Ⓑ Ⓒ Ⓓ Ⓔ
8 Ⓐ Ⓑ Ⓒ Ⓓ Ⓔ		28 Ⓐ Ⓑ Ⓒ Ⓓ Ⓔ
9 Ⓐ Ⓑ Ⓒ Ⓓ Ⓔ		29 Ⓐ Ⓑ Ⓒ Ⓓ Ⓔ
10 Ⓐ Ⓑ Ⓒ Ⓓ Ⓔ		30 Ⓐ Ⓑ Ⓒ Ⓓ Ⓔ
11 Ⓐ Ⓑ Ⓒ Ⓓ Ⓔ		31 Ⓐ Ⓑ Ⓒ Ⓓ Ⓔ
12 Ⓐ Ⓑ Ⓒ Ⓓ Ⓔ		32 Ⓐ Ⓑ Ⓒ Ⓓ Ⓔ
13 Ⓐ Ⓑ Ⓒ Ⓓ Ⓔ		33 Ⓐ Ⓑ Ⓒ Ⓓ Ⓔ
14 Ⓐ Ⓑ Ⓒ Ⓓ Ⓔ		34 Ⓐ Ⓑ Ⓒ Ⓓ Ⓔ
15 Ⓐ Ⓑ Ⓒ Ⓓ Ⓔ		35 Ⓐ Ⓑ Ⓒ Ⓓ Ⓔ
16 Ⓐ Ⓑ Ⓒ Ⓓ Ⓔ		36 Ⓐ Ⓑ Ⓒ Ⓓ Ⓔ
17 Ⓐ Ⓑ Ⓒ Ⓓ Ⓔ		37 Ⓐ Ⓑ Ⓒ Ⓓ Ⓔ
18 Ⓐ Ⓑ Ⓒ Ⓓ Ⓔ		38 Ⓐ Ⓑ Ⓒ Ⓓ Ⓔ
19 Ⓐ Ⓑ Ⓒ Ⓓ Ⓔ		39 Ⓐ Ⓑ Ⓒ Ⓓ Ⓔ
20 Ⓐ Ⓑ Ⓒ Ⓓ Ⓔ		40 Ⓐ Ⓑ Ⓒ Ⓓ Ⓔ

CUT HERE

PERIODIC TABLE OF THE ELEMENTS

1 **H** 1.0079																	2 **He** 4.0026
3 **Li** 6.941	4 **Be** 9.012											5 **B** 10.811	6 **C** 12.011	7 **N** 14.007	8 **O** 16.00	9 **F** 19.00	10 **Ne** 20.179
11 **Na** 22.99	12 **Mg** 24.30											13 **Al** 26.98	14 **Si** 28.09	15 **P** 30.974	16 **S** 32.06	17 **Cl** 35.453	18 **Ar** 39.948
19 **K** 39.10	20 **Ca** 40.08	21 **Sc** 44.96	22 **Ti** 47.90	23 **V** 50.94	24 **Cr** 51.00	25 **Mn** 54.93	26 **Fe** 55.85	27 **Co** 58.93	28 **Ni** 58.69	29 **Cu** 63.55	30 **Zn** 65.39	31 **Ga** 69.72	32 **Ge** 72.59	33 **As** 74.92	34 **Se** 78.96	35 **Br** 79.90	36 **Kr** 83.80
37 **Rb** 85.47	38 **Sr** 87.62	39 **Y** 88.91	40 **Zr** 91.22	41 **Nb** 92.91	42 **Mo** 95.94	43 **Tc** (98)	44 **Ru** 101.1	45 **Rh** 102.91	46 **Pd** 105.42	47 **Ag** 107.87	48 **Cd** 112.41	49 **In** 114.82	50 **Sn** 118.71	51 **Sb** 121.75	52 **Te** 127.60	53 **I** 126.91	54 **Xe** 131.29
55 **Cs** 132.91	56 **Ba** 137.33	57 *****La** 138.91	72 **Hf** 178.49	73 **Ta** 180.95	74 **W** 183.85	75 **Re** 186.21	76 **Os** 190.2	77 **Ir** 192.22	78 **Pt** 195.08	79 **Au** 196.97	80 **Hg** 200.59	81 **Tl** 204.38	82 **Pb** 207.2	83 **Bi** 208.98	84 **Po** (209)	85 **At** (210)	86 **Rn** (222)
87 **Fr** (223)	88 **Ra** 226.02	89 †**Ac** 227.03	104 **Rf** (261)	105 **Db** (262)	106 **Sg** (263)	107 **Bh** (262)	108 **Hs** (265)	109 **Mt** (266)	110 **§** (269)	111 **§** (272)	112 **§** (277)						

§ Not yet named

***** Lanthanide Series

58 **Ce** 140.12	59 **Pr** 140.91	60 **Nd** 144.24	61 **Pm** (145)	62 **Sm** 150.4	63 **Eu** 151.97	64 **Gd** 157.25	65 **Tb** 158.93	66 **Dy** 162.50	67 **Ho** 164.93	68 **Er** 167.26	69 **Tm** 168.93	70 **Yb** 173.04	71 **Lu** 174.97
90 **Th** 232.04	91 **Pa** 231.04	92 **U** 238.03	93 **Np** 237.05	94 **Pu** (244)	95 **Am** (243)	96 **Cm** (247)	97 **Bk** (247)	98 **Cf** (251)	99 **Es** (252)	100 **Fm** (257)	101 **Md** (258)	102 **No** (259)	103 **Lr** (260)

† Actinide Series

Natural Sciences

Time: 90 Minutes
100 Questions: Biology (1–40), General Chemistry (41–70), and Organic Chemistry (71–100)

1. Which of the following is NOT a characteristic of all living cells?

   A. All cells are self-contained (surrounded by a plasma membrane).
   B. All cells contain DNA.
   C. All cells contain cytoplasm.
   D. All cells contain genes.
   E. All cells contain a nucleus.

2. The process of diffusion involves

   A. the passive movement of substances from a region of higher concentration to a region of lower concentration.
   B. the passive movement of substances from a region of lower concentration to a region of higher concentration.
   C. the passive movement of water from a region of lower concentration to a region of higher concentration.
   D. the input of energy to move substances from a region of higher concentration to a region of lower concentration.
   E. the input of energy to move substances from a region of lower concentration to a region of higher concentration.

3. During growth and tissue repair in humans, new cells are produced through the process of

   A. meiosis.
   B. mitosis.
   C. fission.
   D. budding.
   E. both mitosis and meiosis.

4. The process of cellular respiration involves

   A. the inhaling of oxygen and the exhaling of carbon dioxide through the lungs.
   B. the inhaling of carbon dioxide and the exhaling of oxygen through the lungs.
   C. the uptake of oxygen and the release of carbon dioxide through the skin.
   D. the breakdown of glucose molecules to produce energy in the form of ATP
   E. the formation of glucose molecules through the breakdown of ATP.

5. Which of the following statements best describes the energy conversion that occurs during photosynthesis?

   A. Chemical energy in the form of ATP is converted to light energy.
   B. Chemical energy in the form of glucose is converted to light energy.
   C. Chemical energy in the form of glucose is converted to energy in the form of ATP.
   D. Light energy is converted to chemical energy in the form of glucose.
   E. Light energy is converted into energy in the form of ATP.

6. Enzymes are

   A. a type of protein capable of raising the activation energy of chemical reactions.
   B. a type of protein capable of lowering the activation energy of chemical reactions.
   C. a type of lipid capable of raising the activation energy of chemical reactions.
   D. a type of lipid capable of lowering the activation energy of chemical reactions.
   E. a type of carbohydrate capable of raising the activation energy of chemical reactions.

GO ON TO THE NEXT PAGE

7. The endosymbiont theory is used to explain

    A. the presence of chloroplasts and mitochondria in eukaryotic cells.

    B. the association between green algae and fungi in lichens.

    C. the association between mistletoe and its host tree.

    D. the association between epiphytic orchids and their host tree.

    E. the presence of a membrane-bound nucleus in eukaryotic cells, but not in prokaryotic cells.

8. Which of the following groups of plants is MISmatched with its description?

    A. mosses   nonvascular; reproduce by spores

    B. ferns   nonvascular; reproduce by spores

    C. pines   vascular; reproduce by seeds

    D. lilies   vascular; reproduce by seeds

    E. apples   vascular; reproduce by seeds

9. Which of the following features is NOT considered a characteristic of primates?

    A. opposable thumb

    B. well-developed cerebral cortex

    C. continuously-growing incisors

    D. forward-facing eyes

    E. omnivorous

10. *Homo sapiens* are a member of

    A. class Hominida.

    B. class Vertebrata.

    C. class Erectus.

    D. class Chordata.

    E. class Mammalia.

11. Which of the following hormones is NOT produced by the pituitary gland?

    A. calcitonin

    B. oxytocin

    C. growth hormone

    D. prolactin

    E. antidiuretic hormone

12. The amount of force exerted by blood against the walls of the blood vessels is referred to as

    A. pulse rate.

    B. heart rate.

    C. blood pressure.

    D. systole.

    E. diastole.

13. In humans, organic molecules taken into the body must be converted to a form that is usable by the body through the process of

    A. respiration.

    B. circulation.

    C. excretion.

    D. digestion.

    E. thermoregulation.

14. Which of the following macromolecules provides the most direct form of usable energy by humans?

    A. lipids

    B. proteins

    C. carbohydrates

    D. nucleic acids

    E. fats

15. The primary functional unit of the human excretory system is the

    A. ureter.

    B. urethra.

    C. bladder.

    D. small intestine.

    E. kidney.

16. Chemical coordination of the human body is controlled by hormones produced in a series of glands referred to as the

    A. excretory system.

    B. endocrine system.

    C. hormonal system.

    D. nervous system.

    E. circulatory system.

17. In the human reproductive system, fertilization takes place in the

A. vagina.
B. cervix.
C. uterus.
D. ovary.
E. Fallopian tube.

18. The human central nervous system consists of

A. the brain and the spinal cord.
B. the spinal cord and the peripheral nerves.
C. the brain and the peripheral nerves.
D. the spinal cord and the parasympathetic nerves.
E. the brain and the parasympathetic nerves.

19. Which of the following represents the correct flow of air in the human respiratory system?

A. nose → trachea → larynx → bronchi → alveoli
B. nose → trachea → larynx → alveoli → bronchi
C. nose → larynx → trachea → bronchi → alveoli
D. nose → larynx → trachea → alveoli → bronchi
E. nose → larynx → bronchi → trachea → alveoli

20. The organ in the human body that is composed primarily of lymph node tissue and is the site where red blood cells are destroyed is the

A. pancreas.
B. gall bladder.
C. appendix.
D. liver.
E. spleen.

21. Which of the following statements regarding antibiotics is INCORRECT?

A. Antibiotics interfere with the growth and development of bacteria.
B. Many bacterial strains have developed resistance to commonly used antibiotics.
C. Antibiotics are currently added to many soaps and other cleaning agents.
D. Antibiotics are effective against bacteria, viruses, and other infectious agents.
E. Different antibiotics may need to be used depending on whether the bacterial agent is Gram-positive or Gram-negative.

22. Which of the following organs or tissues is NOT derived from the ectoderm during human embryo development?

A. skeletal system
B. epidermis
C. cornea
D. tooth enamel
E. nervous system

23. In human embryo development, the first series of cell divisions following fertilization results in the partitioning of the zygote into many smaller cells. This series of divisions is referred to as

A. gastrulation.
B. blastulation.
C. cleavage.
D. organogenesis.
E. morulation.

24. Which of the following must occur for an individual to express a particular trait (for example, blue eye color)?

A. Genes must be transcribed directly into proteins.
B. Genes must be translated directly into proteins.
C. Genes must be transcribed onto transfer RNA (tRNA) from which they can be translated into proteins.
D. Genes must be transcribed onto messenger RNA (mRNA) from which they can be translated into proteins.
E. Genes must be translated onto messenger RNA (mRNA) from which they can be transcribed into proteins.

GO ON TO THE NEXT PAGE

25. The genetic make-up of an individual is referred to as his or her

   A. genome.
   B. genotype.
   C. phenotype.
   D. gene pool.
   E. genetic code.

26. If an individual has one allele coding for attached earlobes and one allele coding for free earlobes, that individual is said to be

   A. homozygous for earlobe type.
   B. recessive for earlobe type.
   C. dominant for earlobe type.
   D. heterozygous for earlobe type.
   E. heterogeneous for earlobe type.

27. The existence of the M, N, and MN blood groups in humans is an example of

   A. complete dominance.
   B. complete recessiveness.
   C. codominance.
   D. incomplete dominance.
   E. heterozygosity.

28. Which of the following combinations of children could be produced by a woman with type-AB blood and a man with type-O blood?

   A. AB only
   B. O only
   C. AB or O
   D. A, B, AB, or O
   E. A or B

29. The characterization of an individual's DNA by restriction analysis and gel electrophoresis is referred to as a

   A. DNA fingerprint.
   B. PCR product.
   C. DNA probe.
   D. restriction blot.
   E. transgenic blot.

30. What proportion of offspring resulting from a cross between a squirrel that was homozygous dominant for round ears and a squirrel that is heterozygous for round and pointed ears would have pointed ears?

   A. 0%
   B. 25%
   C. 50%
   D. 75%
   E. 100%

31. Which of the following statements regarding sex-linked traits is INCORRECT?

   A. Daughters will always show dominant sex-linked traits if their father has the trait.
   B. Sons will always show the sex-linked trait if their mother is homozygous for the trait.
   C. Sons cannot inherit a sex-linked trait from their father.
   D. Daughters cannot inherit a sex-linked trait; only sons can inherit sex-linked traits.
   E. Sex-linked traits are carried primarily on the X chromosome; few traits are carried on the Y chromosome.

32. Which of the following statements best describes the process of evolution?

   A. changes in the genetic composition of a population over time
   B. natural selection among individuals in a population
   C. failure of a population to change in genetic composition over time
   D. genetic drift within a population
   E. survival of the fittest

33. A group of related individuals that can interbreed and produce fertile offspring is referred to as a

   A. community.
   B. population.
   C. species.
   D. gene pool.
   E. family.

34. The difference between a community and an ecosystem is that

   A. an ecosystem does not include any abiotic factors.
   B. a community does not include any abiotic factors.
   C. a community only includes a single species type.
   D. an ecosystem does not include interactions among species.
   E. a community does not include interactions among species.

35. The base of every food chain consists of

   A. carnivores.
   B. primary consumers.
   C. herbivores.
   D. decomposers.
   E. producers.

36. Which of the following factors affecting population density would be considered density-independent?

   A. availability of food
   B. availability of water
   C. accumulation of toxins in the ecosystem
   D. prolonged period of drought
   E. availability of shelter

37. When a toxin enters the food chain, it usually

   A. does not move up the food chain.
   B. becomes less and less concentrated as it moves up through the food chain.
   C. becomes more and more concentrated as it moves up through the food chain.
   D. is broken down immediately by the decomposers.
   E. is absorbed and neutralized by the producers.

38. A tapeworm living inside a human intestine would be an example of which type of interspecific relationship?

   A. mutualism
   B. commensalism
   C. predation
   D. parasitism
   E. symbiosis

39. If a mutation occurs in a population resulting in a favorable trait, that trait is likely to increase in frequency in the population due to which of the following forces?

   A. genetic drift
   B. migration
   C. genetic bottlenecking
   D. evolution
   E. natural selection

40. The study of the evolution of social behavior is referred to as

   A. sociobiology.
   B. socialism.
   C. ecology.
   D. microbiology.
   E. mycology.

41. Which of the following categories best classifies silver?

   A. alkali metal
   B. nonmetal
   C. noble gas
   D. metalloid
   E. transition metal

GO ON TO THE NEXT PAGE

42. Which of the following liquids has the highest vapor pressure?

A.

B.

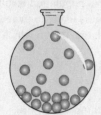

C.

D.

E.

43. What is the total number of valence electrons in sulfur trioxide, SO_3?

A. 8
B. 6
C. 24
D. 22
E. 18

44. Complete the following chemical equation for the incomplete combustion reaction. Include the correct coefficients.

$$CH_3OH(l) + O_2(g) \rightarrow$$

A. $CO(g) + H_2O(g)$
B. $2\ CO(g) + 3\ H_2O(g)$
C. $CO_2(g) + 4\ H_2O(g)$
D. $2\ C(s) + O_2(g) + 4\ H_2(g)$
E. $CO(g) + 2\ H_2O(g)$

45. How many mols of NH_3 equal 3.0×10^{24} molecules of ammonia?

A. 17
B. 0.50
C. 5.0
D. 1.0×10^{22}
E. 6.0×10^{45}

46. Which of the following is the nuclear decay equation for alpha emission by polonium-210?

A. $^{210}_{15} P \rightarrow ^{0}_{-1}e + ^{210}_{16} S$
B. $^{210}_{84} Po \rightarrow ^{4}_{2}\alpha + ^{206}_{82} Pb$
C. $^{210}_{84} Po \rightarrow ^{0}_{-1}e + ^{210}_{85} At$
D. $^{210}_{82} Pb \rightarrow ^{4}_{2}\alpha + ^{206}_{80} Hg$
E. $^{210}_{80} Pt \rightarrow ^{4}_{2}\alpha + ^{206}_{78} Os$

47. Which of the following is NOT a physical property?

A. odor
B. melting point
C. compressibility
D. color
E. flash point

48. Which of the following acids is the strongest?

A. C_2H_2 $pK_a = 25$
B. CF_3CO_2H $pK_a = 0.18$
C. H_2CO_3 $pK_a = 3.7$
D. CH_3CO_2H $pK_a = 4.8$
E. HCO_2H $pK_a = 3.8$

49. Which of the following acids is the weakest?

A. HF
B. HCl
C. HBr
D. HI
E. $HClO_4$

GO ON TO THE NEXT PAGE

50. Which of the arrows in the figure indicates the energy for the transition state along the reaction coordinate?

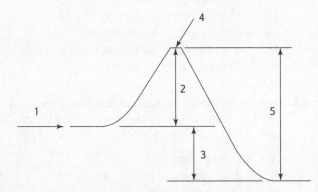

A. 1
B. 2
C. 3
D. 4
E. 5

51. Which of the following pairs of solutes and van't Hoff Factors is NOT correct?

A. CH_3OH (methanol), i = 1
B. NaCl (sodium chloride), i = 2
C. $FeCl_3$ (iron III chloride), i = 4
D. CH_3CH_2OH (ethanol), i = 1
E. $CaCl_2$ (calcium chloride), i = 2

52. What name is used to describe the Group A elements?

A. halogens
B. rare gases
C. representative elements
D. transition elements
E. coinage metals

53. Metallic gold crystallizes in the face-centered cubic lattice. How may gold atoms are "inside" a unit cell?

A. 1
B. 2
C. 3
D. 4
E. 6

54. The angular momentum quantum number ℓ can have values from 0 to n – 1. Which of the following values is correct for a 2s atomic orbital?

A. 0
B. 1
C. 2
D. –1
E. 1/2

55. Which of the following covalent bonds is the shortest and strongest?

A. H-I
B. H-F
C. H-Cl
D. H-Br
E. H-At

56. How many tons of $KClO_3$ are needed to produce 96 tons of O_2? The reaction is $2\ KClO_3 \rightarrow 2\ KCl + 3\ O_2$. The molar masses are 1 mol $KClO_3$ = 123 g/mol; 1 mol KCl = 75 g/mol; 1 mol O_2 = 32 g/mol.

A. 369 tons
B. 123 tons
C. 492 tons
D. 750 tons
E. 246 tons

57. The trans→cis isomerization of 1, 2-dichloroethylene has an energy of activation of 232. kJ/mol. The ΔH for the reaction is 4.18 kJ/mol. What do you predict for the activation energy for the reverse cis→trans isomerization?

E_a forward $- \triangle H = E_a$ reverse

A. +232 kJ/mol
B. –232 kJ/mol
C. 4.18 kJ/mol
D. +227 kJ/mol
E. –227 kJ/mol

58. Which of the following exists as a ferromagnetic solid?

A. lithium, Li
B. iron, Fe
C. calcium, Ca
D. potassium, K
E. silver, Ag

GO ON TO THE NEXT PAGE

59. Which of the following atoms has exactly one outer electron?

   A. Br
   B. Ca
   C. Li
   D. Mg
   E. Sn

60. Which of the following pairs of atoms, molecules, and hybridization is NOT CORRECT?

   A. carbon in carbon monoxide, sp
   B. oxygen in water, sp^3
   C. sulfur in sulfur dioxide, sp^2
   D. nitrogen in ammonia, sp^3
   E. carbon in methane, sp

61. The density of helium is 0.1786 kg/m^3 at STP. The gas is allowed to expand to 1.500 times the initial volume by adjusting temperature and pressure. What is the new density for the helium sample?

   A. 0.2656 kg/m^3
   B. 0.1191 kg/m^3
   C. 0.1786 kg/m^3
   D. 1.6786 kg/m^3
   E. 1.1910 kg/m^3

62. Which of the following combinations of orbital quantum numbers do not go together? $n = 2$, $\ell = 0$, $m_\ell = -1$?

   A. 1s, $n = 1$, $\ell = 0$, $m_\ell = 0$?
   B. 2p, $n = 2$, $\ell = 1$, $m_\ell = -1$?
   C. 2s, $n = 2$, $\ell = 0$, $m_\ell = -1$?
   D. 3s, $n = 3$, $\ell = 0$, $m_\ell = 0$?
   E. 3p, $n = 3$, $\ell = 1$, $m_\ell = -1$?

63. One mol of electrons is usually associated with which of the following terms?

   A. 1 Ohm
   B. 1 Faraday
   C. 1 Coulomb
   D. 1 Ampere
   E. 1 Volt

64. Which set of conditions makes a real gas behave like an ideal gas?

   A. high temperature / low pressure
   B. high temperature / high pressure
   C. low temperature / low pressure
   D. low temperature / high pressure
   E. high density / low temperature

65. In order to balance the half-reaction $MnO_4^- \rightarrow MnO_2$ in acidic solution, how many electrons need to be added and to which side?

   A. 1 to the product side
   B. 2 to the reactant side
   C. 3 to the reactant side
   D. 2 to the product side
   E. 4 to the reactant side

66. Which of the following nuclear processes decreases the atomic number in the daughter?

   A. α, alpha decay
   B. γ, gamma decay
   C. n° decay
   D. β, beta decay
   E. K capture

67. In a reversible chemical reaction, which of the following will "remain after the reaction stops?"

   A. only the products
   B. only the excess reagent
   C. both reactants and products
   D. the percent yield
   E. the limiting reagent

68. Based on the following standard electrode potentials for the two half reactions, what is the standard electrode potential for the reaction $I^-|I_2\|Sn^{2+}|Sn$?

$I_2 + 2\,e^- \rightarrow 2\,I^-$ $E^0 = 0.53$ V
$Sn^{2+} + 2\,e^- \rightarrow Sn$ $E^0 = -0.14$ V

   A. $+ 0.2644$ V
   B. $+ 0.39$ V
   C. $- 0.39$ V
   D. -0.67 V
   E. $+ 0.67$ V

69. What does the term "Q" represent in the Nernst equation, $E = E^0 - (RT/nF) \ln Q$?

A. standard potential
B. non-standard concentrations
C. temperature effects
D. electrons per mol
E. Universal gas constant

70. Which of the following is an amphoteric compound that can act as either an acid or a base?

A. $NaOH(aq)$
B. $Ca(OH)_2(aq)$
C. $Al(OH)_3(aq)$
D. $HCl(aq)$
E. $NH_3(aq)$

71. What is the addition product from the reaction of $Br_2(g)$ with 2-butene?

A. 1,4-dibromobutene
B. 2,3-dibromobutene
C. 1,2-dibromobutene
D. 2,3-dibromobutane
E. 1,3-dibromobutane

72. What is the name for the molecule shown here?

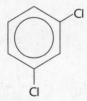

A. m-dichlorobenzene
B. p-dichlorobenzene
C. o-dichlorobenzene
D. o-chlorotoluene
E. 1,4-dichlorocyclohexane

73. According to Markonikov's rule, which carbon will the hydroxide go on in the formation of alcohol from the following hydration reaction?

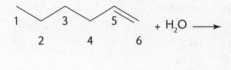

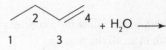

A. 6
B. 2
C. 3
D. 4
E. 5

74. Which of the following functional groups is NOT an ortho-para director?

A. –OR
B. –CH_3
C. –OH
D. –NH_2
E. –C:::N:

75. Which form of spectroscopy would be the best for detecting the types of differently bonded hydrogen atoms?

A. FT-IR
B. MS
C. UV-Vis
D. NMR
E. Raman

76. In the following figure, which carbon atom is most likely to be the site for the formation of a carbanion?

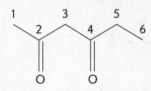

A. 1
B. 2
C. 3
D. 4
E. 5

GO ON TO THE NEXT PAGE

77. What type of amine is formed from the reaction of an alkyl halide and a tertiary amine?

   A. primary
   B. secondary
   C. tertiary
   D. quaternary
   E. cyclic

78. Which of the following molecules has a hydrogen atom in an allylic position?

   A. $H_2C::CH_2$
   B. $HC:::CH$
   C. $H_2C::CHCH_3$
   D. $C_6H_5C:::CH$
   E. CH_3CH_2OH

79. The hydrogen atoms in the molecule are labeled A through E. Which of these hydrogen atoms is NOT labeled correctly?

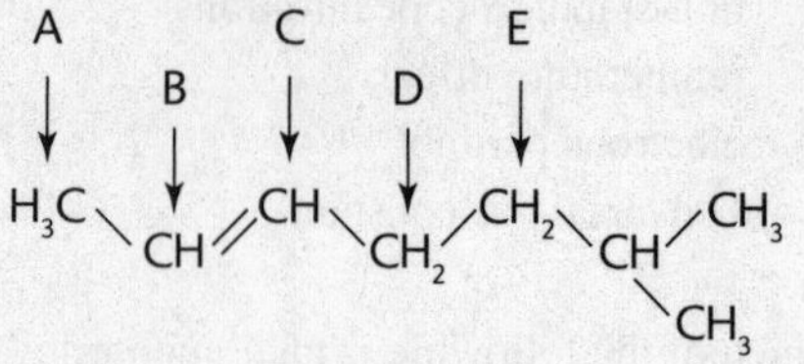

   A. 1°, allylic
   B. 2°, vinylic
   C. 2°, vinylic
   D. 2°, allylic
   E. 2°, vinylic

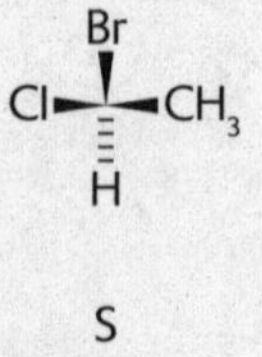

80. Which of the following alkenes will yield only one product on ozonolysis?

   A. $H_2C::CHCH_2CH_3$
   B. $H_2C::CHCH::CH_2$
   C. $H_2C::CHCHC::CH_2$
   D. $CH_3CH::CHCH_3$
   E. $H_2C::CHCH_3$

81. The Cahn-Ingold-Prelog rules are used to assign the configuration of each chiral atom in terms of the symbols R and S. Based on these rules, which of the following is NOT labeled correctly?

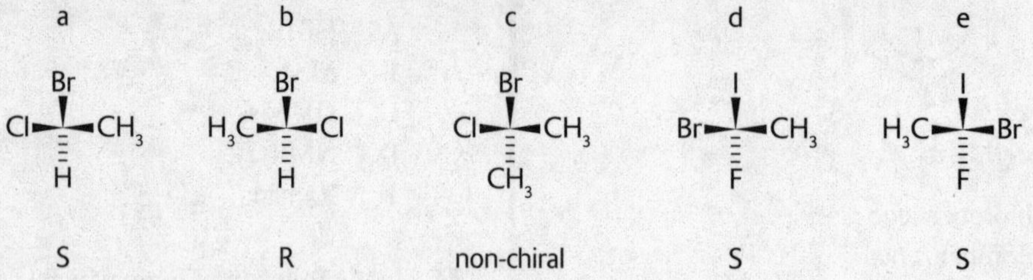

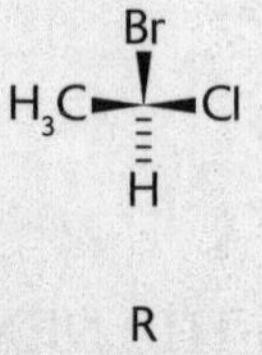

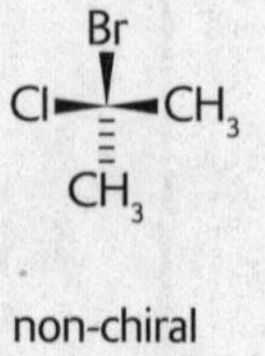

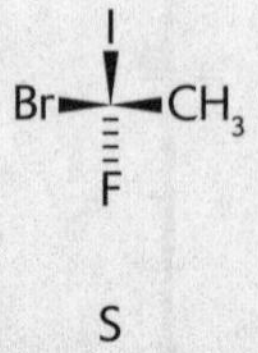

82. Which of the following statements is FALSE?

  A. There are two broad classes of stereoisomers, enantiomers, and diastereomers.

  B. Achiral molecules cannot possess chiral centers.

  C. Racemization of an enantiomer must result in the breaking of at least one bond to the chiral center.

  D. An attempted resolution can distinguish between a racemate and a *meso* compound.

  E. A meso compound cannot be resolved because it does not consist of enantiomers.

83. Which of the following will form 2-butene when treated with concentrated H_2SO_4?

  A. $CH_3CHOHCH_2CH_3$
  B. $CH_3CHBrCH_2CH_3$
  C. $CH_3C:::CCH_3$
  D. $CH_3CHBrCHBrCH_3$
  E. $CH_3CH_2CH_2CH_2OH$

84. Which of the following pairs of general formulas and hydrocarbon classes is INCORRECT?

  A. C_nH_{2n}, cycloalkanes
  B. C_nH_{2n+2}, open chain alkanes
  C. C_nH_{2n-2}, alkynes
  D. C_nH_{2n}, alkenes
  E. C_nH_{2n+2}, alkynes

85. Which of the following is an isomer of 2-methylpropane?

  A. 2-methylbutane
  B. butane
  C. cyclopentane
  D. cyclobutane
  E. cyclopropane

86. Which of the following is the I.U.P.A.C. name for the following compound?

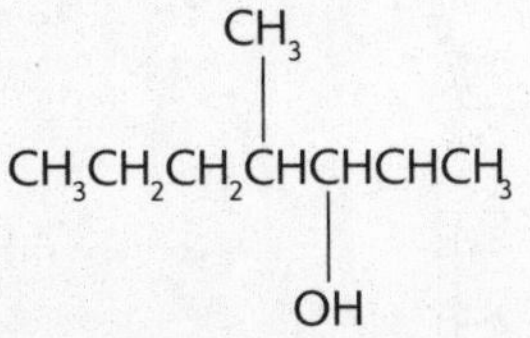

$$CH_3$$
$$|$$
$$CH_3CH_2CH_2CHCHCHCH_3$$
$$|$$
$$OH$$

  A. 2-methyl-3-hexanol
  B. 5-methyl-4-hexanol
  C. 3-methyl-2-hexanol
  D. 2-methyl-3-pentanol
  E. 2,2-dimethyl-3-pentanol

87. Which of the following is the product when CH_3CHO reacts with $KMnO_4$?

  A. CO_2 and H_2O
  B. CH_3COOH
  C. CH_3CH_2OH
  D. CH_3COCH_3
  E. CH_3CH_2COOH

88. What is the product of the reaction of phenylacetaldehyde with $LiAlH_4$?

  A. $C_6H_5CH_2CH_2OH$
  B. $C_6H_5CH_3$
  C. $C_6H_{11}CH_2CH_2OH$
  D. $C_6H_5CHOHCH_2OH$
  E. $C_6H_5CH_2CH_3$

89. Which of the following reactions will NOT produce a carboxylic acid?

  A. $CH_3CH_2CHO + KMnO_4 \rightarrow$
  B. $CH_3CH_2C:::CCH_2CH_3 + HNO_3 \rightarrow$
  C. $CH_3CH_2CHO + LiAlH_4 \rightarrow$
  D. $CH_3CH_2C:::N + H_3O^+ \rightarrow$
  E. $C_6H_5CH_2CH_2 MgCl + CO_2 \rightarrow C_6H_5CH_2CH_2$ $CO_2MgCl + H_3O^+ \rightarrow$

90. What are the products of the reaction of an ester, $C_6H_5COOCH_2CH_3$, with lithium aluminum hydride?

  A. $C_6H_5CH_2OHCH_2CH_3$
  B. $C_6H_5CH_2CH_2CH_3$
  C. $C_6H_{11}CH_2CH_2CH_3$
  D. $C_6H_5CH_2OH$ and CH_3CH_2OH
  E. $C_6H_5CH_3$ and CH_3CH_3

91. Short of being oxidized to carbon dioxide, which of the following functional groups CANNOT be oxidized further?

  A. aldehydes
  B. alkenes
  C. alcohols
  D. ketones
  E. alkanes

92. How many π electrons are in a triple bond?

  A. 6
  B. 4
  C. 2
  D. 1
  E. 0

GO ON TO THE NEXT PAGE

93. Which of the following can react with CH_3CH_2OH to diethylether?

A. H_2SO_4 and heat

B. NaOH

C. Na metal

D. HCl and heat

E. basic aqueous $KMnO_4$

94. Which of the following reactants will convert acetic acid to acetic anhydride?

A. H_2 with Pd

B. NaOH aqueous

C. hot concentrated H_2SO_4

D. $CH_3COO^- Na^+$

E. CH_3COOH

95. Which of the following compounds is an ether?

A. $C_6H_5CH_2COOH$

B. $C_6H_5CH_2CHO$

C. CH_3COCH_3

D. $CH_3CH_2OCH_2CH_3$

E. $C_6H_5CH_2COOCH_2CH_3$

96. What product is expected for the reaction

$$C_6H_5CH_2OH + MnO_4^{1-} \rightarrow$$

A. C_6H_5CHO

B. C_6H_5COOH

C. $C_6H_5CH_2OCH_2C_6H_5$

D. $C_6H_5COC_6H_5$

E. $C_6H_5CH_2OCH_2C_6H_5$

97. Which of the following reagents will convert $CH_3CH_2CHCH_2$ to an epoxide?

A. CH_3COCl

B. CH_3CH_2COOH

C. basic MnO_4^{1-}

D. $CH_3CH_2COCH_3CH_2$

E. CH_3CH_2COOOH

98. Which of the following compounds and the Grignard reagent, C_2H_5MgCl, can be used to produce a carboxylic acid?

A. CH_3CHO

B. CH_3COCH_3

C. H_2CO

D. CO_2

E. CH_3CH_2COOH

99. Formaldehyde has the formula H_2CO. There are 12 valence electrons in formaldehyde. How many electrons are in each of the following classes σ (sigma), π (pi), and n (nonbonding)?

A. $8\,\sigma$, $2\,\pi$ and $2\,n$

B. $4\,\sigma$, $4\,\pi$ and $4\,n$

C. $2\,\sigma$, $4\,\pi$ and $6\,n$

D. $6\,\sigma$, $2\,\pi$ and $4\,n$

E. $6\,\sigma$, $4\,\pi$ and $2\,n$

100. Which of the following structures is expected to be aromatic based on Huckel's $4n + 2$ rule for planar species?

A.

B.

C.

D.

E.

IF YOU FINISH BEFORE TIME IS CALLED, CHECK YOUR WORK ON THIS SECTION ONLY. DO NOT WORK ON ANY OTHER SECTION IN THE TEST.

Perceptual Ability Test

Time: 60 Minutes

90 Questions

Part 1

For Questions 1–15, this visualization test consists of a number of items similar to the sample below. A three-dimensional object is shown at the left. This is followed by outlines of five apertures or openings.

All of the tasks throughout this test are identical. The first step is to look at the object and imagine how it looks from every viewpoint. Then select the appropriate aperture from the five choices that will accommodate the object passing through it, if the object is inserted from the correct side. Then mark your choice on the answer sheet.

Here are the rules:

1. Prior to passing through the aperture, the irregular solid object may be turned in any direction. It may be started through the aperture on a side not shown.

2. Once the object is started through the aperture, it may not be twisted or turned. It must pass completely through the opening. The opening is always the exact shape of the appropriate external outline of the object.

3. Both objects and apertures are drawn to the same scale. Thus, it is possible for an opening to be the correct shape but too small for the object. In all cases, however, differences are large enough to judge by eye.

4. There are no irregularities in any hidden portion of the object. However, if the figure has symmetric indentations, the hidden portion is symmetric with the part shown.

5. For each object there is only one correct aperture.

Example:

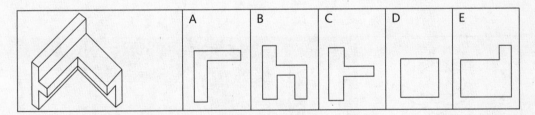

The correct answer is E since the object would pass through this aperture if the side at the left were introduced first.

Proceed to Questions 1–15.

GO ON TO THE NEXT PAGE

1.

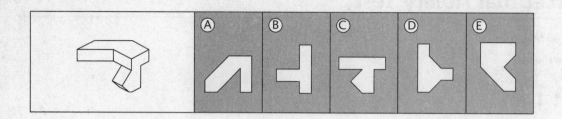

2.

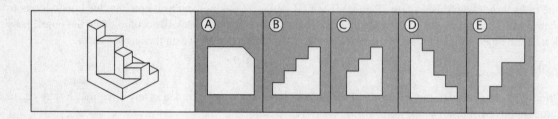

3.

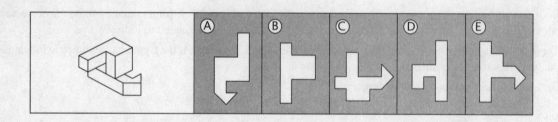

4.

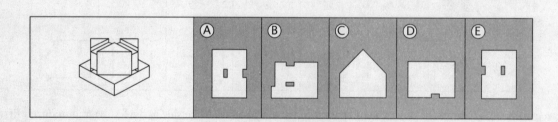

5.

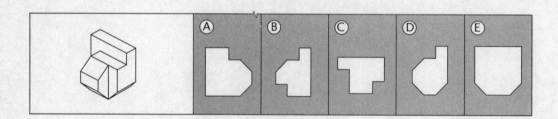

6.

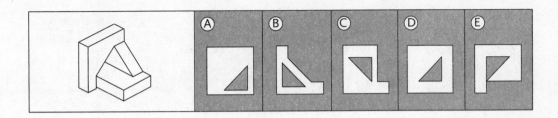

7.

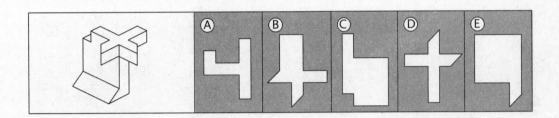

8.

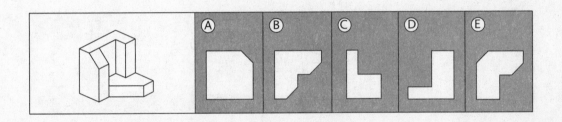

9.

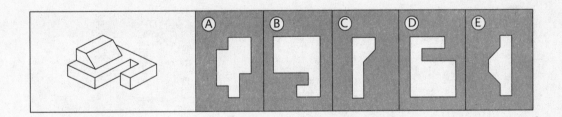

10.

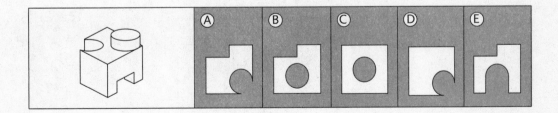

GO ON TO THE NEXT PAGE

11.

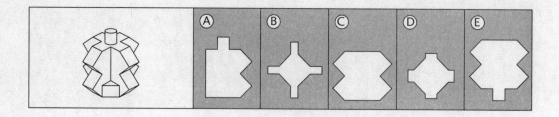

12.

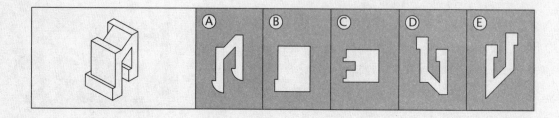

13.

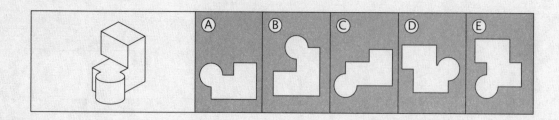

14.

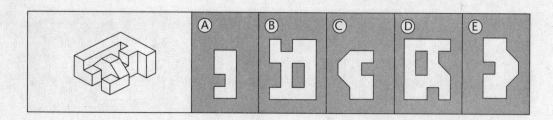

15.

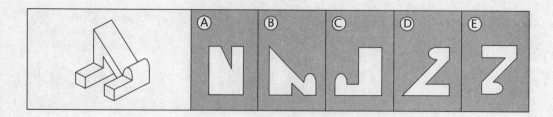

Part 2

For Questions 16–30, the following pictures illustrate top, front, and end views of various solid objects. The views are flat—without perspective, which means that the points in the viewed surface are viewed along parallel lines of vision. In the upper-left corner is the top view and the projection is looking down on it. In the lower-left corner is the front view, and the projection is looking at the object from the front. In the lower-right corner is the projection looking at the object from the end, which is labeled end view. These views are always in the same positions and are labeled accordingly.

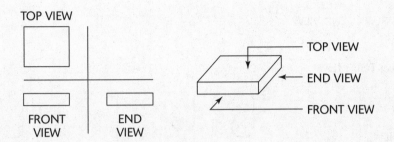

If there were a hole in the block, the views would look like this:

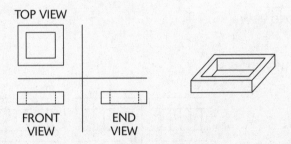

Note that lines that cannot be seen on the surface in some particular view are dotted in that view.

In the problems that follow, two views will be shown, with four alternatives to complete the set. You are to select the correct one and mark it on the answer sheet.

Example: Choose the correct end view.

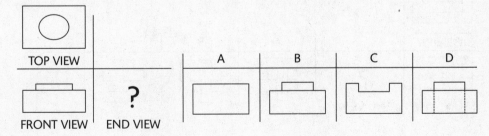

The front view shows that there is a smaller block on the base and that there is no hole. The top view shows that the block is round and in the center of the base. The answer, therefore, must be B.

In the problems that follow, it is not always the end view that must be selected, sometimes it is the top view or front view that is missing.

Proceed to Questions 16–30.

GO ON TO THE NEXT PAGE

16. Choose the correct TOP VIEW.

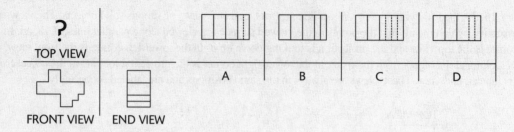

17. Choose the correct TOP VIEW.

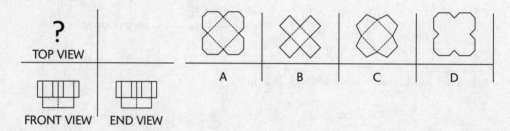

18. Choose the correct TOP VIEW.

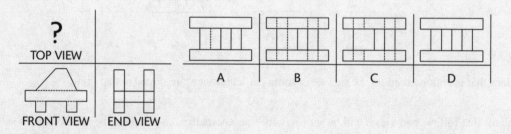

19. Choose the correct END VIEW.

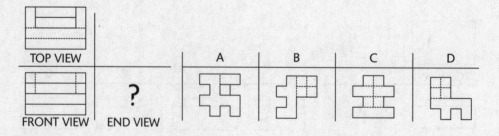

20. Choose the correct FRONT VIEW.

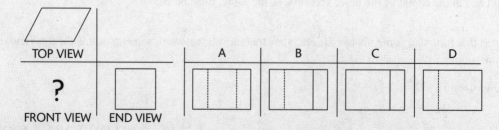

21. Choose the correct END VIEW.

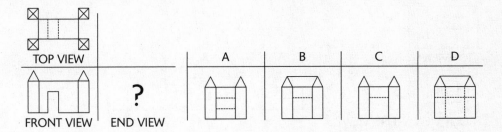

22. Choose the correct END VIEW.

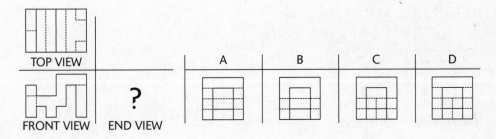

23. Choose the correct END VIEW.

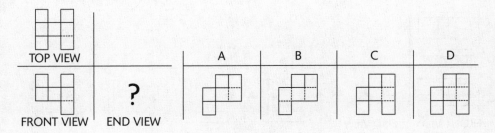

24. Choose the correct TOP VIEW.

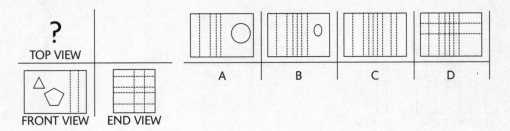

GO ON TO THE NEXT PAGE

25. Choose the correct END VIEW.

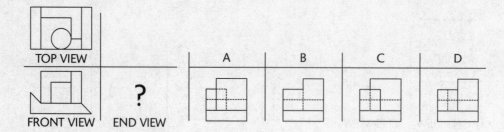

26. Choose the correct END VIEW.

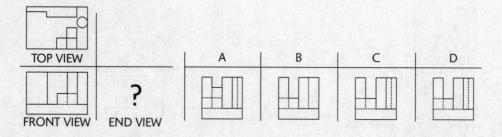

27. Choose the correct END VIEW.

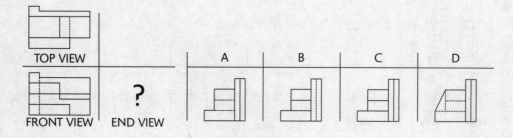

28. Choose the correct TOP VIEW.

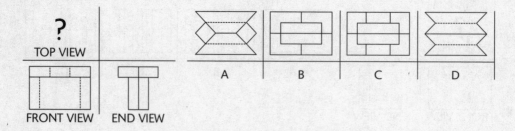

29. Choose the correct FRONT VIEW.

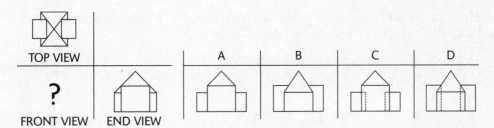

30. Choose the correct TOP VIEW.

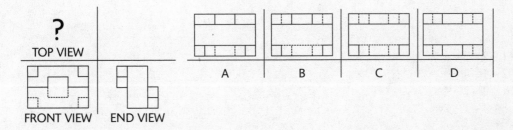

Part 3

For Questions 31–45, you are asked to examine the four INTERIOR angles and put them in order in terms of degrees from SMALL TO LARGE. Select the choice that has the correct ranking.

Example:

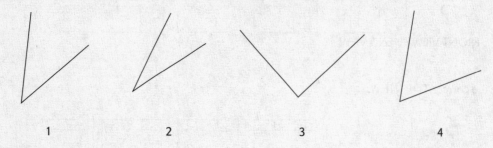

1   2   3   4

- **A.** 1 – 2 – 3 – 4
- **B.** 2 – 1 – 4 – 3
- **C.** 1 – 3 – 2 – 4
- **D.** 3 – 4 – 1 – 2

The correct ranking of the angles from small to large is 2 – 1 – 4 – 3; therefore, B is correct.

Proceed to Questions 31–45.

31.

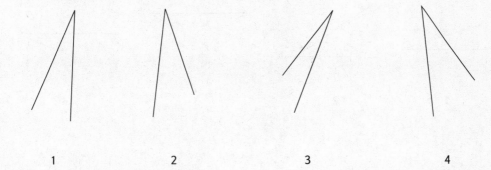

1   2   3   4

- **A.** 3 – 1 – 2 – 4
- **B.** 3 – 1 – 4 – 2
- **C.** 1 – 3 – 2 – 4
- **D.** 1 – 2 – 3 – 4

32.

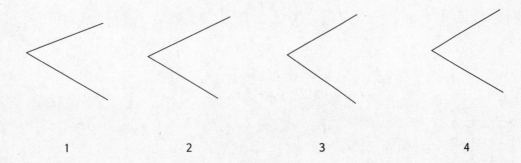

1   2   3   4

- **A.** 4 – 1 – 2 – 3
- **B.** 1 – 2 – 4 – 3
- **C.** 1 – 4 – 2 – 3
- **D.** 4 – 1 – 3 – 2

33.

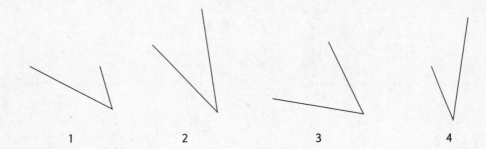

1   2   3   4

- **A.** 4 – 2 – 3 – 1
- **B.** 2 – 4 – 3 – 1
- **C.** 4 – 2 – 1 – 3
- **D.** 2 – 4 – 1 – 3

GO ON TO THE NEXT PAGE

34.

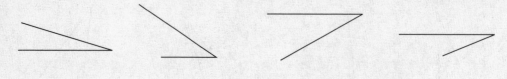

1   2   3   4

    A.   4 – 1 – 3 – 2
    B.   1 – 4 – 2 – 3
    C.   1 – 4 – 3 – 2
    D.   4 – 1 – 2 – 3

35.

1   2   3   4

    A.   4 – 1 – 3 – 2
    B.   1 – 4 – 3 – 2
    C.   1 – 4 – 2 – 3
    D.   4 – 1 – 2 – 3

36.

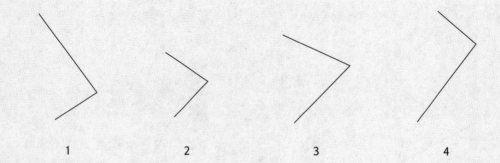

1   2   3   4

    A.   2 – 3 – 1 – 4
    B.   1 – 2 – 3 – 4
    C.   1 – 3 – 2 – 4
    D.   3 – 2 – 1 – 4

37.

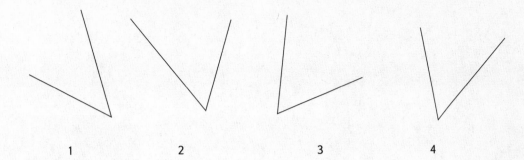

1   2   3   4

A. 1 – 4 – 2 – 3
B. 4 – 1 – 3 – 2
C. 4 – 1 – 2 – 3
D. 1 – 4 – 3 – 2

38.

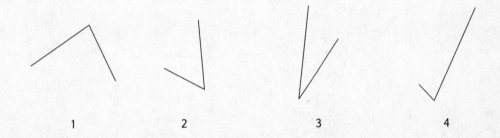

1   2   3   4

A. 3 – 2 – 4 – 1
B. 2 – 3 – 4 – 1
C. 2 – 4 – 3 – 1
D. 3 – 4 – 2 – 1

39.

1   2   3   4

A. 3 – 4 – 2 – 1
B. 3 – 2 – 4 – 1
C. 2 – 3 – 4 – 1
D. 2 – 4 – 3 – 1

GO ON TO THE NEXT PAGE

40.

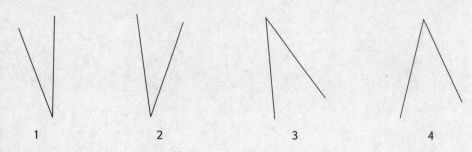

A. 2 – 1 – 4 – 3
B. 2 – 1 – 3 – 4
C. 1 – 2 – 3 – 4
D. 1 – 2 – 4 – 3

41.

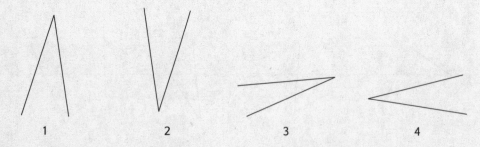

A. 3 – 4 – 1 – 2
B. 4 – 3 – 1 – 2
C. 3 – 4 – 2 – 1
D. 4 – 1 – 3 – 2

42.

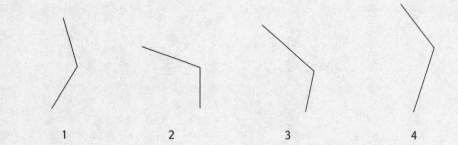

A. 2 – 1 – 3 – 4
B. 2 – 3 – 4 – 1
C. 2 – 3 – 1 – 4
D. 2 – 4 – 1 – 3

43.

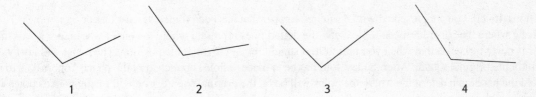

A. 3 – 1 – 2 – 4
B. 3 – 1 – 4 – 2
C. 1 – 3 – 2 – 4
D. 1 – 3 – 4 – 2

44.

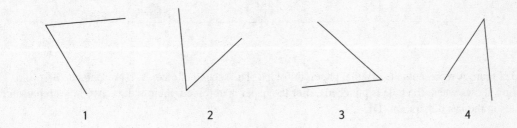

A. 2 – 4 – 3 – 1
B. 4 – 3 – 2 – 1
C. 4 – 3 – 1 – 2
D. 2 – 4 – 1 – 3

45.

A. 1 – 4 – 3 – 2
B. 1 – 2 – 3 – 4
C. 1 – 2 – 4 – 3
D. 1 – 3 – 2 – 4

GO ON TO THE NEXT PAGE

Part 4

For Questions 46–60, you are presented with a square of paper that has been folded at least one or more times. The solid lines indicate where the paper has been folded, and the dotted lines represent where the paper was before it was folded. The paper is never turned so that when you unfold it, it should remain in the same position. The paper will always be folded within the original square. After the last fold has been made, a hole is punched in the paper. Your task is to mentally unfold the paper and determine where the holes will be on the original square. You will be given five choices (A–E) from which to make your choice.

Example 1:

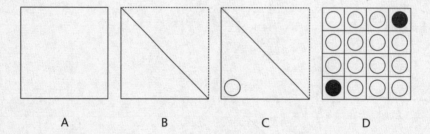

A   B   C   D

In Example 1, Figure A represents the original paper, unfolded. The second choice, B, represents the first fold. The third illustration shows where the hole is punched. After the paper is unfolded, there will be two holes represented by the dark circles in the last illustration (D).

The following example shows how this type of question will appear on the test.

Example 2:

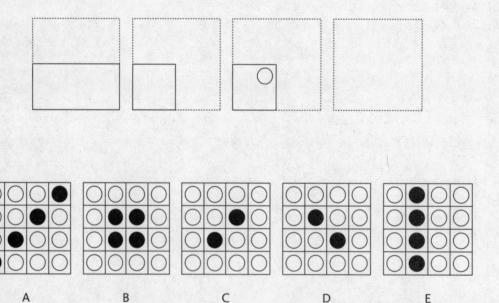

A   B   C   D   E

The correct answer to this example is B. With one fold, you would have two holes punched. With two folds, you will have four holes punched.

Proceed to Questions 46–60.

46.

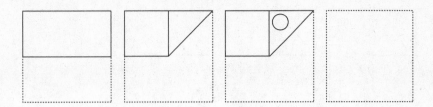

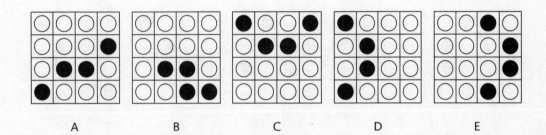

  A   B   C   D   E

47.

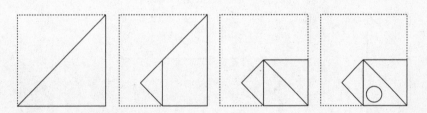

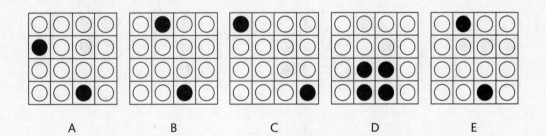

  A   B   C   D   E

GO ON TO THE NEXT PAGE

48.

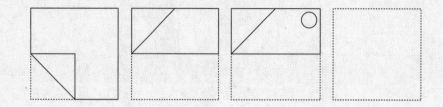

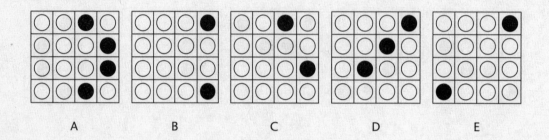

49.

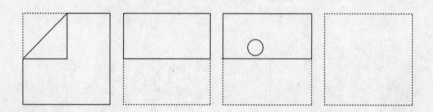

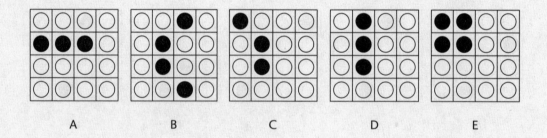

50.

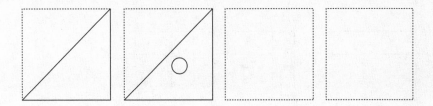

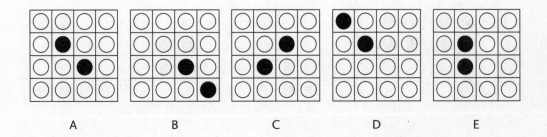

   A   B   C   D   E

51.

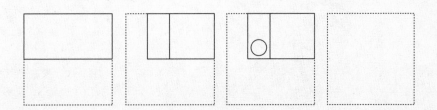

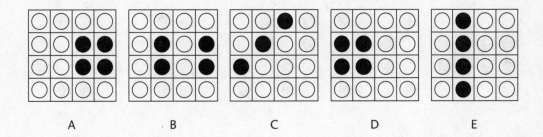

   A   B   C   D   E

GO ON TO THE NEXT PAGE

52.

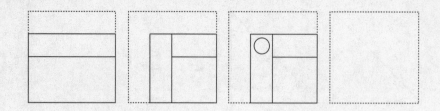

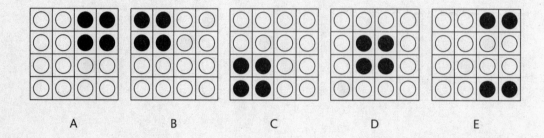

A   B   C   D   E

53.

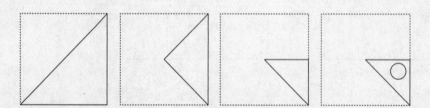

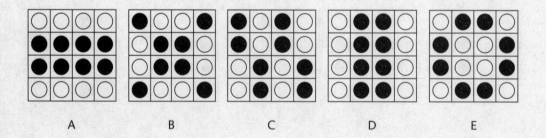

A   B   C   D   E

54.

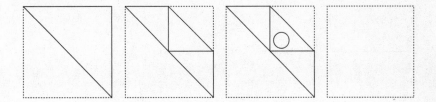

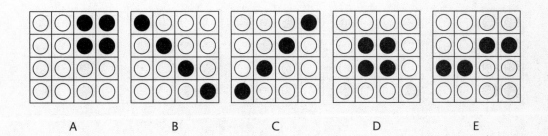

A   B   C   D   E

55.

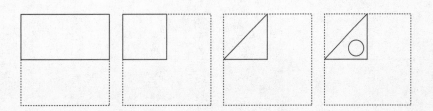

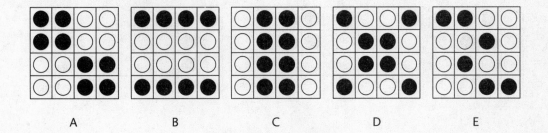

A   B   C   D   E

GO ON TO THE NEXT PAGE

56.

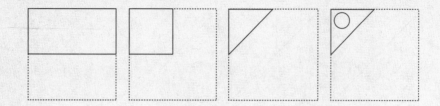

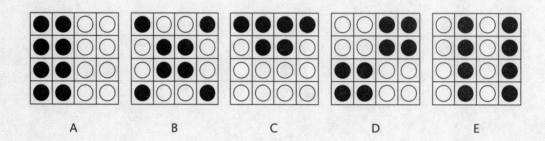

A   B   C   D   E

57.

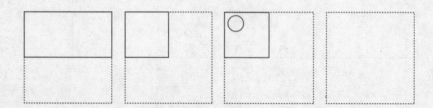

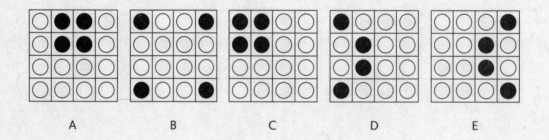

A   B   C   D   E

58.

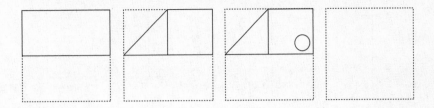

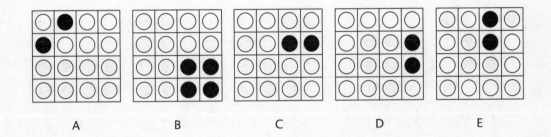

A   B   C   D   E

59.

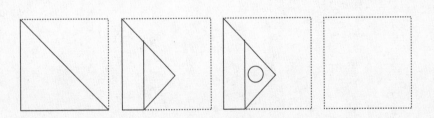

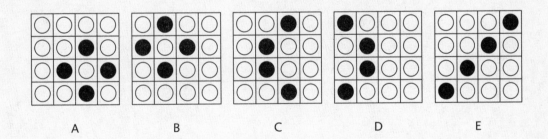

A   B   C   D   E

GO ON TO THE NEXT PAGE

60.

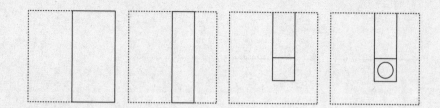

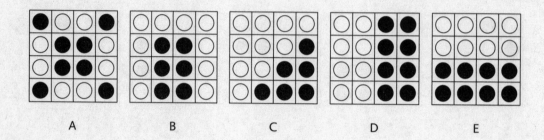

A   B   C   D   E

Part 5

Each figure has been made by attaching cubes of an identical size. After being attached, each group was painted on all sides. Only the bottom sides on which each cube rests were not painted. Hidden cubes are those that support other cubes.

For Questions 61–75, you are asked to answer the following questions based on the related figure:

- How many cubes have only one of their sides painted?
- How many cubes have only two of their sides painted?
- How many cubes have only three of their sides painted?
- How many cubes have only four of their sides painted?
- How many cubes have all five of there sides painted?

There will be no problems for which zero (0) is the correct answer.

In the following figures, how many cubes have two of their exposed sides painted?

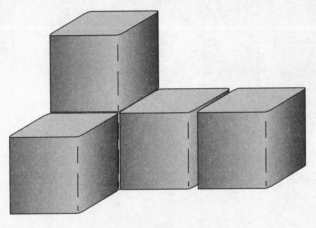

Figure 1

A. 1 cube
B. 2 cubes
C. 3 cubes
D. 4 cubes
E. 5 cubes

There are five cubes in Figure 1. Four cubes are visible and one is hidden, which supports the cube on the top row. The hidden cube has only two sides painted. The top cube has five sides painted. The front cube and the cube on the right each have four sides painted, and the middle cube has three sides painted. The correct answer is A.

Remember that after the cubes have been attached, each figure was painted on all exposed sides, except the bottom.

Proceed to Questions 61–75.

GO ON TO THE NEXT PAGE

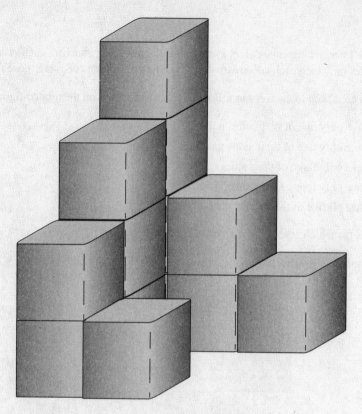

Figure A

61. In Figure A, how many cubes have three of their exposed sides painted?

    A. 1 cube
    B. 2 cubes
    C. 3 cubes
    D. 4 cubes
    E. 5 cubes

62. In Figure A, how many cubes have four of their exposed sides painted?

    A. 1 cube
    B. 2 cubes
    C. 3 cubes
    D. 4 cubes
    E. 5 cubes

63. In Figure A, how many cubes have five of their exposed sides painted?

    A. 1 cube
    B. 2 cubes
    C. 3 cubes
    D. 4 cubes
    E. 5 cubes

Figure B

64 In Figure B, how many cubes have one of their exposed sides painted?

   A. 1 cube
   B. 2 cubes
   C. 3 cubes
   D. 4 cubes
   E. 5 cubes

65. In Figure B, how many cubes have three of their exposed sides painted?

   A. 1 cube
   B. 2 cubes
   C. 3 cubes
   D. 4 cubes
   E. 5 cubes

66. In Figure B, how many cubes have four of their exposed sides painted?

   A. 1 cube
   B. 2 cubes
   C. 3 cubes
   D. 4 cubes
   E. 5 cubes

GO ON TO THE NEXT PAGE

67. In Figure B, how many cubes have one of their exposed sides painted?

    A.   1 cube

    B.   2 cubes

    C.   3 cubes

    D.   4 cubes

    E.   5 cubes

Figure C

68. In Figure C, how many cubes have four of their exposed sides painted?

    A.   1 cube

    B.   2 cubes

    C.   3 cubes

    D.   4 cubes

    E.   5 cubes

69. In Figure C, how many cubes have five of their exposed sides painted?

    A.   1 cube

    B.   2 cubes

    C.   3 cubes

    D.   4 cubes

    E.   5 cubes

Figure D

70. In Figure D, how many cubes have one of their exposed sides painted?

- **A.** 1 cube
- **B.** 2 cubes
- **C.** 3 cubes
- **D.** 4 cubes
- **E.** 5 cubes

71. In Figure D, how many cubes have two of their exposed sides painted?

- **A.** 1 cube
- **B.** 2 cubes
- **C.** 3 cubes
- **D.** 4 cubes
- **E.** 5 cubes

72. In Figure D, how many cubes have four of their exposed sides painted?

- **A.** 1 cube
- **B.** 2 cubes
- **C.** 3 cubes
- **D.** 4 cubes
- **E.** 5 cubes

GO ON TO THE NEXT PAGE

73. In Figure D, how many cubes have five of their exposed sides painted?

    A. 1 cube

    B. 2 cubes

    C. 3 cubes

    D. 4 cubes

    E. 5 cubes

Figure E

74. In Figure E, how many cubes have four of their exposed sides painted?

    A. 1 cube

    B. 2 cubes

    C. 3 cubes

    D. 4 cubes

    E. 5 cubes

75. In Figure E, how many cubes have five of their exposed sides painted?

    A. 1 cube

    B. 2 cubes

    C. 3 cubes

    D. 4 cubes

    E. 5 cubes

Part 6

In Questions 76–90, a flat pattern is presented. Based on your perception of this pattern, you must visualize what it will look like when it is folded into a three-dimensional figure. You are given four choices but only one will be the correct answer. There is only one correct figure in each set. The outside of the pattern is what is seen in the center.

Example:

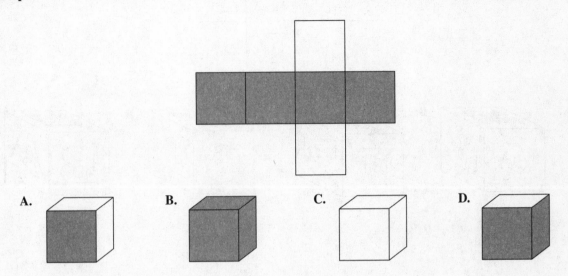

A.　　　　　B.　　　　　C.　　　　　D.

One of the preceding figures (A, B, C, or D) can be formed from the flat pattern in the center. The only figure that corresponds to the pattern is D. If the shaded surfaces are looked at as the sides of the box, then all four sides must be shaded, while the top and the bottom are white.

Proceed to Questions 76–90.

GO ON TO THE NEXT PAGE

76.

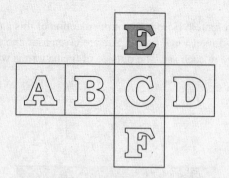

A.  B.  C.  D.

77.

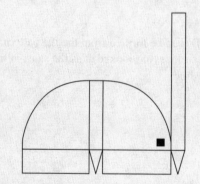

A.   B.   C.   D.

78.

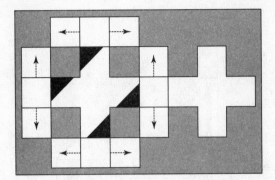

A. 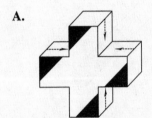 B. 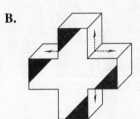 C. 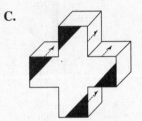 D.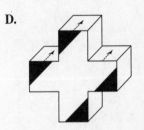

GO ON TO THE NEXT PAGE

79.

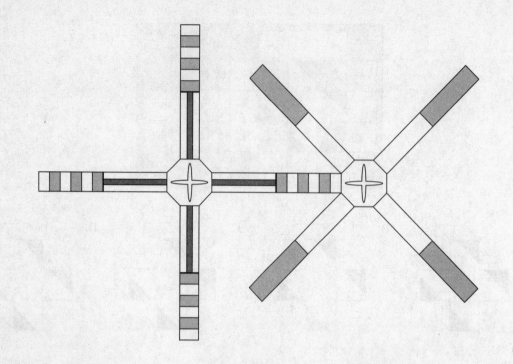

A. 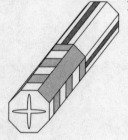 B. 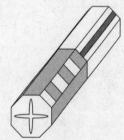 C. 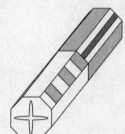 D.

80.

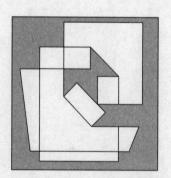

A. 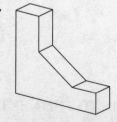 B. 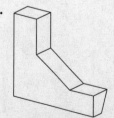 C. 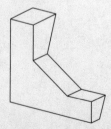 D.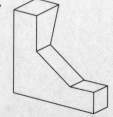

81.

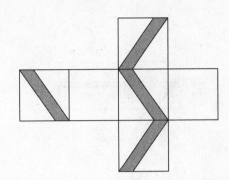

A.

B.

C.

D.

82.

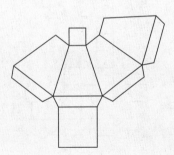

A.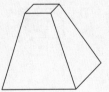

B.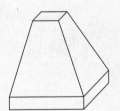

C.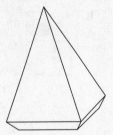

D.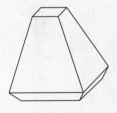

GO ON TO THE NEXT PAGE

83.

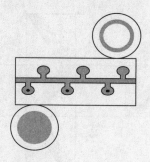

A.   B.   C.   D.

84.

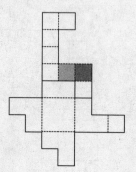

A.   B.   C.   D.

85.

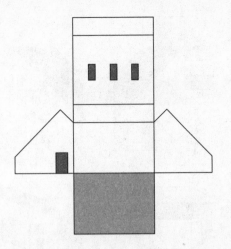

A.    B.    C.    D.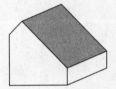

86.

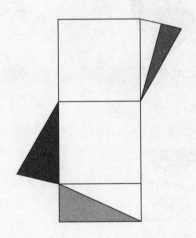

A. 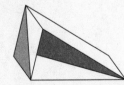   B. 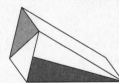   C.    D.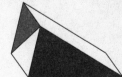

GO ON TO THE NEXT PAGE

DAT Practice Test 2

87.

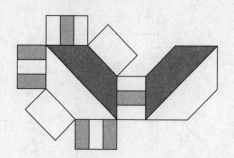

A. 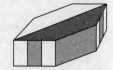   B.    C.    D.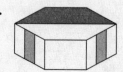

88.

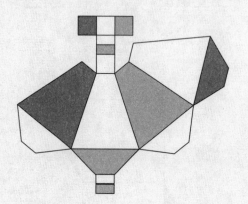

A.   B.   C.   D.

89.

A. 　　B. 　　C. 　　D.

90.

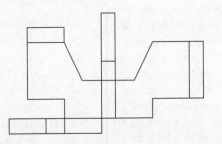

A. 　　B. 　　C. 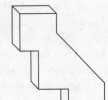　　D.

IF YOU FINISH BEFORE TIME IS CALLED, CHECK YOUR WORK ON THIS
SECTION ONLY. DO NOT WORK ON ANY OTHER SECTION IN THE TEST.

Reading Comprehension

Time: 60 Minutes

50 Questions

Directions: This section measures your ability to read and understand written English similar to what one may expect in a college or university setting. Read each passage and answer the questions based on what is stated or implied in the passage.

Passage 1

Tube worms live anchored to the sea floor, 1,700 feet below the ocean surface, near natural spring vents that spew forth water from the Earth. They live off geothermal energy instead of sunlight. There are two species of the tube worm family, with very different lengths of life and growth rates, but similarities as well.

The slow-growing tube worms are known to live as long as 250 years, making them the longest-living sea invertebrates known. This species lives near cold sea-floor seeps and may not grow at all from one year to the next. Even when they do grow, it is generally from a half an inch to four inches per year. In spite of their slow growth, due to their long lives, they can reach nine feet before they die, although they are thinner than the hot-water worms.

The seeps under the slow-growing tube worms are rich with oily materials. The environment in which they live is slow and peaceful, stable, and low-energy. The cold-water seeps and the tube worms that reside there may live hundreds or thousands of years.

In stark contrast, the fast-growing tube worms live a quick and short life, growing rapidly. They attach themselves near hot steaming vents that force water into the sea, growing about two and a half feet a year, and up to eight feet overall. They live by absorbing sulfur compounds metabolized by bacteria in a symbiotic relationship.

The hot water vents spew forth scalding water filled with hydrogen sulfide, which the tiny bacteria living in the worms' tissues consume. These tube worms live a rapid life, with none of the relaxing characteristics of the cold-water tube worms.

1. The word anchored in the first sentence is closest in meaning to

   A. affixed.
   B. contentedly.
   C. feeding.
   D. above.

2. The expression *spew forth* in the first sentence is closest in meaning to

   A. inhale.
   B. discharge.
   C. control.
   D. eliminate.

3. The author implies that a vent and a seep are

   A. the same.
   B. different in that a vent involves rapid discharge while a seep involves slow discharge.
   C. different in that a vent involves discharge while a seep involves intake.
   D. different in that a vent involves slow discharge while a seep involves rapid discharge.

4. The passage indicates that the two types of tube worms discussed are

   A. from totally different families.
   B. different in that one is not a true tube worm at all.
   C. from the same family but different species.
   D. from the same species and only differ because of habitat.

5. The author states that the cold-water tube worm

   A. grows slower than the hot-water tube worm.
   B. grows faster than the hot-water tube worm.
   C. does not grow as high as the hot-water tube worm.
   D. does not live as long as the hot-water tube worm.

6. The word *stark* in the fourth paragraph is closest in meaning to

   A. complete.
   B. somewhat.
   C. comparative.
   D. interesting.

7. The word *overall* in the fourth paragraph is closest in meaning to

   A. lifetime.
   B. annually.
   C. generally.
   D. rapidly.

8. The word *scalding* in the last paragraph is closest in meaning to

   A. hydrogen-filled.
   B. bacteria-filled.
   C. boiling.
   D. rapidly spewing.

9. The author indicates that the ingredients in the water that come from the two types of vents are

   A. different only because the heat of the hot vents destroys the oil as it spews forth.
   B. different in that one contains bacteria and the other contains oily materials.
   C. the same.
   D. different in that one contains oily materials and the other contains hydrogen sulfide.

GO ON TO THE NEXT PAGE

Passage 2

A new procedure has been developed to treat aneurysms, particularly those that occur near the brain stem, where surgery is dangerous.

Aneurysms are blood sacs formed by the enlargement of the weakened wall of an artery or vein. They are dangerous and, thus, must generally be removed before they cause considerable damage. If one ruptures, it can cause strokes or fatal hemorrhaging, the latter of which occurs in 50 percent of all patients. Before rupturing, an aneurysm frequently shows no sign or symptom that it exists. Brain aneurysms occur in approximately 5 percent of the population. Most patients are between 40 and 65 years old, with hemorrhages most prevalent in those between 50 and 54.

The new procedure involves inserting a soft, flexible micro-catheter through the femoral artery in the groin area and snaking it up through blood vessels to the brain. Inside the catheter is a small, coiled wire, which can be extruded after it reaches its destination. After the coil is outside the catheter, a low voltage electrical current is applied, and the coil detaches at a preset solder point. Additional coils are snaked through the catheter and also detached at the site, creating a basket, or metal framework, which causes the blood to clot around it. The micro-catheter is withdrawn, the clot remains, and the healed aneurysm no longer is exposed to the stress that can cause another rupture.

The procedure lasts two hours, which is half as long as invasive surgery, and recovery time is generally limited to a few days instead of a few weeks. The procedure was discovered in the 1990s, was approved by the U.S. Food and Drug Administration in 1995, and is available in various hospitals where there are advanced neurology departments and specialists trained in the procedure. Many lives have been saved by use of the procedure, because the alternative would have been to watch and wait rather than risk the hazards of surgery.

10. The author implies that the procedure described is useful for

- **A.** all aneurysms.
- **B.** aneurysms that occur anywhere in the brain.
- **C.** aneurysms that occur near the brain stem only.
- **D.** aneurysms that occur near large blood vessels.

11. The word *They* in the first paragraph refers to

- **A.** aneurysms.
- **B.** brain stems.
- **C.** surgeries.
- **D.** procedures.

12. The word *considerable* in the second paragraph is closest in meaning to

- **A.** slight.
- **B.** kind.
- **C.** significant.
- **D.** recurring.

13. The word *one* in the second paragraph refers to

- **A.** brain stem.
- **B.** aneurysm.
- **C.** procedure.
- **D.** surgery.

14. The word *snaking* in the third paragraph is closest in meaning to

- **A.** meandering.
- **B.** extruding.
- **C.** living.
- **D.** damaging.

15. The word *withdrawn* in the third paragraph is closest in meaning to

- **A.** removed.
- **B.** too large.
- **C.** charged.
- **D.** inserted.

16. An aneurysm is most similar to

- **A.** an ulcer.
- **B.** a hernia.
- **C.** a heart attack.
- **D.** cancer.

17. The author indicates that half of the patients who have a brain aneurysm could also have

- **A.** a stroke.
- **B.** a seizure.
- **C.** a heart attack.
- **D.** hemorrhaging that results in death.

18. The author indicates that the point of creating a basket near the aneurysm is to

   A. catch the aneurysm when it breaks off.
   B. serve as a base for a blood clot to form.
   C. dissolve the aneurysm.
   D. provide a means of studying the aneurysm.

19. The author indicates that the femoral artery is

   A. small.
   B. in the upper thigh.
   C. in the brain.
   D. connected to the brain.

20. The author states that the electrical charge is applied in order to

   A. stimulate the brain.
   B. stimulate the aneurysm.
   C. dissolve the aneurysm.
   D. separate the coil from the wire.

21. The author implies that the wire breaks off

   A. randomly.
   B. by being cut with an additional tool.
   C. at a predetermined and prepared location on the wire.
   D. inside the micro-catheter.

22. According to the passage, traditional surgical techniques take

   A. longer and require more recuperation time than the new procedure.
   B. longer but require less recuperation time than the new procedure.
   C. less time and require less recuperation time than the new procedure.
   D. less time but require longer recuperation time than the new procedure.

23. The author implies that the new procedure

   A. can be performed at any hospital.
   B. is performed only at hospitals containing the required equipment and certified doctors.
   C. is performed by certified doctors but requires no special equipment.
   D. is performed by any surgeon using special equipment.

GO ON TO THE NEXT PAGE

Passage 3

Scientists have discovered the bones of what may be the largest meat-eating dinosaur ever to walk the Earth. The discovery was made by a team of researchers from Argentina and North America in Patagonia, a desert on the eastern slopes of the Andes in South America. Besides the interesting fact that the dinosaur was huge and horrifying, it is even more astounding that the bones of a number of the dinosaurs were found together. This discovery challenges the prior theory that the biggest meat-eaters lived as loners and instead indicates that they may have lived and hunted in packs. The Tyrannosaurus Rex lived in North America and was believed to hunt and live alone.

The newly discovered meat-eater appears to be related to the Giganotosaurus family, being as closely related to it as a fox would be to a dog. It is actually not of the same family at all as the Tyrannosaurus Rex, being as different from it as a cat is from a dog.

The fossilized remains indicate that the animals lived about 100 million years ago. With needle-shaped noses and razor sharp teeth, they were larger than the Tyrannosaurus Rex, although their legs were slightly shorter, and their jaws were designed to be better able to dissect their prey quickly and precisely.

24. The author states that the newly discovered dinosaur remains are evidence that it was the largest

    A. dinosaur ever.
    B. carnivorous dinosaur.
    C. herbivorous dinosaur.
    D. South American dinosaur.

25. The word *besides* in the first paragraph is closest in meaning to

    A. in spite of.
    B. in addition to.
    C. although.
    D. mostly.

26. The word *horrifying* in the first paragraph is closest in meaning to

    A. frightening.
    B. large.
    C. fast.
    D. interesting.

27. The word *astounding* in the first paragraph is closest in meaning to

    A. terrifying.
    B. pleasing.
    C. displeasing.
    D. surprising.

28. The author implies that the most interesting fact about the find is that this dinosaur

    A. lived and hunted with others.
    B. had a powerful jaw and sharp teeth.
    C. was found in the Andes.
    D. was larger than Tyrannosaurus Rex.

29. The passage indicates that prior to this discovery, scientists believed that

    A. meat-eating dinosaurs lived alone.
    B. there were no meat-eating dinosaurs in the Andes.
    C. Tyrannosaurus Rex lived in the Andes.
    D. meat-eating dinosaurs were small in stature.

30. The word *it* in the second paragraph refers to

    A. newly discovered meat-eater.
    B. relationship.
    C. *Giganotosaurus*.
    D. dog.

31. The author states that the newly discovered meat-eating dinosaur is

    A. closely related to Tyrannosaurus Rex.
    B. not closely related to Tyrannosaurus Rex.
    C. not closely related to Giganotosaurus.
    D. closely related to the large cat family.

32. The word *dissect* in the last sentence is closest in meaning to

    A. dismember.
    B. swallow.
    C. chew.
    D. escape.

33. The word *prey* in the last sentence of the passage is closest in meaning to

    A. victim.
    B. enemy.
    C. dinosaurs.
    D. attacker.

Passage 4

Scientists have developed a new bionic computer chip that can be mated with human cells to combat disease. The tiny device, smaller and thinner than a strand of hair, combines a healthy human cell with an electronic circuitry chip. Doctors can control the activity of the cell by controlling the chip with a computer.

It has long been established that cell membranes become permeable when exposed to electrical impulses. Researchers have conducted genetic research for years with a trial-and-error process of bombarding cells with electricity in an attempt to introduce foreign substances such as new drug treatments or genetic material. They were unable to apply a particular level of voltage for a particular purpose. With the new invention, the computer sends electrical impulses to the chip, which triggers the cell's membrane pores to open and activate the cell in order to correct diseased tissues. It permits physicians to open a cell's pores with control.

Researchers hope that eventually they will be able to develop more advanced chips, whereby they can choose a particular voltage to activate particular tissues, whether they be muscle, bone, brain, or others. They believe that they will be able to implant multiple chips into a person to deal with one problem or more than one problem.

34. The word *mated* in the first sentence is closest in meaning to

    A. avoided.
    B. combined.
    C. introduced.
    D. developed.

35. The word *strand* in the second sentence is closest in meaning to

    A. type.
    B. thread.
    C. chip.
    D. color.

36. The author implies that scientists are excited about the new technology because

    A. it is less expensive than current techniques.
    B. it allows them to be able to shock cells for the first time.
    C. it is more precise than previous techniques.
    D. it is possible to kill cancer with a single jolt.

37. The author states that scientists previously were aware that

    A. they could control cells with a separate computer.
    B. electronic impulses could affect cells.
    C. electric charges could harm a person.
    D. cells interact with each other through electrical charges.

38. The word *bombarding* in the second paragraph is closest in meaning to

    A. barraging.
    B. influencing.
    C. receiving.
    D. testing.

39. The author implies that up to now, the point of applying electric impulse to cells was to

    A. kill them.
    B. open their walls to introduce medication.
    C. stop growth.
    D. combine cells.

40. The word *particular* in the third paragraph is closest in meaning to

    A. huge.
    B. slight.
    C. specific.
    D. controlled.

41. The word *others* in the third paragraph refers to other

    A. researchers.
    B. chips.
    C. voltages.
    D. tissues.

42. The author indicates that it is expected doctors will be able to

    A. place one large chip in a person to control multiple problems.
    B. place more than one chip in a single person.
    C. place a chip directly inside a cell.
    D. place a chip inside a strand of hair.

GO ON TO THE NEXT PAGE

Passage 5

The immune system aids the human body in defending itself against pathogens and infectious diseases. The first lines of defense are nonspecific—they do not distinguish between invading organisms. The nonspecific lines of defense include the skin, the outer layer of which is composed of thick dead skin cells that bacteria and viruses cannot penetrate; the mucous membranes lining the digestive and respiratory tracts; the hairs lining the nasal cavity, which filter out invading organisms; and the strong stomach acids, which kill most bacteria on food. Any organisms that get past these nonspecific barriers encounter the next line of nonspecific defenses—various white blood cells. The neutrophils and monocytes are phagocytic, engulfing bacteria and viruses in infected tissues. Some monocytes develop into large phagocytic cells called macrophages that move throughout the body engulfing any bacteria or viruses they encounter along the way. Other white blood cells, called natural killer cells, attack and destroy cancer cells and body cells infected with viruses. Other nonspecific lines of defense include various antimicrobial proteins, such as interferons, that either attack microorganisms directly or inhibit their reproduction. The human body's inflammatory response is yet another line of nonspecific defense. The inflammatory response is initiated following any kind of damage or physical injury, which triggers the release of chemical signals, such as histamine. These chemicals may induce nearby blood vessels to dilate and become leaky, causing more blood flow to the area. Other chemicals may attract phagocytes to the area, which consume any bacteria or cellular debris. The accumulated white blood cells and their breakdown products cause localized swelling of the infected tissue.

When the nonspecific defense systems are inadequate to eradicate the invading organisms, a specific defense system takes over. White blood cells, called lymphocytes, are responsible for producing the specific immune system response. The immune system defends against invading microorganisms and cancer cells, which the body recognizes as foreign, by producing a specific response to each invading agent. As such, the immune system must initially be stimulated by a foreign agent, referred to as an antigen. When an antigen is detected, the immune system produces chemicals, called antibodies, that attach specifically to that antigen and counter its effects.

Not only can the immune system provide a specific response, but it has the ability to recognize an invading agent as having been encountered previously and, therefore, can respond to the agent much more quickly the second time it is encountered. This recognition system is referred to as immunological memory. The first time an antigen is encountered, the immune system elicits a primary immune response, which typically takes several days to become effective against the invading organism. A subsequent exposure to the same antigen elicits a faster and stronger immune response, referred to as the secondary immune response. The secondary immune response is possible because of the long-lived memory cells produced by the immune system during the first exposure to the antigen.

We can take advantage of this secondary immune response with the use of vaccines. Vaccines are made from a killed or inactivated version of a specific invading agent, such as the flu virus. When we receive a vaccination, our immune system is stimulated to respond as if the actual virus has been encountered and produces antibodies to the antigens delivered in the vaccine, as part of the primary immune response. If we are later exposed to the real agent (flu virus), our immune system responds quickly with a strong secondary immune response, inactivating the invading agent (flu virus). Thus, vaccines are effective because they act as antigens, stimulating both primary immune response and immunological memory.

While we usually must rely on the work of the immune system, often with the help of vaccines, to fight off viral infections, we can sometimes use antibiotics to help fight off bacterial infections. While a healthy immune system will usually eventually kill off invading bacteria, the use of antibiotics—chemicals that interfere with bacterial growth and development—allow the body to rid itself of the bacterial infection, and the accompanying unpleasant effects of that infection, much more quickly.

43. Antibodies are produced by the immune system when it is stimulated by

    A. phagocytes.
    B. lymphocytes.
    C. nasal cilia.
    D. antigens.

44. Which of the following components of the body's defense system against pathogens and infectious agents is nonspecific?

    A. lymphocytes
    B. antigens
    C. antibodies
    D. neutrophils

45. The purpose of vaccinations is to

 A. make us ill so that we can fight the illness in the future.
 B. create antibodies in our immune system.
 C. eliminate influenza.
 D. develop internal vaccines.

46. A physical injury may result in the release of histamines. Its purpose is to

 A. attract phagocytes to the area of injury.
 B. create swelling of the infected or damaged tissue.
 C. dilate the blood vessels.
 D. prevent the growth of cancer cells.

47. What is the secondary immune response?

 A. the second line of defense by the body's immune system, specifically the development of interferon.
 B. the development of antimicrobial proteins.
 C. the engulfing of bacteria by macrophages.
 D. immunological memory, and the ability to "remember" previously encountered antigens.

48. When the body is invaded by cancer cells, the immune system responds by

 A. sending white blood cells to destroy the cancer cells
 B. releasing histamines to flood the cells.
 C. developing strong stomach acids.
 D. expanding the mucous membranes of the respiratory system.

49. When an antigen is recognized by the immune system as having been encountered previously, the immune system

 A. develops more antigens.
 B. responds with a faster immune response.
 C. hibernates until it can process the information.
 D. destroys memory cells.

50. Which of the following components of the body's defense system against pathogens and infectious agents is specific?

 A. neutrophils
 B. monocytes
 C. macrophages
 D. lymphocytes

IF YOU FINISH BEFORE TIME IS CALLED, CHECK YOUR WORK ON THIS SECTION ONLY. DO NOT WORK ON ANY OTHER SECTION IN THE TEST.

Quantitative Reasoning

Time: 45 Minutes

40 Questions

1. Janice buys a quart of milk and two dozen eggs. If milk costs $1.39 and eggs are $1.28 a dozen, how much change will Janice get back if she pays with a $10.00 bill?

   A. $3.95
   B. $4.06
   C. $5.94
   D. $6.05
   E. $7.33

2. If 400 people can be seated in 8 subway cars, how many people can be seated in 5 subway cars?

   A. 200
   B. 250
   C. 280
   D. 300
   E. 350

3. Devin throws a football $7\frac{1}{3}$ yards. Carl throws it $2\frac{1}{2}$ times farther. How much farther did Carl's throw travel than Devin's?

   A. $2\frac{1}{2}$ yards
   B. $7\frac{1}{3}$ yards
   C. 11 yards
   D. 12 yards
   E. $18\frac{1}{3}$ yards

4. Solve for m: $3m - 12 = -6$

   A. -6
   B. -4
   C. -2
   D. 0
   E. 2

5. If the area of a square is 400, what is the length of its side?

   A. 20
   B. 40
   C. 80
   D. 100
   E. 200

6. Roger collects bottle caps. Each cap can be traded for 5 cents. If Roger receives $40.50, how many bottle caps did he trade?

   A. 810
   B. 405
   C. 202
   D. 200
   E. 8

7. The cube of 8 is

   A. 2.
   B. 24.
   C. 256.
   D. 512.
   E. 8,000.

8. Fencing costs $4.75 per foot. Posts cost $12.50 each. How much will it cost to fence a garden if 10 posts and 34 feet of fencing are needed?

   A. $472.50
   B. $336.50
   C. $315.50
   D. $294.50
   E. $286.50

9. $\dfrac{\cos \theta}{\sin \theta} =$

   A. $\tan \theta$.
   B. $\cot \theta$.
   C. $\sec \theta$.
   D. $\csc \theta$.
   E. $\sin^2 \theta$.

10. Jared rents 3 videos for $8.00. What would the cost of 2 video rentals be?

    A. $1.33
    B. $5.00
    C. $5.33
    D. $5.67
    E. $6.00

11. Multiply $(2x + 1)(2x + 1)$.

    A. $2x^2 + 1$
    B. $4x^2 + 1$
    C. $4x^2 + 2x + 1$
    D. $2x^2 + 2x + 1$
    E. $4x^2 + 4x + 1$

12. A batch of cookies requires 2 cups of milk and 4 eggs. If you have 9 cups of milk and 9 eggs, how many batches of cookies can be made?

    A. 9
    B. 6
    C. 4
    D. 2
    E. 1

13. On a map, 1 centimeter represents 4 miles. A distance of 10 miles would be how far apart on the map?

    A. $1\frac{3}{4}$ cm
    B. 2 cm
    C. $2\frac{1}{2}$ cm
    D. 4 cm
    E. 5 cm

14. If $a^{\frac{1}{3}} = 2$, then what is the value of a?

    A. 4
    B. 8
    C. 16
    D. 32
    E. 64

15. Sandy bought $4\frac{1}{2}$ lbs of apples and 6 kiwi fruits. Brandon bought $3\frac{1}{4}$ lbs of apples and 9 kiwi fruits. If apples cost \$1.39 per lb and kiwis are 2 for \$1.00, how much more money did Sandy spend than Brandon?

    A. \$0.24
    B. \$0.34
    C. \$0.94
    D. \$1.54
    E. \$2.32

16. $\frac{24}{96} - \frac{8}{12} =$

    A. $-\frac{5}{12}$
    B. $-\frac{1}{4}$
    C. $\frac{5}{96}$
    D. $\frac{4}{21}$
    E. $\frac{1}{4}$

17. $\frac{3}{4} \div \frac{4}{3} =$

    A. 0
    B. 1
    C. $\frac{9}{16}$
    D. $\frac{4}{3}$
    E. $\frac{16}{9}$

18. A taxi ride costs \$3.00 for the first mile and \$1.00 each additional half mile. What is the cost of a 10-mile ride?

    A. \$10
    B. \$12
    C. \$13
    D. \$21
    E. \$23

19. What is the value of $64^{-\frac{1}{3}}$?

    A. $-\frac{1}{4}$
    B. $-\frac{1}{8}$
    C. $\frac{1}{16}$
    D. $\frac{1}{8}$
    E. $\frac{1}{4}$

20. If $\sin x > 0$ and $\sec x < 0$, then which quadrant must $\angle x$ lie in?

    A. I
    B. II
    C. III
    D. IV
    E. I and II

GO ON TO THE NEXT PAGE

21. What is the area of the figure shown?

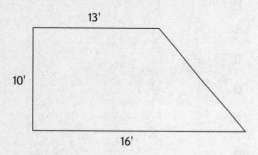

- **A.** 130 ft^2
- **B.** 145 ft^2
- **C.** 154 ft^2
- **D.** 160 ft^2
- **E.** 164 ft^2

22. Mr. Triber earns a weekly salary of $300 plus 10% commission on all sales. If he sold $8,350 last week, what were his total earnings?

- **A.** $835
- **B.** $865
- **C.** $1,135
- **D.** $1,270
- **E.** $1,835

23. If $7^{2x-1} = 7^{5x+8}$, what is the value of x?

- **A.** −3
- **B.** −1
- **C.** 1
- **D.** 3
- **E.** 9

24. Staci earns $9.50 an hour plus 3% commission on all sales made. If her total sales during a 30-hour work week were $500, how much did she earn?

- **A.** $15
- **B.** $250
- **C.** $285
- **D.** $300
- **E.** $315

25. Solve the following equation for x: $5^9 = 5^{4x+1}$

- **A.** −2
- **B.** 1
- **C.** 2
- **D.** 3
- **E.** 4

26. If the diameter of a circle is increased by 100%, the area is increased by

- **A.** 50%
- **B.** 100%
- **C.** 200%
- **D.** 300%
- **E.** 400%

27. What is the amplitude of the function $f(x) = 3 + 2\sin(7x)$?

- **A.** 2
- **B.** 3
- **C.** 5
- **D.** 7
- **E.** 12

28. Which of the following is an equation of a line parallel to the line $4x + 2y = 12$?

- **A.** $y = 2x + 6$
- **B.** $y = -2x + 7$
- **C.** $y = \frac{1}{2}x + 4$
- **D.** $y = -\frac{1}{2}x + 4$
- **E.** $y = 2x + 4$

29. A card is selected at random from a standard deck of 52 cards. What is the probability that the card is an ace?

- **A.** $\frac{1}{52}$
- **B.** $\frac{1}{26}$
- **C.** $\frac{1}{13}$
- **D.** $\frac{2}{13}$
- **E.** $\frac{4}{13}$

30. Temperatures in degrees Fahrenheit can be converted to temperatures in degrees Celsius by means of the formula $C = \frac{5}{9}(F - 32)$. Which of the following statements is TRUE?

- **A.** 41° Fahrenheit is hotter than 5° Celsius.
- **B.** 41° Fahrenheit is colder than 5° Celsius.
- **C.** 50° Fahrenheit is hotter than 10° Celsius.
- **D.** 50° Fahrenheit is colder than 10° Celsius.
- **E.** 50° Fahrenheit is the same as 10° Celsius.

31. Janet has seven coins in her purse: a penny, 2 nickels, a dime, 2 quarters, and a half-dollar. If she selects a coin at random from her purse, what is the probability that the value of the coin is at least 25 cents?

    A. $\frac{1}{7}$

    B. $\frac{2}{7}$

    C. $\frac{3}{7}$

    D. $\frac{4}{7}$

    E. $\frac{5}{7}$

32. If the average (arithmetic mean) of 82, 74, and w is 76, what is the value of w?

    A. 71
    B. 72
    C. 73
    D. 74
    E. 75

33. A right triangle has an area of 24 feet. If one leg is 3 times as long as the other, what is the length of the longest side?

    A. 12.6
    B. 12
    C. 8.4
    D. 6.3
    E. 4.2

34. There are five more boys in the kindergarten class than girls. If there are 27 children all together, how many are boys?

    A. 10
    B. 11
    C. 16
    D. 17
    E. 22

35. If $2^{3x} = 4^{x+1}$, then what is the value of x?

    A. 0
    B. $\frac{1}{2}$
    C. 2
    D. 4
    E. 8

36. Simplify $\dfrac{15\sqrt{3}}{\sqrt{5}}$.

    A. $3\sqrt{3}$
    B. $3\sqrt{15}$
    C. $5\sqrt{15}$
    D. $15\sqrt{15}$
    E. $75\sqrt{3}$

37. Given that the point $(x, 1)$ lies on a line with a slope of $-\frac{3}{2}$ and a y-intercept of -2, find the value of x.

    A. -2
    B. -1
    C. 0
    D. 1
    E. 2

38. At a neighborhood grocery store, the three stock workers earn $28,000 a year, the two department managers earn $31,000 a year, and the store manager earns $34,000 a year. What is the average (arithmetic mean) salary of these employees?

    A. $29,000
    B. $30,000
    C. $31,000
    D. $32,000
    E. $33,000

39. Which of the following values of x is a solution to the equation $\sin x = \frac{1}{2}$?

    A. $x = 30°$
    B. $x = 45°$
    C. $x = 60°$
    D. $x = 75°$
    E. $x = 90°$

GO ON TO THE NEXT PAGE

40. If the area of the circle is 121π, find the area of the square.

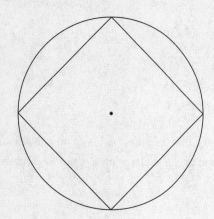

    A. 121
    B. 242
    C. 363
    D. 484
    E. 726

IF YOU FINISH BEFORE TIME IS CALLED, CHECK YOUR WORK ON THIS SECTION ONLY. DO NOT WORK ON ANY OTHER SECTION IN THE TEST.

Answer Key for Practice Test 2

Natural Sciences

Biology

1. E	11. A	21. D	31. D
2. A	12. C	22. A	32. A
3. B	13. D	23. C	33. C
4. D	14. C	24. D	34. B
5. D	15. E	25. B	35. E
6. B	16. B	26. D	36. D
7. A	17. E	27. C	37. C
8. B	18. A	28. E	38. D
9. C	19. C	29. A	39. E
10. E	20. E	30. A	40. A

Chemistry

41. E	56. E	71. D	86. C
42. A	57. D	72. A	87. B
43. C	58. B	73. E	88. A
44. E	59. C	74. E	89. C
45. C	60. E	75. C	90. D
46. B	61. B	76. D	91. D
47. E	62. C	77. D	92. B
48. B	63. B	78. C	93. A
49. A	64. A	79. E	94. C
50. D	65. C	80. D	95. D
51. E	66. E	81. E	96. B
52. C	67. C	82. B	97. E
53. D	68. E	83. A	98. B
54. A	69. B	84. E	99. D
55. B	70. C	85. B	100. D

Perceptual Ability Test

Part 1

1. C	5. C	9. C	13. C
2. D	6. D	10. D	14. B
3. D	7. B	11. E	15. D
4. B	8. D	12. D	

Part 2

16. D	20. B	24. B	28. A
17. A	21. C	25. A	29. D
18. B	22. D	26. C	30. B
19. A	23. B	27. C	

Part 3

31. A	35. B	39. B	43. A
32. B	36. D	40. C	44. B
33. C	37. A	41. C	45. D
34. C	38. A	42. B	

Part 4

46. E	50. A	54. C	58. D
47. A	51. D	55. D	59. A
48. B	52. C	56. B	60. E
49. C	53. E	57. B	

Part 5

61. A	65. C	69. A	73. C
62. E	66. D	70. A	74. D
63. A	67. B	71. C	75. B
64. C	68. E	72. B	

Part 6

76. C	80. B	84. D	88. B
77. B	81. B	85. C	89. D
78. A	82. D	86. A	90. A
79. D	83. C	87. B	

Reading Comprehension

1. A	14. A	27. D	40. C
2. B	15. A	28. A	41. D
3. B	16. B	29. A	42. B
4. C	17. D	30. C	43. D
5. A	18. B	31. B	44. D
6. A	19. B	32. A	45. B
7. A	20. D	33. A	46. C
8. C	21. C	34. B	47. D
9. D	22. A	35. B	48. A
10. C	23. B	36. C	49. B
11. A	24. B	37. B	50. D
12. C	25. B	38. A	
13. B	26. A	39. B	

Quantitative Reasoning

1. D	11. E	21. B	31. C
2. B	12. D	22. C	32. B
3. C	13. C	23. A	33. A
4. C	14. B	24. D	34. C
5. A	15. A	25. C	35. C
6. A	16. A	26. E	36. B
7. D	17. C	27. A	37. A
8. E	18. D	28. B	38. B
9. B	19. E	29. C	39. A
10. C	20. B	30. E	40. B

Answers and Explanations for Practice Test 2

Natural Sciences

Biology

1. **E.** Only eukaryotic cells have a membrane-bound nucleus and other organelles. Bacterial cells are prokaryotic and lack an organized nucleus or other membrane-bound organelles.

2. **A.** Diffusion involves the passive movement of substances down a concentration gradient (from a region of higher concentration to a region of lower concentration). Osmosis is a special form of diffusion that involves the movement of water from a region of higher concentration to a region of lower concentration. The passive nature of diffusion and osmosis does not require the input of energy. However, an input of energy is required for the movement of substances against a concentration gradient (from a region of lower concentration to a region of higher concentration). This type of energy-requiring movement against a concentration gradient is referred to as active transport.

3. **B.** In humans, and most other organisms, growth and tissue repair involves the production of new cells through the process of mitosis, a type of cell division that produces two identical daughter cells from each parent cell. Meiosis (A) is a type of cell division that occurs only in the germ cells that give rise to gametes (for example, eggs and sperm in humans). Meiosis results in the formation of four genetically unique daughter cells from each parent cell. Fission (C) is a type of asexual reproduction that occurs in bacteria. Budding (D) is a type of asexual reproduction that occurs in yeast and hydra.

4. **D.** Cellular respiration takes place in the mitochondria of the cells of most organisms and results in the production of energy (ATP) through the breakdown of glucose molecules.

5. **D.** During photosynthesis, light energy is absorbed by the pigment chlorophyll (found in the chloroplasts of plant cells, algal cells, and some bacterial cells) and is used to produce chemical energy in the form of glucose, from carbon dioxide and water.

6. **B.** Enzymes are a type of protein that speed up the rate of chemical reactions by lowering the activation energy required for the reaction to take place. The enzymes themselves are not directly involved in the reaction, so they are not altered or destroyed by the reaction they catalyze.

7. **A.** According to the endosymbiont theory, mitochondria and chloroplasts originated as small prokaryotes living as endosymbionts within larger cells. The proposed ancestors of mitochondria are aerobic, heterotrophic prokaryotes, and the proposed ancestors of chloroplasts are photosynthetic prokaryotes.

8. **B.** Ferns have vascular tissue (xylem and phloem).

9. **C.** The teeth of primates (which include lemurs, monkeys, apes, and humans) have finite growth. Certain teeth (primarily the incisors) of some groups of organisms (including most rodents) continue to grow throughout the life of the organism and must be worn away through chewing or gnawing.

10. **E.** *Homo sapiens* (humans) are members of *phylum* Chordata, *sub-phylum* vertebrata, *class* Mammalia.

11. **A.** Calcitonin, which lowers the calcium levels of the blood, is produced by the thyroid gland.

12. **C.** Blood pressure is a measure of the amount of force exerted by the blood on the walls of the blood vessels. By taking your pulse (A), you can measure your heart rate (B), or the number of times your heart beats per minute. The diastole (E) is the relaxation phase of the cardiac cycle, and the systole (D) is the contraction phase of the cardiac cycle.

13. **D.** Digestion is the process through which humans transform organic molecules taken in as food into a form that is readily usable by the body.

14. **C.** Carbohydrates, primarily glucose, provide the most basic, direct source of energy for use by the human body. Other macromolecules such as lipids (fats), proteins, and nucleic acids are broken down and used for energy after the body's stores of glucose have been used up.

15. E. The kidney serves as the primary functional unit of the human excretory system. The function of the vertebrate excretory system, which includes the ureters (A), urethra (B), bladder (C), and kidneys (E) is to rid the body of metabolic waste products and regulate the osmotic balance of the blood. The small intestine (D) is part of the vertebrate digestive system, which functions in the ingestion, digestion, absorption, and elimination of food.

16. B. The endocrine system is composed of a series of glands that produce hormones that are responsible for coordinating the various systems in the human body. The human excretory system (A) is responsible for eliminating wastes from the body and maintaining osmotic balance of the blood. The human nervous system (D) controls the body's responses to internal and external stimuli. The human circulatory system is responsible for transporting gases, nutrients, and waste products throughout the body.

17. E. In human reproduction, fertilization takes place in the Fallopian tubes, which lead from each ovary to the uterus. The vagina (A) receives the penis and sperm. The cervix (B) is the constricted region at the base of the uterus. The uterus (C) is a muscular organ within which the fetus develops. The ovary (D) is the organ in which eggs form.

18. A. The brain and spinal cord make up the central nervous system of vertebrate organisms. The peripheral nervous system is composed of the nerves and ganglia leading from the central nervous system to the rest of the body. The somatic nervous system carries signals to skeletal muscles, usually in response to an external stimulus. The autonomic nervous system conveys signals that regulate involuntary control of the cardiac muscles and the smooth muscles of the digestive, cardiovascular, excretory, and endocrine systems. The autonomic nervous system is divided into two divisions: the parasympathetic division controls activities that conserve energy, such as digestion and a slowing of the heart rate; the sympathetic division controls activities that consume energy, such as increasing heart rate or metabolic function, preparing the body for action.

19. C. When air is inhaled into the human respiratory system, it passes from the nasal cavity into the larynx. From the larynx, air moves into the trachea, also called the windpipe. The trachea branches into two bronchi, one leading to each lung. Within the lung, the bronchi branch into finer and finer tubes called bronchioles. The smallest bronchioles terminate into air sacs referred to as alveoli, the surface of which serves as the primary site for gas exchange in the human respiratory system.

20. E. The spleen is composed primarily of lymph nodes and is responsible for destroying old red blood cells. The liver (D) helps to sequester and remove toxins from the body. The pancreas (A) and gall bladder (B) produce enzymes that aid in digestion. The appendix (C) plays a small role in the human immune system but is functionally dispensable.

21. D. Antibiotics are only effective against bacteria; they are not effective against viruses or other infectious agents.

22. A. The skeletal system is derived from the mesoderm layer during human development.

23. C. After fertilization, a special form of cell division referred to as cleavage occurs. Cleavage involves a rapid succession of cell divisions in which the cells undergo DNA synthesis and mitosis, but not the two growth stages of the cell cycle. The result is a partitioning of the zygote (a single large cell) into several smaller cells, called blastomeres, without an overall increase in the size of the developing embryo. This multicellular embryo is called a blastula. Different parts of the cytoplasm are partitioned into different blastomeres during cleavage, setting up the cells for future developmental events. Following cleavage, gastrulation occurs, resulting in the formation of a three-layered embryo called a gastrula. The next stage of development, organogenesis, results in the production of rudimentary organs in the embryo.

24. D. For a given trait to be expressed, genes on DNA in the nucleus of the cell must be transcribed onto a molecule of mRNA (messenger RNA) and carried out of the nucleus into the cytoplasm. The mRNA attaches to a ribosome in the cytoplasm, while tRNA (transfer RNA) molecules add appropriate amino acids to the growing polypeptide chain, according to the message encoded on the mRNA, translating the DNA message into protein.

25. B. The genetic makeup of an individual is referred to as his or her genotype. The physical appearance of an individual is referred to as his or her phenotype (C). The genetic code (E) refers to the triplet of nitrogen bases that code for amino acids. A gene pool (D) refers to the genetic constitution of a population. A genome (A) refers to the entire genetic complement of a particular type of organism.

26. D. An individual with two different alleles for a given trait (in this case, earlobe type) is said to be heterozygous for that trait. If both alleles for a given trait are the same (for example, two alleles for attached earlobes), the individual is said to be homozygous for the trait (A). Dominance (C) and recessiveness (B) refer to the expression of alleles when present together in an individual. In this example, a person with one allele for free earlobes and one allele for attached earlobes would have free earlobes because the allele for free earlobes is dominant over the allele for attached earlobes. Heterogeneous (E) refers to genetic diversity among individuals at the population level, not the genetic make-up of an individual.

27. C. The M, N, and MN blood groups in humans are an example of codominance, in which both alleles are expressed equally in the phenotype. With complete dominance (A), the dominant allele masks the recessive allele. With incomplete dominance (D), the phenotype is usually intermediate between the dominant and recessive phenotypes, with neither allele fully expressed. There is no condition referred to as complete recessiveness (B). Heterozygosity (E) refers to the allelic make-up of an individual with two different alleles for a particular trait.

28. E. A woman with type-AB blood and a man with type-O blood could produce children with either type-A or type-B blood. The woman would carry one A allele and one B allele for blood type, and the man would carry two O alleles. The A and B alleles are codominant, and the O allele is recessive to both the A and B alleles. Because the children would receive one allele from their mother and one allele from their father, the children could have the genotypes AO (with type-A blood) or BO (with type-B blood).

29. A. Using restriction digestion of a sample of DNA from an individual and subsequent electrophoresis of the restricted sample (Restriction Fragment Length Polymorphism–RFLP–Analysis) a DNA fingerprint of the individual can be produced. Such fingerprints can then be used for identification in paternity suits and analysis of crime scene evidence.

30. A. All of the offspring would inherit at least one dominant allele from the homozygous dominant parent and, therefore, have round ears.

31. D. The sex chromosome complement of human females is XX, and the sex chromosome complement of human males is XY. Daughters receive one X chromosome from their mother and one X chromosome from their father. With two X chromosomes, sex-linked recessive disorders are less common among females than males, as there is a chance that a female will carry at least one unaffected X chromosome (with the dominant allele), masking the presence of the recessive allele. However, it is possible for a daughter to inherit the recessive allele from both parents and show the homozygous recessive trait. Sons inherit their X chromosome from their mother and their Y chromosome from their father. Thus, even an unaffected, heterozygous mother has a 50-50 chance of producing an affected son. Because all known sex-linked traits are carried on the X chromosome, males cannot inherit a sex-linked trait from their father through the Y chromosome.

32. A. Evolution involves changes in the genetic composition (allelic and genotypic frequencies) of a population over time. Several factors influence the rate of evolution in a population, including mutation, genetic drift, population size, migration into or out of the population, and natural selection. Natural selection is based on the relative reproductive fitness of individuals within a population and is sometimes referred to as "survival of the fittest."

33. C. A species consists of a group of related individuals who are capable of interbreeding and producing fertile offspring. A population (B) refers to a group of individuals of the same species that share a common geographic area. A community (A) refers to all of the populations of different species that share a common geographic area and have the potential to interact with each other. A gene pool (D) refers to the total complement of genes in a population at any given time. A family (E) is part of the taxonomic hierarchy used to define relationships among organisms.

34. B. A community includes all the organisms living in a given area, which have the potential to interact with each other. An ecosystem includes a local community and the physical surroundings (abiotic factors) with which the organisms interact.

35. E. Producers are organisms that are capable of manufacturing their own food, usually through the process of photosynthesis. Producers in terrestrial ecosystems include any plant that is consumed by another organism. Producers in aquatic ecosystems are usually small, often single-celled forms of algae and photosynthetic bacteria (phytoplankton). Organisms that feed on the producers are referred to as primary consumers (B). Because they eat plant material, the primary consumers are often referred to as herbivores (C). Organisms that feed upon the primary consumers are referred to as secondary consumers. The secondary consumers, which feed on other animals, are also referred to as carnivores (A). There may be several trophic levels of consumers present in a given food chain. Many organisms feed at several layers of the food chain—for example, a hawk might consume a mouse, or it might consume a snake that has consumed a mouse. Organisms that feed on both producers and consumers are referred to as omnivores. Decomposers (D), which include fungi, bacteria, and slime molds, break down dead and decaying material and recycle the nutrients back into the ecosystem. The decomposers are often depicted as being at the end of a food chain; however, they actually operate at all levels of the food chain, breaking down waste.

36. D. A prolonged period of drought would cause a decrease in population size, regardless of the initial density of the population and, thus, would be considered a density-independent factor affecting population size. The availability of food, water, or shelter, and the level of toxins present in the ecosystem, would affect denser populations to a greater degree than less dense populations, and would thus be considered density-dependent factors affecting population size.

37. C. When consumed, toxins are usually sequestered and stored in the liver and fatty tissue of the organisms that consumed them. Thus, when a toxin enters the food chain, it becomes more and more concentrated at each trophic level. This increase in toxin concentration at subsequent levels of the food chain is referred to as *biological magnification.*

38. D. Parasitism involves one organism (for example, tapeworm) living in or on a host organism (for example, human). Predation (C) involves one organism (for example, mountain lion) killing and consuming another organism (for example, deer). Mutualism (A) is a type of symbiotic relationship in which both organisms benefit from the relationship (for example, green algae and fungi living together as a lichen). Commensalism (B) is a symbiotic relationship in which the symbiont benefits, but the host is neither helped nor harmed.

39. E. Natural selection will help to increase the frequency of favorable traits in a population. Evolution (D) is the result of changes in the genetic make-up of a population over time. The rate of evolution is affected by the degree of natural selection operating on various traits. Genetic drift (A) and genetic bottlenecking (C) are both associated with small population size and a decrease in the amount of genetic variation within a population. Migration (B) into or out of the population also affects the relative allelic and genotypic frequencies within the population and, as such, also affects evolution of the population.

40. A. Sociobiology examines the evolution of social behavior, which includes competitive behaviors, mating behaviors, diverse modes of communication, and social interactions within and between species.

Chemistry

41. E. Silver is a metal. It is in Group 11 and is one of the coinage metals.

42. A. Copper and chlorine are a metal and nonmetal, respectively. Normally this type of combination will form an ionic substance. The other combinations all have pairs of nonmetals.

43. C. There are 24 valence electrons in sulfur trioxide. All four of the atoms are in Group 6A, and each has six valence electrons.

44. E. Incomplete combustion of a hydrocarbon always yields $CO(g)$ and $H_2O(g)$. The coefficients must be "1" for $CO(g)$ to balance the carbons and a "2" for water to balance the 4 hydrogen atoms. The odd number of O atoms in methanol matches the odd number of O atoms in CO.

45. C. The mols of ammonia depend on Avogadro's number and the count of ammonia molecules. Convert molecules to mols using Avogadro's number: mols = $(1 \text{ mol} / 6.02 \times 10^{23} \text{ molecules}) (3.0 \times 10^{24} \text{ molecules})$.

46. B. Polonium-210 has atomic number $Z = 84$ and mass number $A = 210$. Alpha particles have a mass number of 4 and $Z = 2$. Loss of an alpha particle will decrease the charge by two units and the mass by four. The product has $Z = 82$ and mass number $A = 206$.

47. E. The flash point depends on the compound's reactivity with oxygen.

48. B. The lower the pK_a, the stronger the acid. The *p* indicates the negative logarithm base 10. Very strong acids will actually have negative values for pK_a.

49. A. Binary acids formed by the halogens increase in acid strength from top to bottom of the group, HF < HCl < HBr < HI < HClO₄. Perchloric acid is stronger than any of the binary halogen acids. The larger the anion, the weaker the bond between the proton and the anion resulting in a stronger acid.

50. D. The transition state exists at the maximum of the energy path.

51. E. Calcium chloride produces three ions per formula unit. This means $i = 3$, not 2.

52. C. Group A elements are the representative elements.

53. D. There are four atoms in an fcc unit cell. One eighth of an atom from each of the eight corners contributes one atom. One half of an atom comes from each face. Since there are six faces, there are three more atoms inside the cube.

54. A. All "s" atomic orbitals (1s, 2s, 3s, 4s, 5s, and so on) have an angular momentum quantum number equal to zero.

55. B. The covalent bond length between hydrogen and halogens, HX, increases HF < HCl < HBr < HI < HA. The shorter the bond, the stronger the bond.

56. E. Decomposition of KClO₃ yields O₂. 246 tons KClO₃ = (96 tons O₂)(1 ton mol O₂/ 32 tons O₂)(2 ton mol KClO₃/ 3 ton mol O₂) (123 tons KClO₃ /1 ton mol KClO₃).

57. D. The reverse activation energy equals Eₐ reverse = Eₐ forward – ΔH. For this reaction +227. kJ/mol = 232. kJ/mol – 4.18 kJ/mol.

58. B. A ferromagnetic solid like iron has domains of unpaired electrons. The electrons in these domains have similarly oriented spins.

59. C. Lithium is in Group 1A with one unpaired outer electron.

60. E. Methane has a central carbon atom with four attached H atoms. These are bonded to the central carbon by overlap of a 1s atomic orbital with a lobe of an sp³3 hybrid orbital.

61. B. The density of a gas will decrease as a gas expands. The density is inversely proportional to the amount of expansion. D final = (Density initial) (volume initial / volume final) = (0.1786 kg/m³) (1 / 1.5)

62. C. The absolute value for the m_ℓ quantum number can NEVER be larger than the value for ℓ.

63. B. The charge carried by an Avogadro's number of electrons is a Faraday, 96,500 coulombs.

64. A. Real gases follow the ideal gas law more closely at high temperatures and low pressures. The ideal gas law assumes that gas molecules have no intermolecular interactions and have no volume. These assumptions are approximated better when the particles have high average kinetic energy at high temperatures (above 273 Kelvin) and at high volume (low pressures, below 1 atmosphere).

65. C. The oxidation number for Mn changes from +7 in MnO₄⁻ to +4 in MnO₂. This reduction requires that Mn gain 3 electrons. The 3 electrons must be added to the reactant side of the equation.

66. E. The atomic number of an atom decreases by one unit when a K shell electron is captured by the nucleus. One proton is converted to a neutron.

67. C. Both reactants and products are in the reaction mixture when a reversible reaction reaches equilibrium. The relative amounts are determined by the equilibrium constant.

68. E. The cell voltage must be positive. The cell voltage is determined from the sum of the reduction potential as written for one half-cell and the voltage for a half-cell reversed as oxidation. $E^0 = E^0_{reduction} + E^0_{oxidation}$; $E^0 = 0.53$ V – (– 0.14 V) = 0.67 V

69. B. The Q term is the reaction quotient. It equals the nonstandard state concentrations or pressures for reactants and products. It equals the mass action expression with concentrations or pressures for the existing conditions. It equals equilibrium constant, K, when the system reaches equilibrium.

70. C. Amphoteric compounds can act as both an acid and a base. Aluminum hydroxide can release hydroxide ions acting as a base. The H atoms bonded to the O atoms can be released so the compound acts as an acid.

71. D. Addition of Br2 to an alkene replaces the double bond with single bonds to the Br atoms.

72. A. The meta dichlorobenzene has the Cl atoms in the 1 and 3 positions.

73. E. Markonikov's rule predicts that hydration of an alkene will yield the most branched (substituted) alcohol.

74. E. The carbon in the $-C:::N:$ group is relatively electron poor with a partial positive charge. Ortho-para directors are able to donate an electron pair that can be delocalized in the aromatic ring.

75. C. Explanation of the answer: FT–IR is best for functional groups, MS for molecular fragments, and NMR for bonding structure.

76. D. Carbons 2 and 4 have no hydrogen, and being flanked by carbonyls, the hydrogens on carbon 3 will be far more acidic than those on carbons 1, 5, and 6.

77. D. Reactions between alkyl halides and primary and secondary amines are replacement reactions. The alkyl group from the halide replaces a hydrogen on the nitrogen of the amine. The reaction between an alkyl halide and a tertiary amine is an addition reaction. The alkyl group adds to the lone pair of the amine.

78. C. Allylic hydrogen atoms are bonded to carbon atoms bonded to the doubly bonded C atoms.

79. E. The two H atoms are $2°$.

80. D. The double bond is cleaved in ozonolysis. Attach a $= O$ to each of the formerly double-bonded carbon atoms. The ozonolysis of $CH_3CH::CHCH_3$ produces two molecules of CH_3CHO.

81. E. The C-I-P rules place higher priority on atomic number. The lowest priority atom projects back from the plane of the page. When the decreasing priority is counterclockwise the configuration is "S."

82. B. A meso compound is achiral but contains chiral centers.

83. A. Dehydration of the primary alcohol gives 1-butene. The secondary alcohol gives 2-butene.

84. E. Alkynes have a triple bond and are short four hydrogen atoms. The general formula is C_nH_{2n-2}.

85. B. Both butane and 2-methylpropane have the formula C_4H_{10}.

86. C. There are six carbons in the longest carbon chain so it is a hexane. The –OH group is in the 2 position with the methyl in the 3 position.

87. B. Aldehydes are oxidized to carboxylic acids by $KMnO_4$.

88. A. Lithium aluminum hydride is a reducing agent; it will reduce an aldehyde to an alcohol.

89. C. Lithium aluminum hydride is a reducing agent. Aldehydes are reduced to primary alcohols by $LiAlH_4$.

90. D. Esters are reduced to alcohols by $LiAlH_4$.

91. D. The position of the carbonyl oxygen is important, which is why we distinguish between aldehydes (terminal carbonyls) and ketones (non-terminal carbonyls). Aldehydes can be oxidized to carboxylic acid, which is a common property that chemists use to distinguish between different types of sugars (aldoses versus ketoses).

92. B. The triple bond consists of two π bonds and one σ bond. Each of the π bonds contains two π electrons.

93. A. Hot sulfuric acid will dehydrate an alcohol to form a symmetric ether.

94. C. Hot concentrated sulfuric acid will dehydrate a carboxylic acid to yield an acid anhydride.

95. D. Symmetric ethers have the general formula R-O-R.

96. B. Oxidation of arenes, $ArCHR_2$, with acidic $KMnO_4$ will yield a carboxylic acid such as $ArCO_2H$.

97. E. Epoxides can be made from alkenes using peroxyacids such as $RCOOOH$.

98. B. Grignard reagents and carbon dioxide react to extend the carbon chain of the R chain in the Grignard to yield a carboxylic acid after hydrolysis.

$$CO_2 + C_2H_5MgCl \longrightarrow C_2H_5CO_2MgCl \xrightarrow{H_3O^+} C_2H_5CO_2H$$

99. D. In formaldehyde there are 6 sigma electrons in single bonds, 2 pi electrons in the double bond, and 4 nonbonding electrons in unshared electron pairs on the O atom.

100. D. The $4n + 2$ rule predicts that monocyclic hydrocarbons will be aromatic if they have a π electron count of 6, 10, and so on. Structure D has 6 π electrons where 4 come from the two double bonds and 2 come from one of the lone pairs on the S atom. Structure A has 8 π electrons. Structure B has 4 π electrons. Structure C has 4. Structure E has 4.

Reading Comprehension

1. A. Affixed is correct. Tube worms attach to the bottom.

2. B. Discharge is correct. Natural spring vents discharge water.

3. B. Different in that a vent involves rapid discharge while a seep involves slow discharge. The author uses the two words in different contexts.

4. C. The two types of worms are from the same family but different species.

5. A. Grows more slowly than the hot-water tube worm. See paragraphs two and five, which distinguish between the growth rates of the two worms.

6. A. Complete is correct and is used as an adjective.

7. A. The implication in the passage is that these tube worms will grow to 8 feet in the lifetime.

8. C. Boiling is correct since the first part of the sentence states that these are hot water vents. Boiling water is scalding.

9. D. The two types of water differ in that one contains oily materials, and the other contains hydrogen sulfide, resulting in two different types of tube worms.

10. C. Aneurysms that occur near the brain stem only is correct. The first paragraph explains that these aneurysms are dangerous to repair with surgery.

11. A. Aneurysms is correct. The noun is found in the previous sentence, and no other noun in the sentence could make sense.

12. C. The paragraph discusses the danger of aneurysms, and therefore they can cause significant damage. The other choices in this context are not relevant.

13. B. Aneurysm is correct. The noun to which one refers actually appears two sentences before the reference.

14. A. Meandering is correct. The idea is that it moves slowly and deliberately toward its destination.

15. A. Removed is the only logical choice in the context of the sentence. One would not leave a catheter of this sort inside the patient.

16. B. A hernia is caused by a weakening of the muscle wall. An aneurysm is caused by the weakening of the arterial wall.

17. D. Hemorrhaging that results in death is correct. The second paragraph states that this can occur in 50 percent of patients.

18. B. Serve as a base for a blood clot to form is correct. This is explained in the second paragraph.

19. B. In the upper thigh is correct. In the reading, it states that the femoral artery is in the groin area. The word "femoral" is related to femur, which is the thigh bone, and the groin area is where the thigh meets the hip area.

20. D. Separate the coil from the wire is correct. This is explained in the second paragraph. After the coil is outside the catheter, a low-voltage electrical current is applied, and the coil detaches at a preset solder point.

21. C. At a predetermined and prepared location on the wire is correct. The same sentence that answers Question 20 says it is a preset location.

22. **A.** Longer and require more recuperation time than the new procedure is correct. This is explained in the last paragraph where it says: The procedure lasts two hours, which is half as long as invasive surgery, and recovery time is generally limited to a few days instead of a few weeks.

23. **B.** Is performed only at hospitals containing the required equipment and certified doctors. This is also explained in the last paragraph where it says . . . is available in various hospitals where there are advanced neurology departments and specialists trained in the procedure.

24. **B.** Carnivorous dinosaur is correct. Carnivorous means the same as meat-eating, which is stated in the first sentence.

25. **B.** The sentence presents two facts, thereby implying that the second fact is in addition to the first fact.

26. **A.** Frightening is correct, since dinosaurs are frightening creatures.

27. **D.** It is unusual to find a collection of bones from several different dinosaurs together—it's a surprising event.

28. **A.** Lived and hunted with others is correct. The first paragraph states that it is more astounding that the bones were found with other bones, because that indicates they were not loners.

29. **A.** Meat-eating dinosaurs lived alone. The same sentences say that this discovery challenges the prior theory that they were loners.

30. **C.** The newly discovered dinosaur is related to the Giganotosaurus.

31. **B.** Not closely related to Tyrannosaurus Rex is correct. The passage states that it is as close to T. Rex as a cat to a dog, which is not close.

32. **A.** To dissect is to take apart, or dismember.

33. **A.** The dinosaurs killed their victims, which were their prey.

34. **B.** To mate is to put pieces together to fit. Thus, combined is correct.

35. **B.** Hair is like a thread.

36. **C.** It is more precise than previous techniques. The passage indicates that they will have control, whereas they previously did not.

37. **B.** Electronic impulses could affect cells. The first paragraph indicates that they have known this for a while.

38. **A.** The word bombarding is similar to "bomb". Even if you don't know the other words, barraging is the only one that makes sense within the paragraph, and among the choices. Barraging is correct.

39. **B.** Open their walls to introduce medication is correct. The passage states that they have used electrical charges in an attempt to introduce foreign substances such as new drug treatments or genetic material.

40. **C.** If a choice is made to select a particular voltage, the implication is that it is a specific choice.

41. **D.** Tissues is correct. The passage indicates that others is a pronoun for other tissues, because it says . . . to activate particular tissues, whether they be muscle, bone, brain, or others.

42. **B.** Place more than one chip in a single person. The last sentence of the passage answers this question: They believe that they will be able to implant multiple chips into a person to deal with one problem or more than one problem.

43. **D.** Foreign bodies that invade the immune system are known as antigens.

44. **D.** Nonspecific lines of defense are those that do not distinguish between invading organisms. Neutrophils (and monocytes) are phagocytes, and will attack both bacteria and viruses. Lymphocytes are specific. Antigens are foreign agents that attack the body, and antibodies are the chemicals that fight them.

45. **B.** The vaccine stimulates our immune system into creating antibodies. These antibodies are quick to recognize the actual agent (disease) when encountered, and can now respond to it quickly, because of immunological memory.

46. C. Specifically, histamines cause the blood vessels to dilate, helping blood to flow quickly to the damaged area, which helps the healing process.

47. D. The ability of the immune system to remember previously encountered antigens is the body's secondary line of defense by the immune system. The chemical interferon (choice A) is an antimicrobial protein, which is also a choice in choice B—and thus, a duplicate choice. Be aware of clues like this to help eliminate certain answers.

48. A. There are different kinds of white blood cells, whose role it is to destroy cancer cells. Some cells are called natural killer cells, and their function is to kill the cancer cells. Histamines, stomach acids, and mucous membranes do not destroy cancer cells.

49. B. Known as immunological memory, the recognition of the previously encountered antigens results in a faster and stronger immune response to new antigens invading the body.

50. D. Lymphocytes are part of the specific immune response. Neutrophils, monocytes, and macrophages are all nonspecific lines of defense against pathogens and infectious agents.

Quantitative Reasoning

1. D. The cost for milk and 2 dozen eggs is $1.39 + (2 \times \$1.28) = \$3.95$. The change is $\$10.00 - \$3.95 = \$6.05$.

2. B. If 400 people fit in 8 subway cars, then $400 \div 8$, or 50, people fit in one subway car. Therefore, 50×5, or 250, people fit in 5 subway cars.

3. C. Carl's throw went $7\frac{1}{3} \times 2\frac{1}{2} = \frac{22}{3} \times \frac{5}{2} = \frac{110}{6} = 18\frac{1}{3}$ yards. The difference between the two throws is $18\frac{1}{3} - 7\frac{1}{3} = 11$ yards.

4. C. $3m - 12 + 12 = -6 + 12$ so that $3m = 6$. Dividing both sides by 3 results in $m = 2$.

5. A. The area of a square is s^2 where s is a side of the square. If $s^2 = 400$, then $s = \sqrt{400} = 20$.

6. A. Let c represent the number of caps traded in. Then $0.05c = 40.50$ and $c = \frac{40.50}{0.05} = 810$.

7. D. The cube of 8 is $8^3 = 8 \times 8 \times 8 = 512$.

8. E. The total cost for the posts and fencing is $(10 \times \$12.50) + (34 \times \$4.75) = \$125.00 + \$161.50 = \$286.50$.

9. B. One of the fundamental trigonometric identities is that $\frac{\cos\theta}{\sin\theta} = \cot\theta$.

10. C. Using the ratio $\frac{\text{price}}{\text{video}}$, the proportion $\frac{8}{3} = \frac{x}{2}$ can be used to find the cost to rent two videos. Cross multiply. $8 \times 2 = 3x$ so $16 = 3x$ and $x = \frac{16}{3} = \$5.33$.

11. E. Using the distributive property, $(2x + 1)(2x + 1) = 4x^2 + 2x + 2x + 1 = 4x^2 + 4x + 1$.

12. D. With 9 cups of milk, $\frac{9}{2} = 4\frac{1}{2}$ or 4 full batches can be made. However, with 9 eggs, only $\frac{9}{4} = 2\frac{1}{4}$ or 2 full batches can be made. At most, only 2 batches can be made with the given ingredients.

13. C. The proportion $\frac{1\text{ cm}}{4\text{ miles}} = \frac{x\text{ cm}}{10\text{ miles}}$ models this situation. Cross multiply. $1 \times 10 = 4x$ so $10 = 4x$ and $x = \frac{10}{4} = 2\frac{1}{2}$ cm.

14. B. This equation is solved by the number whose cube root is 2. The number with this property is 8.

15. A. The cost of Sandy's purchase is $(4\frac{1}{2} \times \$1.39) + (6 \times \$0.50) = \$9.26$. The cost of Brandon's purchase is $(3\frac{1}{4} \times \$1.39) + (9 \times \$0.50) = \$9.02$. Sandy spent $\$9.26 - \$9.02 = \$0.24$ more.

16. A. The least common denominator of 96 and 12 is 96, so $\frac{24}{96} - \frac{8}{12} = \frac{24}{96} - \frac{64}{96} = \frac{-40}{96} = -\frac{5}{12}$.

17. C. $\frac{3}{4} \div \frac{4}{3} = \frac{3}{4} \times \frac{3}{4} = \frac{9}{16}$

18. D. In a 10-mile trip, after the first mile, there are 9 additional miles. If each additional half mile is $1, then an additional mile is $2. The cost of the trip is $3 for the first mile + ($2 \times 9$) for the additional miles. $\$3 + \$18 = \$21$.

19. E. $64^{\frac{1}{3}} = \sqrt[3]{\frac{1}{64}} = \frac{1}{4}$.

20. B. The sine function is positive in the first and second quadrants, and the secant function is negative in the second and third quadrants. Thus, $\angle x$ must lie in the second quadrant.

21. B. Divide the figure into a rectangle and triangle as shown.

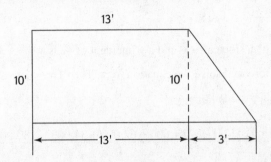

The area of the figure equals the area of the rectangle plus the area of the triangle. The rectangle = length × width or $10 \times 13 = 130$ ft²; the triangle = $\frac{1}{2}$ base × height or $\frac{1}{2} \times 3 \times 10 = 15$ ft². Together, the area is $130 + 15 = 145$ ft².

22. C. The amount of commission is $10\% \times \$8,350 = \$835$. Total earnings are $\$300 + \$835$ commission $= \$1,135$.

23. A. For this equation to be true, it must be the case that $2x - 1 = 5x + 8$. This is true when $x = -3$.

24. D. For a 30-hour week with $500 in sales, total earnings are $(30 \times \$9.50) + (3\% \times \$500) = \$285 + \$15 = \$300$.

25. C. This equation can only be true if $9 = 4x + 1$, that is, if $x = 2$.

26. E. The radius $r = \frac{d}{2}$. The area of the circle is $\pi r^2 = \pi \left(\frac{d}{2}\right)^2 = \frac{\pi d^2}{4}$. If the diameter is increased 100%, the diameter is $2d$ and $r = \frac{2d}{2} = d$. The area of the enlarged circle is $\pi r^2 = \pi d^2$. The enlarged circle is $\frac{\pi d^2}{\frac{\pi d^2}{4}} = \pi d^2 \div \frac{\pi d^2}{4} = \pi d^2 \cdot \frac{4}{\pi d^2} = 4$ or 400% bigger.

27. A. The amplitude of a sine curve is the coefficient of the sine term, which in this case is 2.

28. B. Begin by writing the line $4x + 2y = 12$ in slope-intercept form as $y = -2x + 6$. The slope of this line is the coefficient of the x-coordinate, which is -2. Since parallel lines have the same slope, we need to find an equation with a slope of -2. All of the answer choices are in slope-intercept form, and the choice with x coefficient of -2 is (**B**).

29. C. There are four aces in a standard deck of 52 cards. Therefore, the probability of selecting an ace is $\frac{4}{52} = \frac{1}{13}$.

30. E. Using the conversion formula reveals that 41° Fahrenheit is the same as 5° Celsius and that 50° Fahrenheit is the same as 10° Celsius. The only correct statement, therefore, is (**E**).

31. C. There are 7 coins in her purse, and three of them are worth 25 cents or more. Therefore, the probability that the value of the coin is at least 25 cents is $\frac{3}{7}$.

32. B. $\frac{82 + 74 + w}{3} = 76$. Cross-multiply

$156 + w = 228$

$w = 72$.

33. A. The area of a triangle is $\frac{1}{2}bh$. Let b represent the length of one leg. Then $h = 3b$, so the area is $\frac{1}{2}bh = \frac{1}{2} \cdot b \cdot 3b = \frac{3}{2}b^2 = 24$. Therefore, $\frac{2}{3} \cdot \frac{3}{2}b^2 = \frac{2}{3} \cdot 24$ and $b^2 = 16$. $b = \sqrt{16} = 4$ and $h = 3 \times 4 = 12$. The longest side of a right triangle is the hypotenuse. Using the Pythagorean Theorem, $\text{leg}^2 + \text{leg}^2 = \text{hypotenuse}^2$, so $4^2 + 12^2 = c^2$ and $16 + 144 = c^2$. Therefore, $160 = c^2$ and $c = \sqrt{160} = 12.6$.

34. C. Let b represent the number of boys in the class and g represent the number of girls. Then $b + g = 27$. If $b = g + 5$, then $(g + 5) + g = 27$. $2g + 5 = 27$ and $2g = 22$, so $g = 11$. Therefore, the number of boys is $27 - 11$ or 16.

35. C. In order to solve the equation, rewrite 4^{x+1} as $2^{2(x+1)}$. Thus, we are given $2^{3x} = 2^{2(x+1)}$, which is only true of $3x = 2(x + 1)$ or when $x = 2$.

36. B. $\dfrac{15\sqrt{3}}{\sqrt{5}} = \dfrac{15\sqrt{3}}{\sqrt{5}} \cdot \dfrac{\sqrt{5}}{\sqrt{5}} = \dfrac{15\sqrt{15}}{5} = 3\sqrt{15}$.

37. A. The equation of a line with a slope of $-\dfrac{3}{2}$ and a y-intercept of -2 is $y = -\dfrac{3}{2}x - 2$. To find the value of x in the point $(x, 1)$, substitute 1 for y and solve the equation for x. Then $1 = -\dfrac{3}{2}x - 2$ and $3 = -\dfrac{3}{2}x$. So $(3)\left(-\dfrac{2}{3}\right) = \left(-\dfrac{2}{3}\right)\left(-\dfrac{3}{2}\right)x$ and $x = -\dfrac{6}{3}$ or -2.

38. B. $\dfrac{3(28{,}000) + 2(31{,}000) + 1(34{,}000)}{6} = \dfrac{84{,}000 + 62{,}000 + 34{,}000}{6} = \dfrac{180{,}000}{6} = 30{,}000$

39. A. The value of $\sin x$ is $\dfrac{1}{2}$ when $x = 30°$.

40. B. The area of the circle is $\pi r^2 = 121\pi$. So $r^2 = 121$ and $r = 11$. The radius represents half the diagonal of the square, so the diagonal is 22 units long. If x represents the length of a side of the square, then x^2 is the area of the square. Using the Pythagorean Theorem, $x^2 + x^2 = 22^2$ and $2x^2 = 484$. Therefore $x^2 = \dfrac{484}{2} = 242$.

Wiley Publishing, Inc.
End-User License Agreement